THE
San Francisco Opera
1923-1961

Gaetano Merola
1879–1953

THE
San Francisco
Opera 1923-1961

ARTHUR J. BLOOMFIELD

APPLETON-CENTURY-CROFTS, INC.
NEW YORK

PRINTED IN THE UNITED STATES OF AMERICA

FOR

ANNE

PREFACE

It is scarcely news at this late date that San Francisco has long boasted of its high culture quotient and cosmopolitan, *European* atmosphere. Not unnaturally, opera has thrived by its bay. Specifically it has thrived for the past thirty-eight years in the activities of the San Francisco Opera. This company now gives more performances annually than any other in the country outside New York, it has operated over the years without a break, and today its fame and reputation are higher than ever before.

The simple facts of the company's existence and long record of performance make a history worthwhile. But what has especially prompted the author to reconstruct and interpret the past seasons of song is this: the San Francisco Opera has had, in its best years, a personality in its productions which has lifted it way out of the "branch of the Metropolitan" category. And in its genial founder Gaetano Merola there is a subject to tempt any writer.

I have sought to combine reference and entertainment values in this book. The founding of the company is traced; the building of the company's ultimate home, the War Memorial Opera House, is recounted in detail; each season is discussed; and then, in an appendix, all the casts of San Francisco performances are given (those of the Los Angeles performances are mostly identical but any important changes are noted in the text).

Many acknowledgments are in order. The chapter on the founding could not have been written without the help of Mrs. Horace Clifton, and I am also highly indebted to her for the use of many old photographs. Mrs. Stanley Powell, John Stine, Guglielmo Torchia, Marsden Argall and Fortune Gallo are among the others who were of great assistance in connection with this chapter. Frank De Bellis' help in introducing the author to friends and associates of Merola is greatly appreciated. Acknowledgment is also made to Millie Robbins.

To James Cleghorn and his staff in the Music Department of the San Francisco Main Public Library—and to Dolores Cadell and her associates in the Reference Room—many thanks. Herbert Scholder, publicity chief of the San Francisco Opera, was of invaluable assistance, and I must also thank manager Howard Skinner and Evelyn Crockett of the business office for some details.

The author was happy to have the opportunity to consult Kurt Herbert Adler, general director of the San Francisco Opera, several times on matters of production which might escape one from the audience side of the footlights. His permission to use a number of candid photos from company files is gratefully acknowledged. A number of consultations on singers of the early years with critic Alexander Fried and collector Anthony Boucher were highly productive, and William Kent III lent me records from his fabulous vocal collection most generously. Albert Goldberg of the *Los Angeles Times* was also of assistance.

Harold Rosenthal, the editor of *Opera,* published in London, provided some elusive biographical material with startling speed and precision. Clade von Besser, one of Merola's secretaries, kindly contributed some pictures. I am indebted to G. Albert Lansburgh for showing me early blueprints of the Opera House. And to Dean Wallace for opening *San Francisco Chronicle* files to the author.

Veteran choristers Paul Guenter, Colin Harvey and Max Lorenzini have helped with many points, and also former members of the company, among them Amerigo Frediani, Anita Olmsted, Nino Comel, Louis Ford, the late Julius Haug and Flossita Badger. My thanks to Charles Kendrick for reading the Opera House chapter. I also profited from conversations with Mrs. Milton Esberg, Sr., Austin Morris, Earl Anderson, Jesse Colman, and, from the Opera House technical staff, Thomas Colangelo and Ed Zettel. Visits to the *Examiner* and *News-Call Bulletin* libraries were also productive.

The Pisani Printing Co. kindly lent the photo on the dust jacket.

San Francisco
1961

CONTENTS

THE
San Francisco Opera
1923-1961

1 ⁊

THE BEGINNINGS

On September 26, 1923, 5,000 persons made their way into the big, boxy and unaesthetic Civic Auditorium on Grove Street to attend the first night of the first season of the San Francisco Opera. The performance of Puccini's *La Bohême* starred Giovanni Martinelli as Rodolfo and Queena Mario as Mimi, and also on stage was a local girl, Anna Young, as Musetta. The top price was four dollars, the evening a near-sellout. The auditorium, not basically a home for artistic events, had been modified and spruced up for the season—the stage was extended seventy-seven feet out toward the audience, the non-plush main floor seats were cushioned and arranged on a sloping platform, and an arc of so-called boxes was constructed behind the last row. There was a big false proscenium, and curtains hid from view the empty sections of the huge balcony at each side of the stage. The total effect was that of a theater within an auditorium, and if the transformation had elements of improvisation, it served.

On the conductor's podium that September night was a forty-four-year-old Neapolitan named Gaetano Merola.[1] Son of a court violinist, he had arrived in the United States in 1899, fresh from the Conservatorio San Pietro a Majella in his home city, where piano and conducting were his major studies. He had become an assistant to Luigi Mancinelli at the Metropolitan for a season and then joined the Henry W. Savage Opera Company. Savage took his troupe through the East and Midwest during these pre-television days, giving six and seven week engagements of opera in English, and it was in Buffalo that young Merola conducted his first opera, *Lucia di Lammermoor*. In February, 1906, he came to San Francisco for the first time, as accompanist to the mezzo Eugenia Mantelli. The concert did not come off, because an opera company starring Luisa Tetrazzini was having such a success at the Tivoli Theater that there was no room in the city for anybody else. But the trip served a certain purpose. The city

[1] To be precise, he was born January 4, 1879.

of San Francisco began to weave a spell over Merola. "If destiny wants you not to return to Italy," he thought, "this is the place to settle down."

As things turned out, the night of the slated Mantelli program Merola went to hear her competitor, Tetrazzini, and liked her very much. His recommendation later helped her get an engagement with Oscar Hammerstein's Manhattan Opera in New York.

And, fifteen years later, Merola was to settle in San Francisco and provide the spark for the founding of a home opera company—an institution which, after troublesome birth pains, emerged from its "experimental" first season in healthy shape and, following some relatively adventurous early years, found a solid artistic place in the world of opera.

After returning from San Francisco in 1906, Merola went to work for Hammerstein's company as chorus master—and an unusually youthful, precise and good-looking chorus it was. The summer of 1909 found him visiting San Francisco again, as conductor for the extensive engagement at the Princess Theater[2] of W. A. Edwards' International Grand Opera Company. *Otello, Fedora, La Gioconda* and *L'Amico Fritz* were performed, with *Aida, La Traviata, Lucia, Il Trovatore, Carmen, Cavalleria Rusticana* and *I Pagliacci*. Between two San Francisco series of performances, there were presentations in a number of other California cities and towns: Oakland, Sacramento, Stockton, Santa Cruz, Fresno, Bakersfield, Riverside and Los Angeles. Merola's nephew Armando Agnini, who was later to serve the San Francisco Opera for many years, was the stage director.

According to a newspaper clipping of that time, Merola resigned from the International while it was in San Francisco, and "the Italian quarter" was reported as interesting itself in the problem of finding means whereby "Merola, the competent director from Rome, may be constrained to remain and be content." The young Roman from Naples undoubtedly was content to remain, but the means were apparently not there. His association with Hammerstein continued in New York, where he led the premiere of Victor Herbert's *Naughty Marietta* in 1910, and in London where he conducted during the great Oscar's last operatic fling in the spring of 1912.

He was also the first to conduct Rudolf Friml's *The Firefly*. Work with the Shuberts followed, and for them he presided over *Maytime*. Then Fortune Gallo hired him as the conductor of the San Carlo Company: the war was on and Gallo had lost his maestro—Carlo Peroni—to the U. S. Army. Since Merola's main interest was in

[2] On Ellis street near Fillmore.

heavier fare than *Maytime*, he was pleased. He doubtless would have spent more time in so-called grand opera prior to the San Carlo engagement had not Hammerstein's rivalry with the Metropolitan resulted in the impresario's 1910 agreement—for a $1,200,000 settlement—not to produce opera in New York, Boston, Philadelphia or Chicago for ten years. At all events, the San Carlo Company provided Merola with several more trips to San Francisco, and the thread of destiny wound closer to the most important events in his career.

Merola returned in February, 1919, for a well-attended two-week season in the Curran Theater with such artists as Queena Mario, the Japanese-American soprano Haru Onuki and San Francisco's own Doria Fernanda. He was in the pit February 2, 1920, when the San Carlo went into the Curran again, with Mario, Anna Fitziu, Alice Gentle, Maud Fay—another San Franciscan—and the Spanish baritone Vincente Ballester on the roster. A special third week was added to the season to take care of the ticket demand. In January, 1921, when he returned again with the company, *Examiner* critic Redfern Mason noted that "Merola conducted (the opening) and the audience greeted him like a friend." Again there was an added third week, and Merola had extra time to indulge his love for San Francisco, "my other Italy."

He not only liked San Francisco for its charms. He hoped he could benefit the city, and himself of course, by producing opera by that famous Golden Gate. He knew San Franciscans paid a lot of money to hear visiting troupes—the Chicago Opera, the Scotti Opera, the San Carlo—and he knew that that money would be more than enough to give San Francisco what he thought it ought to have: its own company.[3] The fact that a new War Memorial Opera House was projected was of vital interest to him—it should, he thought, be opened by a locally organized production outfit.

Following the San Carlo tour, Merola was back in New York in the spring of 1921. He reminded his employer of an invitation from San Francisco. It was extended by Mrs. Oliver Stine, a music patron and something of a composer herself. She had developed an interest in Merola—she had consulted him on a San Carlo visit regarding some music she'd written for an opera on a Japanese theme—and now she wanted Merola to come West that summer and give lessons in voice. Mrs. Stine promised to help get him pupils.

Merola borrowed a sum from Gallo for transportation, and with his

[3] In September, 1921, 6,313 persons paid $30,652 to hear Geraldine Farrar in *Butterfly* with the Scotti Opera in Civic Auditorium, and, according to the press of the day, this was the highest box office registered for a single performance of opera in the United States.

wife Rosa set out for San Francisco. He left the door open for continued employment with the San Carlo, but, when Gallo corresponded with him about returning as a regular conductor the next season, Merola asked for a raise of $50 plus transportation. Gallo offered a $35 raise and no fares: this Merola refused. Obviously the possibilities which San Francisco offered were so favorable that he would not return to the San Carlo on other than his own terms.

Settling in San Francisco had long interested him, and 1921 saw Merola becoming a permanent resident. He found more friends—many of them in the Italian community, with a smaller number outside it. Eating in restaurants in the heavily Neapolitan North Beach district, he did not have much trouble forming new friendships there. To make a living he gave lessons, and for recreation, he played cards with his fellow Italians. Meanwhile, remaining relatively less active than during his touring days, he nursed his idea of producing opera in the San Francisco area. And in November of 1921 something happened which set Merola thinking about that subject in more specific terms than previously.

The Merolas were invited to a football game—the "Big Game" between Stanford University and the University of California—in Stanford Stadium, thirty miles south of San Francisco, and when he heard the band music down on the field he was immensely stirred. The acoustics were impressive. With tenors more on his mind than quarterbacks, he decided the stadium had excellent possibilities for the production of opera. It reminded him of the Verona Arena and the Baths of Caracalla in Rome. The idea was not the most practical in the world, but, even if some thought it a romantic dream, Merola was determined to go ahead anyway and try to execute it. He wanted to make an impression producing local opera, and the opportunity to do so, a daring one, was at hand. A meeting was arranged with Dr. Ray Lyman Wilbur, the Stanford University president. Dr. Wilbur referred him to Dr. Williams, the chairman of the Board of Athletic Control; the latter gave the youthful, charming and enthusiastic Italian just the permission he wanted: the stadium was his. So, ready to wear the hats of conductor, chorus master, impresario and backer, Merola went ahead with plans for a short June season.

Early 1922 found him guest conducting part of the San Carlo's engagement in San Francisco, at the Century Theater. That company's new chief conductor was the German Ernst Knoch, listed on the prospectus of the emphatically Latin San Carlo as Ernesto Knoch.

The funds for the Stanford season—singers, chorus and orchestra, not to mention the special stage—obviously posed a big problem.

Merola was reluctant to ask for money from people he did not know too well, so he did not go outside the Italian community for his financial help. Cashing in his own Italian bonds, he persuaded his North Beach friends—small businessmen, white collar workers, an artist—to contribute to his project. None of these men was particularly affluent. Some of them had just a little more than nothing salted away. But the operatic idea appealed to them; Merola was very convincing, and there seemed good reason to believe the venture could be an artistic and financial success. The Italians put in their initial contributions: some were $1,000, some $500. A handful of men helped Merola set the project in action: Guglielmo Torchia, Giuseppe Brucia, Antonio Farina, Giulio Stradi, Alfonso and Amedeo Napolitano, Milano Milani and Amedeo, Amalio and Anacleto Paoni.

Merola went East and engaged such well-known singers as Martinelli, Leon Rothier and Ballester. He wired back that guarantees were needed, so the more prosperous Italians found themselves at a bank and a note was signed for several thousand dollars (twelve or thirteen, depending on the source). San Francisco Symphony players were engaged, and Merola rounded up a large chorus. It rehearsed in vocal teacher Frank Carroll Giffen's well-remembered early Victorian house at the northeast corner of Hyde and Chestnut Streets on Russian Hill.[4] A visit to this corner in the spring of 1922 would have found Merola at the piano, playing with one hand, conducting with the other, working with a green but willing band of choristers who at least knew their director was a dynamo.

The preparations continued. A stage was constructed at the north end of the stadium, redwood trees were set decoratively at each side thereof, and seats on the greensward and in the semicircular balcony formed by the north end zone were sold. Capacity was 17,000, and the price scale one to five dollars. To accommodate patrons special train service to Palo Alto was arranged.

As if enough money had not been spent prior to the day of the first performance, June 3, an extra several hundred dollars had to be provided at the last minute for insurance because of a prediction that it would rain that night. But there was no need for cancellation or postponement. The weather was balmy and *I Pagliacci,* followed by a ballet divertissement, was successfully presented. There were a number of vocal delights that night under the stars, but none was more memorable than the climactic A flat which the powerful-voiced Ballester rolled out at the end of the Prologue, holding onto it as he

[4] When the Hyde Street cable car stopped at Chestnut, the gripman would yell out: "Rue de l'Opéra."

sauntered across the stage. Only about 6,000 persons were in the *Pagliacci* audience, but the figure grew to approximately 8,000 for *Carmen* on June 7. The *Faust* on the 10th had an estimated 10,000— and a natural assist in the garden scene from a rising moon. For the second *Carmen* there was an even larger audience.

Yes, there was growth in attendance, but it wasn't enough. Hoped-for patronage by Shriners convening in San Francisco failed to materialize, and there was further loss of a sort due to the fact that some of the audience would buy cheap seats and then go to sit in more expensive ones. Fog in San Francisco discouraged potential travelers. After the season, one of the artists asked Merola, "Maestro, did you go in the hole?" And the answer, in characteristic Neapolitan accent, was "Yes, a beega hole!" Merola and his North Beach friends were liable for the stack of bills, but amid some grumbling there was warm feeling that the artistic success had justified the financial hardship. At the same time, at least one of the backers suggested to Merola he get help from richer men the next time.

Ballester, incidentally, joined the Metropolitan the season of 1924–1925, singing several leading roles there. His career was unfortunately cut short by a fatal disease, and this was his only season at that house.

CASTS—STANFORD SEASON

June 3: *I Pagliacci* (Leoncavallo)

Canio	Giovanni Martinelli
Tonio	Vincente Ballester
Nedda	Bianca Saroya
Silvio	Marsden Argall
Beppe	Aristide Neri

Followed by:

Ballet divertissement

Conductor: Gaetano Merola

June 7 and 16: *Carmen* (Bizet)

Carmen	Ina Bourskaya
Micaela	Bianca Saroya
Don Jose	Giovanni Martinelli
Escamillo	Vincente Ballester
Zuniga	Leon Rothier
Dancairo	R. Agni
Remendado	Aristide Neri
Morales	U. Rovere
Frasquita	Constance Reese
Mercedes	Georgianna Strauss

Conductor: Gaetano Merola

June 10: *Faust* (Gounod)

Marguerite	Bianca Saroya
Faust	Giovanni Martinelli
Mephistopheles	Leon Rothier
Valentin	Vincente Ballester
Wagner	U. Rovere
Siebel	Doria Fernanda
Marthe	Georgianna Strauss

Conductor: Gaetano Merola

Following the season, Mrs. Sigmund Stern, a philanthropically minded San Franciscan, gave an elaborate barbecue at her summer place in nearby Atherton. Since some wags had been wondering what happened to the bull from *Carmen*, an animal alleged to have been Escamillo's adversary found itself on the menu. A number of wealthy and influential people were at this affair, and in the warm afterglow of the season some of them offered Merola future help. Since he wanted very much to continue the summer seasons at Stanford and initiate a series of performances in San Francisco itself, he was extremely happy to hear that he would have some new and wealthier angels. One of his good friends, Horace Clifton, a San Francisco insurance man, made a note of those who had offered support, but back in the city after the festivities many hoped-for angels thought it over and were less interested.

A few staunch supporters, though, such as Mrs. Stine and Clifton, joined Merola in working toward his goal of a permanent San Francisco company.[5] They decided that approximately $75,000 was needed to go about the business of preparing for a two-week season in Civic Auditorium. There was no Opera House yet, and a large capacity was needed for box office success. The idea conceived was that seventy-five men should be found to contribute $1,000 each. Robert I. Bentley, a prominent businessman, had a group of potential sponsors to lunch at the Pacific Union Club, Merola made a strong speech, and a committee was appointed to explore ways of getting the money. But the memory of a visit of Mary Garden's Chicago Opera in the spring of 1922 did not sit well with the moneyed men of San Francisco. The spendthrift Garden regime had brought the Chicago company to the West Coast with an expensive list of singers and a pretentious repertoire which included *Tannhäuser, Lohengrin, Louise, Salome, L'Amore dei Tre Re, Monna Vanna* and *The Girl of the Golden West*, not to

[5] Meanwhile, in some quarters interest had been expressed in former Met conductor Giorgio Polacco as musical director of future opera production—indefinite, of course—in San Francisco.

mention a few more standard items. The San Francisco backers lost $700 each on the venture.

On February 5, 1923, Bentley wrote a letter to Merola in which the Chicago fiasco was noted. "I have made inquiry of a number of the names we had under discussion the other day," the letter said. "Some have declined absolutely to come in at all and with all of them it was a case of being very reluctant about it." Bentley's conclusion was that it certainly looked inadvisable to go ahead with the opera plan at that time. Merola was extremely depressed by the letter, but, as it turned out, this seeming message of doom was simply the needed spark to set off the next, and fruitful stage in the progression of events toward realization of the goal. The evening of February 6 the Merolas dined with Clifton and his wife. While Merola sulked, Clifton thought. "I have it," he said. "It's simply a matter of mathematics. If we can't get seventy-five to give $1,000 each, we'll get 750 to give $100, and they'll get something in return. We'll give them a season ticket to the opera for each $50." The idea met with immediate favor, hope was renewed, and work toward the season started zipping along at tempo presto.

The first meeting was held February 7, with Mrs. Stine, Judge George Crothers, patron of the arts Albert Bender and impresario Selby Oppenheimer among those present. Solicitation of pledges was organized and almost daily meetings were held. A "party with a purpose" was given at Miss Edith Livermore's home February 13 with Merola offering a one-man preview performance of *Gianni Schicchi* at the piano. In March he went East and engaged Martinelli, Beniamino Gigli, Giuseppe DeLuca and others. Then came a climax, April 4, at the St. Francis Hotel, when a meeting attended by more than one hundred persons was called to formally announce detailed plans of the company for an autumn season. Merola told the assemblage that the auditorium could be remodeled in a manner reducing acoustic faults to a minimum, and the seating arrangement could be improved by raising the chairs like those in a conventional theater. Members of the San Francisco Symphony would be engaged, and a resident chorus would participate in the performances.

"We shall prove," he said, "that there is ample talent in and about San Francisco that only awaits an opportunity to obtain adequate training and experience to prove itself capable to vie with artists of distinction."

Governing officers were elected: Timothy Healy chairman, A. W. Widenham and Clifton vice chairmen, Mrs. James R. Miller secretary, and Edward F. Moffatt treasurer. Merola's title was general director;

Oppenheimer was the business manager. The executive committee consisted of: Bender, Bentley, Crothers, Milton Esberg, Charles Field and B. F. Schlesinger; Mesdames William Fitzhugh, Marcus Koshland, W. H. Mills, M. C. Porter, William Sesnon, Ernest Simpson, M. C. Sloss and Oliver Stine; and the Misses Louise Boyd, Mary Dunham, Edith Livermore and Sallie Maynard.

Work on ticket pledges continued through the spring, the chorus meanwhile beginning its rehearsals in early May. At times the campaign seemed to be dragging, but actually a lot of quick activity was getting some results. By the end of May solicitors could account for more than $30,000. Bentley, who had hoped as much as anybody that his February letter reflected too much caution, was at the head of the solicitors' list, accounting for thirty-six subscriptions totaling $3,464. Next was Mrs. Sloss, with thirty-one totaling $2,950. Clifton was third, with twenty-nine adding up to $2,850. Others with $1,000 or more were Mr. and Mrs. Healy, Widenham, Mrs. Porter, Mrs. Koshland, Mrs. Stine, Mrs. Simpson, Mr. and Mrs. Esberg and Merola himself.

The ticket money was just in promises, though, and early in May some of it was needed in the bank to take care of contractual arrangements. So Clifton wrote a check for $1,000 on May 9, asked for others to match his, several other checks were written, and this particular problem was eased. On the basis of the good names of those involved, a substantial bank loan was negotiated to ease the larger problem of securing the money to go ahead with all the arrangements for the season. Scenery had to be built, the special stage constructed. By June 26 the pledges had reached $40,000.

The ultimate prospects were good enough to insure that the project would go on. But still more money was needed to make up for the lack of sufficient operating backlog. Bentley invited a group of men to dinner, took them to a chorus rehearsal at ballet master Natale Carossio's Sutter Street studio, and won some additional backers. At the close of the season he was able to repay each of fifty underwriters $500.

When the idea of contributions was first broached, there was some consternation at the size—reputedly $2,000 per performance—of Martinelli's fee, but Merola turned that consternation into something approaching awe when he asked, "How many bankers are there in the world—and how many Martinellis?"[6]

[6] Speaking of top tenordom those days in San Francisco, Gigli—according to his memoirs—was escorted from the Ferry Building to his hotel by a squad of motorcycle policemen. The sirens whirred *fortissimo*.

Merola imported many of his artists from New York and Chicago. The aim of his company was to build up an organization to present the best available singers, and the program front billed "World Famous Principals and Leading California Artists." There was not sufficient talent in San Francisco, a musical city but hardly a highly developed opera-producing center by the standards of New York, Chicago and the musical meccas of Europe, to form the basis of the artist list. In this country, incidentally, Chicago held an especially high position in the operatic scene during the twenties, maintaining as it did a winter season of approximately three months. Many important singers—Galli-Curci, Ruffo, and Tito Schipa, for instance—sang for some years with the Chicago Opera before joining the Metropolitan.

While New York and the midwestern metropolis were the prime sources which Merola tapped for his leading singers, he reached out to Europe more and more in later years for some of his best talent, and the direct importation of artists from Europe by him and his successor, Kurt Herbert Adler, has helped to give the San Francisco Opera a particularly cosmopolitan and independent flavor.

Merola's artist lineup in 1923 was a bit thin, but he did have three of the greatest singers of the century, the tenors Gigli and Martinelli, and the baritone DeLuca. And there was that veteran, well-regarded bass, Adamo Didur. All of these, plus the up-and-coming tenor, Armand Tokatyan, were from the Metropolitan. Merola also made much use of Alfredo Gandolfi, a reliable and versatile Italian baritone then singing with the Chicago Opera, who later went to the Metropolitan where in general he sang roles less starry than those he was assigned in San Francisco. Figuring prominently, too, were well-routined *comprimario* performers from the Metropolitan: tenor Giordano Paltrinieri and basses Louis D'Angelo and Paolo Ananian. The lack of reserves was especially noticeable in the stellar soprano list which was composed of only Bianca Saroya, a handsome, big-voiced lyric-dramatic, and the more intimate-toned Queena Mario, the latter from the Metropolitan. Saroya, for instance, was called upon to follow a Giorgetta in *Il Tabarro* with a *Suor Angelica* on the same evening, having sung the female lead in *Andrea Chenier* two nights before, and with an appearance in *Mefistofele*—as both Margherita and Elena— scheduled for two nights later, and one in *Tosca* the evening after that.

The inclusion of Puccini's *Trittico* (*Il Tabarro, Suor Angelica* and *Gianni Schicchi*) was a notable element in the far from insubstantial repertoire which, if almost exclusively Italian, did also include such a relatively rare item as Boito's *Mefistofele*. (This opera, incidentally, had been revived at the Metropolitan during the 1922–1923 season.)

The complete list of operas was: *Rigoletto, La Bohême, Tosca, I Pagliacci, Il Trittico, Mefistofele, Andrea Chenier* and *Romeo and Juliet.*

Rigoletto and *Bohême* proved the most popular at the box office; *Mefistofele* was at the bottom of the popularity list, and a scheduled repeat was replaced by an extra *Chenier.* A generation later audience taste ranges wider, and Boito's opera—with a good cast—can outsell some of the oldtime popular favorites. As a matter of fact, it is one of the few operas performed three times in a single San Francisco Opera season—this was the case when it was revived in 1952.

On opening night, with *Bohême* on stage without benefit of a dress rehearsal, the critics found the chorus nervous at times, and there were a few other reservations, but in general it was a night for rejoicing. Martinelli was in mellow mood, and, according to Ray Brown in the *Chronicle*: "Although he was so deliberate in the delivery of 'Che gelida manina' as to lag a bit behind the orchestra at times, it was a deliberateness that served to accentuate the ease with which he sustained notes and linked them in unbroken sequence." Merola, Brown wrote, conducted "con amore" and was not to be held responsible for the "not completely successful experiment of placing the orchestra in a semicircular pit extending the full width of the stage. There was a lack of tonal blending and the individuality of the instruments stood out prominently."

The "house" for *Rigoletto* was crowded and three fishermen reportedly paid five dollars apiece for extra chairs which box holders had allowed to be placed in their boxes. And, so the story goes, a young Italian in Senator James D. Phelan's box became so excited during a Gigli aria he fell off his seat and was knocked unconscious. It was after the first act of this performance, the last of the season, that Merola was feted with a *tusch* from the orchestra. He thanked all who had participated, citing the yeoman service of the choristers who had rehearsed that spring and summer without remuneration.[7] There were also thanks to be given the faithful women who had undertaken the finding of props for the operas.

One of them, who was assigned *Chenier*, remembers that the only item which gave her trouble was Marat's bust. All she could find in the junk shops was Dante's Beatrice, but when she brought her back to stage director Agnini, he took out a pen knife, added various features, and soon Marat emerged. Pacific Heights mansions provided

---

[7] Chorus pay was minute and irregular in the early days. Less than $10 per performance was customary. In the middle thirties, with AGMA coming on the scene, rehearsal pay was added and there were other increases. Today the average chorister can make $1,500 a season.

other more elegant props. For several years faithful subscribers helped out with furnishings as the company built up its stock. Mrs. X would proudly exclaim, "That was my best rug in the center of the last scene!" and Mrs. Y would shudder when it looked as if an impetuous prima donna might drop one of her treasured pieces of stemware.

Merola could be thankful that his first season was not only an artistic but a great financial success. At the end of the season he actually had a small profit.[8] The total seat sale for the season was $124,000.

There was one near-fatal postscript to the season, however. Following the last performance, the scenery was transported to a warehouse. It was not insured. At a post-season party, Horace Clifton sat worrying about the lack of insurance and tried to figure how to expedite improvement of the situation. The following day he and his wife were to escort the Giuseppe DeLucas to Santa Rosa, fifty miles to the north, on a visit to Luther Burbank. And they had to leave early. What to do? Clifton asked his friend Charles Christin to be sure to go to his office the next morning and ask his secretary to insure the sets. When the party returned from Santa Rosa the next afternoon, they saw headlines describing a fire which had seriously damaged the warehouse. The sets had been destroyed. More worry. But it was dispelled when Christin assured the Cliftons the insurance had been taken care of.

Merola was exhaused at the season's close—he had conducted all the performances. However, there was the happy occasion of returning the $500 backers' money. As he told Bentley's contributors, "Gentlemen, I don't want your money. I just want your support—as subscribers, box holders." The businessmen, innately suspicious of artists' financial acumen, were more than impressed. And the relatively cloudless monetary picture created a warm, confident atmosphere. In 1924 about 2,000 persons and firms were enrolled as "founders" of the company by buying one or more founderships of $50. The company was now incorporated under the laws of California as a nonprofit organization with Merola as general director and Bentley as president. The new endowment of $120,000 enabled the company to operate until 1936 without resorting to elaborate annual campaigns for funds.

[8] Various figures have been given, but $1,800 turns up most often.

2

THE OPERA HOUSE

In a review of a *Tosca* performance midway through the first season, Mason wrote that Merola "has proved to San Francisco that she can produce opera that will compare favorably with that of New York and Chicago. Now we must have an opera house and it is for the public to kindle new life in the dead bones of the trustees of the War Memorial." The problem of building an opera house was an acute one, with the successful new company obviously ready to do more business in the years to come, and the prospect of more seasons in Civic Auditorium, with its lack of permanent stage machinery, not the happiest. True, the huge building had been tamed somewhat for opera performances, but certain refinements were impossible there. For instance, to anyone sitting in the side balconies near the stage, an offstage chorus would sound nearer than one on stage, because offstage in the Civic Auditorium was simply behind a curtain rather than behind a wall.

Construction of an opera house was a major matter on the post-1906 earthquake reconstruction agenda. San Francisco had always been an opera town—nearly 800 performances were registered in the 1860's, and more than 1,000 in the 1880's—and the operatic current by the Golden Gate, despite fluctuations of intensity, was not to be stopped.[1] The Grand Opera House built by Dr. Thomas Wade, a dentist, on Mission Street near Third in 1873 was rather extravagant for San Francisco's needs, but when it went with the 1906 catastrophe, a void was left. The Tivoli, a former beer garden, had become a home to opera light and heavy in the years before 1906, but it was lost, too. Though a new Tivoli opened in 1913, with performances of the Chicago Opera, the theater was soon turned into a movie palace.

In the years 1911–13 there was a campaign by the Musical Association of San Francisco, sponsors of the newly founded San Francisco

[1] For the record, the first opera played in San Francisco was Bellini's *La Sonnambula*, at the Adelphi Theater February 12, 1851.

13

Symphony Orchestra, to raise $1,000,000 for a grand music hall ac-
comodating opera and symphony on a one-block site at the eastern
end of the Civic Center. Envisaged was a structure modeled somewhat
on the Paris Opera with a grand staircase leading to the auditorium.
A legal question arose as to whether the city could donate property to
the Association, a private enterprise, and in settling a "friendly suit"
testing the validity of the proposed undertaking, the California Supreme Court decided the city could not do so. Mayor James Rolph
was obliged to veto the project, even though the Board of Supervisors
had originally promised the land.

In 1918 a small group of prominent San Franciscans renewed efforts
toward the erection of a hall for symphony and opera. The project
would further include an art museum[2] and a small memorial court
(8,000 square feet or thereabouts in size) dedicated to peace and
celebrating the termination of World War I. W. H. Crocker, Herbert
Fleishhacker, John Drum, John D. McKee, Templeton Crocker, Milton Esberg, M. H. de Young and Walter Martin led the campaign.
During 1918 and 1919 they gathered pledges, and on September 1,
1919, an option was taken on the block bounded by Van Ness Avenue,
Franklin, Hayes and Grove Streets—the former site of St. Ignatius
Church, destroyed in 1906. Their goal was $2,000,000, but by the end
of 1919 they had less than half and the great project appeared to be
drying up. At this time Drum and Charles Kendrick, a cultured,
fortyish businessman, met by chance one day. Major Kendrick,
recently home from the War, and influential in the American Legion,
asked Drum how the fund-raising was going and Drum had to admit
not so well. The matter remained in Kendrick's mind. When he saw
Drum on other business a few days later he said to him, "You know,
I think if you turn this whole project into a War Memorial I can get
the veterans' support." So Drum's associates and Kendrick got together. The merging of private and veteran fund-raising machinery
seemed hopeful indeed, and the board gave him carte blanche to work
out the alliance. Kendrick met with fifty representatives of veterans'
posts, they approved the intriguing idea, and it was put into effect. As
far as the returned soldiers were concerned, the suggestion that quarters be provided for their meeting purposes seemed a more practical
plan than the simple erection of a court as originally conceived.

The merger began smoothly, then—it was to run into very troubled
waters later. Musical and Art Association representatives were joined

[2] The old museum of the San Francisco Art Association in the Hopkins
Mansion on Nob Hill had been destroyed in 1906. The Association carried
on in the roofed-over foundation.

by those from the veterans on the fund-raising committee, and plans went forward. The St. Ignatius block was bought February 28, 1920, with $300,000 contributed by the Art Association. Forty thousand square feet of space for veterans' use was agreed upon. May 19, 1920, a mass meeting was staged in the Civic Auditorium to arouse public interest in the War Memorial.

The general plan for the War Memorial at the time of the meeting was for what might be called a complex of buildings: a 3,000-seat rectangular auditorium with a stage suitable for opera purposes situated on the rear or western half of the block, with a U-shaped structure to take care of the Art Museum and the veterans' quarters in front of it, and an interior court. There was also talk of a drama school and conservatory—these never materialized. In retrospect, the plan looks squeezed indeed.

The meeting was an inspirational event, complete with blare of brass band. Pledges were called out to "auctioneer" Lawrence Harris amid much happy tumult. Acting Mayor Ralph McLeran announced the city's $100,000 pledge. By the end of the meeting, the kitty was swelled to, in round figures, $1,650,000. The drive was taken out onto the streets, pup tents were set up on corners, and contributors dropped their money into cans with holes big enough for silver dollars. The hat was passed in theaters, too. After these activities were concluded, the grand total take was approximately $2,150,000.[3] The cash and pledges were handed over to the care of the Regents of the University of California, in nearby Berkeley, and a board of trustees was appointed August 19, 1921, to administer it. The board consisted of: W. H. Crocker, Templeton Crocker, Drum, Esberg, Fleishhacker, E. S. Heller, Kendrick, Martin, McKee and Frank Kilsby.

It looked—in 1920—as if the War Memorial Opera House would soon be a reality, and there was a confident ground-breaking that year. Actually, however, it was twelve years before the building was ready. And from 1923 through 1931 the San Francisco Opera performed in Civic Auditorium, with the exception of 1928 and 1929, when the company was in Dreamland Auditorium (now Winterland). Many factors contributed to the delay. The first stumbling block came when the attorneys for the Regents determined that the pledges signed by the subscribers were legally insufficient. New signatures on new pledge forms were needed. As there were several thousand sub-

[3] By this time the figure needed was set at about $2,500,000. Still, the gap had shrunk. Meanwhile, it might be noted that there is some disagreement among sources as to whether the amount pledged prior to the May meeting was a little less than $1,000,000 or $1,400,000.

scribers, this re-signing took two years, and some of the original subscribers had cooled in the interim. The trustees were specifically obligated by the Regents not to enter into any expenditures or contracts for the War Memorial until at least $1,800,000 in subscriptions had been signed up on the new forms. And it was not until October 11, 1922, that an Architectural Advisory Committee was named— with Bernard Maybeck as chairman, Arthur Brown Jr., Ernest Coxhead, Galen Howard, G. Albert Lansburgh, Fred Meyer, Willis Polk and John Reid Jr. This committee soon reported unanimously that the St. Ignatius block was too small to carry out the War Memorial project. Many felt that it should have more nobility and greater pretensions than were originally sought, and there was, after all, the variety of interests to be taken care of: opera, symphony, the art museum and the Legion.

Meanwhile, a storage firm, the Lyon Fireproof Warehouse Company, bought a large lot on the southwest corner of Van Ness Avenue and McAllister Street across the avenue from City Hall, and proceeded to have plans drawn and execute building contracts for the construction of a warehouse thereon. The warehouse, so far as some of the city fathers were concerned, would hardly be the most aesthetically satisfying structure across the street from City Hall. At the same time the War Memorial project was running over the sides of the drawing board. So Drum conceived a plan which had the enthusiastic cooperation of Supervisor McLeran. It had always been the hope of the city authorities that the two blocks immediately west of the City Hall be part of the Civic Center. Drum proposed that the trustees exchange their St. Ignatius block for one of the two blocks west of City Hall if the city would purchase the other one. The War Memorial could then adorn the two blocks. Mayor Rolph and the Supervisors' Finance Committee agreed that they could authorize the city to buy one of the blocks.

Numerous conferences were held with the Lyon firm, which finally agreed to accept $188,231 from the city for the property and damages accruing because of interrupted plans and cancelled contracts. Supervisor James B. McSheehy, a builder, thought the $140,000 asked for the lot itself "an elegant price," but discussion among the Supervisors brought out that the figure was not so outrageous, and the Board voted to pay. The trustees paid nine nineteenths, the city paying ten nineteenths and repaying the trustees the other nine following a couple of tax levies.

At the end of January, 1923, the Supervisors ordered condemnation proceedings against the balance of the two blocks under a plan of fifty-fifty purchase between the city and the trustees. Actually, the trustees advanced all the money. Another long period of slow process began as parcels of land were purchased. In the years 1923, 1924 and 1925, twenty-eight of these were bought by negotiation and suit. Meanwhile, on October 4, 1924, the trustees sold the St. Ignatius block to the Board of Education.

With a new working space of two blocks instead of one, original architectural plans were scrapped. But since the single block had obviously provided a tight fit, the new elbow room facing City Hall was a blessing. A plan was put forward to expand the St. Ignatius format into a duplication in miniature of the City Hall, complete with dome in the center. This elaborate building or complex would have sat in the middle of the two blocks. An impressive staircase was part of this idea, and the conception also provided for museum facilities including the display of pictures in foyers adjacent to the auditorium itself. Naturally there were veterans' facilities, too, but influential men of this fraternity strongly opposed the plan and wanted to be off in their own building, so the architects returned to the drawing board. The two-building idea was developed—one, of course, being the Opera House, and the other taking care of the veterans and the art museum. The buildings would be similar, the perimeter of the Opera House, with its special stage and seating demands, determining the perimeter of the second building.

Polk and Lansburgh were put in charge of plans for the Opera House, Brown and his partner John Bakewell those for the Veterans' Building. While the plans were still in the early stages, Polk died and Bakewell withdrew, leaving Brown and Lansburgh as the War Memorial architects. Brown, who had designed the City Hall, with which the new structures would harmonize, was the overall chief. But Lansburgh was responsible for more of the design, including the interior of the Opera House, than his somewhat lesser fame in connection with the War Memorial would indicate. Lansburgh's title was Collaborating Architect for the Opera House.

During part of the considerable time plans were being drawn, Brown was also at work on the Department of the Interior Building in Washington. And Lansburgh, an experienced theater architect, was asked to submit plans for Otto Kahn's proposed new Metropolitan Opera House at the end of West 57th Street and Eighth Avenue in New York.

An *Examiner* illustration of July 14, 1924, gives an idea of what the architects were thinking about in connection with the San Francisco War Memorial. It pictures idealized matching buildings on each side of a court, the buildings rectangular with seemingly endless rows of arches along the side façades, a tall column crowned with a sculptured figure emerging from a lagoon in the court. Stairs led to the court from each building. There were other and more grandiose ideas at this time—one of them to run a mall out Fulton Street from the War Memorial Court to Golden Gate Park. Interior studies continued, and a 1925 blueprint of the Opera House shows a semi-circular foyer wrapped around the auditorium, in distinction to the U-shaped, right-angled promenade area which later emerged.

In this year Pericles Ansaldo, a technical expert from La Scala, visited San Francisco and conferred with architects on the matter of stage design of the Opera House. And in 1926 veterans' representatives examined plans of the adjacent building in connection with provision for veterans' occupancy, and their space was set at 65,000 square feet.

Two buildings on two blocks, obviously enough, were going to cost more than the contents of the one-block plan. By 1926, after estimates were taken on what the architects had drawn up, it was determined that the funds subscribed were entirely inadequate to construct a War Memorial of "the dignity and grandeur the people of San Francisco have a right to expect." A ground-breaking took place on Armistice Day, with Louise Homer singing "The Battle Hymn of the Republic," but the trustees were approximately $4,000,000 short of the funds to go beyond any symbolic shoveling. On February 18, 1927, the trustees informed the publishers of the five San Francisco newspapers that there were these alternatives: either the construction could go on piece by piece over the years in Gothic cathedral-style as the funds became available, or, should the money be found more quickly, for instance by bond issue, then construction could go on in the conventional manner. The publishers felt that by all means the latter procedure was preferable: when the trustees mentioned the idea of building a "concrete shell" for performances which could be finished later, Edmond Coblentz of the *Examiner* objected strenuously. He reminded them that the 1906 fiasco had furnished San Francisco with more than enough "ruins." So the question of the bond issue was carefully discussed, and the figure of $4,000,000 agreed upon.

In March, 1927, City Attorney O'Toole advised the trustees that he had eliminated from the resolution for the bond issue all direct mention of the museum and opera house in order to make sure it conformed to California statutes (remember the problem fifteen years earlier in connection with the city donating property to a private association), and when, on May 2, 1927, an ordinance was passed by the Supervisors submitting a proposition to the voters for the bond issue, it referred to the construction of "permanent buildings in or adjacent to the Civic Center to be used as a Memorial Hall for War Veterans and for educational, recreational, entertainment and other municipal purposes." A lawyer could look at that statement and not see an opera house anywhere. As it happened, some of the veterans were to look at that statement and see only a very dim view of an opera house.

In the arguments for Progress Bonds put out by the Civic League of Improvement Clubs and Associations of San Francisco, the following was set forth:

"The utilitarian value of these buildings, alone, merits their construction. One of them will be the Veterans' Building, housing all the veterans' organizations in San Francisco. . . .

"The other building will contain San Francisco's long-needed Symphony Hall and Opera Auditorium. . . . We have one of the finest Symphony Orchestras in the United States, and it should have a fitting place to perform. The San Francisco Opera Chorus, with the Municipal Chorus, foreshadow the day when the musical productions here will rank with those produced in Chicago and New York; and a home for all the future will be provided, second to none in beauty. . . . The War Memorial deserves unanimous support. Vote yes."

Despite this quaint description of the musical picture in San Francisco—the opera company seemingly denuded of all but its chorus—this argument makes it obvious that an opera house is included in the plans.

In any event, the wording of the ordinance was unfortunate, and it was invoked many a time during the several years of wrangling which followed the bond election. Bonds for the War Memorial were voted June 14, 1927, with approximately 2,000 persons more than the necessary two thirds taking the affirmative view. But argument over plans and control of the War Memorial consumed time into 1930, and the Opera House did not open until October 15, 1932.

Several days before the bond election, Supervisor Frank Havenner introduced a resolution that, should the bonds be voted, the Board of Supervisors would not appropriate money for construction of the War Memorial until official plans received the formal approval of the majority of duly constituted representatives of all the war veterans' organizations in San Francisco. It was adopted eleven to seven. Now this was an entirely democratic resolution, but at the same time it acted, in a sense, as a sort of strangulator of progress, because it paved the way for the interminable bickering over details of the Veterans' Building plans.

There were, of course, two ways of looking at the War Memorial: there was the view from the board of trustees, mindful of its multi-partite purpose, its original artistic emphasis, and the fact that the original subscriptions were aimed at a project centered on a hall for symphonic and operatic purposes. The other view was that of some influential, outspoken veterans, mindful of the wording of the ordi-nance, the dedication of the project as a War Memorial, and desire for space for their organizations. Picture two sides, each more or less suspicious of the other, the veterans' spokesmen now emerging as less sympathetic, on the whole, than the trustees.

John Drum, one of the latter, reported at a public meeting in 1928 that plans had been discussed with veterans' representatives prior to the bond issue and there was no apparent dissatisfaction with the space alloted for their purposes. Just before the bond election, Drum said, some veterans became worried their rights might not be taken care of—a rumor was circulating that the trustees were going to put up a grand opera house and leave the veterans only some architectural scraps—and the Havenner resolution followed. After the bonds passed, a number of veterans' groups previously unheard from decided, as Drum put it, that they qualified under the resolution as critics of the plans.

The veterans' space, he continued, was duly enlarged by approxi-mately 40,000 square feet. At first the veterans had had a great area on the first floor and a number of impressively large rooms in the base-ment. The museum entrance was on Van Ness Avenue and into a multiple-story sculpture court, with galleries on the second and third floors. When the veterans demanded an auditorium, the sculpture court evaporated in the tug of war which consumed plan after plan of the companion building to the Opera House. It was decided to push the museum up to the fourth story, a floor which had been planned in part as an outdoor promenade.

As 1928 wore on without resolution, the veterans disapproved plans, then tentatively approved, then disapproved again. One aspect of the proposed Veterans' Building continued to irk representatives of the posts: this was a "temporary" indentation of 50 x 235 feet on the McAllister Street side, an indentation which would have made the building L-shaped—an L, this is, with a wide vertical piece. It is certainly true that matching buildings—and matching buildings were ultimately constructed—are preferable to two not quite matched.

The veterans were absolutely right. But at the same time they didn't show much appreciation of the growth in their exterior and interior space over the years. And those of them who were indignant that their building would cost less than the Opera House (in various planning stages the Veterans' Building price tag was $1,000,000 or so lower than the figure for its neighbor) failed to take into account the greater complexities of an opera house with its elaborate theatrical production demands.

It might be noted parenthetically that another Civic Center building—the Main Public Library, which dates from 1916—has a large indentation in its side along McAllister Street, and the outer façade therein is unfinished. An interesting point is that many San Franciscans never notice the jog: actually, a small office building has been set inside the indentation.

Milton Sapiro, a prominent legionnaire, and later a San Francisco Superior Court judge, had the feeling as 1928 drew to a close that the history of the War Memorial should have taken an entirely different, and quicker, direction. "If we (the veterans) had gone out for a private War Memorial Building in 1920," he said, "we would have had a building and we would have secured subscriptions from the same groups that had provided the other million and a half for your musical purpose, because they are just as patriotic as we are." Patriotism aside, some people interested in an opera house undoubtedly were not as interested in a Veterans' Building. As Sapiro continued, with a good deal less than complete appreciation of the trustees' charge, "You (the trustees) had money on hand all the time (from 1920). You had more than a million dollars. You could have put up a building to house us, and then gone out and put up the other building (the Opera House), or you could have started something that indicated there was going to be progress in the work."

Mayor Rolph, who appears through the War Memorial battle smoke as an especially upstanding public official, tended to favor the trustees. He rarely said things which didn't make good sense, but he was guilty at one point of a remark in which he stated that the Opera House would be of more lasting value than the Veterans' Building because the veterans would be gone in a half century or so. Perhaps he was thinking in terms of the "war to end all wars." In any case, Rolph's questionable remark brought a particularly debatable answer from Sapiro, who said, "An Opera House is more apt to become a lodestone on the back of the city than is a War Memorial."

Parallel to the argument over plans there ran another over control of the War Memorial. On September 18, 1928, Herbert Hall, attorney for the Regents, issued an opinion to the effect that they could not turn over the privately subscribed money to the Board of Supervisors as such, but they could to a group of trustees formed to carry out the terms of the trust. On the other hand, Hall said, the land should not be in the Regents' name. A charter amendment was suggested, and at a special election on November 6 the people adopted an amendment providing for the appointment of a new group of trustees to watch over the composite War Memorial project. The strangulating item in this matter was provided by an unprecedented clause in the amendment making the nomination of trustees by the Mayor subject to confirmation by the Supervisors. As Rolph put it, this was an unfortunate and unnecessary clause, as he was perfectly capable of carefully selecting the men. And he was.

Rolph offered his eleven names on August 26, 1929. They were: General Hunter Liggett, U. S. A., retired; Frank N. Belgrano, state commander of the American Legion; James I. Herz, 363rd Infantry (San Francisco's own); Charles Kendrick, World War veteran; Herbert Fleishhacker, president of the Anglo and London Paris National Bank; Kenneth R. Kingsbury, president of Standard Oil of California; Robert I. Bentley, president of California Packing Corporation; George Cameron, publisher of the San Francisco Chronicle; George Hearst, publisher of the San Francisco Examiner; Colonel Jesse Colman, Supervisor; and J. W. Mullen, publisher of the Labor Clarion.

This added up to only five veterans out of eleven, and a number of prominent veterans felt they should have a majority. A communication to the Supervisors from the Advisory Board to Veterans' War Memorial Committees "emphatically protested confirmation," and in so doing quoted the bond issue ordinance with its phrase "Memorial Hall for War Veterans." The veterans were not claiming the entire use of the War Memorial—all they wanted was sufficient space so arranged as a practical response to their minimum needs. But it warmed up to this: "The veterans of San Francisco demand that the purposes for which the War Memorial Fund was created be carried out. The main purpose was to erect a building to house the veterans' organizations of San Francisco. Other uses and purposes were incidental. . . . If it is your intention to disregard the law and build an art museum and/or other buildings, leaving to the veterans such scraps of space as may be available and which some of their bodies can use, the best and most conclusive way for your Board to manifest such intention is to confirm these appointments." The Supervisors voted against confirmation thirteen to four.

Redfern Mason breathed some fresh air into the close situation in an *Examiner* piece October 13, suggesting that the eleventh member of the new board be neither a veteran nor precisely a non-veteran, but a war worker, for instance a person with Red Cross or Salvation Army experience. This person, he wrote, could act as a moderator, a harmonizer. Mason went on to say, with great rising-above-the-turmoil logic: "The Museum is for the veterans as much as for the civilians. The same is true of the Opera House. But the Legion has this advantage over the Symphony—that, whereas the musical organizations will have to pay whenever they use the Memorial, the Legion gets its quarters for nothing.[4] The War Memorial's purpose is to honor the dead, but the best way to do that is to help the living. Its purpose is, through the gentle ministrations of art, to bring up a generation that shall have outgrown the brutalities of war."

On February 28, 1930, Rolph submitted his new nominations. They resulted in the same board, with the exception of one substitution, Richard Montgomery Tobin, a Navy veteran, for Fleishhacker. There was now a so-called veterans' majority. But it must be remembered, of course, that being a veteran by no means can be equated ipso facto with a cool-to-culture attitude, and the Mayor had wisely chosen men who not only carried a gun in the War but had cultural interests, too. The new board was confirmed March 3, and from then on the pace of constructive activity hastened. The unemployment problem had helped mellow some of the arguing, and by January, 1931, construction was beginning. Late in the month trucks bearing the words "Hello Prosperity! Here Comes the War Memorial" could be seen carrying materials to the long deserted site.

The cornerstones of the two buildings were laid on Armistice Day, 1931—and this was not a premature ceremony, like the ground-breakings five and eleven years before. "The Battle Hymn of the Republic" had its place again, this time voiced by Myrtle McLaughlin, a local singer. Sealed in the cornerstones were two boxes, their contents including, among other things, a silver spade used in the 1926 ground-breaking, the Navy Cross awarded posthumously to the first San Franciscan killed in the war, the history and a file of programs of the San Francisco Symphony, and a copy of the charter amendment providing for the War Memorial board. Came October 15, 1932, and the Opera House opened with a performance of *Tosca*.

Deflation had been a critical factor in facilitating the construction and furnishing of the War Memorial, which cost approximately $5,-500,000; this figure, considerably below the architects' minimum esti-

[4] A $15,000 subsidy from the city's Publicity and Advertising Fund has helped the Opera Association substantially in paying its rent to the city.

mates of 1929, excludes cost of land purchase. Further, a five-figure price was saved by postponement of installation of an organ.[5] The happy ending of the story found the buildings matched: neither, actually, a rectangle as earlier conceived, but both with attractive lateral projections twenty-five and one-half feet wide on each side near the fronts. These were the result of Lansburgh's feeling that plans to put stairways within a rectangular Opera House scheme—roughly where the elevators and water fountains now are at each end of the main promenade—were aesthetically unsatisfactory. The story *is* ended, but the book has now gotten eight years ahead of itself. A modulation is necessary back to 1924, and the activities of the San Francisco Opera itself.

[5] It has never been installed.

3 🐍

MAKING THE AUDITORIUM DO

1924

"It is hardly possible," an unidentified *Chronicle* writer said, "to expect a fashionable audience to arrive punctually for a performance that is plainly advertised to commence at 8:15 P.M. But after the initial disturbances of late and dilatory 'fashionables' there were several isolated incidents of ranker vulgarity. Some minutes after the last act was in progress a youth, correctly attired in the habiliments of a gentleman, walked noisily down the center aisle accompanied by a brilliantly attired 'flapper,' both talking loudly and deliberately ignoring the feelings either of the performers or of the audience."

This rather dated-sounding and supremely quotable knuckle rapping was occasioned by an incident at the performance of *Madam Butterfly* on September 26, the musical side of which did not elicit any hosannas. Butterfly would have been sung by the girlish-voiced but authoritative Toti Dal Monte had her engagement in San Francisco been fulfilled, but it was not. Thalia Sabanieeva was her replacement.

The season had opened several days earlier with *Andrea Chenier.* Gigli, DeLuca and Claudia Muzio were starred. This well-remembered dramatic soprano was to sing in the performance of *Tosca* which would open the new Opera House eight years later. She sang her superior Tosca later this season, and also her equally memorable Violetta. Those who know Muzio's famous recording of "Teneste la promessa" and "Addio del passato" from the fourth act have a good idea of the pathos she brought to this role. She had a way of throwing herself into a character so intensely she *became* the woman she was portraying, and when she clutched the Annina in this San Francisco *Traviata* she was trembling and crying—as if she were indeed Violetta.

The versatile Gigli was busy in the tenor leads this year, as was Tito Schipa, who came from the Chicago Opera for his first of many seasons. The third leading tenor was another member of the Chicago troupe, Jose Mojica, a handsome Mexican who had a way of getting mixed reviews.[1] DeLuca had the cream of the baritone parts.

Among the sopranos was a local girl named Myrtle Donnelly who had sung in small Italian opera houses. She was given the roles of Lauretta in *Gianni Schicchi* and Mimi in the second *Bohème*. After the latter one critic praised her for the "freshness, purity and lovely transparency" of her tone, but he also wished for more warmth. In addition, she was inexperienced in making her way around the stage convincingly.

There was nothing novel in the repertoire for 1924 except Mascagni's *L'Amico Fritz*, a not very distinguished choice, particularly in view of the shortness of the season. It was paired with *Schicchi*.

The *Traviata* of October 4, with the alluring cast of Muzio, Schipa and DeLuca, and with Merola on the podium (he again conducted all the performances), brought in the biggest box office to date, $19,-615, and there was a modest profit on the season as a whole. Top price this year was one dollar higher than that previously charged. The boxes, it might be noted, were placed in a U in the middle rather than at the rear of the orchestra.

1925

With the main floor seating capacity reduced to allow more space between seats in the company's not particularly comfortable home, the third season of the San Francisco Opera opened September 19. Castwise, it was a particularly notable beginning for a particularly notable season. Rosina Torri of La Scala made her American debut as Manon in the Massenet opera with Schipa as Des Grieux and that aging but still vocally resplendent bass, Marcel Journet, as his father. Yugoslavian Antonio Nicolich of the Chicago Opera sang Lescaut, and the De Bretigny was a local baritone who had sung in the Stanford season, Marsden Argall. It was Argall who had the first words to be officially sung from the new Opera House stage seven years later: the wonderfully appropriate "Ah, finalmente" of Angelotti in *Tosca*. Journet had not sung at the Metropolitan since 1908, at the Chicago Opera since 1919. He was, of course, busy in Paris.

Torri's appearance marked the christening of Merola's importation

---

[1] When he turned up in San Francisco thirty years later, it was as a member of the Franciscan Order attending a religious conclave. He had joined the Order in Peru in the early forties, following a not yet exhausted career on the operatic stage and in the films.

of singers directly from Europe. An artist who deserves to be better remembered, Torri possessed a pure lyric instrument which she used perfectly to convey a touching sense of fragility. She had a real Puccini voice—for Liu, Mimi and Butterfly. And she was, in fact, Rome's first Liu—in 1926. She continued to sing at La Scala until 1934, and is now living in retirement.

Torri was further featured in a specialty of hers, the role of Consuelo in *Anima Allegra*, a four-year-old opera by Franco Vittadini (1884–1948) which never made much of an impression. A sweetly tuneful, somewhat Puccinian work—disjointed and with a slim story —it had been produced at the Metropolitan two and a half years earlier with Lucrezia Bori.

Other female stars this year were Muzio; coloratura Elvira De Hidalgo, who sang at the Metropolitan in 1910 and returned the seasons of 1924–1925 and 1925–1926; and mezzo Marguerite D'Alvarez, who had sung in Oscar Hammerstein's old Manhattan Company a decade and a half earlier and with the Chicago Company in the early twenties.

The tenor territory was populated by an especially starry group. Besides Schipa there were the Belgian Fernand Ansseau and the Spaniard Antonio Cortis, both of whom were singing in Chicago and neither of whom ever joined the Metropolitan. Riccardo Stracciari and Cesare Formichi, also with Chicago associations, led the baritone contingent.

For the first time Merola shared the baton this season, and his colleague was Pietro Cimini, a vigorous Italian maestro who had conducted at the Chicago Opera.

A large opening night audience greeted the Torri-Schipa-Journet *Manon.* The next day San Franciscans read in the *Examiner* that the young prima donna from Italy "had something of the charm of Pavlova and the spontaneity of Nazimova." Becoming more specific musically, Mason went on to say that "vocally she charmed by the sustained delicacy of her cantilena. In moments of lyric rapture she has tones of pearly beauty." Schiapa was awarded an encore for his distinguished singing of "Le Rêve." Two days later there were reports of Ansseau's debut in *Samson* and his vibrant, powerful voice, his impeccable French and his handsome bearing. D'Alvarez was an intense Delilah. Some of Ansseau's recordings, it might be noted, remind one a little of the youthful Bjoerling. The Cortis instrument was distinctly more Latin: both had strong lyric and dramatic qualities in their vocalism.

In those early days of the company the press carried frequent re-

ports of the box office status, and the box score after three performances—*Manon, Samson* and *The Barber of Seville,* was: attendance,
14,781, and the take $47,221. The performance of *The Barber* made
a particularly good impression. As Mason reported, the Spanish De
Hidalgo is "that rara avis among prima donne, a coloratura with
brains and character . . . here was no female music box." Journet's
"La Calunnia" began "like a breeze and ended like a storm."

Muzio was delayed in getting to San Francisco because the Buenos
Aires season was extended for the Prince of Wales, but she did arrive
in time for postponed *Aida* and *Tosca* performances. The Scarpia was
Stracciari, who, to Mason, showed "flinty hardness and Roman
severity" as opposed to Scotti's "'cold malignity and Machiavellian
subtlety." Another end-of-season delight was the combination of
Torri, Ansseau and Journet in Montemezzi's *L'Amore dei Tre Re.*

Besides being the most interesting of the company's first three
seasons vocally, the 1925 series was a highly successful one financially.
Of the twelve performances in the large auditorium, six were sold
out, and the total receipts amounted to $154,058. In an atmosphere
of prosperity it is not surprising that prophecies were made—prophecies which time has shown as unduly optimistic. In one of Mason's
editorials—they were often of a commendably crusading nature—he
quoted the Los Angeles impresario L. A. Behymer as predicting that
within three years the West Coast would have twenty-four weeks of
opera divided between the principal coast cities.

"If we can," Mason wrote, "offer great artists a sufficient number
of engagements to induce them to come and sing for us, we shall be
able to compete for their services in the same field and on equal
terms with the Metropolitan and Chicago."

In the next thirty-five years there was a gradual and pleasing enlargement of the San Francisco Opera's activities, but the total length
of time consumed by them each year in San Francisco, Los Angeles
and other cities has by no means reached twenty-four weeks. The
"California season" of the San Francisco Opera has, however, been as
long as ten weeks[2] and remains close thereto. A respectable length—
unrivalled in the United States outside New York! The recent expansion—prior to its dissolution—of the Cosmopolitan Opera, a smaller,
rival organization, added an extra six weeks or so to the list in San
Francisco, but it must be pointed out that the Cosmopolitan's schedule
was less concentrated than the San Francisco's. Now there are three
weeks of Spring Opera.

[2] In 1959, when the San Francisco season of six weeks was preceded by six
performances in Portland and followed by a Southern California season of
approximately three weeks. No Portland appearances took place in 1960.

During 1925, as in the year previous, there was a Los Angeles season: six performances in Olympic Auditorium, produced by Merola and Behymer. Choristers from Los Angeles were used, and the Los Angeles Philharmonic contributed musicians. These southern ingredients formed important parts of the San Francisco Opera-conceived performances. Los Angeles seasons continued; a pact was signed in February, 1926, assuring that there would be no rivalry between the home association and that offering the operas in the southern California city. After a break in the mid-thirties, the San Francisco Opera traveled south in toto in 1937, under the name of the home association. Such seasons have continued regularly, and if they are not discussed in this book in detail it is because, in general, they repeated the attractions which San Francisco witnessed.

Many would like to see that twenty-four-week idea work out. It is unfortunate that it has not. Only by development of a solid core of resident artists to form a vital and virtually independent nucleus of the company could a half-a-year concept come to fruition. There have been good young singers, Californians or otherwise, who could be snatched up before too much demand pressed them into service as "airplane singers" rushing here and there. But there have not been enough of them to maintain an extended season in the manner to which the San Francisco Opera is accustomed. The brevity of West Coast opera activity has, naturally enough, not always persuaded singers interested in that area to establish a home along the Pacific shore.

In the twenties, with visits on and off of the Chicago Opera, the San Carlo and other companies, there were often five or six weeks of opera in a year, and sometimes more. Merola felt that his activities might well be expanded into two seasons a year, and he was the musical chief of a two-week series at the Columbia Theater in January, 1926. One of the special features of this season was an opera called *Fay-en-Fah*, the outgrowth of a 1917 Bohemian Club musical play, *The Land of Happiness*, with libretto by Templeton Crocker and music by Joseph D. Redding, prominent San Franciscans both. Their opera had premiered in Monte Carlo the year before, and three of the singers from that production, Lucy Berthrand, René Maison and Edmond Warnery,[3] were imported, the first two making American debuts in the San Francisco performances.

Toti Dal Monte was starred in *Lucia* and *Rigoletto*, the title role of the latter being sung by Joseph Schwarz of the Chicago Opera.

[3] The Pelléas of the first London performance of Debussy's opera, at Covent Garden in 1909.

Augusto Beuf was the leading tenor in *Lucia*. The repertoire further included *The Tales of Hoffmann*, with Berthrand as Olympia and Antonia, Maison as Hoffmann and Schwarz as Dr. Miracle. The season was not a great financial success, and this was the last winter series produced by Merola.

1926

Claudia Muzio was late again for her appearances with the company during the 1926 season, causing a postponed opening night. Of course she was worth waiting for. This time her ship, sailing from Rio de Janeiro to New York, was caught in a hurricane. After arriving she sang a busy season which included performances as Mimi, Manon Lescaut in the Puccini opera, Aida, Tosca and the *Trovatore* Leonora.

Marcel Journet sang his thousandth Mephistopheles in *Faust* during his San Francisco engagement, and appeared with Muzio in *Tosca*—as Scarpia. The role had been planned for Formichi, whose suave baritone was not heard again this year as scheduled. Actually Journet's basso had enough flexibility, notably in the later years of his career, to allow him entry into the baritone or bass-baritone realm. He did not sing Scarpia in his years at the Metropolitan (1900–1908) but he did appear as Escamillo during that period.

The 1926 repertoire was not especially adventurous beyond the building up of staples. There was, however, a well-attended performance of Auber's *Fra Diavolo*, not seen at the Metropolitan in a decade and a half. This light-textured affair was given with Schipa, Journet, the Chicago-based buffo Vittorio Trevisan, and Florence Macbeth, an American coloratura who made her debut abroad and returned to sing principally with the Chicago Opera. Luella Melius, an Australian who also sang in the midwest city, shared the soprano roles with Muzio, Macbeth and the local Myrtle Donnelly. Miss Macbeth, incidentally, was a substitute for the Polish lyric soprano Claire Dux.

Louise Homer, in her middle fifties, appeared as Delilah opposite the Samson of Charles Marshall, the dramatic tenor from the Chicago. Besides Schipa and Marshall, Paul Althouse, Aroldo Lindi and Cortis were in the tenor lineup. Lindi, who was really a Swede, named Harold Lindau, was to breathe his last on the stage of the War Memorial Opera House eighteen years later—he died just as he was finishing the first act of a San Carlo performance of *Pagliacci*. His ringing, light-colored voice was Italianate enough in sound to match his *nom de chant*.

The 1926 season also marked the company debut of the fine American lyric baritone Richard Bonelli. He appeared on the roster numerous times into the forties.

1927

The 1927 season acquainted San Franciscans with Ezio Pinza, Lawrence Tibbett and Puccini's *Turandot*.

The repertoire, more interesting and mature than previously, also included Wagner's *Tristan und Isolde* and Verdi's *Falstaff*. The former was the first Wagner presentation attempted by the company. The thirty-five-year-old Pinza bowed in as Timur in *Turandot*, which Merola presented only a little less than a year following its American premiere (November 16, 1926, at the Metropolitan) and indeed, only a year and a half after its world premiere (April 25, 1926, at La Scala in Milan). Young Tibbett made his first appearance with the company in the role which sealed his success at the Metropolitan, Ford in *Falstaff*, and the fat knight he clinked the coins at was the veteran Antonio Scotti, whose span of service at the New York house stretched from 1899 to 1933.

Another Tibbett special was Neri in *La Cena Delle Beffe*, Giordano's operatic version of Benelli's gruesome play. Boasting a strong if melodramatic libretto by Sem Benelli, it was more compelling dramatically than musically—although it might be noted that the simple, winding theme at the beginning of the fourth act is hard to forget. With Tibbett appeared Peralta and Tokatyan in parts sung in New York by Alda and Gigli.

Pinza and Tibbett were to have long records of San Francisco appearances. *Turandot*, however, disappeared—following repetition in 1928—for many years, but made a more than ordinary comeback in the fifties, being presented in three seasons of that decade: 1953, 1954 and 1957.

Alfred Hertz, the conductor of the San Francisco Symphony, members of which form most of the San Francisco Opera Orchestra, was a guest on the podium for *Tristan*. Elsa Alsen of Chicago experience and Rudolf Laubenthal of the Metropolitan were the lovers—the latter an unusually ascetic-looking knight. For a Latin touch, there was Pasquale Amato as Kurwenal. His voice had unfortunately faded prematurely, and stylistically he was a misfit on the Cornish scene. The overall production indicated that there was definitely room for artistic expansion insofar as the company's adventures in Wagnerland were concerned.

Manon Lescaut opened the season on September 15, with Frances Peralta (real name: Phyllis Partington), a big-voiced, California-raised soprano who had gone on to a modest success at the Metropolitan via the Scotti company.[4] The *Turandot* cast, including the Hungarian Anne Roselle, Tokatyan, Pinza and Myrtle Donnelly, was almost completely different from the Metropolitan's, which had been headed by Maria Jeritza, Giacomo Lauri-Volpi, Pavel Ludikar and Martha Attwood. Only Angelo Bada as Pang was in the eastern and western productions. Roselle had created the title role in Germany. As demonstrated in her recording of "In questa Reggia," she was a stunning Turandot from the vocal point of view, singing cleanly with a light, creamy tone and a relaxed manner stressing suavity over power. Hers was a bel canto approach to this difficult role. She sounded younger and altogether less haughty than many later Turandots, and it was possible to understand how a Calaf could fall in love with her.

Scotti, Tibbett and Bada, who had been on the Metropolitan stage January 2, 1925, when *Falstaff* had a New York revival after many years, were on the boards in San Francisco for the company's first excursion to Windsor Forest on September 27. This was to be the only *Falstaff* for many years, but happily this extremely subtle masterpiece has returned fairly frequently in recent years: in 1944, 1948 and 1956 —each time conducted superbly by William Steinberg, who knows the score well enough to rehearse this opera without one. Scotti's voice was well beyond its prime, but it mattered less in *Falstaff* than in *Tosca.* His acting was superior.

Puccini's opera brought forth as Cavaradossi the young American tenor Mario Chamlee,[5] the possessor of an appealing lyric-dramatic voice not unreminiscent of Richard Tauber's. Emphatically an above-average actor, he was short, but knew how to move around the stage, and how to engage sympathy.

Although her story is not strictly within the scope of this book, 1927 was also the year that a noted San Francisco coloratura made her operatic debut—not with the San Francisco Opera, nor even in the United States. Her name was Lina Pagliughi and she had been brought from New York to San Francisco as an infant. Her father was an upholsterer, and she had sung as a child in the Civic Auditorium. Tetrazzini and Gigli both encouraged her, and her regular

[4] She died in 1933.
[5] His career included performances at the Vienna Volksoper.

studies at Galileo High School were supplemented with music lessons from Domenico Brescia. Redfern Mason pointed out at least once that the San Francisco Opera was cautious about her; at all events, a fund drive sparked by Ettore Patrizi, editor of the newspaper *L'Italia*, raised enough money to send her to Italy for further study in 1926. Her debut was at the Politeama in Milan, and she later achieved La Scala. Pagliughi married an Italian tenor and pursued her career in Italy, never singing with either the San Francisco or the Metropolitan Opera. Her stout figure didn't help her, but her voice was a superb instrument, and she will be remembered, of course, as one of the top coloraturas of the century.

4

AN ELEMENT OF REVERIE

1928

There was talk of "an atmosphere of intimacy" in describing Dreamland Auditorium (now Winterland), the large neighborhood arena which became the home of the San Francisco Opera in 1928. But the building, which has served the Ice Follies troupe for the past two decades, was only a slightly smaller barn than the Civic Auditorium as far as opera was concerned. A number of reasons were cited for the move to Post and Steiner Streets. The capacity was smaller (4,600), the setting up of the special stage was less costly than at the Civic Auditorium, and, as the press of the day reported, "The new hall has been built with a careful view to the housing of music . . . acoustics have been given much consideration." Two seasons were played at Dreamland, but there had indeed been an element of reverie in the optimistic welcoming of the new home, not especially refined in decor, apt in location, nor notable for sonic excellence, and it was not with reluctance that the company moved out following the 1929 performances.

An unusual aspect of the 1928 series was the large place held by composer Umberto Giordano in the repertoire. *Andrea Chenier*, *Fedora* and *La Cena Delle Beffe* (at this point four years old) were all given. Considering that twelve operas were performed during the season, the traditional twins together, three out of eleven bills by Giordano seemed undue consideration. He was sometimes compelling as a puller of heart strings and a strong painter of atmosphere, but not the sort of consistently inspired composer who makes his connecting passages as interesting as the arias on each side of them.

Maria Jeritza, whose showmanship is better remembered than her voice, sang Fedora and Turandot, and also Tosca, this including her famous "Vissi d'arte" sung from a prone position. Elisabeth Rethberg began her long and happy association with the company during this

season, and the other of the three hard-worked prima donne was Elda
Vettori, a Metropolitan soprano of considerably less fame than her
sister performers. Backing them up was Myrtle Donnelly, who sang
Micaela besides Olga in *Fedora* and Lisabetta in *Cena*.

The season opened September 15 with *Aida*—this was the first of
a number of seasons to begin with this classic and appropriate season-
starter. Rethberg was cast with Edward Johnson, then a well-known
tenor, and later, of course, the Metropolitan's general manager. Tibbett
stepped in on short notice to sing Amonasro, a role he had taken only
once before. Giuseppe Danise, who was indisposed, made his first
appearance later in the season in *Fedora*.

A greater maturity was noted in Miss Donnelly's performance in
Cena, which, understandably enough, was sung to a smaller audience
than the *Aida* of two nights before. *Tosca* brought Jeritza and her
famous Floria before an SRO crowd. She was described by Alexander
Fried of the *Chronicle* as "a woman of royal beauty and magnetism."
Her plan of the character, Fried continued, "could not be called subtle,
but it was artistic and effectively credible throughout the story."
Jeritza, he said, "does not pretend to the perfection of bel canto," and
her full voice was rarely used with memorable beauty. It sometimes
dropped to "dramatic prose speech, forced beyond mellifluousness."
In *Carmen*, the soprano was, according to Mason, a "human panther"
as she defied the traditions of the role. Her Turandot was especially
striking: she brought out the willfulness of the princess vividly.

Rethberg scored a hit in *Butterfly*, and her tenor, Gennaro Barra,
making his American debut, was praised by one critic for his "excellent voice." There was far from unanimous enthusiasm about his vocal
quality, however. *L'Amore dei Tre Re*, given September 24, drew
the second smallest audience of the season, but those who were there
heard the highly effective Archibaldo of Ezio Pinza, who, incidentally,
sang the role under the composer's baton in San Francisco nineteen
years later. Pinza also appeared as Ramfis this year, and Escamillo and
Mephistopheles. *L'Amore* and *Carmen* were led by a young Metropolitan conductor, Wilfred Pelletier. As usual, Merola and Cimini did
most of the conducting.

1929

The 1929 pre-crash season of the San Francisco Opera was an
unusually happy one: almost half of the operas were comedies. *The
Barber of Seville, The Elixir of Love, Don Pasquale, Gianni Schicchi,*

Martha and *Hansel and Gretel* joined hands in a chain of merriment. Cutting through, of course, were the blood-spillers and thunder-sounders, but never again was there to be such a large proportion of works whose leading characters live happily ever after.

Tito Schipa and Giuseppe DeLuca, along with Nina Morgana and Pompilio Malatesta, were on hand to lend voice and charm to the comic proceedings. Rethberg, whose duties were all in the non-comic part of the list, sang Aida, the *Trovatore* Leonora, Marguerite and Mimi. The experienced French bass, Leon Rothier, returned for the first time since the Stanford season, and he was exceedingly conspicuous during 1929, a year that was missed by a company regular named Ezio Pinza. Rothier's roles were Sparafucile, Ferrando, Basilio, Colline, Ramfis, Mephistopheles and Count Des Grieux! Meanwhile, back East, Pinza was preparing for, among other things, the Metropolitan's overdue revival of *Don Giovanni.*

There was lots of enthusiastic applause this year, and the man who grabbed an especially large amount of it was that indisputably thrilling tenor, Giacomo Lauri-Volpi. He stopped the show—*Rigoletto*— opening night, and although he didn't encore "La donna è mobile" it looked as if he might. This ovation remains one of the longest in company history. Merola, in the pit, stuck to the rulebook, and after a few minutes Lauri-Volpi turned his back on the audience. At this point there were some boos from the gallery.

Some of the patrons were wondering just why this particular member of the Big Four of Italian tenors (Gigli, Martinelli and Schipa were the others, of course) had been so long in coming to San Francisco. After all, he was about to go into his eighth season at the Metropolitan. As one critic reported it, DeLuca innocently quoted Merola to some patrons as having said Lauri-Volpi was too expensive. Although a bright and ringing, sweet and pulsating tenor was his chief selling point, he was an artist of no mean histrionic ability.[1] His Canio was especially well thought out—one particular thought had to do with stumbling on a discarded handbill from the opening of the village scene just before "Vesti la giubba." The handbill served as only too positive a reminder of the fact that the show must go on.

Opposite Lauri-Volpi as Gilda opening night was Merola's old favorite Queena Mario, a pure lyric soprano whom some connoisseurs consider to have gone through her career with rather less than the lustre she deserved.

Merola and Cimini again conducted the majority of the per-

[1] Actually, at the time of writing the mid-sixtyish Lauri-Volpi is still singing in Italy.

formances, with aid at the podium from Wilfred Pelletier, Karl Riedel (second-stringers from the Metropolitan) and Antonio Dell'Orefice, the company's chorus master. Note was taken of improvement in the chorus—Merola's decision to employ a group of selected singers combining the best available voices in San Francisco and Los Angeles as the chorus for performances in both cities met with strong favor. This system endured for three seasons.

The tenor Barra reappeared briefly this season, overshadowed by Lauri-Volpi and Schipa. Incidentally, he is now living in Milan where, it is reported, he is a much sought-after teacher.

5

A PREMIERE AND SOME WAGNERIANS

1930

San Francisco gave an American premiere in the 1930 season. It was Ravel's wispy five-year-old, *L'Enfant et les Sortilèges*. Also on the boards was Puccini's *The Girl of the Golden West*, which had been revived at the Metropolitan during the previous season. *Salome, Tannhäuser* and *Mignon* were other newcomers to the company's repertoire.

Introduced to American audiences were Clare Clairbert, an elegant Belgian coloratura with a dramatic edge to her ebullient, silvery, and sometimes showy vocalism, and Gaetano Viviani, an American-born, Italian-educated baritone with international experience.[1] Also new to San Francisco audiences were Hope Hampton, a movie star ill-advised to try heavy opera, and Sydney Rayner, a New Orleans tenor whose career took him to the Paris, Metropolitan and American San Carlo companies.

With the troupe back in Civic Auditorium after two years on another stage, *Manon* opened the season September 11. Merola conducted a cast which boasted the presence of Beniamino Gigli. The French diction, Fried reported, would have raised many an eyebrow in Paris. But there was more good news that night. It was noted that "an excellent new seating arrangement, the lately provided canopy and an efficient stage all served to balm age-old wounds of disappointment at the lingering non-existence of the War Memorial Opera House."

The inflammable combination of Jeritza and Salome was unfolded for the first time in America the following night, in a performance which conductor-producer Merola, to quote Mason, "made organic and thrilling despite utterly inadequate preparation." Jeritza, he said,

[1] Record collectors may remember Viviani's presence as Barnaba in a European Columbia *Gioconda*. He continued to sing into the late forties, according to *Opera*'s files, appearing as Scarpia in Verona in 1946.

38

carried the last scene "to the white heat of horror," although perhaps some of the horror was taken away with the covering of Jokanaan's head with an opaque veil—a concession to certain pressures. Rayner and John Charles Thomas, the Herod and Jokanaan, were praised, but their voices were on the light side for these parts. Jeritza repeated her Salome in Chicago in 1934.[2]

A large crowd turned out for Puccini's helping of Latinized old Californiana September 15. Mason suggested the overwrought Jeritza dispense with her "bag of tricks" which included a spectacular fall prefaced by crude gyrations. But forgetting these, and the difficulty of Californians suspending disbelief at Puccini's California, there was much good singing from Viviani, Frederick Jagel and Madame Jeritza herself. An unintentionally amusing bit of action occurred when the active prima donna knocked off Viviani's wig and he slapped it on again—backwards!

The largest audience of the season to date turned out for Bohême on September 17. The Musetta was the young local singer, Audrey Farncroft, who sang creditably among her more famous colleagues: Gigli, Mario and Viviani.

The artistic piece de resistance of the year came September 19 when the Ravel was premiered. The whimsical little opera, never given professionally elsewhere in America, was cleverly staged by Agnini with settings by the local artist Lucien Labaudt. The furnishings in the indoor scene—its walls were patterned with red apples and wide blue stripes—were exaggerated in size to make Mario, as the *enfant*, look appropriately diminutive.

John Charles Thomas triumphed as Tonio in *Pagliacci* the following evening, which saw Jeritza singing both Nedda and Santuzza. There was some disagreement as to just how good Madame Clairbert was as Philine in *Mignon* September 22. But Hope Hampton was adjudged simply not ready for such a pretentious part—Marguerite in *Faust*—as she was given on the twenty-fifth. Her entrance caught her literally voiceless. Gigli sang in *Mignon* under the hardship of having just been informed of his mother's death in Italy.

A performance of *Tannhäuser* on the twenty-third surely included one of the most southerly-oriented Wagnerian casts ever assembled. Messrs. Paltrinieri, Sandrini, Oliviero and D'Angelo sang the roles of the four knights, and Pinza was the somewhat uncomfortable Landgrave. The production featured Jeritza as Elizabeth, Dorothee Manski

[2] This was also the year in which *Salome* returned to the Metropolitan repertoire for the first time since the famous first performance in that house, in 1907. Göta Ljungberg took the title role. Jeritza had left the Met.

as Venus. Rayner as Tannhäuser and Thomas as Wolfram. Merola
found it difficult, of course, to arrange for Teutonic Wagnerian casts
when there was so little Wagner given. Riedel conducted this performance.

Cimini was absent this year, and the combination of Riedel,
Pelletier and Dell'Orefice as Merola's podium partners was hardly
electrifying. He was slow to engage conductors of any great brilliance
or expense. Of course it is also true that many top conductors were
not interested in traveling such a long way to serve a company whose
rehearsal schedule was skimpy. Travel in later years was quicker,
rehearsal time somewhat more plentiful.

On the twenty-seventh there was an afternoon *Salome* and an evening *Lucia* to close the season. The next day Mason wrote in a curtain-
lowering piece that, in spite of the depression, fears of a deficit "have
evaporated." The general public, he reported, attended the opera in
larger numbers than ever.

The title role of *Lucia* was assumed by Clairbert, whose autumn
schedule also included an engagement with the Philadelphia Opera. She
did not sing much, however, in this country. According to authoritative reports she now manages a restaurant near the Monnaie, the Royal
Opera House in Brussels.

1931

Mârouf, by Henri Rabaud, the French composer-conductor-con-
servatory director, opened the 1931 season. Yvonne Gall, a forty-six-
year-old Parisian soprano with Chicago Opera experience, and Mario
Chamlee, the Los Angeles tenor with Paris Opera experience, were
starred. This light, pleasant score, vintage 1914, with its fairly corny
exoticisms and ornateness was the French pastry on this year's menu,
which also included such solid viands as *Tannhäuser*, *Lohengrin* and
Meistersinger.

Mârouf was inspired by *The Arabian Nights*. It's the story of a
poor cobbler cursed with a shrewish wife who passes himself off to a
sultan as a rich merchant and wins the sultan's daughter's hand. The
concoction, a rarity in this country (the Metropolitan, which first
produced it in 1917, revived it in its spring season of 1937) won
enthusiastic applause from the first night audience. Mason wrote of
the "languor and sweetness and melancholy of it all" in describing the
music, which was sung against a lavish background.

This season, for his Wagnerian frontal attack, Merola gathered together singers whose reputations were made north of the Alps. They were among the best available, and he was going to get plenty of mileage out of them. Wagner was in the San Francisco air, what with a couple of visits (in early 1930 and 1931) by the German Grand Opera Company, an aggregation including such oldtime Wagnerians as Johanna Gadski, Carl Braun and Johannes Sembach.

Merola's choices were the incomparable baritone, Friedrich Schorr; the appealing soprano, Maria Müller; and the interesting tenor, Gotthelf Pistor (he in his American debut). Not to mention an established San Francisco favorite, Elisabeth Rethberg. The Wagner conductor was one Hans Blechschmidt, who had appeared in the Civic Auditorium the previous January conducting *The Flying Dutchman* with the German Grand Opera. His work was highly efficient if not the last word in interpretative distinction.

Müller managed the stylistic changes and summoned the vocal endurance necessary to sing Mimi and Butterfly besides Elsa and Eva. Her performance of the Japanese girl called forth from Fried this comment: "The deeply expressive quality of her song, and the conviction and logic of her acting thrust from importance the question of whether a tall German soprano of heroic voice should impersonate a fragile, sad daughter of Japan."

Pistor's heldentenor was not the most consistently beautiful imaginable, nor was his production always effortless, but he was capable of producing a good deal of dark, suave tone, he was impressive-looking, and further, he was a man of no mean interpretative gifts.

The trio of Rethberg, Martinelli and that distinguished, seductive-toned high baritone, Giuseppe Danise, carried the leads in *Aida*, *Chenier, Masked Ball* and *Trovatore*. There was a Gallic Tosca in Gall, a relatively dainty one who killed Scarpia, one critic said, "from impulse rather than heroic desperation." Her soft tones were particularly lovely, her louder ones sometimes forced.

Among the new members of the company were Maxine Castleton, a Los Angeles soprano who undertook Venus; Luisa Silva, a La Scala mezzo originally from California whose voice had "a dark vigor of quality" apt for Azucena; and Faina Petrova, a Metropolitan mezzo from Moscow whose Carmen was, for Mason, "a graceless animal." The veteran bass Andres DeSegurola turned up as Sharpless and Marcello, but not so happily, for he was well past his prime.

Once launched, the San Francisco Opera had pursued a pleasant financial course, operating virtually without deficit. The depression and diminished patronage caught up with the company, however, and there was a spot of red ink adding up to approximately $18,000 in 1931.

The founders' fund could take care of that, of course. At the same
time, Mason noted that repeats of *Lohengrin* and *Meistersinger*, had
they been available, would have helped reduce the deficit. And looking
beyond the special financial problem, he cited the obvious artistic
advantages of repeat performances. In time there would be seasons
with practically the whole repertoire repeated, but in 1931 patience
was needed along with appropriate criticism.

The visits of the German Grand Opera, in early 1930 and 1931,
have already been mentioned. The winter of 1931 also saw a short
visit of the Chicago Opera to Civic Auditorium. *Der Rosenkavalier*
was given for the first time in San Francisco, at a Saturday matinee,
with Frida Leider as the Marschallin, Maria Olszewska as Octavian,
Alexander Kipnis as Ochs, and Thelma Votipka, later known at the
Metropolitan and in San Francisco for *comprimario* parts, as Sophie.
Frank St. Leger conducted. The season was also interesting for the
presence, in small roles, of one Jenny Tourel. Other conductors were
Emil Cooper and Roberto Moranzoni.

At this point the history of the Chicago's sporadic bay region
activity following the 1922 "fiasco" might be recapitulated. The troupe
came to the Casino Theater at Ellis and Mason Streets for four performances March 6–8, 1924, the list including a *Boris Godounoff* with
Chaliapin as Boris, Kipnis as Varlaam. Mary Garden sang in *Cléopâtre*
of Massenet. When the company appeared in Oakland, for four March
performances, in 1928, she sang in Alfano's *Resurrection*. Rimsky-
Korsakoff's *Snow Maiden* was also among the operas presented. There
were four Oakland presentations in 1929.

6

THE NEW HOME

1932

The great day came at last, on October 15, 1932—the first performance by the company in a home worthy of its best efforts: the War Memorial Opera House. The opera was *Tosca*, the cast headed by Muzio, Dino Borgioli and Gandolfi. The first act was broadcast nationally over NBC's Red Network.

The choice of opera reflected Merola's love of Puccini, his admiration of Muzio's art and the demand for a sure-fire hit.

Those who tuned in the broadcast heard an announcer read a ten-minute prepared script in which many of the hall's measurements and details of its decor were given. The night's musical fare, the announcer read in a sentence which dotted every i, would be *"Tosca,* an Italian opera in three acts by Giacomo Puccini, brilliant Italian composer of opera"; the evening, he said, marked fulfillment of "a dream long denied."

Warm applause greeted Merola coming into the pit, and before the announcer had quite finished his introduction, the "Star Spangled Banner" was struck up. It was a deliberate and highly moving performance of the anthem that carried through the house, the audience joining in fairly lustily. A short pause, and then the opera itself began.

Merola had a particular way with Puccini, and he was at the top of his form this night—the music was given a characteristically plastic, unrushed, mellow treatment, the rallentandos receiving all their due, and the results from the pit were gripping indeed. Muzio was excellent. She brought to the role the combination of her warm, limpid, well-modulated voice and her strong, honest, dramatic conviction. This was a Tosca who could be tigerish, but few have surpassed Muzio in the gentleness and subtlety she put into this part. The pianissimo effects were memorable.

Borgioli was an exciting dulcet-toned Cavaradossi, and Gandolfi, if not first class vocally, was at least a persuasively sinister Scarpia, cadaverous in look and dark in voice. The opening marked his first appearance with the San Francisco Opera since the 1923 season: he had also participated in the first performance of the company.

Among those tuning in the broadcast were some of the thousands who had been unable to obtain tickets for the opening. Some whose checks were returned were rather miffed to find tickets available from brokers at premium prices. Actually, a ticket problem applied to the whole season, which offered the usual dozen performances in a hall approximately 2,000 seats smaller than the previous home. An increase in single seat ticket applications caused difficulties as eighty per cent of the seats to the main series of performances were taken by subscribers.

After the broadcast, during the first intermission, there was a speech by Wallace M. Alexander, the new president of the Association—Bentley had just died, without having the pleasure of seeing the company he had helped so much into its new home. "Italy has her Toscanini, New York her Gatti-Casazza, San Francisco her Gaetano Merola," said Alexander. He cited a mixture of "grasp of vocation, resourcefulness and indomitable perseverance" as the qualities which had enabled Merola to bring exciting opera to San Francisco for nine successive years. Armando Agnini, his "tireless co-worker," was also saluted. And then he concluded: "Ladies and gentlemen, this is YOUR Opera House, your own rich heritage."

Now what was this new home, the War Memorial Opera House, like? A detailed report on the structure would include mention of these facts: the building is 180[1] feet by 282 feet on the ground, its external appearance similar to that of the adjacent Veterans' Building. But with the difference that the Opera House's stage block rises 150 feet above ground level, or higher than a twelve-story building. The exteriors of the two buildings are in rusticated terra cotta, with granite bases and steps and free-standing columns of granite on the front façades.

The architecture of the Opera House and its near-twin is classic, harmonizing with that of other buildings in the Civic Center complex, notably the City Hall directly across Van Ness Avenue. It is somewhat reminiscent of Palladio's Basilica in Vicenza. The main façade gives entrance through five pairs of doors to the lobby, and then to the foyer, with its marble floor, walls of cast stone and vaulted and

[1] This figure does not include the lateral projections, which result in an overall front façade 231 feet wide.

coffered ceiling thirty-eight feet high. At each end broad main stairs of marble rise to the upper levels.

The auditorium itself is not wholly traditional. There is a golden horseshoe of boxes—twenty-five in all, each with a separate inner room —but there are no other semicircular tiers.[2] Two wide and deep galleries cut across the hall, the lower one divided into the Grand Tier and the Dress Circle by a crossways aisle, the upper divided similarly into the Balcony Circle and Balcony.

The Opera House has a seating capacity of 3,252, which means that it is not exactly an intimate house—the Paris Opera seats only two thirds as many, for instance—but there is this advantage: there are none of those blind view seats found in the rears of side boxes in old-style opera houses. Had acoustics experts not discouraged it, the capacity might have been 4,000 plus.

Thirteen hundred of the seats are on the main floor, which is 113 feet wide and 116 feet long from curtain to rear wall. The distance from the curtain to the rear wall of the second gallery is 161 feet. Boxes A, B, Y and Z, at each end of the horseshoe, officially contain six seats, the other twenty-one, eight seats each (total: 192), but more can be squeezed in. There are 274 seats in the Grand Tier, 578 in the Dress Circle, 290 in the Balcony Circle and 618 in the Balcony.

The proscenium arch is 52 feet wide and 51 feet high in the center. Relief figures in the spandrels—two horses ridden by trim Amazons —are by sculptor Edgar Walter. The principal feature of the ceiling is the great elliptical surface from which the big chandelier hangs. Twenty-seven feet in diameter, it produces the effect of a huge, illuminated star, the color of which can be changed, or so it was stated in the 1932 program, "to suit the lighting of the stage or the mood of the music being played (!)." Much of the main ceiling is formed of acoustical plaster, the balance of wall and ceiling surfaces of lime plaster.

The arches of the side walls above the boxes are faced with plaster grillwork intended to conceal the organ loft on each side. There is a projection room behind the Dress Circle. And a loggia at the front of the building on the Grand Tier level which might well be utilized on warm evenings. But large doors onto it were never provided.

As for the stage itself, it is 83 feet deep and 131 feet wide, with 140 feet between stage level and roof. Underneath the stage there is a rack

[2] A number of the War Memorial trustees—Kendrick, Kingsbury and Tobin for instance—were opposed to the idea of having boxes because they seemed like relics of bygone ages of aristocracy.

for rolling up and storing scenery. There are four fly galleries at each side of the stage and two gridirons extending over the entire stage area, all for the purpose of operating scenery and properties. Lifting and lowering of scenery is automatically controlled at stage level by an electronic push button system: there are facilities for raising and lowering seventy-seven backdrops. The stage floor can be set up with twenty-nine sections at different heights.[3]

The entire lighting of the hall and stage is controlled from a thirty-foot-long switchboard located at stage right just behind the proscenium. It permits pre-setting of all lighting combinations for an entire performance.

At the time of writing, three artist's dressing rooms are available on the first floor—the leading tenor is always given No. 11, at stage left, and the leading lady occupies No. 14 across the house. No. 10, also on stage right, is the conductor's. There are eight dressing rooms on the second floor, four on the third, most with tub and shower. The chorus dresses in the basement. Calls to all rooms come over a speaker system.

The orchestra pit as customarily used seats about sixty-five comfortably and seventy-five sardine-packed. The basic orchestra for the opera consists of sixty to sixty-five members of the San Francisco Symphony (sometimes a few players are not members of the Symphony); that number is swelled to a figure between seventy and eighty for elaborate Wagner and Strauss scores. The pit was designed in two sections, the two together accommodating a grand total of about 120 players, but such an arrangement is only possible when the first two rows of seats are removed from the auditorium. The opera management has not chosen to forsake the revenue of the customers in those two rows, and its point deserves sympathy. But how much better it would have been if the pit had been built with one total in mind—say, about ninety-five players—instead of two, one of them inoperable.[4]

It is interesting to further record that the Old Mission Bay Creek from Hayes Valley runs underneath the War Memorial. There is continual subbasement seepage, but a special drain gutter running along

---

[3] In general the San Francisco Opera uses portable levels because productions must also fit the less elaborate stage of the Shrine Auditorium in Los Angeles.

[4] Actually, the space under the stage behind the basic pit to the left and right of the prompter's box can be used to accommodate an extra twenty-five or thirty musicians, but acoustical, atmospheric and visibility conditions are not optimum. During some seasons this space has been used in various ways.

the passageway between the Opera House and the Veterans' Building has been set up to deal with this persistent and not unhumorous liquid malady.

After opening night, the season continued highly successfully at a five dollar top, with the SRO sign hung out for all performances but *Hansel and Gretel* and the second *Meistersinger*. The matinee of *Lucia* with Lily Pons was not only heard by an audience in the Opera House but also by another which listened to it piped into the Civic Auditorium and by still another in City Hall Plaza which listened from a second sound system. With Muzio, Pons, Schorr, Pinza, Bonelli and others kept busy, there were plenty of vocal delights this season. A visual low point was reached, however, with the mise-en-scene of *Lohengrin*: it was disturbed by such mishaps as a trumpeter taking a spill, a swan refusing to disappear, footlights going out, and four none-too-husky choristers almost toppling Maria Müller to the stage when they hoisted Elsa on the King's Shield. Not to mention big peepholes in the nuptial chamber.

This was one of those unlucky nights. But speaking in general, in spite of the new facilities, there was room for improvement in the overall stage picture, and need for insurance that a high standard could be maintained. One thing Merola did about it was to ask for a permanent ballet school, which was created at a meeting of the Opera Association's Women's Committee in December. The school would keep the company supplied with dancers; they would dance in the productions as the San Francisco Opera Ballet. Adolph Bolm of Diaghileff fame was secured as ballet chief, and thus was launched the special history of what has come to be known as the San Francisco Ballet. Until 1957 the outside activities of the troupe were limited, with the Christmas presentations of *The Nutcracker* its most conspicuous achievement. But then three State Department foreign tours brought the dancers international fame, and a substantial season of repertoire was launched at the downtown Alcazar Theater in February, 1960.

The forty-five-year-old *tenore robusto*, Francesco Merli, sang his one and only appearance in San Francisco in 1932's first *Lucia*. As record collectors know, his way with the role of Calaf in *Turandot* had a rugged and moving ring to it. His Edgardo was not so appropriate. "Merli had a good grasp of his duties," wrote Fried. "When he was not singing vigorously, he tended to lapse from pitch. When his music permitted his upper tones to unleash themselves, he was forceful. An Edgar, however, should look more romantic." Audience reaction was not enthusiastic. Merli was having trouble with his voice, and it was decided to make substitutions in his other performances. Tandy MacKenzie, a Scotch-Hawaiian tenor, was his replacement in *Trovatore*, gaining mixed reviews. Chamlee assumed his Turiddu, Borgioli the tenor lead in the second *Lucia*. Indisposition aside, Manrico undoubtedly would have been a better introduction for Merli than the more subtly elegant Edgardo.

1933

Louis Gruenberg's somber and harrowing *The Emperor Jones* was rather too much for some of the subscribers when it was unfolded on November 17, ten months following its premiere at the Metropolitan—there were even some boos. But Lawrence Tibbett scored a hit in his tour de force role, and the second performance was more warmly received than the first. There were two other items in English this season: *The Secret of Suzanne* by Wolf-Ferrari, which served as curtain raiser for *The Emperor*, and *Le Coq d'Or* of Rimsky-Korsakoff, which was given as pantomime cum vocal accompaniment in a new and expensive production with a light scenic touch. Emily Hardy and Nathan Stewart sang the leading parts, while Maclovia Ruiz and Adolph Bolm mimed them.

Fried provided a succinct estimate of *Emperor Jones*, writing: "Eugene O'Neill's text is effectively curt, but at the same time it is prosaic and shallow.... The success of Louis Gruenberg's modernistic music is that, added to the distant tireless drumbeat of the original play, it works well together with O'Neill's devices of theatrical tension. To build an opera for the ages, however, a composer has to conceive some musical eloquence of his own. Gruenberg's score is not eloquent. His use of voices in declamation heightens the vividness of speech a little, but it never glorifies diction into really thrilling utterance. His orchestra, for the most part, is energetically and cleverly busy with tight-lipped dissonant tricks of accompaniment. Only when Jones falls to his knees to sing the spiritual, 'It's me, O Lawd,' does the music cast over the listeners' spirit a spell of large beauty."

The fact remains that it was worthwhile doing something new and provocative—although, to be sure, *The Emperor Jones* is more a "play with music" than an opera. When Richard Tobin, president of the Musical Association of San Francisco, sponsor of the San Francisco Symphony, let out an irate broadside against it in the *Call-Bulletin*, Tibbett took time out from a *Pagliacci* rehearsal to remind Mr. Tobin in another *Call-Bulletin* article that "one can't live on sweets."

The 1933 season opened with lustrous-toned Cyrena Van Gordon in *Samson and Delilah*. The audience listened not without appreciation to this and the *Coq D'Or* which followed, but it was with the third performance, *Aida* with Muzio and Martinelli, that the patrons became wildly enthusiastic, at least in greeting the artists. There was lots of excitement over a subsequent *Bohême*, too—one which featured Lucrezia Bori, who made her debut with the company this season. While three thousand-odd saw and heard her in the Opera House, another several thousand listened to the performance as relayed to the Civic Auditorium. This was another public service of the Art Commission. Following the performance, Bori was whisked from garret to auditorium, there to be presented with a bouquet by Mayor Angelo Rossi. Bori made more news this season singing Act 2 of *Pagliacci* on points.

The precedent for the pantomime-with-accompaniment *Coq* would be Fokine's version prepared for London and Paris in 1914 after the idea was voiced by Diaghileff's scenic collaborator, Alexandre Benois. When Pierre Monteux conducted the Metropolitan premiere of this version in 1918, the part of the King was danced by Adolph Bolm. And so it was in San Francisco in 1933—Bolm, of course, being the director of the ballet. He was credited with the choreography for this presentation, which found the singers sitting in narrow double-decked grandstands at each side of the stage. The sets and costumes—delightful ones—were by Nicholas Remisoff, of Chauve-Souris fame.

The singers in *Coq D'Or*, it can be pointed out, were all San Franciscans. The cast of *Emperor Jones* was all-Californian.

Issay Dobrowen, the San Francisco Symphony's conductor, had been engaged to lead *Tristan*, but a nervous disorder prevented him from doing so, and Alfred Hertz, the orchestra's conductor emeritus and likewise a podium figure of some eminence, filled in. Paul Althouse was the Cornish knight, and his virile tenor was highly praised. Four months later he became the first American to sing the role of Tristan at the Metropolitan. Gertrude Kappel's Isolde, considered one of her best roles, met with favor for its sweeping top tones. Hertz was criticized for letting the brass blare too loudly, but his forthright approach won praise.

Another addition to the repertoire this year was Verdi's *La Forza del Destino*. Its coming-in coincided, alas, with Muzio's going-out. December 1, 1933, marked her last appearance with the San Francisco Opera. Exactly a month later, she returned to the Metropolitan from which she had been absent for nearly a dozen years, her affiliation having been switched to Chicago. She died in 1936.

The relatively limited capacity of the Opera House, the expense of adapting old productions to the new theater, the cost of elaborate new productions of *Coq D'Or* and *Tristan:* these factors contributed to the whopping $36,000 deficit which the company chalked up in 1933. Actually, the ten performances of the main subscription series had been sold out, and the five repeats enjoyed a heavy sale, but sale of the most expensive seats for the five extra performances lagged. In retrospect, the emphasis on Sunday matinees, plus the Thanksgiving matinee, proved a strategic error in the time-setting of the repeats. At all events, $6,000 of the losses were recouped at a post-season concert for which artists volunteered their services.

One of the most interesting seasonal résumés written during the early years of the company came not from the daily press but *The Argonaut,* a now-defunct San Francisco magazine which showed strong signs of life in the musical criticism of one Covington Enderly. On December 8, 1933, he suggested that the San Francisco Opera (1) hire fewer stars, (2) employ local conductors who were just as good as Metropolitan "hacks," (3) utilize economical modern scenic designs instead of expensive realistic sets and (4) have more rehearsals, "toward which the visiting stars might contribute by arriving in town earlier."

Further, he said, with heroic optimism, "in the field of American opera, it is time the San Francisco Opera Company created the precedent of including at least one premiere of a new American work each season." Mr. Enderly wrote about one generation too soon: in 1959 the Ford Foundation announced a program whereby the San Francisco Opera, along with the Metropolitan, the New York City Opera and the Chicago, is given the financial aid to produce new American operas. But even in 1933 there was a good deal of point, if not necessarily practicality, to his recommendations.

Perhaps a very modern-minded general director would have initiated a consistent program of modern sets, economic or otherwise, but in 1933 there were many opera managements that were conservative. Greater length of season was needed to facilitate Enderly's program, and greater length of season came in later years. A real modern spirit did not come immediately upon the extension of the seasons, but in time it came, and today the man from *The Argonaut* would probably be quite happy.

What is especially intriguing about Enderly's suggestions is that they are exactly the same ones which in early 1960 could logically be directed toward the Cosmopolitan, the rival troupe which performed during late winter and early spring for several years. In the mid-thirties one didn't really expect modern sets in this country (although the crusading work of the Philadelphia Orchestra opera productions must be noted, and there were other examples of modernity), but by 1960 the new visual aesthetic of opera production had become a widespread living force.

1934

The 1934 season opened with a gay *Bartered Bride*, continued with an estimable *Tosca*, let down briefly with a questionable *Carmen*, and caught its stride again with an exquisite *Manon*. And on through a total of fifteen performances a particularly high average was maintained.

The Bartered Bride, sung in German, was especially notable for the clever way Bolm integrated the dances with the stage movement. The unusually interesting Tosca was Lotte Lehmann, and of her performance Redfern Mason wrote, "Her Tosca had not the sculptured beauty of Muzio; she did not wallow as Jeritza had when she sang 'Vissi d'arte.' What she did was to give us a Tosca evolved out of her inner consciousness, and in that scene with Scarpia, she touched a note of beautiful humility which neither Bernhardt nor Muzio can give us." Fried wrote, "She is a personality. Her voice, opulent and beautiful, but not necessarily restricted to the charm of honeyed tone, bespeaks a penetrating expressive intelligence. She constructs the role as it should be constructed with human conviction and with a controlled and flexible sense of its form."

The *Carmen* suffered, many thought, from forty-eight-year-old Ninon Vallin's cool, intimate and straight-laced projection of the cigarette girl. She was not interested in being tough or vulgar. There was a certain amount of disappointment among opera-goers over Madame Vallin, who was, after all, a highly regarded member of the Paris Opera, but her lovely Marguerite was better received than her Carmen. This famous singer never sang at the Metropolitan or the Chicago Opera. It should be noted, too, that Micaela, besides Carmen, was in her repertoire: she was more a Micaela type.[5]

Richard Crooks made his first San Francisco Opera appearance in *Manon* opposite Bori, and his lyric voice, elegant phrasing and handsome appearance won him warm applause. He was not, however, an imaginative actor.

[5] But not so starchy as to refuse a Paris music hall engagement.

Lehmann continued her activities in the Italian repertoire with a Butterfly which, Marjory Fisher wrote in the *News*, was "more Italian than Japanese." The acting, she said, "verged on the melodramatic in tragic moments, but she was amazingly youthful and girlishly animated in the first act, and in the second, the matured woman who has known much agony." Others felt more strongly that this was a serious case of miscasting.

Lauritz Melchior was introduced to San Francisco opera with performances in *Tannhäuser* and *Otello*, the latter, incidentally, missing from the Metropolitan's repertoire from 1913 to 1937. The Wagner was conducted with a great deal of fire by Hertz, and the cast further boasted Rethberg's presence. She also sang her touching Desdemona to Melchior's decidedly un-Italian Moor, which he never sang at the Met. In the second *Tannhäuser*, the Wolfram was one Nelson Eddy, up from Hollywood as a replacement for Bonelli.

Puccini's *La Rondine* was brought into the repertoire for Bori, and had a minor success. This "afternoon off of a genius," as W. J. Henderson once called it, mingles humor, show and tender emotions in good proportions, but it never returned to the boards in San Francisco, nor has it really found a firm place elsewhere. Bori was also welcomed in the title role of *Mignon*—a specialty of hers although a mezzo part. Transpositions upward gave the performance something of the quality of a nervous elevator.

Providing Emily Hardy, a relatively inexperienced local lyric-coloratura, with a good starring opportunity, Delibes' *Lakmé* began its unduly long association with the company this season. The most serious opera lover might well have asked at that point, Why *Lakmé* when the company has not even touched Mozart?

What *had* the San Francisco achieved with regard to repertoire in its first dozen years of operation? One could credit Merola with the American premiere of Ravel's *L'Enfant et les Sortilèges*. One could thank him for keeping San Francisco informed of the later and less popular Puccini: *Turandot*, the complete *Trittico*, *The Girl of the Golden West* and *La Rondine*. He could draw praise for bringing *Emperor Jones*, a provocative work at least, to San Francisco shortly after its world premiere. One could admire his ambition in performing Wagner.

At the same time, one could question bringing out *Anima Allegra* and *Mârouf* when the Strauss of *Ariadne*, the Bartok of *Bluebeard's Castle*, the Prokofieff of *Love for Three Oranges* and, above all, the Mozart of *Cosi fan Tutte*, *Don Giovanni* and *The Marriage of Figaro*

Exterior, War Memorial Opera House

Carolyn Mason Jones

Charles Keerdrick

Original plan for opera house
on Van Ness Avenue

G. A. Carsburgh

Grand staircase,
original project

Foyer, present opera house

Morton

Claudia Muzio as Violetta, 1932

Queena Mario as Juliette, 1923   *Davis*

Rosina Torri
as Manon, 1925

S. F. Opera Ass'n.

Fernand Ansseau
as Cavaradossi, 1925

Mrs. H. Clifton

Pasquale Amato
as Kurwenal, 1927

Hartsook, Courtesy Mrs. H. Clifton

Rudolf Laubenthal
as Tristan, 1927

Hartsook, Courtesy Mrs. H. Clifton

De Gueldre, Courtesy Mrs. H. Clifton

Elisabeth Rethberg,
1928

Ezio Pinza, 1927   Mrs. H. Clifton

Gretchen Dick

Yvonne Gall, 1931

Mrs. H. Clifton

Clare Clairbert, 1930

Setzer
Wien

Setzer, Vienna

Maria Jeritza in *Eine Nacht in Venedig*, 1931

Marôuf, Act 3, 1931   *Morton*

Morton

Die Meistersinger, 1931,
with Pistor, Schorr, Pinza, Müller, Grüninger

Garden Party at Milton Esberg's, Ross, 1925. Standing, left to right: James D. Phelan, William T. Sesnon, Charles W. Fay, Charles Lauwers, Milton Esberg, Gaetano Merola, Robert I. Bentley, Armando Agnini, Riccardo Stracciari, Marcel Journet, Fernand Ansseau, Horace Clifton, Antonio Cortis, Vittorio Trevisan. In foreground: Tito Schipa, Lodovico Olivero, Gennaro Papi.

Lily Pons,
1933

Metropolitan Musical Bureau,
Courtesy Mrs. H. Clifton

Dino Borgioli,
1932

Mrs. H. Clifton

Morton

Lauritz Melchior
as Otello, 1934

Set Svanholm
as Otello, 1948

Paul Tracy

Kirsten Flagstad as Leonore, 1939

Merola and Agnini in the forties

Standard Hour Broadcast, 1947, left to right:
Baccaloni, Pinza, Quartararo, Merola, Conner, Kullman

Backstage at *Aida*, 1950, Posz, Bing, Nikolaidi, Del Monaco,
Merola, Tebaldi, Agnini

went untapped. With these operas Merola could have kept at a higher pace the crescendo of imaginative operatic activity which was building up. To be sure, the shortness of the season, the remoteness of San Francisco, the fact that the Metropolitan in some respects (Mozart, for instance) was not particularly adventurous cast shadows of limitation. But the courage seemed to be there—intermittently—for great things.

7

COMING OF AGE

1935

By far the most newsworthy event of the 1935 season, and the most ambitious and expensive project the company had undertaken, was the presentation of the complete *Ring* cycle of Wagner. For this impressive series of performances Merola gathered together a list of artists prominently associated with the Wagnerian realm. It included Kirsten Flagstad, Elisabeth Rethberg, Friedrich Schorr, Emanuel List, Kathryn Meisle, Dorothee Manski, Marek Windheim, Hans Clemens and Gustav Schützendorf. There were also the American basses Chase Baromeo and Douglas Beattie, the latter from nearby San José with experience in Italy.

Artur Bodanzky, who had presided over the German wing at the Metropolitan for twenty years—he followed Hertz in this position—was the conductor. The augmented orchestra, including Wagnerian tubas and bass trumpet, was rehearsed for several weeks prior to the season with assistant conductors Karl Riedel and Hermann Weigert aiding in the preparation. Bodanzky himself arrived two weeks before the *Rheingold* was performed. Part of the orchestra for *The Ring* was seated under the stage.

The sets were, of course, in traditional style. They were designed by Julian Dove, who had worked for impresarios Conried and Hammerstein in New York and held an important post with the Chicago Opera. The prop list included a large segmented aluminum and canvas dragon for *Siegfried* which was capable of some fairly realistic thrashing about.

The four operas were given consecutively to make up the first four performances of the regular subscription series, and *Walküre* was repeated as a non-subscription event. *Rheingold* was a somewhat uncomfortable choice for opening night with its single long act, and perfect Wagnerites legitimately raised eyebrows at the intermission placed following the second scene.

The cycle called forth many superlatives from the critics, Flagstad for instance being hailed by the *Chronicle's* Alfred Frankenstein as "a kind of Nordic Winged Victory" at her local debut in *Walküre*. Melchior not only sang well but was also a forceful actor, despite what Frankenstein called "an occasional touch of ponderous kittenishness." Flagstad sang the *Siegfried* Brünnhilde for the first time in her career November 6. Of the orchestra's performance on this occasion the *Chronicle* critic wrote that it had "fierce energy and subtle atmosphere." Bodanzky's Wagner was classic and clear-cut, moving at a relentless pace but never lapsing, he said, into "vulgar blare of brass."[1]

From the box office view, *The Ring* was a smashing success. It was sold out a month in advance. Enthusiasm ran high as the performances progressed, and at the end of *Götterdämmerung* there was a standing ovation for Bodanzky. The orchestra tendered him a *tusch*. Despite a ten per cent raise in ticket prices for the season, there was a hefty deficit thanks to *The Ring* and its extra expenses, but no one was too unhappy about it in view of the hit the tetralogy made.

The production of Wagner's epic could be said to symbolize the coming of age of the company. The thirties saw the San Francisco Opera emerge more and more from the cozy "family affair" status of its early years to the fully assured, more pretentious atmosphere of its maturity. But lest there be great concern that early performances lacked the ultimate refinement, imagination and sophistication of production, veteran followers will tell you that there was a spontaneity about the best performances which was hard to beat. Some of the castings speak for themselves.

An ironic, shadowy footnote to *The Ring* appeared after the cycle was concluded, when word got back to San Francisco of an interview Bodanzky had given *The New York Herald-Tribune*, some of which could easily be construed as patronizing toward San Francisco. The tremendous turnout and enthusiasm for *The Ring* in the western city he took as an example of "an unsophisticated audience." Those who felt San Francisco provincially chauvinistic clucked, but others were disturbed about the conductor's probably innocent but not brilliantly tactful statement.

In any case, some people were undoubtedly relieved when, the following year, negotiations directed toward reengagement of Bodanzky fell through. He wanted a raise in fee, more rehearsal time than seemed

[1] Warmth, instrumental clarity and purposeful pacing are nicely audible on a representative air check of Bodanzky's *Tristan* from the Met January 2, 1937. Although in general his tempos are by no means notably slow, the Liebestod is taken very deliberately.

profitable to the company, and he wanted the pit expanded. There was certainly merit in his demand about the pit; judging the rest of the matter is impossible from this distance. But it seems that Bodanzky did not have quite the flexibility the situation asked for.

The non-Wagnerian repertory did not benefit from the presence of such variously slim operas as Massenet's *Werther*, Flotow's *Martha* and Halévy's *La Juive*. If there were any anti-Wagnerians around, they had only *Aida, Rigoletto, La Bohême* and *The Barber of Seville* as really solid consoling fare. There remained the strange combination of *Coq d'Or* with *Suor Angelica*. Helen Gahagan, the actress and politician, made her American opera debut in the latter. It was rather less than a complete success. Fried, now with the *Examiner*, wrote: "Miss Gahagan gave the title role some life because she is a seasoned actress. Her voice is strong and she sings feelingly. But neither in timbre nor in development is her soprano a first rate opera instrument."

Martinelli, Schipa, Bonelli and Pinza were on hand this season to give strength to the non-Wagner wing. Nelson Eddy made another excursion from his activities in southern California, and his Amonasro, the *Chronicle* said, was "vengeful, barbaric . . . sung with a suave, aristocratic voice." Fried found his performance "beautifully, nobly sung." Schipa wasn't able to redeem the *Werther*, which suffered basically from dullish music and secondarily from the Charlotte, Coe Glade, who was unable to project well her "contralto of beautiful, dusky quality." Schipa, incidentally, sang in Italian while the rest of the cast used French. Such bilingual performances have thankfully been rare in San Francisco. Also those in which the leading tenor is seriously late for an entrance. This performance ground to an unscheduled halt in the third act, while the audience waited for Schipa.

This was a year for fledgling soprani, and Josephine Tumminia, from San Francisco's North Beach, made a successful if unremarkable appearance as Rosina in *The Barber*. Helen Jepson had a modest success in *Martha* and *Bohême*. The latter two operas were conducted by Richard Lert, who had settled in southern California following many years' experience in German opera houses. Of Tumminia Fried wrote: "She is young, pert, gay . . . her voice is a natural coloratura . . . what it lacks in mellowness it balances in the sparkle and skill of its agility." The Gilda of San Francisco's Emily Hardy was judged uneven. She was more of a lyric soprano than a coloratura, and her handling of the more acrobatic aspects of the score was wanting. The following year she appeared briefly in the spring season of the Metropolitan.

A special comic interlude in the season occurred on November 15 when a sort of variety show called "Opera-Tunities of 1935" was put on. It was aimed at bolstering the company's production fund, and it did by $7,000. Emperor Jones, Aida and Butterfly collected fifty cents apiece in the lobby for souvenir programs, Tito Schipa conducted the Schipa Jazz Band, and the *William Tell* Overture was conducted by two conductors. Lots of fun was had by many, but at least one critic found this "production" too improvised. Rehearsal time had been skimped, and numbers that would have been better left out were offered anyway.

1936

The so-called endless melody of Wagner's *Ring* lingered on into the 1936 season, which offered performances, not in any particularly meaningful sequence, of *Rheingold, Walküre* and *Götterdämmerung*. There were two of *Walküre* and one each of the others. More important than this continued interest in Wagner was the belated introduction of Mozart to the repertoire. The excursion into this particularly subtle area took the form of one traversal of *The Marriage of Figaro*, with at least two artists of great Mozartean experience, Rethberg and Pinza, in the cast. Unfortunately the performance, conducted by Lert, was not consistently sparkling, and two of the principals, Perry Askam as the Count and Chicago's Gina Vanna as Cherubino, were not so well versed in the Mozartean phrase. Askam's experience was mainly in light opera. Study with Margarete Matzenauer had led him to heavier work.

Fritz Reiner began his three years' association with the company during this season, taking over the Wagner, which was sung by familiar casts including Flagstad, Rethberg, Lehmann, Melchior, Schorr, List, Meisle, Manski, Clemens and Arnold Gabor. Reiner handled the Wagnerian repertoire with distinction.

There was opera in English again this year: Puccini's *Gianni Schicchi* in Percy Pitt's translation. Tibbett assumed the title role. The consensus of critical opinion was that the words could be understood about eighty-five per cent of the time, but the presentation was coolly received. Tibbett also sang his first Iago during this season, and Martinelli his first Otello. The tenor won from Fried this praise: "In few of his roles is he so penetrating a histrion. Quickly in turn and by contrast he expressed Otello's imperiousness, his lovable sincerity and his maddened pathetic fury." When Martinelli became the Otello of the Metropolitan revival thirteen months later, he again won high praise, and a generation later he is perhaps best remembered for his interpretation of the Moor.

The mezzo Bruna Castagna joined the artists' list for *Carmen* and *Trovatore*, making a particularly notable impression in the latter. Marjory Fisher wrote in the *News* that "the vocal opulence she brought to the part seemed, at the time of hearing, unparalleled in local annals."

Lotte Lehmann sang another Tosca opposite the Cavaradossi of the young American tenor Charles Kullman (then Kullmann), fresh from European successes. In those days his lovely voice was in full bloom, but it was not, of course, a large instrument.

Merola conducted only *Otello*, *The Barber* and *La Juive* this year, giving over the majority of the Franco-Italian repertoire to Gennaro Papi, long associated with the Metropolitan. Papi is panned in Irving Kolodin's history of the Metropolitan as a sluggish routinier, but in San Francisco he fared better with the critics. In general they found him an authoritative maestro, chiding him only occasionally for sacrificing the basic pace of his performance to make a particular musical point.[2] Also new to the company was the lusty baritone, Carlo Morelli, whose diverse background included Chilean birth, engineering study at the University of California and vocal training in Italy.[3] The German soprano Charlotte Boerner also appeared with the company for the first time, singing Eudoxia in *La Juive* and the Countess in *Figaro*.

An important development in the makeup of the San Francisco Opera's seasons came this year with the initiation of a special package in the form of a popular subscription series of performances scaled at prices somewhat lower than those regularly charged. Instead of the six dollar top asked for the main subscription performances, four dollars was the highest price for a seat to one of the three events of the series. *The Barber*, *Trovatore* and *Rheingold* made up the list. The experiment was a pronounced success, and today there are two popular subscription series of six operas each. The initiation of this sort of series was overdue, considering that some of the opera-loving public shied away from the formality and expense of regular subscription performances.

[2] The author agrees. Air checks of old Met broadcasts and recordings of excerpts from a couple of his San Francisco performances indicate that Papi had the punch, wit and lyrical feeling of an exciting, imaginative opera maestro. Sometimes he *did* allow the singers more than maximum leeway for making fussy virtuosic effects.

[3] The brother of Renato Zanelli, originally a baritone and later one of the great Otellos of the century (Covent Garden in 1928 and 1930). He died in 1935.

The *Ring* production having drained off what remained of the founders' fund—approximately $50,000—in 1935, it was necessary this year to provide some financial damming. A new membership classification of so-called Guarantor Members of the Association was set up, each pledging assistance should a deficit materialize, and one of $20,000 was not impossible. The original hope was for two hundred guarantors, each pledging up to $100. But about four hundred signed up. The whole idea was to spread out the carrying of financial responsibility in the face of a deficit, for in 1935 only a relative handful of backers had wiped up that season's red ink. Soon guarantor status became an obligation of season ticket holders to the regular series in the orchestra, boxes and Grand Tier.[4] This was not accomplished without some grumbling—for a few it meant possible financial hardship. But it must be said that the system is not undemocratic.

As a result of a new understudy cast system, there were—for the first time in the company's history—principals rehearsing with the chorus two months before season opening. The plan, which put resident artists in the main roles at rehearsal sessions, was conceived in large part as a benefit to the chorus, but the solo singers benefited from appearing in a couple of previews of scenes from operas of the season. They were presented before invited audiences in Veterans' Auditorium. At the second of these one of the "stars" was Mona Paulee, who later went East for larger success. Unfortunately the previews petered out. The Merola Training Program presentation of *The Tales of Hoffmann* at Stern Grove in 1959 marked a return to a profitable sort of experience for young artists before an audience.

1937

The season of 1937 was the most generous to date, offering fourteen operatic bills in eighteen performances: *Fidelio, Tristan* and *Lohengrin* in German; *Norma, Aida, Masked Ball, Traviata, Rigoletto, Bohème* and *Butterfly* in Italian; and *Romeo and Juliet, Manon* and *Lakmé* in French. Ticket demands ran high, and there was even some talk that enlargement of the opera house might become a vital necessity. The two balconies could extend arms over the boxes along the sides of the house, it was suggested in the press. But the answer came

---

[4] Prior to 1958 the maximum guarantee was $50 per seat in the Orchestra and Grand Tier, and $100 per Box seat. In 1958 the $50 maximum was raised to $75, the $100 maximum to $150. In 1960 the Orchestra and Grand Tier maximums were raised to $100 in the centers of these sections.

with later years: not enlargement of the house, but enlargement of the season's length, without increase in the size of the repertoire. In other words, more breathing space was to be created with a larger proportion of repeat performances. There was logical feeling you could only crowd so much heavy work into so short a time. The skillful way in which this work was carried out under Merola's energetic, determined direction deserves praise indeed—the circumstances were not especially comfortable. But the company was going through a stage toward a more flexible format.

Italy and France contributed important soprano talent this year in the voices of Gina Cigna and Vina Bovy, both of whom had been singing the previous season at the Metropolitan. Cigna, a powerful if variable artist, was the Norma when this riot of bel canto was given for the first and, lamentably, the only time in company history. In the opening night *Aida*, her warm, dramatic tones appealed, and her mezza voce made its expressive points, but her full low tones were tremulous. She made a better impression in *Masked Ball*, then went on to a Violetta which lacked the necessary vocal control. This part, incidentally, she did not sing in her two seasons at the Metropolitan.

Bovy, a warm, elegant-voiced lyric soprano of Belgian origin, was an unqualified hit in *Bohême*, singing, according to Fried, with "intelligent sensibility," and making, so far as Frankenstein was concerned, "perhaps the most successful debut of several seasons." He meant, most likely, "since Flagstad." Bovy's other assignments were along expected lines: Juliet and Manon. Her Violetta would have made an interesting comparison with the heavier product of Cigna.

Progressive strides were made in scenery this year, for instance with Agnini's atmospheric, non-literal sets for *Romeo and Juliet*. But there was still a great deal that was old-fashioned or becoming so. Herbert Graf joined Agnini in the stage direction, and the mass movements he sent the prisoners through in *Fidelio* resulted in one of the best such effects in company history. This opera, of course, was one of the artistic hits of the season. It had a strong cast led by Flagstad, with the smooth, villainy-colored bass of Ludwig Hofmann in the role of Pizarro. As a further example of San Francisco's "unsophistication" as Bodanzky might have put it, Beethoven's opera brought in the most money of all performances during the year. The second *Lohengrin* produced the most standees, with *Lakmé* as runner-up—thanks, without doubt, to Pons.

It is very likely that the second *Lohengrin* was particularly well patronized because of an announcement which appeared in the press the day before. It was an announcement which reads strangely indeed today. Flagstad, it said, was planning curtailment of her career, would not appear in opera again in San Francisco following her last Elsa and, further, she would not sing at the Metropolitan after 1938–1939. Well, as we all know, she returned to San Francisco in 1939, was still at the Metropolitan in 1940–1941, and returned triumphantly to the San Francisco Opera in 1949, the Met in 1951.

Following the home season, approximately two hundred persons boarded a train for Los Angeles, where the company launched its first southland season under the name of the San Francisco Opera Association. The engagement of the complete troupe was guaranteed against loss by the Los Angeles Musical Foundation, a division of the Junior Chamber of Commerce. Five operas were on the slate at Shrine Auditorium—four from the home repertoire plus a *Tosca* with Jeritza, Frank Forrest and Bonelli. The crowded opening was *Tristan* with Flagstad and Melchior, then *Lakmé* with Pons, *Aida* with Cigna, and *Lohengrin* with the popular pair of Wagnerians. Ticket demand ran high, and chartered buses from as far away as Phoenix and Tucson in Arizona brought opera-hungry passengers. Los Angeles seasons have continued without break.

The auditorium in Los Angeles is cavernous, like the Civic Auditorium of San Francisco's earlier operatic history, but its acoustics are better, and even a distant seat affords clear sound. Despite the far from elegant atmosphere and surroundings, the Shrine has seen openings no less gala than those at home, and seated audiences far larger and no less cosmopolitan.

The San Francisco Opera Association's new president this year was Robert Watt Miller, a businessman and opera lover who had served as first vice-president for five years. He continued in the president's post until the United States entered the Second World War, returning following hostilities as a director, and in 1952 to the president's chair where he remains today. Kenneth Monteagle was president during and after the War years.

1938

The season of 1938 marked an advance, if an isolated one, in the direction of greater independence from the Metropolitan Opera, an institution of which the San Francisco Opera was sometimes said— not completely in jest—to be a branch. There are two ways to give an artist list independence from the Metropolitan: either one can bolster it with local singers, or one can import singers directly from abroad. During this season Merola looked to Europe and garnered a large amount of imported talent from the continent.

The great mezzo Ebe Stignani, whose 1938 voice was of undiminished freshness, made her American debut. So did Alessandro Ziliani, the La Scala tenor, and Mafalda Favero, remembered for her expressive, light soprano. Favero went on to sing a couple of Mimis at the Metropolitan on her way home, but the other two never appeared at that house. Two young artists, Janine Micheau and Georges Cathelat, were specially brought from Paris on the recommendation of Pierre Monteux, the San Francisco Symphony's conductor, for the company's first performance of Debussy's *Pelléas et Mélisande*. Cathelat was called up for the French Army shortly before he was due in San Francisco, but, as things worked out, he made it to the Golden Gate, and earned a success. *Pelléas* was conducted by Erich Leinsdorf, then only twenty-six, and the boy wonder of the podium during that era. Merola cautiously scheduled only one performance of this subtle, fragile work, and it was not heard again until 1947.

Besides the singers new to America, Merola added to his roster Rose Pauly, Irene Jessner and Kerstin Thorborg, who formed the estimable leading female contingent in Strauss' *Elektra;* the lovable basso buffo, Salvatore Baccaloni, who had sung in Chicago 1930–1932 and was to join the Metropolitan in the season of 1940–1941; and the American bass-baritone, Carlton Gauld.

The tenor roster took on special lustre with the presence of Beniamino Gigli, who was making a brief return to the United States, having left under rather disagreeable circumstances in 1932 after refusing to take a pay cut at the Metropolitan. He was one of the stars of the opening night, October 7, when *Andrea Chenier* was given with Rethberg and Bonelli. Merola, who again relinquished most of the French and Italian works to Papi, was at the conductor's stand.

In *Martha,* on the twelfth, Gigli achieved one of the few encores in company history, repeating "M'appari." And applause was so great following the third act of the first *Forza*, October 28, that the hero was roused from his dressing room to accept it. He appeared onstage in what one of the lady scribes thought might be a "nightie": he was changing for the next act. At the second *Forza*, November 1, the applause following "Solenne in quest' ora" was so thunderous that Gigli got off the stretcher to bow, thereby leaving the bearers jobless.

Galliano Masini, the forty-two-year-old Rome tenor who had sung the previous season in Chicago and was to go on to the Metropolitan for a year, made a big impression with his stirring, passionate, decidedly Italianate performances. He was not a subtle artist or a great master of phrasing—the sobs could be objectionable—but he was one of those singers who make you sit up and take notice.

Favero was the first major debutante of the season, in the second performance of the year: *Don Giovanni* conducted by Reiner. Two nights later she was Lady Harriet in *Martha*, and she followed this with appearances as Norina in *Don Pasquale* and Mimi in *La Bohême*. Her full lyric soprano and her sensitive phrasing met with favor, but when she pushed her tones into harshness she was less than fine.

The *Pasquale* was paired with *Cavalleria* to form what was surely one of the longest double bills ever devised. It was in the latter that Stignani made her only appearances of the season. Her debut was an auspicious one, and Frankenstein found her to have a "perfect grand opera voice." Although it was felt she wasn't much of an actress, her singing, he said, "completely voiced Santuzza's sulphuric emotion, yet she tore no passion to tatters and never indulged in unmusical ranting for the sake of sensational effect." Ziliani was the Turiddu, and met with a mixed press. The Alfio was Carlo Tagliabue, the Italian baritone, who made his local debut in a repeat of *Andrea Chenier*, demonstrating for Fisher "a commanding stage presence and a rugged baritone of excellent quality."

When *Pelléas* was given on October 19, Micheau's performance as Mélisande was hailed by Fisher as "beautifully sensitive," and Frankenstein felt her portrayal had "just the right note of small, pathetic strangeness." Cathelat, he wrote, was "surely one of the great light tenor voices of the day." Gauld was a fine Golaud, and Leinsdorf conducted outstandingly. The latter's ability with another twentieth century score, Poulenc's *Dialogues of the Carmelites*, which has something of the same refinement and understatement of sound, was to be noted nineteen years later. There was special praise for the stylized, suggestive sets of Jane Berlandina and William Gaskin, which came to the Opera House stage as the result of a competition among local artists. They provided a dose of modern theatricality not so often seen during the company's early seasons.

A distinct find for 1938 was the basso buffo broad in girth and action, Baccaloni, who appeared as Leporello, Fra Melitone and Don Pasquale. Baccaloni's inimitable services in roles of this sort won him a fond audience, and he has been with the company almost without break ever since. He was with the Cosmopolitan for a short time between San Francisco Opera engagements. Incidentally, during his early Chicago days he sang Masetto in *Don Giovanni*, to Virgilio Lazzari's Leporello. In the early years of Baccaloni's career, in the twenties, he sang serious roles. Records show, for instance, that he appeared as Timur in *Turandot*—difficult as it might be to imagine— at Covent Garden in 1928.

The *Elektra* production boasted an orchestra of unprecedented size: ninety-nine musicians, some of them sitting under the stage in the six-foot-deep areas to each side of the prompter's box. The Strauss opera was one of the special hits of a season with a particularly strong repertoire. The *Meistersinger* had some notable merits, too, if an insufficiently powerful Walther in Kullman and a fair amount of imprecision of ensemble. Pauly, incidentally, should be credited with an heroic job of vigorously pursuing Elektra's wild histrionic course in the Los Angeles performance after falling and seriously hurting her ankle early in the proceedings.

Anne Jamison of Los Angeles was this year's Musetta, and one of the better ones. A plug for unused local talent was put in after the *Barber of Seville* matinee, in which the dependable Metropolitan *comprimario* Lodovico Oliviero sang two small roles. It was entered by Marie Hicks Davidson of the *Call-Bulletin*, who indicated there seemed little reason to import Oliviero when surely good voices could be found locally. Presumably Kurt Herbert Adler, Merola's successor, was thinking somewhat in the same direction when, in the late fifties, he stopped bringing the excellent, but over-used *comprimarios* De-Paolis and Cehanovsky from the East. The *Barber* performance was aimed at the children, and the reaction indicated that a regular program of young people's performances might be followed. The new Opera Guild pursued this matter.

Coq d'Or was revived this year—as an opera with incidental dances rather than a pantomime with voices, and in French instead of English. The presence of Pons naturally dictated the changes.[5]

The 1938 deficit came as something of a shock, although it was obvious that *Elektra* and *Meistersinger* and imported stars don't come cheap. A big problem was that not as many seats were sold for the repeats as expected. The guarantors, who had been billed for sixty-seven per cent of the guarantee in 1936, and thirty-one per cent in 1937, received one hundred per cent assessments this year for the first time. And any contributions beyond this were welcome: the deficit was $88,000.

The Los Angeles season, November 5–11, brought at least two important cast changes: Rethberg sang Eva instead of Jessner, Gigli Rodolfo instead of Masini. In 1938 also was the company's first visit to the state capital, Sacramento. It has returned often, on a one-night stand basis from San Francisco. Pasadena was added in 1939 in the same way.

[5] This opera, it might be noted, has an especially delightful prop list. Sample item: one box false noses.

8

THE WAR YEARS

1939

Hitler and Mussolini were the leading villains of the 1939 season. And history was the most hapless tragedy presented. Merola had planned to show off his "Italian" company again: Favero, Stignani, Ziliani, Tagliabue and Baccaloni, plus the young and exciting dramatic soprano, Maria Caniglia. The state of world affairs decreed otherwise, however. None was available to San Francisco. Merola had further planned to use Favero, Stignani and Baccaloni, along with Schipa, in a Leinsdorf-conducted production of Cimarosa's *The Secret Marriage*. But this delightful opera buffa did not make its way into the company's repertoire—in 1939 or any other year.

Caniglia had been slated for Desdemona, Tosca and Leonora in *Trovatore*. Rethberg was her more than adequate substitute, as things turned out, in *Otello* and *Trovatore*. *Tosca*, planned with Caniglia, Ziliani and Tibbett, was dropped, and there was *Traviata* instead. There was a *Lucia* instead of *The Secret Marriage*—a much less happy wedding. Favero was replaced by the distinguished Brazilian soprano Bidu Sayao in the opening night *Manon* and by Jarmila Novotna in *Butterfly*. On this occasion the Czech soprano made her American debut, but it was an American debut which San Francisco won by default. Novotna had arrived in New York earlier in the year in connection with a projected, but unrealized series of operatic performances planned for the World's Fair there.

Stignani's inevitable Santuzza—she sang it in each of the two seasons she did appear with the company, 1938 and 1948—went to Dusolina Giannini, the American soprano who developed her operatic career abroad. And her scheduled Azucena was assigned to Kathryn Meisle. Ziliani's Pinkerton was taken over by the young American of Hollywood fame, Michael Bartlett. He was to have sung in *Don Pasquale* on a double bill with *Cavalleria*, but with all the reshuffling the projected *Pasquale*, to have starred Favero, was eliminated. *Cavalleria* appeared with its customary mate, *I Pagliacci*. Dezso Ernster, the Hungarian bass, was unable to fulfill his engagement, so King Marke in *Tristan* and Rocco in *Fidelio* were assumed by Alexander Kipnis, Hunding in *Walküre* by Norman Cordon. Julius Huehn, frequently associated with Wagner, took over Tagliabue's Sharpless.

Merola must be credited with quick work in more than salvaging the season, which opened just a month and a half after hostilities began.

I Pagliacci brought with it the most newsy event of the year from the human interest point of view. This was the debut of "The Singing Cop," an erstwhile Highway Patrol officer named George Stinson. His move from patrol to *Pagliacci* was a tailor-made story for the press, and much was written about him in the newspapers. *Pagliacci* preceded *Cavalleria* the night of October 21, doubtless so the critics could hear him before deadline called them away. Stinson was able to deliver the goods. Fried wrote that whereas his acting was green his voice was "brilliant, powerful, broad of range, thrilling in its top tones," and had "intrinsic emotional content." Frankenstein declared that Stinson's voice was "extremely large and powerful, fresh and youthful in its clarion ring . . . he carried his assignment through to an ovation richly deserved." The new Canio was greeted with cheers, and a second *Pagliacci*, at popular prices, was scheduled with the ballet *Coppelia* rounding out the bill. On this occasion Stinson offered, following a nervous start, what was in sum a smoother performance than his first triumphant one.

As the story goes, several years earlier Stinson had been giving a traffic talk to some grammar school students in nearby Santa Rosa. The youngsters wouldn't settle down, so Stinson went to the piano, boomed out some songs, and all was quiet in the auditorium. Soon, all his traffic talks had musical accompaniments. In any case, Merola heard Stinson in 1937, coached him and saw him off to Italy for study. The reshuffling of the 1939 season in San Francisco precipitated his debut. He was heard again in 1940, but not thereafter. Well along in his thirties, Stinson realized he had started very late, and had a long way to go in acting, repertoire and calming of stage nerves. He returned to law enforcement.

The two performances of *Walküre* brought an interesting switch. At the first one, the young Australian soprano Marjorie Lawrence sang Brünnhilde and Flagstad Sieglinde. But their roles were reversed at the repeat. It was generally agreed that, from a vocal point of view, the second was the better performance, for Flagstad, while a very fine Sieglinde, was a fabulous Brünnhilde. The first *Walküre*, with Lawrence's estimable Brünnhilde, was conducted in good style by Leinsdorf, but the second went to the baton of Edwin McArthur, Flagstad's accompanist, and his leadership was neither inspired nor well-schooled. Unfortunately some of his inferior Wagner conducting was saved for latter-day audiences in several badly engineered recordings made in Los Angeles featuring Flagstad and Melchior in popular excerpts.

Novotna's Butterfly was poignantly sung, and *The New York Times'* Olin Downes, who was in San Francisco at the time, wrote: "Miss Novotna has given proof of being not only a singer, but also a musician and interpreter of true dramatic instinct." While he felt that Butterfly was probably not her greatest role, he found that "there is grace, warmth and communicative feeling in all that she does."

The afternoon of November 3 a special children's matinee of *Madama Butterfly* was sung. The sponsor was the San Francisco Opera Guild, an outgrowth of the Women's Committee of the Opera Association founded in 1938 for the purpose of developing wider public interest in opera. The Guild continued providing student performances at low prices in 1940 and 1941, and resumed the practice following the War. During hostilities it purchased tickets to the opera at box office prices for distribution to members of the Armed Forces at greatly reduced rates. Three student performances per season have been the recent standard, and at the time of writing the number was swelled to four.

During the 1950's an Opera Ball and Fol-de-Rol became an annual event, artists of the season engaging in serious song and humorous skits, the proceeds going to the Guild's fund for new settings. Guild dues are used to meet the cost of buying the student performances. Admittance to an opera dress rehearsal has been a yearly privilege offered Guild members. Dedicated as it is to the musical youth of the San Francisco area, the Guild originated in 1959 a non-profit agency called the Talent Bank. Through it various local engagements can be obtained for young singers who have proved their stature by qualifying in the San Francisco Opera Debut Auditions.

The Guild's first chairman was Mrs. Stanley Powell, the daughter of Robert I. Bentley, a leading figure in the founding of the company. Vice chairmen were Mrs. Edward Otis Bartlett and Mrs. Henry Potter Russell. In 1961 the following officers were elected: Mrs. Andrew W. Simpson III, chairman; Mrs. Dewey Donnell, first vice chairman; Mrs. Allen E. Charles, second vice chairman; Mrs. Paul

Bissinger, third vice chairman; Mrs. Richard P. Cooley, secretary; Mrs. James E. Durkin, treasurer; and Mrs. Richard C. Ham, liaison.

1940

The San Francisco Opera debuts of Strauss' *Der Rosenkavalier*, tenor Jussi Bjoerling and baritone Robert Weede took place during the 1940 season, a rather light-textured one which included no Wagner but two Mozart operas, *The Marriage of Figaro* and *Don Giovanni*. There were also *Manon, Carmen, Lakmé, A Masked Ball, Aida, Rigoletto* and *Bohême*. The projected *Simon Boccanegra* and *Girl of the Golden West* were dropped because of Tibbett's inability to appear due to a throat ailment.

It had been announced in the spring that *Rosenkavalier* would be given in English, but the artists turned thumbs down on this idea, and it was performed in German. In the fairly regular revivals of the last fifteen years the language usually has been German, but there was one exception: a very sound production with John Gutman's English translation in 1952. It did not, however, meet with great audience approval.

Lotte Lehmann was on hand in 1940 to sing her famous Marschallin, and the twenty-seven-year-old Rïse Stevens was Octavian, Alexander Kipnis Baron Ochs. The intricate prelude to the third act was omitted, and this unfortunate practice continued through several *Rosenkavalier* seasons, but the cut has lately been reinstated. Jane Berlandina's light, witty sets "danced to the music," one observer said, and the strong cast under Leinsdorf's spirited direction impressed.

The *Don Giovanni* was to have had the services of that noted Mozart stylist Tito Schipa, but he was detained by bad weather on an air journey from Latin America. His place as Don Ottavio was taken by Alessio DePaolis, the exceedingly adept *comprimario* who has delighted many an audience with such characterizations as his shifty-eyed Spoletta and his rickety, amiable Franz in *The Tales of Hoffmann*. DePaolis omitted "Dalla sua pace," not because he didn't know it, but in apparent obeisance to Schipa, into whose category he was not trying to step. Actually, as a younger man DePaolis was a leading lyric tenor, and recordings indicate that vocally he was a convincing one. Kipnis' Leporello was fairly straight, and good—he portrayed a clever, attractive peasant trying to be a lower class replica of his master.

Bjoerling's debut occurred in *Bohême*, and he followed this with

A Masked Ball. He was rightfully hailed as one of the most striking tenors heard in San Francisco in many years. Power, and the floating freshness of youthful tone which time, alas, partly rubbed away, were gloriously in evidence.[1] Weede was the season's new Rigoletto, and his large, beautiful voice and commanding presence brought him one of the year's bigger ovations and some of the lustiest critical praise.

In *Rigoletto* the Duke was a Cuban tenor, Francisco Naya, who was good-looking and had a good natural voice. But stage ineptitude and faulty intonation marred his work. The Singing Cop's regular series Rhadames was cancelled—some said because Mme. Rethberg refused to appear with such an inexperienced partner—but he did sing a children's matinee, and not without some success. Marjorie Lawrence was this year's Carmen, but there was much feeling she was miscast. If *Girl of the Golden West* had been staged, she would have been the Minnie, and one who mixed vocal and equestrian accomplishments.

The year 1940 further brought the first company appearances of two important artists: the Australian baritone John Brownlee, whose *Bohême* Marcello and *Marriage of Figaro* Count were especially fine; and Raoul Jobin, the reliable Canadian tenor.

1941

The 1941 season saw the first San Francisco Opera performance of Verdi's subtle and somber *Simon Boccanegra*, postponed from the year before, and Donizetti's *The Daughter of the Regiment*, an airy vehicle for Pons and Baccaloni. Italo Montemezzi, now a resident of southern California, was the conductor of his own *L'Amore dei Tre Re*, not presented since 1928. He returned in 1942 and 1947 to conduct his uneven but striking opus—an opera, incidentally, which boasts a truly fine, literary libretto. *Rosenkavalier* was repeated, and although world events eliminated a Flagstad *Tristan*, there was a *Tannhäuser* with Melchior.

The presence in minor roles of a nineteen-year-old southern California college student named Jerome Hines (Biterolf), Christina Carroll (Shepherd) and Wilma Spence (Page) should be noted. All went on to grander things, notably Hines, of course, who has become a leading bass at the Metropolitan and returned to San Francisco in the late fifties singing with the Cosmopolitan Opera. In 1941 he also sang a Monterone, and won extremely favorable notices.

[1] Documentation of this the author has heard from a private recording of part of the *Ballo* performance. It also shows the aging Rethberg in some passages of special loveliness.

When the season was concluded, and the résumés of activity were in, it was *L'Amore, Rosenkavalier, Tannhäuser* and *Boccanegra* which had made the outstanding impressions as total musico-dramatic events. But there were other pleasant things to report about this season, one which had benefited from an out-of-town warm-up by way of a northwest tour including three performances each in Portland and Seattle.[2] Jan Peerce made a notable company debut in *Rigoletto*, Licia Albanese conquered with her Cio-Cio-San. Erich Leinsdorf was basically a German repertoire man during the early days of his career, but he was assigned *Carmen* and *Boccanegra* and did well in their territories.

Grace Moore was the Fiora of *L'Amore* and she sang, according to Fried, with "impulsive fervor," but "her occasional stagey gestures were beneath the dignity of the opera." *The Daughter of the Regiment* was a happy presentation, with Agnini producing a bright, comic setting. The "Marseillaise" was interpolated at the end of the proceedings, but in light of the current events it could hardly do otherwise than cast a shadow of sadness over the gay atmosphere.

Schipa had originally been scheduled for the 1941 opening night, singing Ernesto in *Don Pasquale*. But he wanted to cut things close again coming from South America, and his engagement was cancelled. Franco Perulli took his place.

Gennaro Papi's appearances with the San Francisco Opera this year were his last. He died in New York in late November. In a sympathetic obituary, Fried noted critical disagreements about his merits and went on to say: "Without being the exhibitionistic or arrogant type of conductor, he had an interpretative style that was consistently individual and scrupulous. Indeed, he conceived certain tempos in popular operas—zipping little vivacities in *Rigoletto*, for instance—that were so much his own that such stars as Lily Pons and Tibbett had to be very careful to blend in with them. . . . People who did not care for Papi and who, for mysterious reasons, could not detect his finesse, considered him a routinier. No routinier ever loved music as Papi did."

On the lighter side, an anecdote about Papi is worth recording: one day a San Francisco critic met the conductor in the lobby, and said, "You know, maestro, I admire your conducting very much, but you haven't lost that habit of hissing at the orchestra. You'd be surprised how you can hear it even over the trombones." "All right," said Papi, "the nexa time I putta potato in my mouth."

[2] *Manon*, not in the San Francisco repertoire, was heard in the Northland, with Grace Moore in the title role.

1942

After the United States entered the war, there was discussion of whether or not to continue the opera seasons. Thankfully the vote was to continue. Merola felt that surely this was no time to expand—shortage of materials made new production unfeasible—and the 1942 and 1943 seasons were not especially adventurous. But he also felt that if the seasons stopped, they would not start again, at least not with ease. Suspension of the opera would have hurt the Symphony men, of course.

The Association pursued a cautious path through the spring, announcing tentative plans early in June. President Robert Watt Miller issued a statement that "by means of a series of economies in which all branches of the Association have cooperated, we are gratified to continue."

The tentative plans included the name of Pierre Monteux among the conductors. There had long been hope that the San Francisco Symphony's permanent conductor would lead performances of the city's other major musical organization, but as things turned out, the public had to wait another twelve years for that. The more detailed plans announced late in July included mention of a *Werther* with Rïse Stevens. This, too, failed to reach the Opera House.

At the same time, it was reported that the city had agreed to finance the company's rental of the building, and that August 10 had been set as deadline in a drive to achieve $50,000 in season ticket sales, a supplement to the already purchased $75,000-worth. The indication was that if the sales lagged too seriously, the season would be abandoned. The season seat deadline had to be extended, but by mid-August, with the season to open on October 9, the ticket situation was encouraging enough that the season was assured. As it happened, all but three performances were sold out.

There were three operas in English this year: *The Bartered Bride*, *Die Fledermaus* (*The Bat*) and *Coq d'Or* (*The Golden Cockerel*) in its operatic form. A lot of the diction was excellent thanks to the use of American talent, but sometimes the Europeans flavored the text beyond recognition. The productions were long on spirit, and some of the portrayals, for instance Douglas Beattie's brilliantly acted and richly voiced Kezal, were memorable.

Sayao's classic Violetta, Pinza's towering Archibaldo, Irra Petina's coy, devilish Carmen—these were particularly noteworthy performances of the season.

Fausto Cleva began a long, although interrupted, association with the company this year, conducting *Traviata, Faust, A Masked Ball* and *The Barber of Seville*. Montemezzi returned for *L'Amore*, this time with Jean Tennyson of wide radio experience as Fiora, and not one of the most successful ones. *Fledermaus* and *The Bartered Bride* were conducted by Walter Herbert, at that time a member of the San Francisco Symphony's viola section and more recently a conductor of opera in New Orleans and Houston.

1943

Puccini's *Girl of the Golden West* has had a difficult time taking hold in this country. After all, full-blown Puccinian melody is not the sort of music Americans associate with something as familiar as the Gold Rush in California. The grade C Western quality of the story has not helped, either. Nor, for international audiences, the lack of tightness in the first act. When *The Girl* finally made her way back to the War Memorial stage in 1943 (she had been scheduled for 1940), the strange local color was too much for some of the patrons, especially as it was served up in English. The advance sale for the announced second performance was slow enough that Merola withdrew it from the slate. This was an unfortunate state of affairs, because the opera does boast some winning melody (the vagabond's nostalgic song in the first act, for instance, and Minnie's soulful, pre-Howard Hanson theme) and is shot through with the fascinatingly somber and edgy quality which comes from use of the whole tone scale and the questioning augmented triad, a harmonic cliff-hanger.

Florence Kirk, who made her debut with the New Opera Company in New York in 1941, was praised for dramatic credibility and good diction in her portrayal of the heroine. But Jagel, about a head shorter, was not a romantic Dick Johnson. The mismatch hurt. Some of the smaller parts were difficult to understand because of foreign accents. Weede took over the role originally planned for Tibbett and made Jack Rance properly venomous. The R. H. Elkin translation was used, but reworked into less British English by music critic Fried. He removed some of the colloquialisms which were absurdly British in view of the Gold Rush setting.[3]

Repertoire-wise this was an extremely pale, ill-balanced season,

[3] While on the subject of *GGW*, the author is reminded of the anecdote of the miners' shoes. They came from the costumers at the last minute—all brand new, and light yellow-brown! Some quick aging was indicated.

reflecting a certain wartime austerity and the idea that Wagner might well be rested while things went badly in Europe. *Carmen, Samson and Delilah, Don Giovanni,* and *The Girl of the Golden West* were the only operas on the year's ration card outside the more or less normal Italian fare. A special spark was provided, however, by the presence of Sir Thomas Beecham in the pit for *Carmen* and *Don Giovanni.* Beecham, of course, was an excellent opera conductor of seemingly unlimited versatility, and his appearances were a distinct boon to the season. If on the night of his first performance (*Carmen*) there was any worry that his stiff, deliberate stroll to the podium indicated a lack of energy, such an idea was immediately dashed by his immensely exuberant handling of the "Star Spangled Banner," and by the vibrancy of his work the rest of the evening.

The Carmen was Irra Petina, who offered what one critic described as an "apple-chewing, leg-scratching" version of the role. The Escamillo was Pinza, who had a disagreement with Beecham about the timing of the Toreador's entrance. The upshot was: the audience had a slight unscheduled wait.

The company's new chorus master, Kurt Herbert Adler, who was not to be confused with his counterpart Kurt Adler—sans middle name—at the Metropolitan, made his conducting debut with the company at a performance of *Cavalleria Rusticana* starring Giannini in a great portrayal. He made the Intermezzo sound "truly expressive whereas it usually sounds maudlin," wrote Fried of his well-considered, non-routine performance. Adler was to build the chorus to heights not previously attained, and later became Merola's chief aide. Following Merola's death in 1953, Adler became the company's artistic director, and, later, the general director. John Charles Thomas reappeared after thirteen years' absence as the Tonio of the accompanying *Pagliacci.*

The German tenor John Garris, whose fine reputation at the Metropolitan was built largely on secondary roles, was given the opportunity to sing Ernesto in *Don Pasquale* and made the most of it, singing with a pleasing lyric voice. In one of his more routine assignments, as Lord Arthur in *Lucia,* he made an excellent impression, eliciting from one critic the opinion that this was the "only good Bucklaw in ten years."

One George Burnson followed Hines as this year's Monterone. A few years later the same bass-baritone was singing the title role in *Don Giovanni* at the Vienna State Opera, Scarpia at the Metropolitan and the title part of *The Flying Dutchman* at Bayreuth. By then, of course, this was George London. The 1943 comments are especially interesting in light of what followed: Fried wrote, "George Burnson

. . . whose voice is excellent, though not of largest size, made a striking impression." Fisher said, "Another newcomer, George Burnson, made an unusually impressive Monterone with his commanding presence and excellent bass voice." And Frankenstein opined, "Burnson acted Monterone extremely well and has a very nice voice, but not a very powerful one . . . If Burnson is the boy I think he is, the one who played the stuttering lawyer in the *Rose Masque* (with the San Francisco Civic Light Opera), his voice has time to grow."

The tenor Kurt Baum made his company debut in a matinee repeat of Forza, arousing a huge ovation after the third act aria. His ringing, striking tone was good to hear, but it lacked the ultimate in plasticity of handling. His vocal power was an asset to a *Trovatore* which also boasted Thorborg as Azucena and Zinka Milanov as Leonora. Thorborg, wrote Frankenstein, "swept through Azucena like a whirlwind attached to a rocket," showing off a luscious voice and commanding histrionics. This was Milanov's only season with the company, and there were times in the years immediately following when her services would have helped the Italian dramatic soprano department.

Ivan Petroff, a middle-aged, dark-voiced baritone who had sung with the American San Carlo, made his San Francisco Opera debut as Rigoletto during 1943, thereby initiating a series of performances which had more than solidity to offer. The name of Petroff, on the roster for four seasons, evaporated from the musical scene thereafter, but he was one of the most pleasing baritones the San Francisco had.[4] This was also the first San Francisco season for baritone Leonard Warren, who made a striking impression as the High Priest in *Samson* opening night. A Mexican bass, Roberto Silva, joined the company this year, making several successful appearances. And also from south of the border was Irma Gonzales, who sang an especially good Micaela.

1944

Two new conductors made outstanding contributions to the 1944 season: William Steinberg, who led the revival of *Falstaff*, and George Sebastian, who was in charge of the returned *Salome*.

Forty-five-year-old Steinberg had come to the United States in the late thirties after vast experience conducting in the opera houses of Cologne, Prague, Berlin and Frankfurt, where he was general music director. He brought with him a wonderfully crisp and sensitive

---

[4] He now teaches in Los Angeles. He did appear briefly with the Pacific Opera in San Francisco in 1954.

stick. Although his background might have typed him as a German repertoire man, his assignments in this almost completely un-Germanic season were *Faust, A Masked Ball* and *Falstaff*. The casting worked exceedingly well: his *Falstaff* was as brilliant a piece of precision baton work as had ever come out of the Opera House pit, and the *Faust* had a sensitivity and dynamic control several notches above the average. In later years Steinberg conducted much Wagner, but he never made a better impression than the fine one registered on the non-Teutonic side.

The more expansive Sebastian, a forty-two-year-old Hungarian who had worked under Strauss himself, Karl Muck and Bruno Walter— he also spent five years as conductor with the Soviet Broadcasting System during the thirties—was responsible for the hair-raisingly exciting *Salome*. He also offered a not completely smooth *Carmen*— Sebastian has not been noted for any special clarity about his beat. *Salome* marked his debut as a conductor of stage-produced opera in America, although he had been an assistant conductor at the Metropolitan in the early twenties and had done considerable operatic work on a New York-based radio program.

For the first time in company history, a full season of operas was broadcast this year. Evening broadcasts began at 10 P.M., afternoon ones at 4 P.M., each continuing from a midway point to the conclusion of the particular opera. Safeway Stores was the sponsor, KFRC the home station, and a number of outlets in California, Oregon, Washington and Idaho carried the fourteen transmissions. Safeway offered the last parts of fifteen operas the following year over KFRC; then, in 1946, time was arranged on KYA for the grocery chain to present ten operas complete. Union demand for a raise in the musicians' pay brought an early finale to this broadcasting history.

In *Falstaff*, the title role was assumed by Baccaloni, who naturally made the most of the comedy, but he had trouble with some of the high notes. *Salome*, staged in an effectively icy, austere setting, was dramatically intense and notably well sung. Lily Djanel, the Franco-Belgian soprano, was a warm-voiced Salome, and Jagel offered one of the best performances of his career as Herod. John Shafer, a young California baritone, turned up as Jokanaan, singing the part sonorously if not with the greatest vocal-dramatic power. In *Faust*, the Marguerite was Vivian Della Chiesa, a lyric-dramatic soprano well-known to radio audiences. She met with a decidedly mixed response.

Miss Djanel also sang Giulietta when the company introduced a glittering new production of Offenbach's *The Tales of Hoffmann*. Virginia MacWatters, a light coloratura, was Olympia; Albanese sang Antonia. Claramae Turner, a member of the chorus who had been singing in small-scale Gilbert and Sullivan productions, had her first important assignment as the Voice of the Mother. This was a Voice which had more to say than that in *L'Amore dei Tre Re*, her assignment two years previous. She later went on to the Met, and has become one of the leading performers of the title role in Gian-Carlo Menotti's *The Medium*. MacWatters was joined by baritone Hugh Thompson and a mute Alessio DePaolis in Wolf-Ferrari's pleasant *Secret of Suzanne*, which served as curtain-raiser for *Salome*. It was well conducted by chorus master Adler.

Traviata, with Lily Pons singing Violetta for the first time, was supposed to be a feature of 1944, but as things turned out, this portrayal was not seen until seven years later.

9

CROWDED SCHEDULES AND A
DARK SHADOW

1945

If wartime strictures had unduly lightened the repertorial weight of the 1942, 1943 and 1944 seasons, that which followed sought to bring things back to the earlier-established norm encompassing a fair share of the German along with the Verdi and Puccini. The offerings included *Tristan, Walküre, Rosenkavalier, Salome* and *Don Giovanni*, and also *Boris Godounoff*, which the critics had been calling for longingly and with reason for more than a decade.

This is not to mention that finely etched little masterpiece, Ravel's *Spanish Hour* (*L'Heure Espagnole*) which served as a curtain-raiser for *Salome*. Much of the dry verbal humor amid the hilarity of the clockshop slapstick was missed without the benefit of English translation. At the same time, it was pointed out that some of the French puns would be difficult to capture in another tongue.

From the tick-tock opening to the habanera finale, with Baccaloni squeezing into a grandfather clock in between, *The Spanish Hour* was delightful fun. Albanese, Garris, DePaolis, Baccaloni and the fine American baritone Mack Harrell made up the excellent cast under Merola's direction. The production was something of a coup for the company as the Metropolitan had not played it since 1926. It is overdue for revival at both houses.[1]

Heading the Wagner casts were soprano Helen Traubel and a vocally aging but still powerful Lauritz Melchior. Lorenzo Alvary, the Hungarian bass, who in his many years at the Metropolitan has had few star parts, was given big opportunities in San Francisco this year: King Marke, Hunding and Baron Ochs. A busy man during

[1] It turned up at the New York City Center in 1952.

77

the 1945 activities, he was also cast as Pimen, Masetto, Raymond, Sparafucile, the *Aida* King and Crespel, not to mention his appearance in a small role in *Salome!* Alvary carried off his assignments with distinction, although his Ochs was a bit lean in stature, both physically and musically.

The *Tristan* and *Walküre* baritone was Herbert Janssen, an experienced, well-regarded Wagnerian if not one with a voice of commanding beauty. Steinberg conducted authoritatively, but had to put up with an economy which presented *Walküre* in a reduced orchestration minus the Wagner tubas and other instruments. In later seasons the tubas crowded into the pit and Hunding got a square instrumental deal therefrom.

Boris was introduced in Italian and minus Rangoni, but with the persuasive Pinza, an excellent chorus, expensive new sets and a strong cast led forcefully by Sebastian. The *Boris* production took on greater stylistic virtue later in company history as Rangoni was let in, and the opera was sung in Russian! Dimitri proved, like Herod, one of Jagel's best roles, and little need be added here about DePaolis' incomparably oily Shouisky and Baccaloni's uproarious Varlaam. John Garris was a memorable Simpleton, Claramae Turner had another good opportunity as the Innkeeper. The Frontier Guard Sergeant was entrusted to one Georg Spelvinski.

In *Rosenkavalier*, with Lehmann returning for the Marschallin role, the fanciful rococo-modern sets of Jane Berlandina again made a happy impression, although several of the principals brought along their gorgeous costumes which didn't precisely fit against them. Berlandina's hand-painted costumes were never popular. Also worth remembering from the 1945 season would be Adler's rich-toned, exciting conducting of *Cavalleria* and *Pagliacci*, and an exceptionally good *Traviata* with Albanese on stage, Merola in the pit. A notable feature of Agnini's *Traviata* direction this year was to move a scene usually played inside out and one outside in. Evelynn Corvello, a local girl, made a special impression as Olympia in the held-over *Tales of Hoffmann*. And there was good singing, if not the requisite power, from one Robert Mills, a bus driver (shades of the Singing Cop) who turned to opera, appearing as the *Don Giovanni* Commendatore and *Rigoletto's* Monterone, not to mention less elegant assignments.

A young lady named Lucy Armaganian joined the chorus this year and remained therein for another season. Mention of this affiliation might seem pointless, but Lucy Armaganian later became rather well known under the name of Lucine Amara.

1946

If *Lohengrin* seemed an overly heavy dish for some of the opening night patrons in the War Memorial Opera House September 17, many in the audience that evening were delighted to experience Astrid Varnay's good-looking, beautiful-sounding, movingly conceived Elsa. And they could be very happy about the lyrical, sensitive conducting of William Steinberg, and the special smoothness of ensemble, thanks to pre-season stagings in Portland and Seattle. Set Svanholm, new from Sweden, was a better-than-average Lohengrin if not a great one, and the freshness of his voice was an asset Melchior could no longer offer. The chorus was triumphant.

On the other side of the footlights opening night was back to its peacetime atmosphere of full formality. The evening repeated a pre-curtain script which has been played and played over the years with little variation but much fanfare, plenty of civic pride and journalistic cliché—although the *Chronicle's* Vincent Mahoney was in inspired form when he wrote: "No one was let down. It was a collector's experience—the grandness of a bygone age kept alive by a complex and fascinating city. It was humanity with almost no suggestion of human dreariness, and that is a multiple dream walking."

During the frantic half hour before the first note of music sounded, the action was—as usual—most lively in the hallway by the carriage entrance on the north side of the house. The socially prominent, and some who are just ubiquitous opening nighters, enter here. Photographers collected their quota of shots to fill a page or more of the next day's papers, and society writers scampered around taking names and describing the fashions—stylish and impeccable in the San Francisco tradition.

Meanwhile, the central foyer was populated to the crushing point. Pity the poor man who tried to cross this mass of boiled shirt and ermine with any speed. And outside the glass front doors—and those by the carriage entrance, too—a faithful group of relatively impecunious citizens came to press their noses, sometimes literally, against the barrier and see the show. They were a singularly friendly lot, but such an assemblage always suggests faintly a modern-day contingent from some people's chorus which drifted through time from a scene in *Boris* or *Andrea Chenier*.

A goodly share of the opera's opening nighters have spent the evening in one of the three bars—*Lohengrin* helped the bartenders of 1946 better than some other operas—but the audience is usually well-behaved. The writers of color stories usually return to their offices with colorless stories because nobody provides a really good scandal. True, once there was a lady of questionable repute who wore a full-length cape of fresh carnation petals. Another patron of the fair sex "hung herself," as one opera chronicler remembers, "with diamonds." And a gentleman came to the Opera House in white tie, tails *and* ten gallon hat. But these were exceptions to conformity.

The men who brought transistor radios one year and listened to a crucial *Giants* game in the pennant may be pardoned. But not the man who turned the lights up after a "Ritorna Vincitor" and sent a segment of the season's least informed audience toward the lobby at the wrong time.

The 1946 schedule of the San Francisco Opera was the most elaborate to date. There were four performances each in Portland and Seattle, followed by twenty-seven in San Francisco along with three in Sacramento, these in turn followed by a dozen in Los Angeles, plus two in Pasadena. The grand total was fifty-two. Whereas there were five more performances than the previous season in San Francisco, they were crowded into a space of time only one day longer than that available during 1945. Today, with a six-week season, there is more breathing space, and greater overall artistic success is facilitated. In 1946 the twenty-seven performances occurred within thirty-four days; in 1960, thirty performances were given within forty-two days.

Boris and *Rosenkavalier* were successfully repeated from the previous season, with Sebastian again in the pit. Kurt Baum was a huge-voiced and amusingly foppish Italian Tenor in the first performance of the Strauss, the local Kayton Nesbitt taking the role in the second and making a nice impression. Alvary had broadened his Ochs to good effect. With the second *Rosenkavalier*, Lotte Lehmann bade farewell to this, her most famous role.

The revival of *Fidelio*, in Theodore Baker's clumsy English translation, went a good deal less well than these other matters. The cast had some of the same weak elements apparent in the March, 1945, revival at the Metropolitan: Regina Resnik's not completely pure-toned Fidelio and Kenneth Schon's ineffective Pizarro. And there was no Bruno Walter to produce orchestral excellences to make up for insufficiencies on stage. Paul Breisach, who did much fine work during his several years (1946–1952) with the company, notably in the French repertory, simply did not give *Fidelio* the monumental approach it demands. The unfocused orchestral playing is best forgotten.

A catalog of unfortunate memories need further include only the Florestan of Mario Berini, which was not unpowerful, but hard in sound.

Breisach, along with Sayao, Jobin and Brownlee, helped make the revival of Gounod's touching but gutless *Romeo and Juliet* less pallid than it might have been. But the reappearance of *Lakmé* was *de trop*, and thankfully she disappeared from the repertoire. The Lakmé, of course, was Lily Pons. When she sang Gilda, it was opposite the Rigoletto of Tibbett, returned for a single performance after five years' absence. His voice wasn't quite what it had been, but the portrayal was striking.

The season's first *Bohême* had not one, but two Brazilian sopranos: Sayao singing her excellent Mimi and Maria SaEarp, in her North American debut appearances, offering a shrill Musetta. There were three new Bohemians when the opera was repeated with Stella Roman as a dramatically provocative but vocally uneven Mimi: Bjoerling, Harrell and Nicola Moscona took over the garret from the more familiar tenants Kullman, Valentino and Pinza.

Lily Djanel's Carmen was a gaspy letdown after her fine Salome, and George Czaplicki, the Polish baritone, was not a vocally suave Escamillo. Florence George, Bing Crosby's sister-in-law, was the Micaela in this opera's second performance, showing more promise than actual delivery of the goods. Martina Zubiri, a young lady from the chorus, made exceptionally good impressions in the small roles of Barbarina (*Marriage of Figaro*) and Ellen (*Lakmé*). This was not, however, one of those years notable for a barrage of new and exciting vocal talent.

Shortly after the season was concluded, a dark shadow was cast over the San Francisco operatic scene with the announcement that the Metropolitan would extend its tour to Los Angeles in the spring of 1948. There was immediate concern that the appearance of the New York company in the southern California city would endanger the substantial Los Angeles season of the San Francisco Opera, a season of great financial importance because of the large capacity of Shrine Auditorium, which seats approximately 3,000 more than the Opera House in the home city. Furthermore, rumors were flying that the Met would come right into San Francisco itself, and since the trip west was a long one, the visit at the end of the trip would probably be of some length. When the musical press in San Francisco predicted that this could sink the San Francisco Opera, in some respects a carbon copy of the Metropolitan, and even sink the San Francisco

Symphony, sixty-odd members of which derive helpful income from the opera performances, it was, very possibly, not being simply pessimistic.

The large guarantee for the Metropolitan's Los Angeles season came from an organization called Greater Los Angeles Plans, Inc., or GLAP for short. One of its most conspicuous leaders, Dr. Charles H. Strub, vice president of the Los Angeles Turf Club, operators of Santa Anita Racetrack, felt that Los Angeles had room for seasons by both companies, especially as GLAP was going to underwrite a 6,000-seat opera house. Meanwhile, Fried was wondering in the *Examiner* about "the peculiar sponsorship the Met has accepted for its West Coast plans." How firm a foundation, he asked, would racetrack money, "shrewdly supplied for self-promotional and self-protective purposes" provide for the future of opera in Los Angeles?

On December 21, Strub conferred with officers of the San Francisco Opera. He told them he was authorized to offer the Metropolitan to San Francisco. Naturally, it was pointed out, the New York company would come to San Francisco only if substantial guarantee was raised there. San Francisco stuck by its own company, which was going full speed ahead with plans for its twenty-fifth anniversary season the following fall: Merola had already gone east, earlier than usual, to engage artists. He knew very well that new productions, lively revivals and strong new singers were of strategic importance to upcoming seasons.

One could find some ominous chords in a statement issued in January, 1947, by George A. Sloan, chairman of the Metropolitan board, when he arrived in Los Angeles for an inspection of the Goodyear Tire and Rubber plants in the area. "While the details of our Los Angeles engagements," it said, "other than for the spring of 1948, have not been worked out between our respective managements, Dr. Charles Strub, on behalf of Greater Los Angeles Plans, Inc., has indicated to Mr. Johnson (Met manager Edward Johnson) and to me the desirability of our spending from six to eight weeks here each season after your new home is completed, and with the understanding that some of this time, perhaps, will include visits to other parts of the Pacific Coast. Later when we discuss mutually satisfactory dates, it may be necessary to divide the time as between the early fall and late spring." That talk of early fall was especially worrisome.

But the finale of this shadowy story was unpainful for San Francisco: the Metropolitan gave fourteen performances in Los Angeles the spring of 1948 and 1949, and then withdrew from the Pacific. Neither the artistic quality nor the financial reward of the venture was consistently up to expectations, and in some cases they were downright disappointing. The touring Met was not generally superior to the San Francisco Opera, and sometimes it was distinctly inferior. The second season went less well than the first, and, as Quaintance Eaton puts it in *Opera Caravan*, her history of the Metropolitan's tours, "the dream was over." After the troupe turned eastward, she writes, "Los Angeles expiated her feelings of guilt by turning her full loyalty to San Francisco." A new opera house in the southern city might have altered the situation, but it did not materialize. At the time of writing such an opera house remains to be built, but its realization is much closer than it was in the late forties.

1947

For his twenty-fifth anniversary season Merola offered the public a generous outlay of twenty-nine performances of seventeen operas. There was the customary regular subscription series of ten performances, mostly on Tuesdays and Fridays; the popular series of five, on Thursday nights; five non-subscription "extras" and seven so-called "added" performances. Not to mention two children's matinees.[2]

The productions new to the company were Charpentier's dreamy ode to Paris, *Louise*, and Ponchielli's tumultuous potboiler, *La Gioconda*. The important revivals were *Die Götterdämmerung*, not heard in eleven years; *Otello*, absent since 1939; *Pelléas et Mélisande*, which had been given only in 1938; and *L'Amore dei Tre Re*, last heard in 1942.

Of the revivals, only *Götterdämmerung* had two performances. The accent this year, as in 1946, was on quantity of operas rather than the chances for greater security of presentation which come with repeats. In later seasons the emphasis on pure size of repertoire was to be lessened, to the benefit of tired performers and novelty-hungry ticket buyers. Very likely there was only one *Pelléas* because Merola remembered the hardly enthusiastic manner in which Debussy's model of musical understatement had been received nine years earlier. Times have changed sufficiently that two performances by a good cast in one season would by no means be financially unthinkable today.

Louise may not be a great opera, but it has a special personality and

---

[2] As in 1941 and 1946, there were performances in Portland and Seattle. The company did not return to the Northwest until 1959, when only Portland was visited. Problems of housing (in Seattle) and guarantees have limited the Northwest activities.

deserves a certain place in the repertoire. When it was unfolded October 3, the performance served to introduce Dorothy Kirsten, whose pure lyric instrument and attractive appearance were more than valuable to the title role. In the part of the father, Pinza had the opportunity to show San Francisco another of his brilliantly etched characterizations. Claramae Turner as the mother and Raoul Jobin as Julien were the other stars of a long and strong cast sensitively conducted by Breisach.

Some wondered how *Gioconda* had remained out of the repertoire so long. Perhaps Merola can simply be credited with good judgment. The production, though, was very expensive, and it was repeated the following year. Thankfully, it has remained unheard since 1948. The cast included Stella Roman, Blanche Thebom, Margaret Harshaw, Baum, Warren and Nicola Moscona. The conductor was a youngish maestro from Italy named Dick Marzollo. He conducted only *Gioconda*, in which he made a striking impression. After returning in 1948, he too vanished, but his possibilities had by no means been exhausted. The chorus in *Gioconda* was especially fine, the ballet brilliant, and praiseworthy also was the scenery painted by Eugene Dunkel after designs by himself and Agnini.

The single *Pelléas*, which was postponed from September 22 until October 10 because of "technical difficulties," had a good pair of lovers in Sayao and Martial Singher; but the conducting of Wilfred Pelletier, returned after a long absence, was not as sensitive and mysterious as this halting, evanescent music demands. *L'Amore* received a thrilling performance under the composer's direction, and the effect of the climax at the end of the second act, when Pinza as the blind Archibaldo choked his daughter-in-law and carried her across the stage, was so exciting that the oft-reserved Regular Series audience was moved to applaud vigorously and long.

Otello benefited from Steinberg's gripping conducting, and was interesting for its unusual casting: Albanese in her first Desdemona and Svanholm as Otello. Albanese's lyric capabilities were far from foreign to Verdi's wants for his fragile heroine. Tibbett returned for his famous Iago, but was not in the voice to which his earlier-day audiences were accustomed.

The 1947 season not only had musical delights aplenty, but also provided much material of general news value. Before the opening night *Traviata* began, Merola was presented with a scroll bearing the names of hundreds of San Franciscans who had tendered him a gift in commemoration of the twenty-fifth year of the company and his association with it. From the stage Merola responded with "All I can say is, San Francisco knows how," and at that, the orchestra struck up Happy Birthday and the onstage assemblage, the guests at Violetta's party, joined in.

Then there was the Pinza Family *Faust*, offered to a Sunday afternoon audience September 21. Ezio was Mephistopheles, his daughter Claudia the Marguerite. Her Italianate soprano was a fresh and appealing instrument, but not a great one. The friendly audience, including many long-time followers of father Pinza, cheered the girl on. Giuseppe Valdengo, new to the company, was the particularly strong Valentin on this occasion.

There was also the conquering heroine's return of Florence (or Fiorenza) Quartararo, a North Beach girl who, rather to the San Francisco Opera's embarrassment, had sung at the Metropolitan but not with the company of her own city. Her debut at the New York house occurred January 18, 1946, at which time Howard Taubman, writing in *The New York Times*, opined that "she may be the find of the season." When she appeared as Donna Elvira in San Francisco September 19, 1947, her generous lyric-dramatic soprano gifts were nicely revealed and also, a superior sense of how to move knowingly around the stage and engage sympathy. She received a major ovation, and her subsequent performance as the Countess in *The Marriage of Figaro* was also enthusiastically received. There was a certain amount of indignation among the city's operatic population because Quartararo was only scheduled for two performances. Her fans were not to have many opportunities to hear her: her career was short-lived. She returned to the San Francisco Opera only in 1949 and 1950. She had the vocal and dramatic talents to sustain a long and fruitful career, but she chose marriage—her husband is Italo Tajo, who later sang with her in San Francisco—and gave up singing as a profession.

Illness struck the company two sudden blows toward the season's end. Nadine Conner sang the children's matinee of *Traviata* on October 17 suffering from a stomach ailment, and she fainted away in the final scene. Simultaneously the company was hastily making arrangements to go on with that evening's *Lucia*, threatened with cancellation when Lily Pons came down with a bad cold. In one of those operatic scenes from real life, Josephine Tumminia, an alumnus of the company (1935–1937) and a housewife in suburban San Mateo, rose to the occasion and subbed on extremely short notice. That morning Merola called Nino Comel, Tumminia's teacher. "*Come sta Josephina?*" he asked, in his characteristic *andante legato*. "Does she know Lucia? . . . Have you heard her lately? . . . You know, Lily Pons is quite sick, I don't think she can sing tonight." At that Comel jumped. "Why, you know, maestro, Josephine's been retired for three years. You want her to sing TONIGHT?!" The upshot was that Comel gave Merola Tumminia's telephone number, then quickly called her himself to alert her. When Merola phoned, she consented, rushed to San Francisco, and rehearsed briefly with Pietro Cimara, the evening's conductor. She had sung Lucia a few years earlier in Chicago—subbing for Pons on that occasion also—and in South America. Considering the circumstances, which generated an understandable amount of nervousness, she acquitted herself right well that evening.

Following the 1947 season, the pair-of-seats guarantors pledged to a figure of $100 received their first assessment bill since 1941—for $44. Ever-growing production costs (*Louise* and *Gioconda* had been added to the repertoire in hardly unelaborate guise) were given as the principal cause of deficit. The San Francisco season red ink, in round figures, spilled out to $97,000, but profits on out-of-town performances, mostly in Los Angeles, and other income, including donations, brought the grand total deficit down to $55,000. The concert activities which the Opera Association had initiated in 1939 ran, as usual, at a moderate profit.

There was talk again of enlarging the Opera House as a curb against deficit, but such did not prove feasible, nor has it subsequently.

1948

Merola took his company into its second quarter century with another tightly packed season: the 1948 schedule listed thirty performances of seventeen bills in thirty-four days. There were no new additions to the repertoire, but *Meistersinger* returned after ten years' absence, *Siegfried* after thirteen, and *The Elixir of Love* after nineteen. The previous year's *Otello* was repeated, also *La Gioconda*—each in one performance. And *Boris* returned as a Pinza finale.

Merola recommenced his importation of singers, bringing Tito Gobbi, the young matinee idol baritone, for his American debut. A Swiss lyric tenor from Zurich named Max Lichtegg also came to this country especially for San Francisco appearances. Ebe Stignani returned to the place of *her* American debut a decade earlier,[3] and further luster shone on the roster thanks to the presence of the tenor Fer-

[3] Stignani, for some reason, never sang at the Metropolitan. Her American activities this year included an appearance in *Gioconda* with the Philadelphia La Scala Company in late November. There was also a Chicago recital.

ruccio Tagliavini, basso Italo Tajo and contralto Cloe Elmo, all of whom had been singing in the United States only a short time, Tajo not yet at the Metropolitan.

Verdi's *Falstaff* is a great opera, Merola loved it, and he had the daring to put it on the opening night card, in an apparent effort to put a spotlight on the Windsor doings and make them better known. Naturally some of the tripping delicacies of the score were lost amid the first night festivities. For some the performance was part of a double bill, *A Day at the Races* and *A Night at the Opera*, as racing at Golden Gate Fields had begun that afternoon. But the performance was winning, despite Baccaloni's inexact voicing of the title role. Steinberg's incisive conducting—without score, of course—was a delight, and Stignani's warmly funny Dame Quickly will not be easily forgotten. Her voice wasn't quite as fresh as in 1938, but there was still a lot of lusciousness in it, and the absence of a romantic figure mattered not at all in this role.

The company boasted another first-rate Quickly in Cloe Elmo, who took over the part in the second performance. Elmo had made a tremendous hit with her scenery-shaking, rich-toned Azucena at the Metropolitan the previous spring, and it was in this role that she came to the War Memorial stage September 30, and conquered. She was awarded one of the biggest ovations of the season.

Gobbi's debut occurred in a Saturday matinee repeat of *The Barber of Seville* October 2. His fame as a movie star preceded him, and it was mentioned in the press that whereas he had never sung a note in the United States the Tito Gobbi International Fan Club of South Orange, New Jersey, already existed. It is not surprising that the critics were on the suspicious and impatient side. His Figaro took a very secondary place at the bottom of the Monday reviews, which had some other news—from the Sunday afternoon performance— to relate.

This was the appearance of Astrid Varnay, hitherto associated with Wagner, in an important Italian role, La Gioconda. With a silken voice, and impeccable musicianship, she seemed the best answer to the pressing problem of finding a really satisfying dramatic soprano for the Italian wing. Actually the principal replacement for Roman, who had struggled with much of that repertoire for several years, was an Argentine soprano who had sung in Rome and New Orleans, Sara Menkes. She appeared in *Forza* and *Trovatore* with some success, but not enough to warrant a regular and prominent place on the roster.

Gobbi in 1948 was not the subtle artist he has become, and his Figaro was agreeable in a brash and lusty way. But in retrospect some of the reviews have a strange bite. Frankenstein wrote: "He was a Figaro straight off the cover of a candy box. His dapper little figure, his rolling eyes and his flash of beautiful teeth were accompanied by a light, deft and amusing style, tasteful singing, and a high baritone which is rather shallow in body though big enough in volume. He seemed, in short, like an extremely good musical comedy performer who was acceptable enough in opera without quite belonging there." Fried wrote: "Despite his surprisingly brash, uninhibited manner of singing, the audience liked him immediately. True, he was an exceptionally agreeable Figaro to watch, for he was lively, merry and confident. Maybe when we hear him again he will give more thought to the quality of his tone and musical style." Fisher wrote: "Obviously young, attractive and blond, he may best be described by the teen-agers' comment: 'He's cute!' While his voice was nothing to get excited about, it was pleasant, and his singing efficient."

Italo Tajo made a tremendous impression in his first appearance with an outstanding Basilio, and he repeated his great success with an especially inventive Leporello in the second *Don Giovanni*, a week later. The comparison with Baccaloni, the familiar servant of the earlier performance, was interesting, and not unfavorable to either buffo. The presence of both in the lower male reaches was as much an asset as having both Stignani and Elmo in the deeper female voice department.

Tajo had a narrow escape when the company toured to Bakersfield, near Los Angeles, and the shade of a stage light fell on his head during the second act of *Bohème*. The theater was new and apparently not quite performance-worthy when the opera took the stage. Colin Harvey, who was playing a waiter, recalls hearing a pop as he opened the bottle of champagne for Baccaloni, the Alcindoro. But the cork was still firmly in the bottle *after* the pop. What he heard was the impact of the lighting fixture on Tajo's skull. He continued singing through the act and there were no serious consequences. But at intermission time it was discovered that the instrument had cut full through his wig. There was more consternation that night when, at one point, the flexible orchestra pit suddenly began to rise toward heaven, and the musicians had to jump from this reverse version of a sinking ship.

If Tajo and Elmo won notably enthusiastic responses during the 1948 season, it was Tagliavini who received the most prolonged ovation of all. It happened the night of October 11, at the only performance of *Elixir of Love*. After "Una furtiva lagrima," the applause was loud and persistent. While the audience clapped, Tagliavini smiled anxiously, twisted his cap, shrugged his shoulders. Conductor

Breisach knew that line in the program which reads "No encores permitted," but after five minutes something was needed to stop the flood. The rule was broken, as it had been before and would be again, but not often.

The performance of the aria was not necessarily the best thing that happened during the season. But Tagliavini's voice was unusually sweet and suave in lyric tone. This was the first of two Tagliavini appearances—he sang Alfredo in *Traviata* opposite Kirsten four days later. Gobbi was the Belcore in *Elixir*, and also sang Marcello.

Another new Italian tenor was Mario Binci, who had made his American debut at the New York City Center the previous spring. He sang only one performance, as Turiddu in *Cavalleria* with Stignani. He was not remarkable vocally, and insecure dramatically. He did not return.

Claudia Pinza was back to sing two performances of *Don Giovanni*. Her Elvira was a little lightweight in voice but she created a good sense of pathos. The Ottavio was Lichtegg, whose voice had a slight Germanic hardness but was sure and pleasant.

One of the most important debuts of a local singer in company history was that of Dorothy Warenskjold, a young lady from Oakland, and a graduate of Mills College. Warenskjold had sung in Jan Popper's Stanford University Workshop production of *Der Freischütz* a year and a half before, but her appearance as Anne in the San Francisco Opera's second *Falstaff* October 7 marked her debut with a major company. Her charming lyric soprano won immediate favor. A Micaela followed.

Other good opportunities were provided for Mary Jane Gray of the chorus, who lent good voice and appearance to Flora in *Traviata* and Kate Pinkerton in *Butterfly*. She was a girl going places, and she has, minus the middle name, singing principal roles with success in Germany. Theodor Uppman, who sang Pelléas at the Metropolitan five years later, was the Morales in *Carmen* and the Nachtigall in *Meistersinger*.

The *Meistersinger* revival September 21 was a good try, but hardly realized in ideal fashion. Neither Kullman nor Janssen really had enough voice for their roles, Walther and Sachs respectively, although they were sympathetic enough interpreters. The orchestral playing under Steinberg was better once the tight, wobbly brashness of the prelude was over with. Svanholm appeared as the Franconian knight in the repeat, and also in the successful *Siegfried*.

Leinsdorf returned after seven years' absence to conduct *Siegfried*, *Carmen* and *Boris*—all with above-average results. The *Carmen* starred

Winifred Heidt. Tall, good-looking, sensuous in voice, and relatively refined in interpretation, this was one of the better Carmens. *Boris,* along with *Forza* and *Don Giovanni,* marked the outgoing of Ezio Pinza, who had sung with the company twenty out of twenty-two seasons from 1927. The next autumn found him well established on a *South Pacific* beachhead in New York. The third act of *Boris* was still cut, but Rangoni was no longer left writhing on the cutting room floor.

The late Leonard Warren also departed from the company this season—at least for six years—and *his* leave-taking was considerably less warm than Pinza's. Warren was a top baritone and a conscientious artist, but he was not precisely popular backstage because of his headstrong ways. Before the *Rigoletto* performance he decided he didn't like certain aspects of the staging and made known his displeasure in no uncertain terms. In trying to smooth the argument between Warren and Agnini, Merola reminded Warren that his principal business was singing, not staging, and that if he didn't like the staging in San Francisco he didn't have to come back and sing in the middle of it. The result of this discussion was that Warren did not return so long as Merola was alive. Some are of the opinion that there was mutual regret over the matter, but the fact remains Merola never engaged him again.

Advancing costs, the "exceptional" effort made at brilliant productions because of Met competition in Los Angeles, and an unexpected recession in demand for tickets: these were the leading causes of the 1948 deficit, a larger one than the previous year's. The guarantor assessment was $67. A determined effort would be made, it was announced, to rectify the situation, and the number of operas and performances was cut down in 1949. The season in San Francisco remained the usual length (from 1946 through 1953 it was thirty-four days), so there was more breathing space for performers and audience alike.

10

THE PACIFIC STORY

The year 1948 also saw the first spurt of growth in the re-organized Pacific Opera of Arturo Casiglia. Merola's chorus master during the first season in the Civic Auditorium, Casiglia had struck out on his own, producing low-priced, low-budget opera off and on through the years with local talent. He was a sound musician, a spunky trouper, and many San Francisco singers can remember him today as a good friend to the youthful, local, non-star performer. Some of his artists went on to bigger things.

Following a considerable period of near-dormancy, tentative plans were announced in February for what would be the *New* Pacific Opera Company. "Putting on opera for a dollar a seat (orchestra seat!) plus tax is just like giving opera away," said Casiglia. "That's what we want to do."

Casiglia's advisory committee included Mrs. John Coghlan, Mrs. Thomas Carr Howe, Jr., Mrs. Leon Cuenin, Campbell McGregor, Karl Weber, William G. Merchant and Jack Pisani. At that time most of these were guarantors of the San Francisco Opera, and the Pacific activities had the benediction of the San Francisco Opera Association, which termed the project a "valuable supplement" to its own per-formances. Young local singers had opportunities to sing major roles, and opera was introduced to people who couldn't afford the usual prices.

A projected May season did not materialize, but there was an intro-ductory performance in the Opera House July 29: *Rigoletto* with Splendora Merlitti of San Francisco as Gilda, Ernest Lawrence of New York City Opera experience as the Duke, and Vittorio Weinberg, once of La Scala and a San Francisco resident, as the Jester. Casiglia, of course, conducted. Many were turned away, and a season of nine performances did materialize November 5 through 26. The operas were *Carmen, Traviata, Rigoletto, Bohême, Cavalleria* and *Pagliacci, The Barber* and *Lucia.* Ina Souez, the onetime Glyndebourne great, was announced for Santuzza, but she did not appear.[1] The season was a great success, and another batch of nine presentations, at $1.80 top, was given March 4–13, 1949.

The Pacific was now on relatively solid footing, and a happy adjunct to the city's operatic life. Later, however, the plot of this parallel story thickened. What Casiglia had never intended as a rival institution evolved into a company which had a good deal less than the most friendly attitude toward the San Francisco Opera. The feeling was mutual.

The path of the Pacific had never been precisely easy. When Casiglia, a Sicilian who had reached San Francisco via Boston, started his company in the mid-twenties, sporadic performances—not seasons —were all that could be achieved. The first show was a *Butterfly* performed in a playhouse, the Capitol, which had been closed for some time. The date was December 17, 1925. The original idea had been to call the troupe the Casiglia Civic Opera, but it was as the Pacific Coast Opera that it came to public light. The name must have seemed a bit cumbersome, and journalists took to shortening it to Pacific Opera: this name stuck. With local talent taking a commendably conspicuous part in the proceedings, the company reappeared June 16, 1926 in a performance of *Traviata* which featured Vera Didenco, Charles Bulotti and Albert Gillette, with Max Lorenzini and Evaristo Alibertini in smaller roles. A *Cavalleria* and *Pagliacci* followed November 24, 1926, Bellini's *Norma* (hardly standard opera) was given December 6, 1927, and the double bill was heard again February 28, 1928. There was a certain spirit of adventure about these performances, but if there were rough and ready aspects, there were some delights, too. It must not be forgotten that the San Francisco Opera itself did not enjoy the greatest elegance or security in its early days.

The second chapter of Pacific history opens with its first full season, which began April 16, 1929, at the Capitol. Eight performances of *Norma, Carmen, Rigoletto, Traviata* and the double bill were given. A group of "founders" had been gathered, more than half of them already supporters of the Musical Association and/or the San

[1] Performances by Colorado-born Ina Souez since her return from Europe in 1940 have been rare. Her American career took on a checkered aspect, including a tour with Spike Jones! She appeared successfully with the Werner Janssen Symphony in San Francisco in 1945, singing excerpts from *Wozzeck*, and was again successful in a 1947 recital. There was reason to believe the San Francisco Opera at some time might value her services, but they made no overture in her direction. She has long been a California resident and now teaches in San Francisco.

Francisco Opera Association. Seasons followed in 1930, 1931 and 1932, the repertoire remaining largely standard but containing some decidedly offbeat items. Casiglia went on from *Norma* to *Sonnambula* (in 1930), *Gioconda* (1931) and Catalani's *La Wally* (!) in 1932.[2] The title role in *Norma*, incidentally, was sung by Florence Ringo, the part of Amina in *Sonnambula* by Ione Pastori Rix.

The first major instance of internal dissension in the Pacific came in 1932, when Hugo Newhouse, president of the Pacific Opera Foundation, urged that a subsidy from the city not be paid the company as he and his fellow officers had decided not to give a 1932 season. The municipal budget included appropriation of $7,500 from the old Welfare Fund, and $1,600 had been paid, but $5,900 was held up. The Supervisors honored the Newhouse request, but this was not the end of the matter. With a new set of officers, headed by Ettore Patrizi, Casiglia went to court, and in September, 1933 Judge I. L. Harris decided in his favor.

But for the next fifteen years there was next to no Pacific Opera activity in San Francisco. The records show a few wartime performances in North Beach's relatively minute Fugazi Hall, in May, 1943, and a sprinkling of outdoor presentations at Stern Grove.

Following the rejuvenation of 1948, there were *two* seasons the following year, the first in March and the second in late November and early December—the two accounting for twenty-two Opera House performances altogether. A series of eight San Francisco and three Berkeley performances was begun in late November, 1950, with a *Bohème* which starred Tomiko Kanazawa, the *Butterfly* soprano. Ticket prices by this time had risen to $2.40 in the orchestra, with seats in that section available at $1.80 to patron members.

If you looked closely, you would have seen Campbell McGregor, the Pacific's president and principal backer, blithely assuming the chores of a Cafe Momus waiter in the second act of a *Bohème* performance. McGregor, the son of the president of the old Union Iron Works, had long been theater-struck.

Fortune Gallo's dying San Carlo troupe didn't come to San Francisco in the winter of 1951, and the Pacific, which hoped to concentrate its performances in that time of year rather than the San Francisco Opera's autumn, secured four dates in the Opera House that February. The Pacific's history continues with six performances in March, 1952—at the last one, a *Butterfly*, many persons were turned away. And then there were six performances in March, 1953, the

[2] The avalanche at the end of *La Wally* has always been a staging problem, even in houses like La Scala. It was comically inadequate in this production.

accent, as usual, on popular repertoire with local talent and young singers from other cities. The New York City Center did not go unrepresented.

The 1953 season played to the usual good houses, but the house of the Pacific was not in order. The second major instance of internal dissension came to public light May 1 when it was reported in the press that Casiglia was planning a season in November and "a Pacific Opera Company under a board of directors whose president is Campbell McGregor" was planning another season in the following March. The Pacific board, headed by McGregor, had offered Casiglia a one-year renewal on several conditions: (1) the directors have control of the Pacific name, (2) in out-of-town performances he use some name other than Pacific Opera, and (3) he surrender final say on singers and artistic policy to the directors.

Casiglia insisted the name Pacific belonged to him. After all, he had been producing opera under that name off and on for almost thirty years. The bill-paying McGregor, on the other hand, subscribed to the opinion that the name belonged to the estate of the late Hugo Newhouse, one of Casiglia's former backers, and was lent to Casiglia by the trustees. But the Newhouse estate had recently been settled and ownership of the name would have to be settled in court.

What had happened, really, was this: some feeling had developed on Casiglia's board that he was on the provincial side as an opera company artistic director. Dario Shindell, the company manager, wanted to hire singers in the East, but only Casiglia could sign the contracts. The determined Sicilian, who had always been essentially the sole pilot of what had remained a spunky homegrown organization, felt squeezed, and thought the character of the company might be changed. He wasn't sure how many renewals of contract he could look forward to.

Casiglia now and then took a group of performers out on the road almost on the spur of the moment, and the more formal element in the Pacific control was not so sure these performances were on the level of production pretensions to be maintained. Furthermore, Casiglia would pack his troupe on a bus without insurance, and had there been an accident, McGregor, it was complained, could have found himself with some whopping bills he hadn't planned on.

The whole matter went to Superior Court May 7, when McGregor, with Angelo Scampini as legal counsel, filed a petition asking for an injunction preventing Casiglia from using the Pacific name. His complaint stated that on September 29, 1950, Casiglia secretly incorporated a new society under the name Pacific Opera Company, without the knowledge of the New Pacific Grand Opera Association, that being the incorporated name of the company since 1948.

On August 20, 1953, Judge Harry J. Neubarth decided in favor of Casiglia. The Pacific would go on under his aegis, with a season in February. And McGregor, taking Shindell with him, soon announced plans for the first season of the Cosmopolitan Opera, to take place in March.

What followed the winter of 1954 was probably one of the most curious spectacles in American operatic history. It was tagged by columnists and critics the "Siamese Twin Opera Season" or the "Two Round Opera Season." Enter the Pacific with four performances at three dollar top in the Opera House from February 17 through 26. Enter the Cosmopolitan with six performances at three dollar top in the Opera House from March 2 through 19. Both seasons opened with *Traviata*. The same local *comprimario* sang Benoît and Alcindoro in *Bohéme* for both companies. No wonder the people in the ticket office were awfully confused: "Which *Traviata* will you have, sir?"

At all events, both troupes enjoyed box office success.[3] Casiglia contributed the one repertorial ace—if not a completely winning one—in Franco Leoni's Chinatown opera dating from 1905, *L'Oracolo*. This, of course, was Scotti's old vehicle. It had last been performed in San Francisco by the San Carlo a number of years earlier. The Cosmopolitan's conductor was Anton Coppola, a young maestro with a certain dramatic flair. And the McGregor-Shindell side had the advantage of Walter Fredericks, one of Casiglia's top men, in the tenor lineup. Casiglia had a teen-age Silvio and Schaunard in Ronald Dutro.

By this point the Cosmopolitan story is launched. And that is another story. But suffice it to say in this chapter that the Pacific was entering its last phase. Casiglia died late in 1954, and the company itself never performed after 1956. Meanwhile, the Cosmopolitan proceeded to flourish. In the late fifties Shindell became more and more intensely competitive with the San Francisco Opera, offering big-name artists stupendous fees while the overall production values behind the stars were not given such royal financial attention. By 1960 a dozen performances were offered. The possibility of some sort of collision between the San Francisco and the Cosmopolitan was not impossible.

---

[3] It has subsequently come to light that during the early Cosmopolitan years Shindell on occasion gave away several hundred tickets—considerably more than the normal allotment of passes.

11

PERSONAL TRIUMPHS

1949

There was a long, suspenseful and unmusical overture to the 1949 season. And for a while it looked as if there would be no opera, or more specifically a season of operas, to follow it. This was the Flagstad affair.

On June 27 it was announced that Kirsten Flagstad would appear in two performances each of *Tristan* and *Walküre*. Her return to Norway during the Nazi occupation thereof had been strongly questioned by some, but there was no incident when she appeared in an Oakland concert a year previous. Several weeks of rumors to the effect she would appear during the 1949 season resulted in absolutely no complaint from subscribers. But a stink bomb had been thrown at a Philadelphia appearance. And on July 11, in San Francisco, a verbal bomb was thrown: it came in the form of a resolution, submitted by Supervisor John J. Sullivan, which was aimed at preventing Flagstad from singing in the War Memorial Opera House. Similar resolutions were adopted by the San Francisco County Council of the American Legion and by the County Council of the Veterans of Foreign Wars. The singer was labeled as one "whose immediate sympathies and support were placed on the side of foes of freedom and democracy and with enemies of this country."

On July 14 the War Memorial Board of Trustees voted unanimously to officially "disapprove" of Flagstad's Opera House performances because of "the highly controversial character of her public appearances elsewhere in the United States." Before the vote was taken, however, attorney Herman Phleger, representing the San Francisco Opera Association, warned that loss of the Wagner productions would be a terrific financial blow, and could result in cancellation of the season. Superior Judge Milton Sapiro, of the local Legion, countered with a point of view reminiscent of his peculiar thoughts in connection with the building of the Opera House twenty years earlier. "Her appearance," he said, "would desecrate the War Memorial and the ideals it stands for. We wouldn't want a Benedict Arnold to sing in the Opera House. It would be better for the Opera Association to go out of business than hire a traitor to Norway." Phleger noted that the Association had made a thorough investigation of Flagstad's record during World War II, pointing out that she never sang in Norway or Germany or any German-occupied countries, "contrary to all statements and reports." She returned to Norway prior to the United States' entrance into the war, Phleger said, to be with her sick husband, lumberman Henry Johansen. This husband, Sapiro said, "was one of the leading Quislings and she should have stayed here to raise money for the Norwegian cause." The opera attorney put in that the King of Norway once gave Flagstad the highest decoration of that country, and had not recalled it after the war. Furthermore, he said, the Norwegian government had not refused her a visa to leave Norway and return. Her son-in-law, it was pointed out, was an American Air Force bomber pilot in the war.

Meanwhile, the demand for tickets to the scheduled Flagstad performances was far ahead of that for other operas on the announced list. And Flagstad herself was decidedly concerned when, in Salzburg, she read an erroneous newspaper report that her San Francisco contract had been cancelled. On July 18 the San Francisco Opera made its commendable ploy very clear: the season, the directors said, must proceed as planned, without substitute for Flagstad, or substitute for the Opera House—there had been some talk of moving the Wagner to some other hall.

Mayor Elmer Robinson, who was on vacation, suggested a conference between the Opera Association directors and the War Memorial trustees, and such a meeting was called July 20 by Supervisor, and Acting Mayor, George Christopher. The directors served notice on the trustees that, should their ban not be lifted in a week, the season might be called off. The tide slowly began to turn, but the suspense remained intense. Editorials in the newspapers criticized the trustees. The Mayor's office queried the State Department and found there was no derogatory information from that source on the singer. The Junior Chamber of Commerce urged the trustees to reconsider. The State Commander of the American Legion sent a telegram saying the local legionnaires were "not acting for the Legion" in the matter. The American Guild of Musical Artists pointed out that the San Francisco Opera might be blacklisted by ninety-five per cent of the world's greatest artists should the ban continue.

Another meeting in Christopher's office July 23 resulted in no definite progress, but the trustees were not far from an even split on their vote. The opera directors' deadline was postponed once, then a second time: to August 1. One of the trustees, Sidney Ehrman, was returning from Europe and his vote could be of critical importance. He reported by phone that he would cast his vote in favor of Flagstad, and he did so at the short meeting held by the trustees August 1. As another trustee switched his vote to pro-Flagstad, a 6-4 "against" was turned into a 6-5 "for." The ban was lifted. The opera season would go on as planned.

Two months later, on the night of September 30, Flagstad sang in *Tristan*. There was a midnight ovation, a standing one, and no incident. A special third performance of *Tristan* was added to the schedule. The five San Francisco appearances were her first American opera performances since the war,[1] and they demonstrated that she still had more than plenty to offer.

Many of the elements in the Wagner casts were familiar. But they also brought forth a Hungarian bass, Mihaly Szekely, who turned out to be one of the most distinguished singers in the lowest Wagnerian range in company history.[2] The Wagnerian wing was also the area in which the year's Horatio Alger story took place. Its protagonist was a young baritone named Richard Sharretts. He had come to California the year before with a road company of *Oklahoma* and, while in San Francisco, auditioned for the role of the Night Watchman in the 1948 *Meistersinger* production. He won the part and was singled out for his fine handling of it. Then, for 1949 Merola gave him a promotion—to Wotan! When he appeared in this taxing role along with Flagstad, Svanholm and Szekely, he sang intelligently and well, but without anything near the vocal power and authority needed in this company. It was one of the best tries in the annals of the San Francisco Opera, but an ill-advised bit of daring all the same. Janssen was his replacement at the repeat.

The 1949 season calmed down from the previous year's thirty performances of seventeen bills in thirty-four days to twenty-five presentations of twelve bills in the same amount of time. As an innovation, there were two popular subscription series, and *Tristan* and *Tosca* were given unprecedented third performances. The latter opera, strangely absent for eight years, returned as the opening night fare: one can only assume that Merola didn't have the soprano he wanted in the interim, although Milanov was on the roster one year, and Della Chiesa and Varnay, who were present in others, had possi-

[1] She returned to the Metropolitan, as Isolde, January 22, 1951.
[2] Non-Wagnerian assignments for him in San Francisco and Los Angeles were Ramfis and Sparafucile.

bilities for the title role. The choice in 1949 was a twenty-six-year-old Italian, Elisabetta Barbato, who had risen to stardom three years earlier when she substituted for Caniglia in a Rome Opera *Aida*. This was her American debut. If her performances as Tosca and Aida were not unqualified successes, they showed promise plus. Her voice had warmth and beauty, but at times it wobbled. Youth enhanced the credibility of her performances, but she was not always at ease on the stage.

This was a season unusually strong in tenors, and Merola offered two Cavaradossis of top rank: Bjoerling, who sang opening night, and Tagliavini. When the latter was called upon for heroic pronouncements, his voice could lapse into mere loudness, but the lyrical aspects of the part were exceptionally well-voiced. Ramon Vinay, the dark-voiced Chilean, made his company debut in *Carmen* opposite Heidt, and an impressive one it was. His acting had a conviction about it above the average, and his Rembrandtian tonal quality was striking and expressively put forth, if not always with maximum freedom. Svanholm, Peerce and Jobin were also around this year, lending more strength to the solid tenor line. Giacinto Prandelli was supposed to make his American debut, but this didn't work out.

The major revival of the season was Puccini's *Manon Lescaut*, not heard in twenty-two years. When it returned October 7, Albanese and Bjoerling sang the romantic leads, and Enzo Mascherini, an Italian import, was the Lescaut. Baccaloni sang Geronte. Fausto Cleva, absent for six years, led a performance which was one of the best in company history.

Cesare Curzi of the chorus was a decidedly better-than-average *comprimario* talent in the role of Edmondo in *Manon Lescaut*, and another chorister, Jo Ann O'Connell, gave a good account of herself as Olympia in the second *Tales of Hoffmann*.

Rose Bampton was heard with the company for the first time this year: she appeared as Sieglinde in *Die Walkure* and Donna Anna in *Don Giovanni*. Tajo switched from Leporello to the Don this year, and there was much feeling that he was more the master of the servant's role.

1950

Again this year, Tristan and Isolde almost didn't get their night on stage in San Francisco—at least on schedule. The circumstances were quite different.

The company informed the press September 27 that Ramon Vinay just might not make it to San Francisco in time for needed rehearsals prior to his first appearance in the role of Tristan October 3, and it looked as if some troublesome rearranging of the schedule might be in order. Vinay, it developed, had been delayed on his way from London to Chile, his plane being grounded in Panama. As a result, he had missed two of his four announced performances in Santiago. Since Vinay retained something of the status of a national hero in Chile, his native land, pressure was put on him to stay long enough to make up for the lost performances. Rumor even had it that the Chilean president had been persuaded to withhold Vinay's passport. The tenor was reported as offering to repay the San Francisco Opera Association for any unfulfilled appearances, but the Association didn't consider that much help.

Luckily this little comic opera did not play long. On September 29 it was reported that the situation had been resolved and Vinay would arrive, after all, in time for adequate preparation. Vinay followed this news in person October 1, explaining to reporters that the management of the theater where he was appearing in Santiago had indeed sent his passport to the Secretary of Exterior Relations. And on October 3 he sang as scheduled, opposite Flagstad. He proved to be one of the most moving Tristans of the modern operatic stage, his dark voice finding an especially appropriate home in the somberness and yearning of the score. This performance also served to introduce to America the most impressive-voiced Wagnerian baritone the company had presented since Schorr, Sigurd Bjoerling—no relation to tenor Jussi. And there was an experienced, authoritative King Marke in Dezso Ernster, who had been originally scheduled for the roster in 1939.

The new *Tristan* conductor was a bearded gentleman named Jonel Perlea, a Rumanian-born musician who had worked in Italy and spent a short time at the Metropolitan. His interpretation was remarkably poetic, but not lacking in strong climax: Perlea obviously helped this year's edition of Wagner's opera take on its special quality.

But 1950 will probably be most remembered as the season in which Renata Tebaldi and Mario Del Monaco made their American debuts. Tebaldi, who was, of course, already well-established in Italy, had been enthusiastically recommended by Albanese. When the season's all-but-final plans were announced in March, they included her name, but that of Del Monaco, also rising in Italy, was not among the tenors. It did appear, however, in the revised roster released to the press in May—without any special fanfare. The name of Jussi Bjoerling, which had been in the earlier announcement, was absent.

That spring Merola had visited the office of Frank DeBellis, the patron of Italian arts, for the main purpose of listening to new recordings of Tebaldi, whom he had already engaged. Opera managers can never be too sure, and although he was confident he was bringing a special singer to this country, he was happy to have documentary evidence. "Thank you," said Merola after the audition, "but you know, I'm not really worried about sopranos. Tenors are the problem. I know you buy a number of Italian recordings. If you hear a promising voice please call me." At that, DeBellis played him recordings by several tenors, but Merola was not aroused. The last tenor, however, brought the remark, "*Who* is this singing?" It was not long before Del Monaco's engagement was announced.

The two debuts took place in a starry opening night *Aida* September 26 with Weede, Tajo and Elena Nikolaidi, the Greek contralto of the Vienna Opera, also on stage, and Cleva in the pit—Merola was prevented by doctor's orders from conducting. It was immediately apparent that Del Monaco was an exciting find. His little figure moved with brisk vigor. His eyes flashed. His voice cut through "Celeste Aida" without the early evening uncertainty that plagues many a Rhadames. As the season continued, and the succeeding *Andrea Chenier* and *Manon Lescaut* found Merola's new prize bellowing and hamming things up a great deal, it developed that there were some reservations to be registered about Signor Del Monaco. But there wasn't any question of the eclat of his presence, despite the personalized poses, and the free-ringing tone of his upper register, the dulcet seductiveness of his lower tones when he watched over them. In later seasons Canio and Manrico were notably apt vehicles for his robust talents. And Otello, of course.

The wistful, expressive beauty of Tebaldi's voice and her attractive personality won her a fond audience immediately and deservedly. The new Renata divina let her tone explode a bit at times in *forte* passages, but this was a minor distraction. Merola had finally found a dramatic soprano for the Italian repertoire with the greatness of a Muzio or a Rethberg. Her Desdemona, which came a couple weeks later, was, in fact, an impersonation harder to surpass than her *Aida*. A scheduled Countess in *The Marriage of Figaro* was taken over by Quartararo, however.

Rudolf Bing, the Metropolitan's new general manager, was interested enough in the San Francisco Opera in general and Tebaldi and Del Monaco in particular to fly out from New York for the repeat of the *Aida* opening at the Sunday matinee subscription on October 1. At a press conference he said, "We shall have to pull up our socks to do better than that, or even match it." Well, obviously not all San Francisco Opera performances were like that, but the company had to be taken very seriously.

The 1950 home season was another of relatively comfortable proportions: twenty-five performances of thirteen operas within thirty-four days. The Mozart and Wagner statistics were enlarged with delayed additions of *The Magic Flute* and *Parsifal* to the repertoire.[3] The Mozart singspiel was not mounted with any great distinction: the genuine style that would have best reconciled its comic and serious elements was lacking. With its large amount of spoken dialogue, *The Magic Flute* was wisely performed in English—in the translation by the Martins. But Breisach's somewhat timid conducting, the rather ragged ensemble and the hardly virtuoso cast took a lot of the natural shine out of this flute. Heavily literal sets didn't help either.

Parsifal, presented on the last Friday evening of the regular series—beginning at 5 P.M. with a break for dinner—and the following Sunday afternoon beginning at one, was conducted by Perlea with his accustomed sensitivity: perhaps even too much of it. Flagstad, almost unrecognizable wigged in black, was the authoritative Kundry, and Kullman, returned for such specialized assignments as Tamino and Parsifal, was surprisingly forceful. There may have been times that weekend when one was reminded of the story about the man who went up to the ticket window and asked for a lower berth for *Parsifal,* but the stirring passages were well realized, the productional effort worthwhile. The sets, by Agnini and Dunkel, were contributed by the Opera Guild, which raised money this year at the first annual Opera Ball and Fol-de-Rol in the Civic Auditorium. Many of the company's artists donated their services, and for this gay occasion on October 5, Lily Pons wiggled her hips to a recording of "Diamonds Are a Girl's Best Friend," and Baccaloni introduced the song "Some Unlikely Morning" from the musical *North Atlantic* while an old colleague named Ezio Pinza sat at a table out front.

A note in the program pointed to the difficulty of building "new and necessary" productions without special financial aid. Ticket prices were not being raised, the note said, though production costs certainly were. Regular series orchestra seats remained $7.20.

The tenor department was exceptionally strong again in 1950. Be-

[3] *Parsifal* had last been staged in San Francisco by the Chicago Opera at the Tivoli in 1914. The Kundrys of the two performances were Minnie Saltzman-Stevens and Julia Claussen. Otto Marak sang Parsifal, Clarence Whitehall Amfortas, Allen Hinckley Gurnemanz, and Hector Dufranne Klingsor. Mabel Riegelman, a Californian and a San Francisco voice teacher today, was one of the Flower Maidens. Cleofonte Campanini conducted.

sides Del Monaco, Vinay and Kullman (plus Jagel returning in his best role, Herod), there were two fine young additions in Giuseppe Di Stefano and Eugene Conley. Both sang Edgardos, and Di Stefano was further assigned Rodolfo, and Conley Almaviva. Both were strong lyrics—the Italian tenor's voice was fully in its prime at that time: this was before his ill-advised switch to a dramatic tenor emphasis. *Lucia* further boasted as good a pair of second tenors as company history could record: Cesare Curzi as Arthur and Hubert Norville as Norman.

An unscheduled bit of business in *The Barber of Seville* came under the heading of cheerful avoirdupois—Baccaloni, as Bartolo, sat down hard enough on a chair during the shaving scene to cave it in under him. Claramae Turner must have been happy at the very large hand she received for her singing of Bertha's little aria.

The tenor list further included a young man from Philadelphia named Walter Fredericks. He had been in San Francisco a few years earlier singing with the Ice Follies and caught the attention of Arturo Casiglia, who featured him with the Pacific Opera. His San Francisco Opera debut was as Narraboth in *Salome,* an assignment he carried off well. Brenda Lewis, a young American soprano, made a fine impression in the title role when Strauss' opera was revived.

Del Monaco went to New York after his San Francisco Opera appearances, singing a guest date in *Manon Lescaut* at the Metropolitan November 27. He formally joined the New York company the following season, taking part in the opening night *Aida*. Tebaldi was not to appear at the Metropolitan until the 1954–1955 season. Sigurd Bjoerling was on the roster there only in 1952–1953. Perlea's first season at the Met, 1949–1950, was also his last. According to Kolodin, he and Bing couldn't agree on repertoire.

There was big deficit trouble this year. The fifty-six per cent assessment in 1949 represented a slight dip from the previous year, but that for 1950 was one hundred per cent. New productions and imported artists naturally cost money, but most of it was well spent indeed. There was, unfortunately, a six per cent drop in attendance at the Shrine Auditorium in Los Angeles—the proximity on the calendar of Sadler's Wells Ballet (now called the Royal Ballet) and Civic Light Opera performances doubtless had its effect. Los Angeles income was down approximately $12,000. Meanwhile, the twenty per cent entertainment tax was nearly paralyzing organizations like the San Francisco Opera in the face of rising production costs.

At this time, connections were severed between the Association and Paul Posz, long the manager of the opera company and the concert chief. Posz was succeeded by Howard Skinner, the manager of the

San Francisco Symphony. Artistically the organizations would, of course, remain separate.

1951

A long postponed and not especially successful attempt at a new role by a celebrated artist very well known to San Francisco, and a rousing Boris by a young Russo-Italian bass-baritone in his "second American debut"—these were the newsiest events in a season which was more a reaffirmation of well-tasted items than one noted for the unfolding of novel repertoire.

Lily Pons tried Violetta in *Traviata* for the first time in her career October 5. Seldom has an individual portrayal received so much advance attention in the press, and there was much newspaper talk about it from late summer on. Pons arrived in San Francisco in late August after being coached in the role by Vincenzo Bellezza in Rome. She had, she said, lived with it for six months. And, it was prominently reported, the new Violetta had gone to Paris and ordered some expensive costumes from Balmain and Karinska.

Came the night of her first performance, the audience was as dressy and social as that on opening night. Every important artist not singing in *Traviata* seemed to be there. Pons herself was extremely nervous at the start of the performance, and her tone often became fluttery. But when she relaxed, there were passages of intense feeling and beautiful singing. Although her acting was at first on the studied side, she seemed to identify herself with the role more and more as the evening progressed. She gave of her voice abundantly, but could not persuade many listeners that Violetta is a role for a coloratura: a number of her high *forte* tones were shrill. All in all, then, a not uncommendable entrance into difficult coloratura-lyric-dramatic territory, but an ill-advised one for the artist on the whole. She never sang the role at the Metropolitan.

Jan Peerce was a fine Alfredo, Giuseppe Valdengo an unsubtle Germont. Cleva conducted.

If the Pons *Traviata* was less than a hit, there wasn't any question about the triumph registered by Nicola Rossi-Lemeni as Boris. With more than ample vocal resources, magnificent bearing and lively dramatic ability, the young singer—only in his early thirties—elicited raves. He conceived the Czar as frantically racked with pangs of conscience, and his interpretation, vocally and visually, was intense enough to leave the audience limp. It was climaxed by a brilliant piece of showmanship skillfully wedded to his conception: a sensational corkscrew fall down a flight of steps—a fall so realistic that listeners greeted the tremendous thump on the stage floor with a collective gasp. Actually Rossi-Lemeni fell forward, hitting the floor with his hands and then rolling over so quickly that he seemed to have fallen directly on his back. This fall came at Boris' last words, as he rises from his throne at the top of the steps, clutching the arms of the chair, protesting he is still the Czar. A little earlier, after Pimen's narrative about the shepherd's vision of the child Dimitri, Rossi-Lemeni fell backwards freely and startlingly from the platform, to be caught by two choristers. The stage directions ask for a collapse here, but not necessarily one as daring as this. There was unusual vividness, too, in his entrance in this scene, hurtling on as he did with a wild stare on his face, clutching a handkerchief.

Rossi-Lemeni had come to the United States shortly after the war to appear with a troupe of European artists recruited for Chicago, as the regular company there was temporarily defunct. But alas, this season didn't come off. Rossi-Lemeni did sing, however, at a concert given by the artists to earn money for their passage back to the Continent. This, in reality, was his American debut, though the San Francisco Opera program-makers did not recognize it. Son of an Italian father and a Russian mother, he had a law degree from Padua and, according to a newspaper interview, no formal vocal training. He also sang a Padre Guardiano in *Forza*,[4] and a Colline in *Bohême* in 1951, and returned in 1952 and 1953. He was Merola's last great import, and his American career had a "made in San Francisco" stamp on it. Rossi-Lemeni appeared only briefly at the Metropolitan—in the first part of the 1953–1954 season, opening it in *Faust* conducted by Monteux. After the Chicago Opera was relaunched in 1954, he sang there three seasons. Only San Franciscans saw his *Mefistofele*, in 1952 and 1953.

This *Boris* was sung in Italian, as usual. Walter Fredericks had his best opportunity yet with the company as Dimitri, addressing his remarks to the conductor, Erich Leinsdorf, but singing with soaring tone. San Franciscan James Schwabacher was particularly effective as the Simpleton. This singer, incidentally, had replaced Kullman as Tamino in the Los Angeles *Magic Flute* of 1950.

There was, in 1951, another dose of that suspense which is an all too nerve-wracking prelude to many opera seasons. This time there

[4] Those who own the Callas recording of *Forza* will notice the unusual intensity of vocal characterization Rossi-Lemeni brings to this role: notice in particular the almost but not quite frenzied handling of the recognition—in the second act—that his visitor at the monastery is Leonora di Vargas.

was worry over whether the Japanese Peace Treaty Conference would vacate the Opera House on schedule, only several days before the commencement of the season. Russia's Andrei Gromyko had threatened to keep the conference going for a month. Some wags suggested that perhaps Mr. Gromyko might be set to music and there could be opera after all. At all events, everything went off on schedule and the company's rehearsals were moved from the Downtown Theater into the Opera House as planned.

There were twenty-six performances of fourteen operas this year. The orchestra seat price for a regular series performance now stood at $8.75. Nothing in the repertoire had been off the boards very long: there was *Rosenkavalier, Boris, Parsifal, Fidelio, Carmen, Manon, Romeo and Juliet, Traviata, Rigoletto, Forza, Otello, Bohême, Butterfly* and *Tosca*. There was, however, besides the Pons Violetta, Dorothy Kirsten's first Tosca, Blanche Thebom's first Carmen and Octavian, and Astrid Varnay's first *Fidelio* Leonore. Del Monaco, opening the Met, was unavailable, but Bjoerling returned, in superb voice. Tebaldi didn't return either this year, and Italian-born, American-trained Herva Nelli, favored by Toscanini, was a competent and attractive but not electrifying substitute. Stella Roman came back to sing the Marschallin, which she had done at the Cincinnati Summer Opera, and this turned out to be one of the better things achieved by her in San Francisco.

Kirsten's Tosca was a relatively lyric performance. Thebom's Carmen was almost stolen from her by Dorothy Warenskjold's radiantly pure-toned Micaela. But if the latest cigarette girl overdid the histrionics, the voice was sumptuous. Anna Lisa Bjoerling, the tenor's wife, sang opposite her spouse in the second *Romeo*, displaying an exceedingly sweet and pleasant if hardly exciting voice. Varnay mixed good voice with youthful good looks as Kundry, but *Parsifal*, given on a non-subscription evening beginning at seven o'clock, without so much as a dinner break, was a longer haul than even aficionados could manage. Warenskjold, steadily maturing, also sang the Sophie in the second *Rosenkavalier*.

An interesting addition to the tenor ranks was the Dutchman Frans Vroons, who had sung at the New York City Center. His Des Grieux in *Manon* was noteworthy for its style, handsome appearance and interpretative imagination. The voice was far from great, but the performance had unusual merits.

Fidelio was given in German this time, with Alfred Wallenstein, at that time conductor of the Los Angeles Philharmonic Orchestra, making his operatic conducting debut—sans score. His baton work was not without authority, but sometimes lacked punch, and the production, with an uneven cast onstage and wobbly brass in the pit, didn't come off as well as it deserved. For some reason the opera was only scheduled in one performance, at the end of the season.

The 1951 guarantor assessment was down to 61.3 per cent. The top price had been raised, and there were no new productions. But the twenty per cent entertainment tax continued to be a bother right up to November 1 when, too late to help the San Francisco Opera's activities, it went out of effect. The Los Angeles picture was happier this year: five of fourteen performances were sold out, and the total gross was $225,000. Average attendance in the Shrine Auditorium was almost 5,000. For the record, the smallest houses were drawn by *Otello* and *Fidelio*. Conspicuous cast changes in the southland included Dezso Ernster's Sparafucile and Ralph Herbert's Iago. Merola himself conducted *Traviata*. For the first time, the Southern California Symphony Association was the sponsor of the San Francisco Opera Association visit. It has continued this function.

12☙

REMINISCENCES AND DEATH

1952

Merola, excusably nostalgic in 1952, decided, to the great benefit of those attending the thirtieth anniversary season, to revive two operas not heard since the first year. They were Boito's *Mefistofele*, with its cataclysmic prologue and fantastic Witches' Sabbath scene, and Puccini's *Il Tabarro*, with its poignant and punchy verismo. The Boito was brought back, of course, thanks to the availability of Rossi-Lemeni; the *Tabarro* returned as part of the complete *Trittico*, the other two parts being the *Suor Angelica* and *Gianni Schicchi* which had been presented now and then as parts of double bills following their original presentation with *Tabarro* in 1923. While there was great point in these reminders of how far the company had come since the first performances of these operas, there was also pathos. For this, it turned out, was Merola's last season.

Oldsters remembered a cooler reception for *Mefistofele* in 1923, when lengthy scene changes in the technically ill-equipped Civic Auditorium dragged the performance on beyond midnight. During that season, a projected repeat had to be dropped because of lack of interest, but the total impact of the first performance in 1952 was so shattering that not only was there a scheduled repeat, but an added third performance. *Mefistofele* revisited was obviously one of the top events in company history.

What caused the excitement? Undoubtedly at the heart of the matter was the score itself—a refreshing change from Gounod's high sugar content. The music is not all good, but much of it is very good, and students of music history can be fascinated by the echoes of Berlioz and Liszt, the foreshadowings of late Verdi, the hints of Wagner. The production itself was magnificent. Fausto Cleva led all the forces with great spirit and authority. Rossi-Lemeni, catlike in his fluid movements, was a sonorous menace from his first emergence, bat-winged, out of the scenery. And Bidu Sayao and Tagliavini were lyrically sympathetic colleagues in a strong cast. For the most part the visual effects served up by Agnini and Dunkel were appropriate, and the staging of the Witches' Sabbath was fast, vivid and enthusiasm-provoking, even if on one occasion a gremlin turned on the steam too soon and the chorus lost Cleva's beat for a bit. This episode is supposed to have a nightmarish effect on the audience; it can, alas, also provide nightmares for the stage director.

No less exciting, really, than *Mefistofele* was *Tabarro*, conducted with tremendous intensity by Glauco Curiel, who maintains to this day the reputation of having been the company's best prompter. The little box was his usual working place during his several years with the company, but out on the podium he did some fine things—notably with Puccini, for whom he obviously had tender feelings. At times in this *Tabarro* he let the orchestra well up over the voices, but it was a flood of sound so exciting you couldn't argue with it. Brenda Lewis, Del Monaco and Weede were excellent in the main roles, and Claramae Turner made much of the part of La Frugola. In the second performance Fredericks replaced the lustrous Mario as Luigi and the comparison was by no means unfavorable.

One of the most worthwhile "experiments" in the history of the company was the *Rosenkavalier* presented this year in an English translation by Met assistant manager John Gutman. Said he of his work: "I didn't presume to rewrite Von Hofmannsthal, whose libretto is a literary masterpiece. I sought always to find the right natural meaning and fit it to the music syllable by syllable, stress by stress. Then each line had to pass a further test: it had to sing well." It was not a bad translation at all, and if understanding of it varied depending on where one sat, a good number of the audience heard a lot of the words and found the talky parts less so than usual. Briesach kept the orchestra subdued, and his approach was commendable in that it let the words flow out over the pit unobstructed. But there was, lamentably, some loss of the expected Straussian richness of sound. A real problem of how to have your Sacher Torte and eat it, too! It cannot be reported that the production was received with great enthusiasm, although Brenda Lewis was a fine Marschallin, Blanche Thebom sang Octavian and Dorothy Warenskjold Sophie. Also admired were the baroque-surrealist settings "suggested by" film and theater designer Tony Duquette of Los Angeles, with this qualification, however: some of the fussy details were questionable. The English language somewhat impaired the Ochs of Alvary, but his interpretation had its points, too. Gutman had had the advantage of knowing who the singers would be while making his translation, and of working with them in San Francisco. Subsequently *Rosenkavalier* has returned to German, in performances crowned by the presence of Elisabeth Schwarzkopf, but the English version deserves another try some season.

Another experiment, and a less successful one, took place with *Don Giovanni*. It consisted of scenery painted onto slides and projected from backstage machines onto translucent screens placed behind three archways. This device, reportedly being used in opera in America for the first time, was the work of Richard Rychtarik, a CBS art director in New York. He was brought to San Francisco by Herbert Graf, returning after several years' absence to share staging duties with Agnini and Carlo Piccinato. Much of the action was played in and out of the archways, which were approached by stairs and platforms, there being ample space downstage for props but not for the ballroom crowd. The main trouble was that the lighting had to be very subdued to allow the projections to shine forth, and it was hard to see what was going on in what one critic so aptly termed the "twilight zone." Some people wondered which scenes were supposed to be inside and which outside. The new staging facilitated speedy moves from scene to scene, but the price of pace was high.

The 1952 season brought more new ideas on staging than usual. Some of them may not have been the best ideas, but the sometime static nature of the company's productions was relatively energized. The repertoire was predominantly Italian, but had some fresh touches, as the reader has seen. Actually, Merola was toying with the idea of producing Alban Berg's *Wozzeck*, and there was report of a Los Angeles patron of the arts offering to subsidize the production, but this did not come to pass. Time was a big problem, said Merola. One wonders if a little more daring and a little less caution on his part and the board's would have made *Wozzeck* possible in the early fifties. The schedule of new productions after the wartime austerity period could have been rather more adventurous. *Louise, Parsifal, Gioconda* and *Magic Flute* were given; the latter two might have been delayed so that newer things could make their way. Merola, aging and in frail health, had clearly lost some of his early fire, and he was, of course, a man of the so-called old school.

It is interesting to note that Merola was also thinking of doing Richard Strauss' *Capriccio*, a work rather intimate for the War Memorial Opera House and not easy to cast. A work, too, which is perhaps best performed in the tongue of the audience.

Rossi-Lemeni was this year's Don Giovanni, blond and effective—although perfectionists worried about his playing the mandolin with

gloves on. He delved further into the old Pinza repertory with a compelling Archibaldo in *L'Amore dei Tre Re*, worthily revived after five
years' absence.[1] The composer, Montemezzi, had planned to attend, but
he died early in the year. Cleva conducted, Kirsten repeated her excellent Fiora, and Brian Sullivan, a young Metropolitan tenor of California origin, made his company debut as Avito. He revealed a not quite
fully matured but excitingly romantic lyric-dramatic tenor. At times
he put forth a sort of sublimated whine which made its point in this
chilling, highly charged score.

Lily Pons repeated her Violetta in a non-subscription performance
this year, but the role still wasn't really right for her. She was, in fact,
not as sure of her part as she might have been—Curiel practically sang
a duet with her from the prompter's box. A much happier vehicle for
the French Lily was the revived *Daughter of the Regiment*. But there
was a transportation problem here. In the matinee repeat, the horse
drawing her carriage charged from its resting place on stage and
crashed out into the wings, meanwhile knocking into a side flat which
some choristers promptly propped up before greater damage could
result. The horse had been fidgeting and backing off, and at one point
the man holding the reins let go and the driver urged the animal forward. But too far forward it went. Pons was supposed to get in the
carriage, but minus it, she went off in a huff instead. And who could
blame her? Frans Vroons, the happily received Dutch tenor of 1951,
was supposed to return for the role of Tonio, but did not appear. His
place was taken by a reedy-voiced local tenor, Ernest Lawrence, who
did a competent but far from star-caliber job.

The biggest new vocal sensation of the year was Fedora Barbieri,
who took over where Ebe Stignani and Cloe Elmo had left off in
letting the Italian dramatic mezzo repertory sing forth in the grand
native manner. She was introduced as Azucena at the second *Trovatore*, at which she was notably well applauded, and later, like Stignani,
sang Santuzza. Del Monaco returned, finding outlets for his lusty,
suave talents in *Trovatore, Aida, Tabarro, Tosca, Pagliacci* and
Mefistofele. He had conspicuous trouble with intonation, and needed
to learn greater subtlety, but the *brio*, style and ringing top were a
joy. One especially remembers his Canio as just about unbeatable.

Americans filled out the tenor department this year: Conley, who
sang a subtler if less powerful Cavaradossi at the second Tosca; Peerce,
who sang the first Turiddu of his career at a children's matinee of
Cavalleria; and the previously mentioned Sullivan, Fredericks and

[1] In 1951 there had been talk that Rossi-Lemeni would return to sing
Philip II in Verdi's *Don Carlo* and Scarpia in *Tosca*.

Lawrence. Tagliavini added a Rodolfo to his two Fausts in the second *Bohême*, a performance which saw Brenda Lewis move very convincingly from Giorgetta's barge to Musetta's Latin Quarter a few blocks away. Merola conducted the first *Bohême*, following a heart-warming standing ovation. President Miller made a speech before the curtain went up citing the genial director's guiding force through the thirty years. No one knew, of course, that this was the last evening Merola would enter the Opera House pit.

Although 1952 was distinctly a challenging season, the guarantor assessment managed to slip down to thirty-six per cent. The breaking of attendance records in Los Angeles obviously helped soften any financial blows. The total patronage was 72,119, this marking an increase of 7,613 over the previous year. There was a twenty per cent increase in box office intake, *Tosca* as a matter of fact capturing the box office record for opera in Los Angeles. *Bohême, Aida, Cavalleria* and *Pagliacci*, and also the attentively witnessed opening night *L'Amore*, were other favorites, with *Don Giovanni* and *Traviata* not far behind. Weakest in public interest were *Daughter of the Regiment* and Puccini's *Trittico*. The company came back from the southland with San Diego added to its list of cities. Three operas are now given there each year.

1953

It was a cold Sunday morning at Stern Grove August 30, 1953. Heavy dew dripped from the eucalyptus trees as musicians from the San Francisco Symphony shivered in their seats on the outdoor stage. It was so cold, in fact, that there was talk of moving the rehearsal for the afternoon's scheduled concert to some indoor place—Merola, who was to conduct, was not in good health. But the gaunt maestro said no. Don't fuss. We will carry on in the usual manner.

And they did. That was the afternoon Gaetano Merola died.

He conducted the first half of the "pops" program. Then, after the intermission, he was accompanying Brunetta Mazzolini, a Portland soprano, in the aria "Un bel di" from *Butterfly*. She sang the beginning of a sentence: "Io, senza dar risposta me ne starò nascosta un po' per celia, e un po' per non . . . ("I, without answering will stay hidden partly for fun, and partly so as not . . .) At this point, there is a downbeat, on the second syllable of "morire al primo incontro" ("to die at the first meeting"). Merola's baton was upheld. In a moment the downbeat would come. The singer awaited her cue. But it never came. His baton remained upheld, and a strange, dazed look came into his face. It seemed as if he might spring into the air. Suddenly he fell forward, and onto the stage floor. There was dead silence. Orchestra and audience arose, standing motionless. A doctor in the audience came on stage. But there was no commotion, everyone knew what had happened.

Merola died conducting the music of his favorite composer, leading the musicians he had known so well. It was, after all, a death that perhaps he might have chosen for himself, had he been given the opportunity. As a kind fate would have it, Merola in dying defied the old Italian superstition which decrees that a man should not die with his feet on the ground. In falling from the conductor's stand he turned around and landed with his feet up on the podium.

Though Merola's health had been poor for several years, his generalship of the company had not basically faltered, and he had, in fact, constructed for 1953 a season of strong variety and freshness. A major problem had beset him just a few days before his death: the cancellation of Del Monaco, who did not feel well enough to come for his assignments. The season had been built, if not around him at least in an adjacent semicircle. He was slated to sing in *Turandot, Manon Lescaut, Otello, Masked Ball* and *Carmen*. When word from Del Monaco's manager arrived several days before Merola's death, he wanted to make doubly sure that what the notification said was irrevocable. The manager was called, but this was unproductive. So Merola attempted to get in touch with the tenor himself. He thought he might well be able to persuade him to come. Meanwhile, all possibilities of replacement and rearrangement were considered and necessary machinery set in action. The night of August 29—the night before Merola's death—a cable was received at the Opera House by his chief aide, Kurt Adler. It was from Del Monaco. He could not come. This was the ultimate answer. Adler, knowing how much Merola was depending on a yes from Del Monaco, decided not to show him the communication until after the Stern Grove concert. So at least Merola never knew.

Otello tenors are as rare as *Turandot* sopranos, and when an international search proved fruitless Verdi's opera left the schedule. *Manon Lescaut* also had to be scratched. But the problem was being attacked quickly and skillfully—the season was due to open September 15. Orchestra rehearsals began on schedule August 31. Meanwhile, messages flowed in—from Lotte Lehmann, Lily Pons, a number of artists. The official announcement of Del Monaco's indisposition was in the papers September 2 and it was further announced that *Bohême* and

Traviata would be inserted for *Otello* and *Manon Lescaut*. What was not spelled out was the fact the chorus had already spent lots of time on *Otello* and *Manon Lescaut* and had not looked at the other operas. This was not so much a problem for the old-timers, but every year there is some turnover in the choral personnel. The announcement also informed the public that David Poleri, a young tenor who had sung with the Pacific, would appear in *Carmen*, *Traviata* and *Bohême*. Kenneth Neate, an Australian, would take over Calaf in *Turandot* and Riccardo in *Masked Ball*.

The Neate story was full of ironies. Some months earlier, en route from Sydney to Ottawa, he had stopped over in San Francisco. Since he was interested in singing with the company, an audition was arranged. Merola liked him, but had no spot for him on the roster. Later, after the unhappy Del Monaco cancellation, Neate was contacted, and engaged. But illness forced him in turn to regretfully withdraw. Roberto Turrini was the Calaf and Riccardo when *Turandot* and *Masked Ball* were performed.

There was no eulogy for Merola on opening night. This is as he would have preferred it. The company which he had created—and whose growth was largely due to him—could speak for itself. One of his major successes—*Mefistofele*—was the opening night opera. That was Merola's choice, and a good one. With Rossi-Lemeni starred, it was received with a good deal more enthusiasm than opening night audiences had been able to muster for many other operas.

There was no official talk yet of a successor: it had been announced after Merola's death that all consideration of a new director would wait till the season was over. There was a mission to accomplish, a trust to fulfill. Speculators, of course, speculated. Some figured the new man would be Kurt Herbert Adler, assistant to the general director. There was also talk of Agnini, or Cleva, or Karl Ebert, the noted producer of Glyndebourne fame.

Merola had liked importing fresh talent from Europe. He had enjoyed encouraging young Americans. Both enthusiasms were strongly reflected in the 1953 season. Six singers were introduced to this country: sopranos Inge Borkh and Gertrude Grob-Prandl, mezzos Giulietta Simionato and Margarete Klose, and tenors Cesare Valletti and Ludwig Suthaus. Also the conductor, Georg Solti. Three young Americans, Ellen Faull, Beverly Sills and Barbara Gibson had good opportunities, forming together the trio of female stars in *Don Giovanni*. Faull was to have been the Desdemona. Of the imports, only Valletti went immediately on to the Metropolitan.

Valletti's elegant style was introduced in *Werther*, revived after eighteen years, and there was not much question that he carried on the Schipa tradition very nicely. Valletti has, of course, built a fine reputation as a singer of lieder besides opera, so perhaps a better overall classification for him would be chamber singer. His soft and medium-loud singing is beautifully suave, well-rounded and delicate. His *fortissimos* may occasionally sound a little like cultured yells, but lusty tones have been something of an occupational hazard for singers of his leggiero type. Valletti's superior qualities as a musician and actor were noticed during his first San Francisco season, which also found him appearing in *The Barber of Seville*. He later demonstrated them as a member of the Cosmopolitan troupe.

Simionato's now-famous gifts were most brilliantly put forth in Rossini's opera, which she sang in the original mezzo key. The virtuosity of her cleanly executed vocal fireworks and the spirit of her presence made a marvelous impression. She also appeared in *Werther* to good if less exciting effect, and was an estimable Marina in *Boris Godounoff*. Her projected Carmen was turned over to Turner, who did well with it.

Inge Borkh was the vocal-dramatic crown of the revived *Elektra*, which returned in one of the greatest performances the company has ever given. The young soprano, large but not bulky in figure, had vocal resources to burn and vivid dramatic accents to spare. Solti's conducting was on the same high level of extreme brilliance. Klose was a striking Klytemnestra, and Paul Schoeffler, the excellent Viennese bass-baritone then singing at the Metropolitan, was the Orestes. Faull sang Chrysothemis, Suthaus Aegisthus. Borkh's final dance was designed for her by Harold Kreutzberg. Piccinato was stage director, and deserved praise for the imaginative lighting. The granitic Harry Horner set from 1938 reminded one that it was unusually forceful and simple for its time.

The second performance maintained the high level of the first, and both were cheered, the applause meter jumping as it had when Flagstad returned. A shortened version of Beethoven's ballet, *The Creatures of Prometheus* was the curtain-raiser. To the best of the company's knowledge, San Francisco was giving it its American premiere. As a matter of fact, the record showed only two major performances since the Vienna premiere in 1801. Choreography was by Willam Christensen. The production gave the San Francisco Ballet one of its biggest opportunities, and the presenting of this troupe in performances of its own during the opera season—on double bills—is happily becoming a regular practice today. Meanwhile, there was progress in the direction of leaving out ballet where it is superfluous, and in 1953 *Carmen* was given without the inserted ballet which customarily had interrupted the dramatic course of Act 4.

The other, and more elaborate, new production of 1953 was Puccini's *Turandot*, an opera which Merola had wanted to bring back often. Yet a quarter of a century was allowed to pass between performances.[2] Casting had not been easy—although one might wonder why Cigna, Martinelli and Pinza didn't have a go at it in 1937. At all events, in Borkh he certainly found a striking Principessa with the vocal wattage and the dramatic conviction to do much justice to the musical and histrionic demands of the role. Borkh's Turandot was of the intense, haughty variety. For some it was too intense, and there are other ways of doing it, but in general hers was one of the most opulently voiced and authoritative interpretations.

Turrini was a robust, ringing Calaf. Albanese and Warenskjold were the Lius, the latter singing the role the day after her father's sudden death. The Opera Guild donated the new sets by Horner, which mixed realism and imagination to good effect. Obviously a new production was indicated. As a matter of fact, a by-no-means-bare effect had been created in 1927 when decorative rugging, curtaining, banners, lanterns and high steps were the ingredients of a less architectural, interior approach to the big second scene of the second act. The first act set of the twenties was inexpensive and literal enough in appearance; it might bring a few titters today.

Rossi-Lemeni returned to conquer in *Boris*. In December, 1952, he had sung a concert version in Russian with Stokowski and the San Francisco Opera Chorus at the regular concerts of the San Francisco Symphony, but Italian was the language again this time. Tullio Serafin, the veteran, and generally superb maestro conducted—but not as convincingly as he did *Werther* and *Barber of Seville*. The cast, though, was one of the top ones assembled for *Boris* in San Francisco. Brian Sullivan was the best Dimitri yet, Janice Moudry an unusually good Innkeeper, Guilietta Simionato sang Marina, and Alvary, Baccaloni and DePaolis were in their accustomed places as Pimen, Varlaam and Shouisky respectively. Cesare Bardelli, a solid baritone who had been singing in the East, was the new Rangoni, and more of the third act was heard than ever before. Superlatives continued with the longest clinch remembered at the end of the Polish scene.

Rossi-Lemeni also sang Basilio and the Don. The production of Mozart's opera was again not wholly satisfactory.

[2] The Metropolitan shelved *Turandot* from 1930 to 1961. But New York did hear it in 1950, 1957, 1958 and 1959 at the City Center.

Turandot with Anne Roselle, 1927   *Morton*

Turandot with Leonie Rysanek, 1957   *Robert Lackenbach*

Bada, Picco and Oliviero
in *Turandot,* 1927

Blankenburg, Assandri and Curzi in *Turandot,* 1957

Carolyn Mason Jones
Kurt Herbert Adler,
General Director

Carolyn Mason Jones
Francisco Molinari-Pradelli
and Dino Yannopoulos rehearsing

The *Siegfried* Dragon, 1935   *S. F. Opera Ass'n.*

Nicola Rossi-Lemeni making up as Mefistofele, 1953   *Paul Tracy*

Nicola Rossi-Lemeni
as Boris, 1953

Courtesy William Kent III

Boris Christoff
as Boris, 1956

Robert Lackenbach

Revolutionary Scene, *Boris Godunoff,* 1945

Same scene as staged in 1956, with Raymond Manton

Dorothy McGuire and Lee Marvin in *Joan at the Stake,* 1955

Troilus and Cressida, with Kirsten, Lewis and McChesney, 1955

Cesare Curzi
as Arturo in *Lucia*

Robert Lackenbach

Giuseppe Campora
as Fenton in *Falstaff*

Robert Lackenbach

Clade Von Besser

Ferruccio Tagliavini and Tito Gobbi in *L'Elisir d' Amore*, 1948

Carolyn Mason Jones

Tito Gobbi as Jack Rance, 1960,
in *Girl of the Golden West*

Inge Borkh
as Elsa in *Lohengrin*, 1955

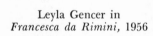

Leyla Gencer in
Francesca da Rimini, 1956

Robert Lackenbach

Leontyne Price,
Dorothy Kirsten
and Sylvia Stahlman
in *The Carmelites,* 1957

Robert Lackenbach

Leontyne Price
and Lawrence Winters
in *The Wise Maiden,* 1958

Bill Cogan

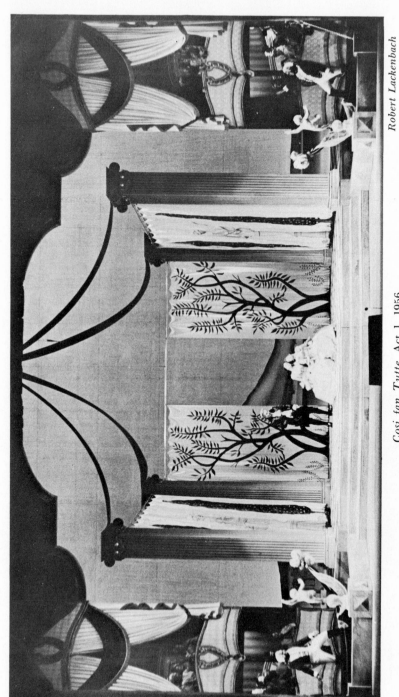

Così fan Tutte, Act 1, 1956

Robert Lackenbach

La Bohème, Act 2, new setting by George Jenkins, 1958

Bill Cogan

Carmen, Act 1,
new setting by Howard Bay, 1959, with Gloria Lane and Lorenzo Alvary

Robert Lackenbach
Ariadne auf Naxos, Manton, Blankenburg,
Alvary, Streich and Curzi

Carolyn Mason Jones
Wozzeck, with Margot Blum and Geraint Evans, 1960

Die Frau ohne Schatten, Act 2, Scene 3,
with Edith Lang and Irene Dalis, 1959

Bill Cogan

Carolyn Mason Jones

La Sonnambula, Act 2, Scene 2,
with Anna Moffo, Giorgio Tozzi, Sylvia Stahlman and Andrew Foldi, 1960

A new departure in the staging of *Traviata* was Piccinato's setting the first act on two levels, minus the clutter of dining tables of old. Champagne was served on the upper level, the guests sauntered back and forth. Poleri was an Alfredo of conviction, but there was need for more subtlety and shading in his tone production. A lively, strong-headed personality, Poleri would fight with the conductor and act rough with his leading lady, but there was more youthful impetuosity than meanness in his temperament.

Wagner was well served this year, with Solti at the helm of *Tristan* and *Walküre*, leading performances remarkable for strong climax and refined lyricism. Grob-Prandl's matronly looks and old-fashioned acting were not much help, but there was vocal power and some exquisite quiet singing in her Isolde and Brünnhilde. Borkh was a winningly warm Sieglinde, Suthaus was in his prime for Tristan and Siegmund, and Schoeffler's beautiful voice and intelligent stage manner were assets to his Kurwenal and Wotan. Klose and Ernster lent further authority to the Wagnerian wing. Grob-Prandl and Klose crossed the Italian border into *Masked Ball*, to close the regular series. It was at this performance, during the second intermission, that a small ceremony in Merola's honor took place. A plaque bearing a bas-relief portrait done by Spero Anargyros was unveiled at the west end of the south corridor of the Opera House.[3] The portrait might well have smiled, for this had been a season which included much that was exciting. It was an expensive one for the guarantors—the assessment was one hundred per cent, partly because the Los Angeles box office was down—but worth it.

Those who watched the unveiling could remember a warm, just and loyal man, a unique figure with many fine qualities of personality. He was, indisputably, a personality—but not a flamboyant one. To the stranger on the street his trim moustache, well-tailored clothes and the expansively but tastefully draped handkerchief in the breast pocket would have indicated the urbane man that he was: a continental gourmet of selective taste, an enthusiastic traveler, a good raconteur, and above all, a gentleman through and through. His manners were impeccable, and as one of his students from the early days in San Francisco remembered, he accompanied her down the street after a lesson—they were both going in the same direction—only after solicitously inquiring if she minded that he wore no hat. Merola liked his artists to act like ladies and gentlemen—most did, though some definitely did not—and the artists in turn recognized his courtly mixture

[3] And subsequently moved to a fittingly more conspicuous place in the main part of the foyer.

of fairness, firmness and friendliness. One singer said, in fact, "He's such a gentleman I feel I don't need a contract."

Those who played, sang and worked for him in other capacities knew the traits which were perhaps his most distinctive: his great diplomacy and his great calm. His board, of course, realized he had a very good business sense, and this is a very important trait in an opera director.[4] Merola's acute feeling of how to handle his artists kept the backstage atmosphere warmer and more easy-going than that in some opera houses. There are those who might say his disinclination to take sides smacked of evasiveness, but he knew as well as any director ever did how to get what he needed artistically from his charges without letting them know he might be strongly displeased with them at heart. He knew the power of time as a great settler, and when his secretary worried how a duel of two artists for the same role would turn out, Merola simply said, "Don't worry. Just let the pot boil." He could be very understanding, and when one of his most reliable violinists reached a Los Angeles performance late, he didn't bawl out the musician—he drawled, in a benign manner, "You sleepa too much?" He knew it wouldn't happen again.

Tantrum was a word Merola did not seem to know, and though he could be angry, his impatience rarely if ever turned to rage. Actually, some of his most characteristic actions were silent ones: he had a way of walking out from the wings slowly at a rehearsal, taking out his watch, putting it away and walking off, without a word. No one needed to be told overtime was creeping up. He sometimes added the visual prop of an overcoat to complete the director's pantomime. If the orchestra was offending, he might walk over to the pit and peer down into it with an unhappy expression, but he wouldn't audibly exhort the musicians if another conductor was on the podium. His manner of speaking itself was musical and Neapolitan; it could have been marked *andante legato piano*. An expressive face and hands, and mastery of the shoulder shrug, amplified his speech eloquently.

Perhaps no better picture of Merola's warmth—and practicality— can be offered than that revealed in a little speech he addressed one afternoon to the audience at a children's matinee. "Good afternoon, young people," he said, "This is a beautiful Opera House. It's here for your enjoyment. We are going to play nice music for you. . . . Please don't put gum under the seats."

Merola played a lot of nice music for a lot of people, young and old. He was not the best conductor in the world, but a sensitive musi-

---

[4] When conducting he would tell the double basses, "I want to hear you bassi. I'm paying for you, you know." He was fond of the instrument.

cian and by all means a great interpreter of the music of Puccini. As a director, he was on occasion more conservative and less imaginative than he might have been, but there was much in the way of his production planning which was exciting and memorable. Had the war and ill health not plagued him and the company, his record of achievement might have been greater. It is very likely that without him San Francisco would have long remained only a host to touring troupes, certainly until the Opera House finally was built. And at that time the depression would not have looked in friendly manner on a new venture. It is to Merola's lasting credit that his company never skipped a season, and never frantically asked for funds.

13 🌿

THE NEW DIRECTOR

1954

Kurt Herbert Adler, Assistant to the General Director, became Artistic Director in November, 1953. As such, he was the chief architect of the 1954 season. This was his season to show what he could do—no General Director had been named to succeed Merola—and the forty-nine-year-old Viennese provided enough freshness in approach to make a very convincing case for his abilities. He was, in effect, launching a new era, one in which staging had greater importance than ever as a basic rather than underlying factor in performance, and one in which productions of contemporary operas became a more or less regular event.

To introduce Adler more specifically, he had studied at the University of Vienna and the Vienna State Academy of Music, served as a coach, accompanist and conductor for Max Reinhardt in that city, and—in the mid-thirties—conducted at the Volksoper. He was an assistant to Toscanini at the 1936 Salzburg Festival, came to the United States in 1938 and served with the Chicago Opera, and in 1943 began his highly efficient work with the San Francisco Opera Chorus. In Merola's last years he was his first lieutenant in the command post, and in that capacity he had become highly familiar with the problems of constructing an opera season. Mixing this experience with ideas definitely his own—plus some unrealized Merola plans —he came up with one of the top seasons in the annals of the opera house.

It began, however, not precisely on a sour note but on a high one which had more altitude than artistry to commend it. Mado Robin, the late French coloratura, made her American debut in *Rigoletto* opening night, September 17. It was well-known backstage that a high B above high C was a specialty of hers, and Cleva, the evening's conductor, was against her using it. But came the end of "Caro nome" September 17 and, without warning, a loud, pointed alarm was sounded. B-stung Cleva restrained himself from walking out of the pit then and there as the audience gasped, but he refused to conduct the repeat. Presumably Karl Kritz, the substitute maestro, felt less strongly on the matter, but as things turned out Robin arrived at the crucial point during the second performance and didn't offend. Opening night, though, was also the night Leonard Warren returned to the company and Richard Tucker joined it. The baritone's portrayal of the jester needs no further comment from this source; the tenor's fresh, facile vocalism was very welcome. The season then progressed to its various pièces de résistance.

There was the company's first performance of Wagner's *The Flying Dutchman*, a Merola pet project and not played in San Francisco since the German Grand Opera Company visited the Civic Auditorium in 1931; the American premiere of Cherubini's 1798 opera buffa, *The Portuguese Inn;* and the first fully staged presentation in the United States of Honegger's *Joan of Arc at the Stake*. There were also *Turandot, Salome, Fidelio, Marriage of Figaro* and *Tabarro*, not to mention more standard items. The *Salome* followed the Cherubini, the *Tabarro* preceded the Honegger.

Perhaps the major coup of all was Adler's procuring of the services of Pierre Monteux in the pit. As the seventy-nine-year-old conductor emeritus of the San Francisco Symphony told the press, he had not felt that the conductor of the Symphony should also conduct the Opera, but now that he had retired from his old post (in 1952), he was ready to join the Opera.[1] His assignments were *Manon*—Monteux is one of the very few who can make this elegant candybox music exciting—*Fidelio* and *Joan*. *Manon*, of course, he had conducted innumerable times. *Fidelio* he had led on only three occasions, but the Monteux Beethoven needed no apology. The score of *Joan* he learned for the San Francisco production.

Adler entrusted the stage direction this year to three men: Piccinato, Horner and Paul Hager, the latter a twenty-eight-year-old who had assisted Wieland Wagner at Bayreuth, worked at the Munich Opera and was a leading stage director of the Nürnberg Opera. Hager has become a regular of the staging department, joined more recently by Dino Yannopoulos. He has had a lot of good ideas, and some not so good, but there has been an underlying inventiveness about this work which keeps it above the routine.

The new spirit of staging which henceforth would be a central

[1] In his days with the Symphony it was his habit not to arrive in San Francisco until shortly before the orchestra's season.

ingredient in the company's production style was implied in Horner's remark at a press conference that "operas in San Francisco and at the Met are still being staged in the style of the 1890's. This is a style in which scenery and direction is based on providing a background for whatever opera star is in the foreground."[2] The state of affairs wasn't quite as antiquated as the statement might have indicated. The Met was taking a new lease on visual life in the Bing regime, by that time four years old, and Agnini, though of the old school, had succumbed a little to the more contemporary spirit in San Francisco. But a major overhaul of scenic ideas was necessary, and it was begun in earnest at this time. Agnini was not in the best of health and had gone on to the New Orleans Opera with its less concentrated schedule. A great deal can properly be said for his pioneering work in facilitating the production of opera in San Francisco. He was a very hard worker, and although Graf, William Wymetal and Yannopoulos came in various seasons during the middle years of the company he always liked to carry a big load. He was inventive and efficient within the context of traditionalism. Frankly, though, the new regime could not fit him in as a central figure.

The Flying Dutchman came to the Opera House stage on October 5 with Hans Hotter in the title role. The new production gave a prominent place to a projection system devised by the Viennese electrical engineer Paul Planer. Whereas the *Don Giovanni* projections came from behind the stage, Planer's machines were set up high on the bridge behind the asbestos curtain. The slides in this production were exact copies of Horner's designs transferred to glass. The system permits stationary and moving effects, so the Dutchman's ship could be seen sweeping up to the shore. The "wide screen" views were altogether more vivid than those of the earlier experiment.

Wagner's not too well-known opera was surprisingly well received. Hotter's dark, haunting vocalism sounding forth from a towering frame was absolutely first class, and Inge Borkh's Senta had vocal charms. But it took her until the second performance to rid her portrayal of agitational-gyrational acting effects more appropriate to Elektra. Alvary's Daland and Curzi's Steersman were likeable, and Brian Sullivan added Eric to his San Francisco accomplishments. The well-schooled but somewhat ponderous conductor was Eugen Szenkar of the Düsseldorf Opera, in his first United States opera engagement.

[2] One is reminded here of a soprano who sang with the San Francisco Opera in the twenties. The local singer who was playing her lady-in-waiting asked, "Madame X, what would you like me to do in this scene?" Madame X replied: "I don't care, as long as you stay at the rear of the stage." Agnini was furious.

The Portuguese Inn came into the repertoire on the hearty recommendation of Lorenzo Alvary, who had sung in it in Europe. Composed in 1798, the score had been left in somewhat fragmentary form, but was revised by Giulio Confalonieri, the Italian composer and critic. It turned out to be a rather Mozartean buffo charmer, by no means great but more than serviceable, capped with a polonaise as finale. The farcical story, about a young woman who flees the amorous attentions of her guardian, has points of similarity with Rossini's *Barber*. It was set by Horner and staged by Piccinato in the *commedia dell' arte* manner, with some of the tallest hats, grandest gowns, and most extravagant wigs, plumes and noses ever seen on the Opera House stage. The cast included—besides Alvary and Curzi, the rising local tenor—a beautiful young Italian soprano named Rosanna Carteri. This warm-voiced singer had made her American debut at the first matinee of the season as Mimi, and by the evening she appeared in the Cherubini the word had gotten around that she was one of the best lyrics in company history.

Honegger's dramatic oratorio of 1938 is sometimes performed in a concert version and sometimes as an "opera." There is an urge on the concert platform for the Joan to act out her role as much as possible. And, conversely, there is a need in staging *Joan* for a certain amount of stylization. Horner staged it with the chorus handled in Greek chorus fashion and moods of the drama heightened by scenic projections of the Planer variety. The ballet had a prominent part in the action. Dorothy McGuire of the movies, replacing Greer Garson, was a touching Joan, and the production had conviction under Monteux' baton.

There was a standing ovation for Monteux when he entered the pit for his first opera of the season, *Manon*. It was performed, according to his wish, with the rarely given Cours la Reine Scene. This addition served two purposes. It gave the story better continuity, and provided the ballet with a good opportunity—not an interpolated one. Monteux had two good Manons in Kirsten and Carteri, and a good Des Grieux in Giacinto Prandelli. But as usual the French diction left something to be desired. Though in this and the following season there were three French operas, there were some casting problems, and doubtless the lack of a force of top-flight native French singers has been a factor in the near-elimination of the French repertoire under Adler's regime since that time. The Austro-German taste in opera production runs north and south of the Alps, but not west of them. *Carmen* is played quite a good deal in Germany and Austria, and *Tales of Hoffmann* has its chance, but to say that the Gounod-Saint-Saens-

Massenet sugar factory is run at full operating force in Vienna, Berlin —or San Francisco—is certainly not true.

A new dramatic soprano in 1954 was big-voiced, Yugoslavian-born Carla Martinis, with experience at New York's City Center. She made a somewhat uneven impression as Leonora in *Forza*, and her Turandot was not one of the best. This role she shared with Borkh, who added Salome to her Straussian conquests this year. Another name worth mentioning is that of Franca Duval, who sang one of the better Musettas.

An innovation this year—not repeated since—was an extra performance in the Opera House titled *Gala Night at the Opera*. Scenes and acts from operas were presented. Altogether there were twenty-six San Francisco performances of thirteen bills in 1954—an average number during the early fifties. The season was one day longer than the thirty-four days customary since 1946, the activities beginning on a Friday and ending on a Thursday instead of beginning on a Tuesday and concluding on a Sunday.

Between the 1953 and 1954 seasons a vital, independent arm of the San Francisco Opera Association commenced its work. This was the Merola Memorial Fund. It was christened by a benefit performance of Verdi's *Requiem* conducted by Cleva on April 2. Proceeds went to the Fund, which set up, in conjunction with the Association, the San Francisco Opera Debut Auditions. This has proved a great advantage to young singers from the western states. When the first five years of the Adler-inspired auditions were recapitulated, it was found that twenty-seven participants had made debuts with the San Francisco Opera, sixteen had been re-engaged for more than two seasons, and a dozen had gone on to Europe to continue their careers in various opera houses. A summer training program for young singers sponsored by the Fund was initiated in 1957, and a number of audition participants have taken advantage of the coaching which the program offers in various phases of opera performance.

1955

On September 8, 1955, a week before the season would open, it was announced that the company was seeking financial support through a public campaign as a supplement to the guarantor system. The appeal for $100,000 was not being made in sudden desperation, President Miller said, but in the cool light of cold facts: even after a full guarantor assessment, the 1954 deficit was only lowered from $157,420 to $89,635, and a small surplus built up over the years had had to be tapped. In order to stem the tide of rising costs, and at the same time maintain and, indeed, extend the range of artistic accomplishment of the company, a fairly agonizing financial reappraisal was necessary. There would be similar drives every year, Miller said, but he reminded guarantors that contributions could be deducted from their normal assessment. As far as box-seat holders were concerned, their guarantor pledge went up from $50 to $100 a seat, whereas that for guarantors in the orchestra and Grand Tier remained at $50 per chair.

Assessments in general were maximum during the second half of the 1950's, but this was an era which saw the company developing its repertoire to the point where it could be termed a truly important international theater. Sir William Walton's *Troilus and Cressida* received its American premiere in 1955, Francis Poulenc's *Dialogues of the Carmelites* was given for the first time in the United States in 1957, and Richard Strauss' *Die Frau Ohne Schatten* reached the American stage in 1959—all at the San Francisco Opera. Carl Orff's *Die Kluge* had its American premiere in San Francisco in 1958 on a double bill with that composer's *Carmina Burana*, which received its first fully staged American performances that season. Alban Berg's *Wozzeck* joined the repertoire in 1960 in its West Coast premiere: it might have come sooner, but the board was dubious prior to the Met's huge success with it.

Meanwhile, Verdi's *Macbeth* joined the repertoire in 1955, Mozart's *Cosi fan Tutte* and Zandonai's *Francesca da Rimini* in 1956, Strauss' *Ariadne auf Naxos* in 1957, Cherubini's *Medea* and Verdi's *Don Carlo* in 1958, and Gluck's *Orfeo* in 1959. No season has been allowed to pass without two or more operas new to the company. Doing new things obviously takes time and money, but any financial burdens have paid off in prestige, freshness and enjoyment. To report these additions is not to take away from the vital groundwork laid and continued by Merola himself. Younger, healthier, and fortunate in working for a president more responsive than some to new ideas, Adler did in the late fifties what his predecessor might have done in the late forties.

Troilus, which had been introduced to the world at Covent Garden the previous December, came to the War Memorial stage October 7.[3] The composer was in attendance. Here was a new opera which can really be called grand. Its music is full-bloodedly neo-romantic, heroic,

[3] The New York City Opera performed it soon thereafter. San Francisco had the first performance rights.

amorous and sumptuous, and its text grandly rhetorical and poetic. Not all of the score is good, but a fair amount of it, notably the love music of Troilus and Cressida, is not only apt but worth remembering. The arching lyrical line, complete with rather ornate ecstatic florid- ities, works notably well in capturing the atmosphere of their desires, joys and frustrations.

Christopher Hassall's libretto, it should be noted, is termed "an orig- inal dramatic variation of the theme Chaucer borrowed from Boc- caccio" and is not based directly on either Shakespeare's or Chaucer's words.

Richard Lewis, the English tenor who created the role of Troilus, was brought over for the San Francisco production and began what has become a continuous association with the company. Kirsten was Cressida, Weede Diomede and Giorgio Tozzi Calkas. Ernest McChes- ney of the New York City Opera was Pandarus, a role originally planned for Kullman, who has been rounding off his career as a character tenor. The cast, singing under Leinsdorf's strong direction, did full justice to Walton, with McChesney perhaps deserving a special vote of praise for his nimble, appropriate portrayal of a fussy fop. The airy settings did not burden the viewers with heavy literalness and enhanced the lyrical aspects of the story. The opera was received with considerable enthusiasm, and a number of persons have requested its revival.

Verdi's *Macbeth*, which entered the repertoire this year, proved one of the most interesting novelties in the history of the company. Now that the Metropolitan has taken it up and broadcast and re- corded it, *Macbeth* is hardly news to American audiences, but one can still marvel at the score, which, for all its earthy, elementally exu- berant—and not displeasing—early Verdiism, has pages and pages of strong imagination and some pointed ironic touches. Some of the most effective music was already in the score of the original version dating from 1847.

Obviously a realistic approach would have underlined the corniness of some of the music, and the designer (Berlin-born Leo Kerz) went off in the other direction to fine effect. The setting was bare and awe- some, nicely suggestive of a fairly dank, barren old castle, with a long curving staircase a recurrent ingredient. Changes of scene were ac- complished in large part by projections. To heighten the sense of bare, chilling spaciousness, the stage opening was literally higher and broader than usual, and the projections seemed to be reaching for the top of the house.[4]

---

[4] Thanks to the Opera Guild, the company had now acquired three pro- jectors of its own.

Weede and Borkh combined the vocal strength and histrionic punch for bringing the Macbeths to life. Indeed, Borkh was a little too explosive dramatically at the first performance, but it is to her credit that the mixture of weight and floridity in the role by no means undid her. Tozzi, an American with Italian experience, and one Metropolitan season behind him, made an excellent impression as Banquo, and Cleva conducted strongly. As a matter of fact, everything Tozzi did during his first San Francisco season—Ramfis was another important assignment—was very successful. Here was a lyric bass of the highest class. He did not return during the following two years, except in one pre-season concert, but he has since become an indispensable member of the roster.

A revival of *Louise* with Kirsten and Sullivan was coolly received, as if Charpentier's love letter to Paris was sealed with too much sentiment. The two performances were led with the appropriate subdued ecstacy by Jean Morel, but this didn't fill seats. Morel's *Carmen* conducting was disappointingly ultra-refined, bloodless and clipped. Nor did Bizet's opera get a fair account on stage. Worst of all was Lewis' tiptoeing vocalism as Don José. One could be thankful for a tastefully quiet conclusion to the Flower Song, but too often the lack of full weight of tone color was extremely tantalizing. Luckily, this demonstration—at Lewis' first appearance in San Francisco—was not typical, and almost everything he has done since has reminded us what a fine artist he is. His voice, basically a lyric instrument with some dramatic tenor possibilities, has a distinctive quality, and he moves around the stage persuasively. The Carmen herself, Nell Rankin, was straight-laced (amorous byplay from the male chorus usually sought by Carmens was rejected) and the toreador was not particularly convincing from the dramatic point of view. But his voice had the ring of great promise. His name: Cornell MacNeil. Another opportunity for him was a Valentin in a Carteri-Siepi *Faust*.

The *Lohengrin* revival, after nine years, had no swan and an Italian conductor. Also a new and modern setting, with projections, paid for by the Guild. A vertical shaft of light signified the swan's presence, and reminded one, incidentally, of Kerz' special interest in "painting with light" instead of on scenery. Brian Sullivan's lyrical performance in the title role was one of the best things he did in San Francisco, and MacNeil was a striking Herald with stentorian power to spare. Borkh was Elsa, her husband, Alexander Welitsch, Telramund. Nell Rankin sang Ortrud, Otto Edelmann King Henry. Edelmann was engaged principally for his well-regarded impersonation of Baron Ochs in *Rosenkavalier*, and his buffo-cantante singing, authoritative jollity and perfect dialect German certainly added up to a fine one.

The Marschallin was sung by Elisabeth Schwarzkopf, who made her American operatic debut on the Opera House stage September 20. In an interview the thirty-nine-year-old soprano noted that she did not sing so much in opera any more, and indeed, she had something resembling a phobia about the supposed pressures of opera engagements in the United States. But Adler had met her after a concert in Los Angeles and persuaded her to come. His persuasion was San Francisco's distinct gain. Her highly inflected and near-youthful interpretation of the Marschallin was, if not agreeable to all, on a very high plane of distinction, and without a doubt better projected from the purely vocal point of view than the final Marschallins of the later Lehmann nine years earlier. With Frances Bible an excellent Octavian, Dorothy Warenskjold a charming Sophie, and Leinsdorf in the pit, this was a *Rosenkavalier* which set a standard for seasons to come.

Schwarzkopf also sang Donna Elvira in a Leinsdorf-conducted *Don Giovanni* which concluded without the jocose final ensemble. There was a new series of projections designed by Kerz, but the slides were too bright, the lighting in front of the three arches from 1952 too dark. Albanese switched from Zerlina to Donna Anna, and if the fioriture were not always impeccable, there were some expressive values to her assumption of this role. This was one of the more controversial assignments of the season, and opinions ranged from extremely favorable to a good deal less than that. Cesare Siepi was the Don.

If *Don Giovanni* lacked only its finale, *Coq d'Or*, which was revived after thirteen years, was stitched together with a number of its parts missing, the abridgement having been dreamed up so *Coq* could be paired with *Pagliacci*. The production, using the vintage Remisoff settings, was a combination of the operatic and ballet versions. If it had little continuity to recommend it, and much less clear English diction than the *Troilus*, there were good elements in the cast: Alvary, whose English was better than some of the others', danced nimbly besides singing as King Dodon, and Raymond Manton, a local lyric tenor with a distinctive, pleasant tone quality and a well-developed top, was a virtuoso, bizarre Astrologer. Mattiwilda Dobbs, the first Negro to join the roster, was a good if not remarkable Queen.

Renata Tebaldi returned after a five-year absence—she had recently joined the Metropolitan—and conquered as Aida, Madeleine and Tosca. The partnership of Tebaldi, Tucker and Warren in *Andrea Chenier* was close to explosive in its excitement: this year's version of the Giordano opera will not be forgotten for a long time. She was less fortunate in her *Aida* tenor, on opening night and in two subsequent performances. Turrini had his merits as a *robusto*, but whether or not his somewhat inflexible style was really gala opening night material was answered in the negative on this occasion.

Tosca had a single performance as a non-subscription event October 19. The first act ended with an under par performance by the chorus of the "Te Deum," and Curiel, the evening's conductor, showed his anger and disappointment during the intermission backstage. But then something happened which stamped the performance as memorable. In excellent voice, and with superb control, Tebaldi put across a "Vissi d'arte" which seemed to hypnotize the audience, and when they recovered from its spell, they broke into wild applause. After several minutes Curiel had to make a decision regarding an encore. Adler was not in his box. So Curiel decided—in favor of one. Weede, the Scarpia, politely turned his back to the audience as Tebaldi began the aria again. And the second time around her performance was more emotional. As usual, there were scoldings in the press, and talk of a claque and ruined continuity. Yes, there is an encore rule, and for good reason, but every few years the bonds have to be broken, and to say that many in the audience were worried about the continuity would be pedantic in the extreme.[5]

Aida was performed this year in "revised" settings with projections by Kerz. The vast figure of the Sphinx projected in the Temple Scene was a notable artistic addition. The Triumphal Scene was less gaudy and gala than usual, and more modern and stylized. The effect was neat and imposing, but there is a good deal to be said for old-fashioned pomp in this context.

The Los Angeles season added *Butterfly* to the repertoire, with an interesting cast which included Richard Lewis as Pinkerton, along with Kirsten as Cio-Cio-San and MacNeil as Sharpless. Curiel conducted. In nearby Pasadena a "gala evening" of operatic scenes included, among other things, Act Two of *Rigoletto* with Dobbs, Peerce and MacNeil, and Act Two of *Traviata*, with Albanese, Fredericks and Weede. The visit to the southland was financially triumphant this year, with the fourteen Los Angeles performances taking in $316,-000 as opposed to the $228,000 which the thirteen shows had brought the previous season. At home, too, attendance was up: to an average capacity of 92.6 per cent. But, as Miller announced, the company was still badly in need of working capital and in spite of a healthy reception to the first fund drive and generous Opera Guild support, the

[5] Speaking of claques, there have been none, the management insists, in recent years. A claque leader who came from the East was politely but firmly told not to operate.

assessment would be one hundred per cent. A second drive was launched—contributions deductible as usual from the guarantor fee.

Following the 1954 and 1955 seasons it was obvious that Adler was carrying the ball without any serious directorial fumbles. Indeed, he was bringing a freshness and excitement to the repertoire and staging which, if not always to everyone's taste, was highly commendable. So, in 1956 his title was lengthened to Artistic and Musical Director, and in 1957 he became General Director, that being the title Merola had held for so many years.

1956

If a production can be said to be lovable, the San Francisco Opera's *Cosi fan Tutte* is that. It was unveiled in 1956 in George Jenkins' admirably light and tasteful rococo-modern settings, and immediately found a place in the hearts of the patrons. The musical genius of Mozart was brilliantly served by a well-knit cast—Schwarzkopf, Rankin, Patrice Munsel, Lewis, Frank Guarrera and Alvary, with Hans Schwieger conducting—and Hager let the rousing humor of the piece come through with a mixture of laughs and style. If every detail of execution wasn't perfect the first time around, this was a production that, in total spirit, really clicked. (As Mozart productions, it must be said, had not often done in San Francisco.) The transparent symmetry of the action, with its pairs of characters, helps, of course, to clarify the comedy for performance in a big house, and with its fabulous score *Cosi* was a natural candidate for success—should the performers be up to and beyond requirements. The victory was positive: ticket demand was so great a third performance was added to the scheduled two.

There was no contemporary opera this year, but there were controversial new stagings of *Walküre* and *Boris,* the first *Boccanegra* in fifteen years and the first *Falstaff* in eight. Not to mention the American debuts of sopranos Leonie Rysanek, Birgit Nilsson and Leyla Gencer, mezzo Oralia Dominguez, baritone Anselmo Colzani, bass Boris Christoff and conductor Oliviero DeFabritiis. Furthermore, Eileen Farrell sang for the first time with a "major" operatic organization and an expatriate American tenor named Richard Martell was given special opportunities to shine. The La Scala baritone Rolando Panerai and the Yugoslavian conductor Lovro Von Matacic were also announced, but didn't make it. Nor did Cleva.

Reappearance of *The Flying Dutchman* served to introduce Munich and Vienna's Rysanek in one of the best of her many good roles. She subtly conquered her audience with the first haunting *pianissimo* and has sustained, with only minor blemishes, a superb reputation in San Francisco ever since. She revealed a big lyric-dramatic soprano rather in the Rethberg-Lehmann tradition if not precisely similar in sound, and also an intelligence, taste and clarity of musicianship which is hardly an every-night commodity on the operatic stage. Following the *Dutchman*, which was excellently conducted by Steinberg, she sang Aida and Sieglinde, the latter in a Kerz-designed production of *Walküre* with Nilsson as Brünnhilde and Hotter as Wotan. Needless to say, it was full of vocal splendors, but at the same time it offered some visual curiosities. Modern man need not worry much over Wotan's having given up his eyepatch, but did Brünnhilde have to wear that dowdy short-skirted institutional dress? And did the rocks of the third act have to be reached by pink onyx steps? The Valkyries had ponytail haircuts which were not unattractive, and Hunding's hut, if it did have touches of the contemporary suburban tract home, had its decorative points. The post-performance prescription, however, was this: get away from the old-fashioned trappings, fine, but make a few amendments next time.

If the sets and costumes of *Walküre* caused a fair amount of near-violent discussion, Nilsson's vocalism resulted in no alarm—only admiration for her exceptionally bright, clear, steely voice, hardly as rich as Flagstad's but with something approaching that crisp northern tonal beauty remembered from earlier days. The complete orchestration was used, and Schwieger's conducting had poetic insight.

The Kerz-set *Boris*, which was sung by Christoff and associates in Russian, was even more problematical. Actually there were some strokes of great artistic beauty—surely the simple Revolutionary Scene with its stark downward daggers and projections had visual merits beyond the fairy-tale literalism of the older version—but removing all the pomp and glitter from the Coronation Scene coldly negated the point of the matter. It had been thought that the music and costumes would provide enough of the requisite peasant color, and that the stern daggers, lowered to different levels in various scenes, would have strong symbolic value. But all the open space worked against the best acoustic interests of the chorus, and when Christoff insisted on certain trappings they collided with the aesthetic of the mise-en-scène.

As far as Christoff's interests were concerned, the company had specifically inquired of the Hurok Office whether the bass would be offended by a modern staging. The answer was in the negative, but it was also incorrect. When the Bulgarian bass arrived he didn't like the production at all. Furthermore, he had an argument with Steinberg, who replaced Von Matacic as conductor, and left a rehearsal to go off and sulk in his dressing room. Swallowing his dissatisfactions somewhat, he came onstage when due and performed according to announcement. The relatively lyric, formal approach was a distinct change from the frenetic Rossi-Lemeni manner with its near-Sprechstimme: both interpretations, of course, have much to offer. The cast had not completely jelled, but taken part by part it had strong merits. Lewis was a vivid Dimitri, Curzi an unusually young-looking Shouisky, Hotter a powerful Rangoni, and Alvary a Varlaam who didn't overdo the clowning.

The *Francesca da Rimini* project stemmed from the fact that Tebaldi was learning the role for the Maggio Musicale in Florence, but when that festival dropped the work, she was less interested. It was more feasible for San Francisco to go ahead with a substitute soprano rather than a substitute opera—the production was already built when Tebaldi made her negative decision—so Leyla Gencer, a Turkish soprano with Naples Opera experience, was imported. She turned out to be an exceptionally interesting if uneven artist. Her physical beauty was marked, her poise sure, her *pianissimo* exquisite and her voice in general, when well-projected, remarkably warm in tone. She did not quite do for this opera what a magnetic Tebaldi might have done, but this was beside the point: *Francesca*, which dates from 1914 and has not been performed at the Metropolitan since 1918, was not really worth doing. It has some sweeping love music of a Richard Straussian sort, and its unfolding at the end of the first act, with the solo viola and lute providing a nice medieval color, is felicitous. But much of the score—related to Puccini, Giordano, Montemezzi, Wagner and Debussy—is simply derivative and not very interesting. Zandonai's opera, which might, incidentally, be called *L'Amore dei Tre Fratelli*, is akin to Montemezzi's *L'Amore dei Tre Re* in that both are romantic-medieval tales set to music at a time when verismo was at its height in the Italian lyric theater.[6] But the Montemezzi is tauter and has held up this special tradition more strongly. Colzani and Curzi as the two disagreeable brothers offered vivid portrayals—the uninhibited Colzani almost chewing the scenery in the fiery finale.

Tebaldi's roles this year were Tosca, which she sang beautifully—and sans encore—and Amelia in *Boccanegra*, a part she learned for San Francisco. She sang much of it well, but there was a disconcerting

[6] Neither is without some of the shock tactics of verismo within its regal setting.

lack of volume control: the tone could get hard and explosive. Martell, an American from Paris, was the Cavaradossi of the first *Tosca*. His compact voice was not quite of ideal size for the house, but his refined, sure, dulcet vocalism had a first-rate thrill to it, and his handsome appearance and solid acting ability helped form a total impersonation of real distinction. He deserved re-engagement. Bjoerling, absent for five years, was the second Cavaradossi. Warren and Colzani, two of the best available Scarpias anywhere, shared that role.

Eileen Farrell was introduced as Leonora in *Trovatore*, and barring some shrill tones she sang the part with great richness. She acted hardly at all, but her stage experience then was limited: her impressive career had been restricted largely to radio and concert. The Mexican Dominguez (with La Scala performances to her credit) was a relatively refined but excellent Azucena. Bjoerling and Colzani helped make this 1956 *Trovatore* an afternoon's entertainment to remember.

Dominguez was also a young-looking Quickly in *Falstaff*, the beautifully revived Steinberg special. Warren took over the title role, singing it sonorously if missing some of the points of joviality, and Schwarzkopf lent her top talents to Mistress Ford. Audrey Schuh, a young soprano who had sung in New Orleans, was a good Nanetta, and the Fenton was Giuseppe Campora of the Metropolitan, who displayed an extremely attractive voice and an occasional coarseness of style. He was also heard in a fairly dismal step-child revival of *The Elixir of Love*. Munsel was Adina and Italo Tajo Dr. Dulcamara. The latter was in particularly bad voice, and conductor Curiel had trouble holding the ensemble together. Some of the magic of 1948 was needed. Panerai's replacement—as Belcore and as Lescaut in the *Manon Lescaut* which opened the season—was Louis Quilico, a Canadian with New York City Center experience. He showed off a beautiful dark baritone, and a far from magnetic stage manner.

Most of the Italian repertory was conducted this year by Oliviero DeFabritiis, the well-known Rome Opera maestro. His work could be summed up by four words: poetic but not punchy. His emphasis on lyricism rather than vigor indicated that he was a sensitive leader of fine ability, but not the man to preside over the Italian wing regularly. With Metropolitan openings moving up into late October, Cleva was no longer available, and a strong substitute was needed.

The Los Angeles season was more profitable than ever—eight of the fifteen performances in the 6,500 seat Shrine Auditorium being sold out. Average attendance approached 6,000! The southern proceedings began with a praiseworthy *Manon Lescaut* which had better pace and fewer kinks than the one which opened the home season.

The dressy and opulent audience which crossed the red carpet into the prosaic, unfashionably located Shrine knew they were hearing a good show. Kirsten and Bjoerling were joined on this occasion by Guarrera, a new Lescaut, and there was plenty of applause for all. But the enthusiasm meter oscillated with special *brio* at the end of Act 1 of *La Bohême* with Albanese and Peerce. The applause welled up from the acres of main floor seats and the wide, colossal balcony. As happens in the Shrine, the first sound of hands coming together was so widespread and great the audience became additionally excited and applauded with renewed vigor, as if no one in the hall wanted to keep his hands still.

In Los Angeles the productions sometimes suffer from the toy look of a normal-sized stage picture set inside an overly large proscenium, but the advantage of prior performances in San Francisco often results in smoother sound. Tebaldi, for instance, caught the stride of Amelia in a *Boccanegra* which was more flexibly sung than those San Franciscans heard. Turrini, ending an inexplicably long attachment with the company, repeated his San Francisco Adorno and added Cavaradossi in Los Angeles.

Continuing an arrangement begun in 1955, the two popular series in San Francisco remained on Thursday and Saturday nights, but the incidence of four extra Sunday matinee performances reminded one of the previous plan, in which one of the popular series always took place on Sunday afternoons (1949–54).

1957

Contemporary opera returned this season with the American premiere of Francis Poulenc's subtle and finespun *Dialogues of the Carmelites*. The date: September 20, eight months following the original premiere at La Scala. Erich Leinsdorf conducted the triadic-beatific score with great sensitivity, and the cast was a strong one which sang clear English. Harry Horner's sets, which sat on a revolving stage, had a fitting austerity and could be swung into place without unduly long waits between scenes.[7]

[7] No wait was more than a minute. The curtain was not lowered during the changes, and the pit lights, which tend to spill over onto the stage, were turned out for the scene shifts from a dimmer by the conductor's stand. When Leinsdorf was sure the orchestra could play the last few bars of a scene from memory, he pushed the button.

As for the sets themselves, Rudolf Bing has expressed interest in using them sometime.

Introduced to San Francisco as Mme. Lidoine, the new Prioress, was a young Negro soprano with *Porgy and Bess* and NBC Television Opera experience. Her name: Leontyne Price. She sang her difficult and ascetic role with rare charm and beauty but there was no clear indication that this girl would turn into one of the greatest Aidas of our time. In San Francisco her opportunities were to grow, as indeed her voice itself evolved into a big dramatic instrument. Another debutante was Sylvia Stahlman,[8] a pure lyric soprano who provided just the right sort of freshness of light-textured tone for the part of Sister Constance. Dorothy Kirsten was in the central role, Blanche de la Force.

She and her colleagues movingly projected the story of a band of nuns who, during the French Revolution, are sentenced to the guillotine. Set against their collective story is that of the timid, confused and complicated Blanche, who joins the Carmelite Order as a refuge from her fear of life, and finally wins over her fear of death by going, in her moment of truth, to the guillotine happily.

Poulenc's score is dedicated to Debussy, Monteverdi, Moussorgsky and Verdi, and there is no question that Debussy and Moussorgsky were influences. In spirit the music is descended, actually, from a long line of French composers including Couperin, Berlioz and Fauré. It is not derivative, but simply a logical and unhurrying follow-up to an old tradition of tastefully sweet musico-religious expression.

The Carmelites was received with enthusiasm—Claramae Turner, the First Prioress, had a big success with her death scene, and Price won prolonged applause for her beautifully spun-out lyric passage in the Prison Scene. There was enough interest to schedule three performances in San Francisco altogether: the last one a special attraction presented in connection with an "International Industrial Development Conference" under *Time-Life* auspices. In the last analysis, *The Carmelites* provided a theatrical experience so freshly moving and penetrating that some of the conventional, less musico-dramatic operas which followed seemed rather more melodramatic and deficient in thought than usual.

The elusive Maria Callas had been signed for the 1957 season in January, and when September arrived the public was anticipating with interest her scheduled appearances in Verdi's *Macbeth* and Donizetti's *Lucia*. But in the papers of September 13—opening night of the season was the seventeenth—San Franciscans read that Adler was checking into rumors Callas planned to cancel her engagement with

[8] Hailing from Tennessee, Stahlman had sung with the Brussels Opera under the name of Giulia Bardi.

the company. She had withdrawn from performances with La Scala at the Edinburgh Festival after an August 29 *Sonnambula* because the cold air in that city had afflicted her and she was not feeling well. The report in the San Francisco papers on September 17 was this: the diva's husband Meneghini said Madame Callas would be happy to sing four performances with the San Francisco Opera beginning October 15! But her first *Lucia* was scheduled for September 27, her second October 5 and her first *Macbeth* October 11. And, the papers continued, as far as the San Francisco Opera was concerned, Madame Callas was fired, and a complaint was being sent off to the American Guild of Musical Artists. The fact that a recording of Cherubini's *Medea* was on the ailing Callas' September schedule—it is mentioned in the album notes that the recording was made in September, 1957— did not sit exactly well with Adler and Miller. Most subscribers felt they were to be commended for their uncompromising action, and after Leonie Rysanek's Lady Macbeth and Leyla Gencer's Lucia— both highly successful—Maria Callas was, if not forgotten, hardly missed.

AGMA, it might be noted, ultimately released a reprimand in which it was concluded that Callas was "not wholly justified" in her failure to fulfill her contract. "There is reason to believe," said the reprimand, "on the basis of medical statements submitted, that Maria Meneghini Callas would have been justified in not performing because of her physical and emotional condition at the time. But the board further finds that, in fact, Maria Meneghini Callas did not rely entirely upon the medical advice, and, in fact, indicated to the San Francisco Opera Association her willingness to perform during a portion of the period covered by the contract. In view of these circumstances and other incidents testified to before the Board demonstrating that she did not rely entirely upon medical advice, the Board concludes, and is of the opinion that she was under an obligation to come to the United States at the time called for by her contract with the San Francisco Opera."

On the heels of the Callas affair came Antonietta Stella's sudden cancellation, reportedly because of an emergency appendectomy. She had been slated for *Aida* and *A Masked Ball*. Rysanek, who had originally been engaged for *Turandot* and *Ariadne*, the title role in each case, took on Callas' two San Francisco Lady Macbeths and one each of Stella's Aidas and Amelias in addition. The Amelia she sang in German to the rest of the cast's Italian, the opera becoming monolingual again when Herva Nelli came out for the second *Masked Ball*. Rysanek handled her taxing assignments with a high degree of effectiveness and one remembers in particular the ease of production and care of musicianship she put into her supreme interpretation of the Chinese princess in *Turandot*. Puccini's opera opened the season and also served to introduce to America the man who has become the chief conductor of the Italian wing, Francesco Molinari-Pradelli. This well-liked little maestro from the leading Italian opera houses would seem to be, in some ways, a latter-day counterpart of Papi. He sometimes stresses lyricism over tautness, and has been damned as a "singers' conductor," but the mixture of fire, authority, sensitivity and just pacing exhibited in his performances—notably of *Aida* and *Otello*—has stamped him as a very good man to have around.

There were, incidentally, three Aidas at home this year. Two were taken by Leontyne Price, who had been planning to sing her first Nile Scene at a later date in Vienna. Her 1957 Aida was not quite her 1959 Aida, but already much more than just promising. *Turandot* was given in the Hearst Greek Theater in Berkeley to initiate a custom of one open-air performance per year.

Ariadne auf Naxos joined the repertoire October 8 in a charming production with scenery by Jenkins of *Cosi fan Tutte* fame, stage direction by Hager and musical direction by Steinberg. The prologue, with its long stretches of marvelously unctuous spoken pronouncement from the Major Domo, was wisely given in English; the more lyrical opera itself was sung in German. The silvery, light vocalism of Rita Streich, a German lyric-coloratura making her first American appearances, was capital in the role of Zerbinetta. On the other hand, her Sophie in *Rosenkavalier* was not as romantic-looking or spontaneously acted as it should be. The 1955 combination of Schwarzkopf-Bible-Edelmann-Leinsdorf was back in this opera, as was that of Schwarzkopf-Lewis-Alvary in the 1956 *Cosi* Revisited. Nan Merriman, the noted mezzo, was a good-looking, vocally superb Dorabella, and Heinz Blankenburg—moving up in the operatic world—a thoroughly first-rate Guglielmo. Streich was Despina. Leinsdorf conducted.

Gencer's *Lucia* was not of the pretty-pretty pyrotechnical variety. She is basically a warm lyric-dramatic soprano who simply happens to have the coloratura equipment as well. The richness of her voice, which, like Callas', seemed to have a certain sonic sex appeal, helped make hers an adult Lucia. Also the vivid acting: she conveyed a real sense of derangement in the Mad Scene. All in all, this was the most memorable portrayal offered in San Francisco by this sometimes remarkable artist. Her success in the part indicated that another re-engagement was in order, and she returned in 1958. Her other 1957 assignments were Violetta and Liu, the latter only in Los Angeles.

The impressive Italian dramatic baritone Giuseppe Taddei made his

American debut this season, taking the title role in *Macbeth* and also appearing as Scarpia. In Los Angeles he added two Lord Henrys. He was a fine addition to the roster, but why an obscure and rough-sounding fellow Italian named Umberto Borghi should be imported made little sense. Robert Merrill was also among the baritones, contributing a beautiful voice if not much dramatic excitement.

The tenor register went through a crisis in the late fifties. Tucker did not return after 1955, and Del Monaco was absent from 1952 to 1959. When Bjoerling did come—in 1956 and 1958—it was only for a few performances. Good tenors appeared, for instance Martell and Lewis, but there was a need during the seasons of 1956–58 for at least one big-league Italian dramatic tenor who combined suavity, fire and magnetism in equal proportions. Eugene Tobin, an American in Stuttgart, was the Calaf and Rhadames in 1957, and while he had many merits and was well worth engaging—Adler's idea of bringing back experienced American singers from Europe deserves commendation—he was not quite the ultra-powerful and polished singer to take all the performances of *Turandot* and *Aida*. The following year Piero Miranda Ferraro was considerably less good. Jon Crain, who also sang in 1957, did not have the vocal size for Cavaradossi in the Opera House. Gianni Raimondi, a highly competent La Scala lyric tenor, appeared often in 1957 and 1958, but he was rarely a success with the press.

The Achilles heel aspect of the somewhat lackluster tenor rosters was this: some of the guarantors are especially conscious of "name" singers. It must be stressed that a number of singers who have appeared in San Francisco have shown themselves to be great artists despite their lack of fame. But Adler did need a little more glamor than he brought into this department, and he left himself open to possible sniping. Sniping there was, when the situation piled up in 1958, and whereas much of it was not justified, a little of it was.

1958

After the war the San Francisco seasons were usually five weeks long, give or take a day or two. In 1957 the length rose to thirty-eight days and in 1958 the duration of home activities was leveled off at a record six weeks. The regular series grew from ten to eleven performances, and each of the "popular" series from five to six. The schedule remained highly concentrated, but by no means as squeezed as some of the early five-week ones in the late forties, when non-subscription performances were piled high within the confines of thirty-four days. The increase in the proportion of Thursday and Saturday evening series performances—slightly cheaper and less dressy than those of the regular series—was a distinct boon to the public.

Not since the *Ring* year of 1935 had there been so many additions to the repertoire in a single season. Verdi's *Don Carlo*, Cherubini's *Medea* and a Carl Orff double bill, consisting of *Die Kluge* (1942) and *Carmina Burana* (1937), were all new. *Medea* and *Carmina* received their first staged performances in America—the concert version American premiere of *Carmina* had taken place in San Francisco in 1954—and *Die Kluge*, presented in English as *The Wise Maiden*, was given its absolute American premiere. There were also two revivals of long withdrawn operas, *The Bartered Bride*, last heard from in 1942 and offered in a new production, and *Tannhäuser*, silent since 1941. In line with the theory that the standard repertory should be visually freshened, *Bohême* was given in a new production financed by the Guild.

Singers in American debuts included soprano Eugenia Ratti, tenor Sebastian Feiersinger, baritone Rolando Panerai and basses Arnold Van Mill and Giuseppe Modesti. Conductors new to the United States were Leopold Ludwig and Jean Fournet. Such San Francisco favorites as Rysanek, Schwarzkopf, Price and Farrell were on hand,[9] and sopranos Lisa Della Casa and Christel Goltz and mezzos Grace Hoffman and Irene Dalis—the latter from nearby San Jose—joined the roster.

Dalis first appeared in what may well be her best role: Eboli in *Don Carlo*. She swung into it with a fiery regality and sang it warmly. She shared top honors in the first two performances of Verdi's masterpiece with Tozzi, whose limping, swaggering Philip was a stage portrait drawn with great imagination and style. Frank Guarrera did the best singing of his San Francisco career as Rodrigo, and though Piero Miranda Ferraro was a choppy-sounding Don Carlo, there seemed reason to believe he might at some time project his dark, dramatic tenor more successfully. No soprano knows better than Leyla Gencer how to stand around looking noble, but her vocal projection was spotty in the role of Elisabetta. As Molinari-Pradelli was unable to return this year—there was illness in his family—George Sebastian was brought back for the Italian wing.[10] In general this was a mistake,

[9] Price and Farrell did not join the Met until 1960–61. Rysanek went on the New York roster in 1958–59; Schwarzkopf has remained unattached as this book is written. Farrell first sang at the Chicago Opera in 1957, Rysanek in 1958 and Price and Schwarzkopf in 1959.

[10] He had been conducting a great deal at the Paris Opera since his earlier San Francisco days.

but he did understand well the somber atmosphere of this score and put it over with grip and thrust. Some of his tempos were slow, but not badly considered in this frame of reference.

Don Carlo is full of subtleties and not basically sure-fire, but evidently the word got around about its merits and there was enough response at the box office to add a third performance. There were some interesting additions and subtractions in character and quality of presentation when a new team took over: Van Mill was a more stolid Philip, but his approach made good sense. His sound, of course, was completely different from Tozzi's—a rounded, deep voluminousness which may be less silken but is not without its beauties. Grace Hoffman sang well as Eboli but simply didn't provide the electricity Dalis put into this role. Goltz was a matronly, tremulous Elisabetta, and one preferred to remember her stupendous Elektra of a few days before. In Strauss' opera she sounded like the owner of the world's richest, creamiest voice, and she romped up and down the Horner set in the appropriate manner. *Elektra* provided Dutchman Van Mill's entry, and his rock-like, grandly sonorous Orestes goes down as one of the great things in San Francisco Opera history.

The *Don Carlo* sets, a mixture of fact and fancy striking for their vastness, were borrowed from the Chicago Opera, thanks to a new exchange agreement which sent San Francisco's *Turandot* production eastward.

Medea was the opening night fare, and not ideal material for that evening: starch is all right in the shirts but not on the stage when the season's curtain is rung up. But there were some cheers for Eileen Farrell, who portrayed the heroine, that tigeress on a hot tin roof for whom the opera is named. At first her extended high tones were thin and tremulous, but as the evening progressed her beautiful voice became more lustrous and secure, its huge tone under control. And plenty of praise was due for her subtle, intense characterization. True, she didn't move around much, but there was action in her singing. Sylvia Stahlman was an excellent Glauce, Claramae Turner outdid past achievements as Neris, and Richard Lewis, if not in his best voice, was a lively, stylish Jason. La Scala's Modesti showed off a truly beautiful lyric bass as Creon, displayed it well during the rest of the season, and regrettably did not return after his 1958 duties were completed.

Medea dates from 1797, and its modern revival from a series of performances with Maria Callas in Italy, the first at the Florence May Festival in 1953. Farrell had sung it in a concert version in New York with the American Opera Society. The score is reminiscent of Cherubini's older contemporaries Gluck and Mozart in the fragile elegance and poignant expressiveness of much of its melody. For all its formality, magnified by the Lachner recitatives replacing original spoken dialogue, *Medea* still lives as a strong musico-dramatic experience and is certainly worth doing occasionally. Waldemar Johansen provided appropriate settings—starkly simple and stylized, and more simply architectural than the more massive sets used at La Scala. Unfortunately, a canopy seemed to have a mind of its own and billowed in the air far more than it was supposed to as Jason entered on opening night.

Carl Orff has become something of a controversial figure, and paradoxically because his music is written in a very simple style. As is well known by now, the oft-repeated rhythm is his trademark, the diatonic scale his favorite. Some people love his music, others can't stand its unsubtle insistence. There doesn't seem to be much question, though, about the Bavarian composer's vivid sense of orchestration: he can make music tinkle with ravishing delicacy and thump with terrific vigor. *Carmina* is, in one opinion, a work of great charm and fire, and judging by the exuberant applause which followed its presentations the audience in large part voted for Orff. *Die Kluge*, with its large percentage of spoken dialogue, would have been a dead loss in German, but in the English of Jane Mayhall and Otto Guth its rustic and rather roguish fairy tale spirit came through. Some of the humor is not especially exportable, but the relationship of the wise maiden and the king is touching and amusing.[11]

Jean-Pierre Ponnelle, a precocious twenty-six-year-old French designer with a romantic-surrealistic bent, was responsible for the Orff sets. *Die Kluge* was staged in "peasant theater" style with boards on barrels and three long-nosed, puffed-cheeked puppet musicians sitting on a rope-hung ladder above the stage. *Carmina* was aptly more elegant, with the all-important choristers placed in small groups around a semicircle and plenty of room in front of them for soloists and ballet. Orff intended *Carmina* to be produced on stage, and it is eminently worthwhile done that way, yet this "scenic cantata" is always more a pageant than an opera of action. So Hager's problem was a big one. He is to be commended for solving it reasonably well: the movements seemed neither unduly forced and cluttered nor static. The lighting was magnificent and the way the costumes were spotlighted on a dimmed stage at the end of the Court of Love Scene will long be remembered. Incidentally, Adler, Hager and Ponnelle conferred with Orff on this production in Munich.

Leontyne Price and Lawrence Winters—the Negro baritone with Hamburg and New York City Center experience—had the leading

[11] At the second performance about ten minutes of the score was cut.

roles in *Die Kluge*: she was altogether enchanting as the wise maiden and he acted superbly the role of the inept, lecherous king. Raymond Manton was amusing and sounded extremely well in the swan imitation of *Carmina*. The sympathetic conductor of the double bill was Leopold Ludwig, the fifty-year-old general music director of the Hamburg Opera, and a real find for the company. He appeared before the San Francisco public for the first time September 30 when he entered the pit to conduct *The Bartered Bride*. All you needed to hear was a few bars of the overture to know that this was a superior talent. The bustling opening was both immensely exuberant and spankingly precise. The conductor drew a glowing tone from the orchestra and demonstrated a warmth of expression and intelligence of pacing which would prove more than valuable. He confirmed the fine impression in the Orff and *Elektra*, and also in *Tannhäuser*, after a somewhat tame-sounding overture.

Schwarzkopf, Lewis, Tozzi and Howard Fried (an excellent Vashek from the City Center) were the leading protagonists in the new and handsome production of *The Bartered Bride*, sung in good English. *Tannhäuser* gave San Francisco its first real opportunity to hear Feiersinger, the new Austrian heldentenor—he had been introduced as Aegisthus in *Elektra*, but this character has little to do. Although his projection was not always perfect, the relatively lyrical phrasing and suave sound he emitted were superior to that of most Wagner tenors. With Rysanek, Hoffman and Van Mill also on stage, this was a *Tannhäuser* production in which those old gremlins, Wobble and Shriek, were chased right out of the Opera House.

Demonstrating that it was by no means simply a friend of the ultra-standard repertoire, the public registered such interest in *The Bartered Bride* and *Tannhäuser* that third performances of these were added. *Bohême*, the popularity of which never surprises anybody, was offered in all three series, and mainly because of the new sets by George Jenkins, who maintained his high batting average in the game of scenic success. Without a doubt he batted .666 here because the second and third act sets were triumphs. For the second he put an elaborate cafe on the left half of the stage which really looked like a Parisian cafe, complete with tables outside and a visible interior bar, from which the waiters get the drinks. The third act set allowed the audience to see inside the tavern by the city gate. The problem with the first and fourth acts was this: the action was played on a sort of puppet platform several feet above the stage with lots of empty space on each side. A lowering and spreading of the set was necessary, and this was done the following season. The atmospheric silhouetting of Paris rooftops in this "open-air" set is effective, and the adjustment has been preferable to abandonment.

Lisa Della Casa was surprisingly cast as Mimi, but at least one viewer thought that her velvety voice, fine technique and better than average acting did great service to the role. She brought out the fact that the frail embroideress has a touch of Manon Lescaut in her. Jean Fournet, the well-known French conductor, was by no means out of his element in *Bohême*—a mixture of shimmering precision, symphonic sweep and warm emotion came out of the pit—but in the home territory of Massenet's *Manon* he was strangely ineffective. Gallic neatness and clarity ruled, and the passion was left singularly untattered: come to think of it, one hears this sort of over-mild performance in Paris often. Gencer's Manon was argued over, and Lewis sang Des Grieux with the same maddening tonal tiptoeing he used in *Carmen* in 1955. But his "Dream" was one of the subtlest in the history of the War Memorial.

Leontyne Price sang her first *Trovatore* Leonora September 26, and once warmed up she performed with rare elegance of style and radiance of tone. Bjoerling, who was scheduled for *Don Carlo* earlier in the season, pleaded delay from Europe but did arrive in time for this performance. He seemed distracted and at times bumbled around the stage absent-mindedly. Furthermore, his voice sounded tired. However, when he sang at the Fol-de-Rol a few days later he was evidently vocally refreshed.

Trovatore and *Forza del Destino* both suffered from the soggy, bumpy conducting of Sebastian: the ill-phrased overture to *Forza* was surely one of the most ill-judged things to be heard in the Opera House. Weede, who had been on Broadway in *Most Happy Fella*, returned as Don Carlo in this opera and as Rigoletto, singing beautifully some of the time and growling at others. Obviously his voice needed a rest following the Broadway grind. Taddei returned, too, but only in the title role of *Gianni Schicchi*. This, of course, is one of his specialties and he did it supremely well. Under Curiel's direction, the *Schicchi* was tossed off perfectly as a curtain-raiser to *Elektra*. Stahlman sang Lauretta well, and the successful Rinuccio was Richard Miller, an American who had appeared at the Zurich Opera. He was hired as a replacement for Curzi, who couldn't obtain release from German obligations. He was rather out of his element singing Almaviva in an Opera House *Barber of Seville*, his delicate diminuendos into something close to silence being altogether too subtle for that auditorium if not unstylish. Eugenia Ratti's Rosina was marred by dainty shrieks of top tones but otherwise commendable. Panerai was a large-voiced and exceptionally lively Figaro who raced to and fro like a kitten intrigued by everything around him. The portrayal looked like a delightfully impulsive improvisation, but for some reason the consensus of reaction in the press was negative.

In Mozart's *Marriage of Figaro* Panerai's impulsiveness, mixed with relaxation, did create a curiously haphazard impression of the same character. Perhaps if Panerai had been assigned serious roles he would have consolidated on the San Francisco stage the excellent impression registered on records. There was a reversal of the usual San Francisco procedure in the Mozart: not only was Figaro sung by a baritone, but the Count was taken by a bass. At first one felt that Modesti's enactment of the Count as a fairly serious haughty nobleman was dramatically acute. But after reconsidering this ill-unified and not especially spirited production, it seemed that his lack of humor was simply a reflection of the whole.

Three of the opera auditions winners had some small but good opportunities this year and sounded well. Robert Thomas, a bright and strong-voiced tenor, was the stentorian herald in *Don Carlo* and formed a third of the Ping-Pang-Pongish trio of vagabonds in *Die Kluge*. Warm mezzos Margot Blum and Frances Groves both sang Inez in *Trovatore*, and Blum was one of the two fairly conspicuous handmaidens in *Medea*. Of the several New York singers brought in, mostly from City Center, some were fine additions and others hardly justified their importation considering the possibilities of California talent.

In Los Angeles performances there were a few noteworthy changes from the San Francisco casts given in the appendix. Bjoerling did sing Don Carlo in that city. Tozzi took over Padre Guardiano from Modesti, Alvary the Rossini Basilio from Tozzi, and Dorothy Kirsten, who didn't appear at all in San Francisco, was heard as Mimi in her city of residence. Farrell was indisposed for her *Trovatore* Leonora, so Price flew back from the East to do it.

While the company was in Los Angeles, a small number of San Franciscans were grumbling about their 1958 season. The absence of Molinari-Pradelli, the late arrival of Bjoerling, the fact that the San Francisco Ballet was off on a foreign tour and had to be replaced—all these things hurt. Following a post-season board meeting, Miller announced that the Association fully recognized, and regretted, certain artistic weaknesses which resulted from these factors. But the nagging continued in some quarters. There had, as a matter of fact, been a strong current of discredit campaigning during the progress of the 1958 season. The morning after *The Bartered Bride* was revived, the newspaper critics received telegrams telling them if they had any courage they would condemn the show as a hopeless waste of time and money. Meanwhile, an excessively fault-finding critique of the San Francisco Opera by Roger Dettmer of the *Chicago American* was being circulated to the press. The irony of the telegram was that the San Francisco critics in general had pulled few punches in recent years, and *The Bartered Bride* was really a good production. Actually, *Medea, Don Carlo, Carmina Burana, Die Kluge, Tannhäuser, Bohême, Elektra* and *Gianni Schicchi* all received performances which in many, if not all, respects would have been hard to surpass. It is true that there were real problems in the *Trovatore, Forza, Barber, Marriage of Figaro* and *Manon,* and this is why 1958 does not add up to one of the greatest all-around seasons. But there were some great things in it. Those who for one reason or another were dissatisfied may feel pleased that Miller and Adler were sufficiently concerned to make sure of engaging a top tenor like Del Monaco in 1959. And with Jon Vickers and Giuseppe Zampieri also on hand, not to mention Lewis and Feiersinger, that department revived markedly. As if to set the right mood, the gentlemen who run the company decided to open the next season with a strongly cast, sure-fire *Aida.*

1959

One of the greatest triumphs of the San Francisco Opera came September 18, 1959, with the American premiere of Richard Strauss' forty-year-old *Die Frau Ohne Schatten (The Woman Without a Shadow).* This is an opera which is supposed to be just about impossible to produce, but there it was on the stage of the War Memorial, a bouncing, strapping wonderchild delayed in its American birth until a day when Strauss' style is that of another era, but also a day when the once-scorned later operas of Strauss are gaining the attention they deserve.

Fate had tried to trip up this production: three of the principle singers cancelled their engagements and the scenic designer was drafted into the French Army before the company had all the designs in hand. But obstacles were hurdled, and the performances indicated that the San Francisco Opera could take on a great challenge and succeed.

In place of the popular Rysanek, who regretfully had to withdraw because of illness, an American singing in Hamburg named Edith Lang took over the role of the Empress. One of the handful of sopranos who sing this taxing part, she turned out to be an eminently satisfactory if not precisely ideal substitute. Eleanor Steber who had been learning the role of Barak's wife also bowed out, so Marianne Schech was brought in from Munich. Her creamy voice and previous knowledge of the role helped her to make an excellent impression. Edelmann, too, not the most logical choice for Barak anyway, was indisposed, and Mino Yahia, an Egyptian-born, New York-raised psychiatrist turned opera singer, got the part. He had been engaged for some important but less elaborate roles than this and the Don Giovanni he assumed for George London later in the season. Since Yahia has a beautiful lyric bass voice—he had been singing in Nürnberg—part of the victory was already won. Insofar as Barak was concerned, he rose to the occasion brilliantly, achieving a by no means unconvincing characterization. Irene Dalis as that cryptic lady demon the Nurse and Feiersinger as the Emperor both filled their scheduled places with distinction.

Reading the libretto of *Die Frau*, with all of Hofmannsthal's elaborate verbal baggage surrounding the essentially simple message of the story, one gets the idea that the opera in performance must sag under all the weight. But in the opera house, under the spell of sympathetic acting, fanciful sets, tricky but effective stage manipulations and, above all, the ravishing score, such dim thoughts tend to brighten a good deal. The reception was most enthusiastic. The public was enthralled, as were the local critics and those who came from the East.

Ludwig, who conducted, was rated as the hero of the evening, next only to Strauss himself. He molded the music with the greatest subtlety, lyrical glow and dynamic control. He took those fantastically beautiful passages such as the Mahler-like hymn at the end of the first act and the interlude based on Barak's music halfway through the first act and spun them out with a kind of subdued ecstacy which made one want to weep.

Ponnelle's decoratively spooky sets were very handsome, and their lightness helped give the production a fairy-tale touch. Hints of surrealism were visible and in the dyer's hut the painted wash hung on the line like Dali watches. Two-level staging was used throughout to accommodate the various worlds of action, and thanks to a scrim curtain and expert lighting the vision of the emperor turning to stone looked as if it were really taking place in midair. The third of the five scenes in the second act was omitted, but this small sacrifice was an anti-fatigue factor.

After the season was over, there was no question about it: *Die Frau* would return in 1960, and with Rysanek herself.

The second addition to the repertoire was Gluck's *Orfeo*, the first opera by this composer to be performed by the company. It was

greeted with a great deal less enthusiasm than the Strauss but not in a
collectively hostile manner. Some critics and patrons thought it was
all wrong, and the production can be entered in the annals as one
of the most controversial the San Francisco company has ever offered.
Remembering the original nature of the legend, stage director Yannopoulos, himself a Greek, decided to let Orfeo kill himself after
Euridice's second death, thereby avoiding the incongruously happy
denouement of the opera. In principle a composer's work should not
be tampered with, but there are many versions of this opera, and that
of Yannopoulos was not beside the point. Orfeo and Euridice were ill-
starred lovers, and the prevailing mood of the opera is sorrowful
and wistful. Perhaps an eighteenth-century European court may have
demanded the happy ending, but does the story?

After "Che faro" and Orfeo's death, the Furies rushed in and
scooped up the dead lover, to exciting effect. Then, after a pause which
was distracting, the audience was taken back to Euridice's tomb and
the opening chorus was repeated. Barring the pause, all of this seemed
logical and inevitable. Of course, the basic problem with *Orfeo* is its
static, ceremonial quality, and it is not surprising that by the third
scene the choristers seemed to be posturing self-consciously as if they'd
been told to avoid being dull. There was a somber beauty about
Waldemar Johansen's basic set, with its Stonehenge effect of rock
above an impressive doorway, and the lighting was a visual symphony
of light and shadow. Silvio Varviso, a thirty-five-year-old conductor
from the Basle Opera, led with great warmth and dignity. The
musical atmosphere was solemn, of course, but *Orfeo* is the reverse
of outgoing, sure-fire entertainment. It is scarcely surprising that the
old opera, along with *L'Amore dei Tre Re*, had the lowest box office
score of the season.

The visual freshening of the standard repertoire continuing, the
Opera Guild donated a new production of *Carmen* in 1959. When the
prelude was struck up the night of September 29, the curtain rose to
reveal a special show curtain of fierce waves of red, pink and black.
That it looked like an abstract expressionist view of a can-can is
beside the point: at the same time it suggested all the energy, blood
and tension of the story, and one knew by this first stroke of color-
shocked originality that the new production would be full of genuine
novelty. Its architects were Howard Bay—like Jenkins, a veteran of
Broadway—who designed the sets and costumes, and Yannopoulos,
who did the staging. Their basic intent was to create a more realistic
atmosphere than one finds in conventional versions, and they took
Carmen back to the war-ravaged 1820's where she really belongs. The
grisly shadows of Goya's Spain hung over Bay's magnificent costumes,

and Yannopoulos filled the first-act stage with a wider variety of "real" people than one usually sees. The ragamuffins were never rowdier and more disheveled.

Bay's actual sets were not in the same vein of realism: devilish fancy, instead, was the thing, the scenery providing a rather fantastic counterpart to the action. The effect was extremely brilliant in the first act with its tall clock tower, and somewhat questionable in the last with its arena taking off like a slow rocket. Of course, this may have been designed to heighten Don José's derangement, but the tenor in this production did not emphasize derangement. Gloria Lane was a superb Carmen who seemed less a product of the dressing room than of history itself. Short, extremely bosomy and not made up to look wildly attractive, here was a Carmen who could sing beautifully the evening through without resorting to that self-consciously throaty sexiness of voice some Carmens love. She suited the production perfectly.

The Carmen—and the Orfeo—was to have been Rïse Stevens. But when, a few months before the season, she demanded a cachet of $100 more than anyone else would get, including that anyone's travel expenses, the company refused. Blanche Thebom was the vocally worn but engaging substitute in the Gluck.

Jon Vickers, the rising Canadian tenor—he had sung in Dallas— was the Don José. As on opening night, when he appeared as Rhadames, he demonstrated distinct personality, loads of taste and some extremely provocative points of dramatic interpretation. His José was unusually iron-nerved. It was with cool dispatch that he knifed the cigarette girl in the final scene. The new and greater manliness was put over consistently and effectively. But there was one rub: after the last curtain you didn't really feel much sympathy for Don José. He seemed, somehow, a less tragic figure than the classic dragoon who showed signs of cracking up. Maintaining his commendable appreciation for dynamic markings, Vickers closed the Flower Song quietly, as he had "Vesti la giubba" in *Pagliacci* a few nights before. In *Aida*, which he sang with great power and beauty if not the last word in liberated top tones, he exhibited a marked sensitivity of phrasing, making "Celeste Aida" more lyrical and deliberate than usual. But the danger sign needed to be hung out here when his warmth of interpretation caused a lag behind the beat. During this aria Rhadames seemed rather troubled and introverted—a refreshing change from the "stand up straight, plant your feet and belt out the tones" manner. But when he arrived onstage in the Triumphal Scene he looked sour and bored. An intriguing artist altogether, one who can be strongly criticized for his questionable points because his good ones are so good.

The *Aida* of the opening night was a hit. Molinari-Pradelli was back on the podium, and Leontyne Price returned with one of the greatest Aidas of our time. The creamy vocal richness of her growing dramatic voice, and the intense conviction of her interpretation added up to a near-perfect score. Dalis, Weede and Tozzi contributed to the sonic pleasures, as did three of the best local talents: Katherine Hilgenberg, Robert Thomas and Carl Palangi.

Two performances of *Aida* were scheduled. When Del Monaco told Adler he was feeling in the vocal pink and would love to sing a Rhadames, a third performance was added. It brought forth San Franciscan Lucine Amara's first Aida in a major house. She almost made one believe a strictly lyric soprano can fill the role satisfactorily. In a dolcissimo passage like that of the third act wherein Aida tells Rhadames of the appeal of life in Ethiopia, her liquid voice was just right. And she dove into less fragile passages with a bright vigor. But at times she was overwhelmed and one yearned for more weight.

Del Monaco's first appearance of the season had already occurred in *Andrea Chenier* a few days earlier, and he later appeared as Otello. His voice was as glorious as ever, and there were some signs of growing maturity and refinement in his art. Rysanek had been scheduled for both Madeleine and Desdemona; her replacement was the rising Italian soprano Gabriella Tucci, who came on Del Monaco's recommendation—they had sung with Gobbi in Tokyo—and made successful if not epical American debut appearances in these roles. The pure, warm, moving tone of her middle register cut through not unlike Tebaldi's, but her voice thinned out somewhat at the top and her temperament thinned out, too, at dramatic points where more was needed. Not an absolutely top performer, but close to one.

Weede had to give up Iago when a family death called him away, and his place was taken by Mario Zanasi, a lightish baritone from the Metropolitan who had offered a pleasant Sharpless and a lackluster Escamillo. His Iago turned out to be something special: here was a slender, youthful one who, praise the change, looked and acted like a real schemer instead of a stock villain. *Otello* audiences are used to darker, richer, heavier voices in the role, but Zanasi put lots of vocal strength and good quality into his performance, and emerged as a meaningful addition to the company.

Tucci was not the only singer to make an American debut in San Francisco this year. Three important artists—soprano Sena Jurinac, tenor Giuseppe Zampieri and baritone Geraint Evans—were added to the roster. All had great successes and were re-engaged. The thirty-eight-year-old Jurinac, for more than a decade a leading soprano light of the Vienna State Opera, was long overdue. She was introduced on September 22 in a somewhat controversial *Butterfly* which began unpromisingly for Cio-Cio-San with a shrill entrance. But once she found her stride, she sang the evening through with a lyric soprano of even-toned melting richness, striking just the right note between the extremes of innocence and sophistication. Her Donna Anna in *Don Giovanni*, her Composer in *Ariadne*, her Eva in *Meistersinger* were all superb. All one could have asked was that she had come a little sooner, before the youthful freshness in her voice had hardened a bit.

Zampieri had begun as a *comprimario*, singing at La Scala, and is today a leading tenor in Italy and at the Vienna State Opera. But few knew about him when he came to San Francisco. His first dulcet *pianissimo* tones in *L'Amore dei Tre Re* indicated he would make a fine lyric Fenton. But later, when he let go with ringing, dramatic tones, one was tempted to think in terms of Otello rather than of Nanetta's lover. In all his assignments—as Avito, Pinkerton and Cassio in *Otello* (this role deserves a tenor with an attractive voice)—he sang not only with tonal beauty but great artistry, too. A fine find!

Welsh-born Evans was hardly better known to San Franciscans than Zampieri—he could be heard on a few Gilbert and Sullivan recordings. But his biography included appearances in the title role of *Falstaff* at Glyndebourne and as Rodrigo in *Don Carlo* at Covent Garden. He had the further distinction of being a Commander of the Order of the British Empire. Some of the German aficionados were wondering how an Englishman could be a good Beckmesser, but they needn't have worried. The newcomer had a triumph as the man with the slate. Beckmesser is not exactly a lovable character, but Evans made such an impression the audience applauded him as if he were the conquering hero himself. He has a baritone of good quality, and a large amount of the vocal distortion traditionally used by Beckmessers could not entirely hide his pure sonic virtues. His characterization recalled an old-time movie villain, except that no matter how hard this villain tried to be snakes and daggers, he was so engagingly inept one couldn't help feeling sympathetic.

The *Meistersinger* revival was marked by the best all-around performances this opera has ever had in San Francisco. Paul Schoeffler, the reigning Sachs of the post-Schorr generation,[12] led a cast which

[12] Actually Schoeffler was sixty-two in 1959, and therefore only about ten years younger than his illustrious predecessor would have been if alive. Edelmann was the originally scheduled Sachs. When he couldn't come, a Czech named Ladislav Mraz was engaged. He in turn could not fulfill his engagement. Schoeffler couldn't have been a happier solution. He should have been selected in the first place.

boasted, besides the afore-mentioned Eva of Jurinac and Beckmesser of Evans, a pair of fine Pogners in Tozzi and Yahia, a lyric Walther in Feiersinger, an excellent Magdalena in Katherine Hilgenberg, a humorously drawn Kothner in Lawrence Winters, and an appealing if vocally Italianate David in Curzi. Ludwig conducted, following a rather humdrum overture, with great warmth and style, and if the first act set looked a little dowdy and that of Act 3, Scene 1 like something left over from Civic Auditorium days, well, nobody cared much when the musical side was so wonderfully taken care of. San Franciscans have had to take their Wagner rationed out, and since this is his most lovable opus it is scarcely surprising there were three performances in the home city.

Don Giovanni, thanks to Ludwig and a superb cast, was another triumph. Price sang her first Elvira on stage and a marvelous portrayal it was. It had charm besides vocal opulence, and many an Elvira has had neither.

In a year of casting difficulties George London was late in arriving for his assignment as the Don because of a case of jaundice. His place was taken by Yahia, who needed to energize his stage movement more but sang with mellifluous tone and good style. Tozzi replaced *him* as the Commendatore in the first performance, but Yahia went back in the part of Don Pedro—who can afford to act like a statue—in the second, London having arrived. Local boy Theodor Uppman returned after eleven years absence with his beautifully sung, jelly-fish-gait Masetto. Jurinac was Anna, and Pierrette Alarie a fine Zerlina, Alvary a good Leporello and Lewis an excellent Ottavio. The staging was more successful than the immediately preceding tries.

Uppman was Arlecchino and Evans the Music Master in *Ariadne*. The sonorities of Strauss' small orchestra were scrubbed as clean and lustrous as could be by Ludwig. Robert Symonds of the local Actors' Workshop was an excellent Major Domo, using a snippy, mincing English accent. But just why in this year the Prologue was performed by the others in German while he spoke in English is incomprehensible. Farrell was Ariadne this time, and at first had considerable trouble with her voice. But, as usual, the powers of vocal characterization were very much there. There had been some talk of her doing an Isolde in 1959, but this didn't work out.

Uppman and Evans further shared the baritone register as Marcello and Schaunard in *Bohême*, presented only as a non-subscription event. Varviso conducted with such warmth and exuberance not a routine phrase intruded. Albanese returned for a remarkably fresh Mimi, and Mary Costa, no stranger to TV's *Climax*, Bernstein's *Candide* or

Bellini's *Norma*, was perhaps the best Musetta ever. This rising talent, who combines coloratura agility with a rich-toned lower register, loves to play naughty women, and she dove into Musetta with great spirit. The *Bohême* tenor was Giuseppe Gismondo, an Italian who had sung at the City Center—a beautiful voice, but not handled with all the necessary plasticity. Costa, who had not sung with a major American company before, also adorned, visually and vocally, the returned and cheered *Carmina Burana*. This time it was paired with *Pagliacci*, and improved through the presence of the San Francisco Ballet itself.

The ballet was given a separate curtain-raiser of its own in 1959 for the first time in six years: Stravinsky's *Danses Concertantes*, paired with *Ariadne*. There was thought of doing the Balanchine choreography, but that gentleman said he had forgotten it, so Lew Christensen, the ballet's present artistic director, and a man of fresh ideas, provided a new one.

The Los Angeles season of sixteen performances broke attendance records, average capacity in the huge Shrine being eighty-seven per cent (close to 6,000 persons). Casts were mostly the same as in San Francisco, but Tucci sang Donna Anna and Del Monaco Canio in that city. When all the activities of 1959 were done, there was little question that the season had been particularly successful. An aura of good feeling surrounded the total presentation, in definite distinction to the atmosphere of dissatisfaction which shadowed the 1958 proceedings. The roster was probably the most strongly balanced of Adler's years, the *Frau Ohne Schatten* was a tremendous success, and only *Orfeo* brought forth unfavorable comment.

The account for 1959 may be closed—but not without mention of another name, that of the company's excellent new chorus master, Vincenzo Giannini of Bologna.

1960

Having shown in 1959 that *Frau Ohne Schatten* was not too burdensome a production within a tight schedule, the company went on in this year to *Wozzeck*, which Adler had long wanted to do. The West Coast premiere took place October 4—the preparation had included 32½ hours of orchestral rehearsal—and it was, on almost all accounts, a great success. The performance went smoothly and the house was nearly filled. If a handful of patrons walked out during the first scenes, there was a tremendous ovation for conductor Ludwig and the orchestra following the sole intermission—after the second act—and the musicians answered the flood of praise with two collective bows. At the end the applause was enthusiastic, and after the performance word of the achievement spread. The second performance was jammed, and a third showing scheduled.[13]

Ludwig conducted with obvious love for the score, balancing its details in crystalline fashion, and shattering the responsive listeners with the inexorable cumulative sweep of its anguished chromaticism. The orchestra was right with him. On stage, Leni Bauer-Ecsy's moderately expressionistic settings and Hager's thorough direction captured perfectly the bleak, oppressive, crazed atmosphere of the drama. The second scene sun was right out of late Van Gogh, the tall skeleton in the doctor's office eavesdropped overbearingly on the conversation of the doctor and Wozzeck, and the endlessly windowed barracks seemed to be falling in on the bunks at the end of the second act.

Geraint Evans, pale-faced in drab fatigues, sang the title role for the first time in his career and was enormously sympathetic—a poor clod who walked around the stage with the heaviness of a man who is crushed just a little more each day. The haunting pathos of his big, dark, plaintive voicing of Berg and Büchner's trampled common man will not leave the memory easily. Some of the less even-keel characters in *Wozzeck* resemble puppets of a contorted world, and the lethargy of Evans' step heightened this resemblance. So did the creaky jerkiness of Richard Lewis' superbly sung Captain, a role new to him, too. One couldn't help thinking of the versatility of these two Britons, both so adept in Mozart, Berg—and Sir Arthur Seymour Sullivan.

Marilyn Horne, a twenty-six-year-old Los Angeles soprano with seventeen German performances of Marie behind her, was as sympathetic in her way as Evans in his, and the vocal demands of the role were tamed by her fiery virtuosity. Horne's opportunity to appear in San Francisco followed Brenda Lewis' cancellation during the summer for reasons of health. Alvary, looking like a character out of an old Fritz Lang movie, was a fine Doctor with an appropriate central European accent. Raymond Manton and Margot Blum were just right as Andres and Margret, and Ticho Parly, a young Danish-American tenor who had sung with the New Orleans Opera, was a histrionically convincing Drum Major if far from ideal vocally. With the exception of Parly, all made themseves as well understood as the chromatic line permits. The Eric Blackall-Vida Hartford Engish translation was used.

A plain black curtain was lowered for scene changes, and these were

[13] With college students taking advantage of a special offer of seats at reduced rate, this performance sold very well if not out.

executed with a nearly cinematic speed. This *Wozzeck* really moved, as indeed it should, and the invisible stagehands deserved some special applause. In short, the production looked like something from the most stylish legitimate theater. Everything was worked out and everything worked.

Wozzeck was closely succeeded on the season's schedule by Bellini's *La Sonnambula,* the company's other first for the year. This fragile flood of *bel canto* and tinkly melody might have been completely over-shadowed by the grip and thrust of the Berg, but it was given a fresh slant. The direction taken was straight into comedy. Nobody can be expected to take *Sonnambula* very seriously these days, and stage director Yannopoulos turned it into a satirical buffo plaything. Elemer Nagy's glorified comic strip sets, complete with seven-towered castle up on the hill, fitted the treatment perfectly—a treatment which found the choristers sitting on spectator benches, sniffing into handkerchiefs, and nodding their heads in unison at appropriate moments for comment.

Doubtless there were some in the audience who would have pre-ferred to let the period of the piece stand out. After all, the pathos of the Sleepwalking Scene is a serious matter, and when the audience is in a laughing mood as Amina makes her doubtful way across the set, a little adjustment is needed. At all events, Anna Moffo, the rising young Pennsylvanian, was a first-rate Amina, providing a model of what beautifully floated, warm lyric tone should be. Her characteriza-tion was not too intellectual: a frail, Giselle-like Amina wouldn't have added up in this *Sonnambula.* Nicola Monti, who had sung in Dallas and Chicago, came from La Scala to help San Franciscans recall the best traditions of light, lyric, liquid tenorism as Elvino. Giorgio Tozzi was an ebullient Rodolfo, looking like Dr. Dulcamara's brother.

The next most newsworthy event of the 1960 repertoire was not strictly a new production, but one which returned after a long absence, with a few alterations and what might be called a certain protective covering. This was *The Girl of the Golden West,* which reappeared as *La Fanciulla del West.* In 1943, the language had been English, the Dick Johnson a head shorter than the Minnie, and too many of the audience thought it was just funny. But people remained—and Adler was one of them—who felt that if the local references were played down, the corn quotient reduced and the cast exceptionally strong, Puccini's problematical western could be revived successfully. As much a gamble as that second act card game perhaps, but worth trying. Because, after all, there is a wealth of exciting music in the score, and if the proper style is struck, the story has an elemental appeal and rude strength which goes over.

Few of the achievements of the San Francisco Opera deserve such praise: this revival was a complete success. Yes, there were some titters (the tossing of the snowflakes outside the second act cabin door reminded one a bit of W. C. Fields' classic line: "T'aint a fit night out for man or beast"), but the second and third act curtains brought warmly enthusiastic applause. The message got through, to audiences which almost filled the Opera House.

The settings were basically those of 1930 and 1943—altogether appropriate one must say, in their handsome realism. A new and happy scenic touch lent a bit of sophistication to the beginning of the opera— a show curtain with a projection thereon of an old photo of a snowy forty-niner scene set in a postmark oval. The language of the production was, of course, Italian. The reference in the first act to Agenzia Wells Fargo was deleted, because that is the name of an established San Francisco bank, and the Indians in the second act sensibly refrained from their Ughs. There were several horses in the last act, and some of them were so speedily and efficiently ridden back and forth across the set that the audience cheered. The equine character who chose to break the calm of the third act opening during the second performance brought possibly the biggest single laugh of the season: he neighed from behind the curtain just before it went up to soft music. But this was one of the few laughing matters.

The *Fanciulla* revival served to introduce Sandor Konya, the rising Hungarian tenor, to the United States. A tallish, sturdy Dick Johnson, he unfolded a relatively light heldentenor voice with a pulsating emotional quality unmarred by bad style. The fact that he tended to lumber about the stage a bit (there are roles more comfortable than Johnson) and the fact that his projection was occasionally a bit insecure or grainy—these mattered hardly at all. Here, obviously, was an appealing and versatile addition to the tenor ranks, exceptionally well stocked this year with Vickers, Zampieri, Lewis, Monti and Konya! Konya is a very hard man to pigeon-hole in a limited category: suffice it to say that he followed the Johnson with an absolutely superior lyric Lohengrin, a fresh Rodolfo, and a Rhadames which called to mind memories of Lauri-Volpi. There were also hints of Bjoerling and Gigli. He was immediately re-engaged.

Minnie provided another role which the versatile Dorothy Kirsten could, as some more celebrated sopranos could not, make visually and vocally believable. Tito Gobbi, returned to the scene of his American debut a dozen seasons and lots of seasoning later,[14] was an absolutely perfect Jack Rance, master of the musical snarl. He looked like a lecherous old cattle baron and when he threw the chair across the room after Minnie *won* the card game, you knew this was one of the angriest, most despicable villains who ever trod the War Memorial boards. Gobbi had been absent far too long, as his rich, powerful voice, the subtlety and intensity of his characterizations, and his sterling presence indicated—in *Fanciulla, Tosca* and *Boccanegra*.

That second act curtain was one of the most exciting ever witnessed in the Opera House, Gobbi throwing the chair and storming out, Kirsten hysterically laughing and letting the cards cascade to the floor. Molinari-Pradelli unleashed a huge well of sound in the pit and the audience answered in force. Yes, it was good to have *Fanciulla* back well done. There haven't been many chances to see it. The Metropolitan dropped it after 1931–32, Jeritza's last season at that house,[15] and when the Chicago Opera revived it in 1956—on opening night —it was after a thirty-four-year absence.

Gobbi's first appearance of the San Francisco season was in the opening night *Tosca*. Tebaldi, absent for four seasons, was due back as Floria, but an indisposition[16] kept her from fulfilling her engagement. Kirsten, scheduled only for Minnie, undertook the opening *Tosca*, Lucine Amara the second. There was a certain amount of concern in musical circles about the advisability of casting Amara in this role, but, as things worked out, her first Floria in Italian—she had sung the part in English in Central City—had many points of merit. To be sure, it was small-scale in approach, and there was no sense of Tosca as an impressive personality. But, after all, the Roman diva was a woman, too, and Amara's Tosca was supremely feminine. When she demanded of Scarpia "il prezzo," it was with a dainty tone, but a tone completely consistent with her lyrical approach. This was one of the most controversial performances in San Francisco history, but of two things one can be certain: Amara's Tosca was beautifully sung and dramatically more apt than her Aida of the previous year. It is too bad the second

[14] He first sang at the Metropolitan during 1955–56 and has recently been a fixture at the Chicago Opera, singing very little in New York.

[15] At the time of writing the Met's Bing was planning a revival with Leontyne Price.

[16] Suffering from an arthritic condition, she was advised in mid-August to rest for sixty days. There was reason to believe she might arrive in time for two *Bohêmes* late in the San Francisco season. She did not. Actually, she still felt quite badly in mid-October, but cynics were saying she didn't want to hurry back to a city where some idol-toppling criticism had displeased her.

act close was ruined by the encore curtains suddenly rushing prematurely to the center of the stage. When before has a Tosca had to agonizingly stage whisper "Aspetta, aspetta"? You could hear it in the last row of the orchestra. At least the curtains didn't obscure the scene completely, but only those in the very center of the house saw the end of the dramatic action.

The rest of the repertoire was largely composed of proven recent successes: the *Cosi* and *Rosenkavalier* last heard in 1957—these, of course, for Schwarzkopf; *Aida* and *Frau Ohne Schatten* for Rysanek; and the newly set *Bohème* and *Carmen*. *Lohengrin* returned after five years, *Boccanegra* after four, *Traviata* after three. The *Traviata* and *Rosenkavalier* are ripe for some new sets.

The *Cosi* danced back into the Opera House with Schwarzkopf, Richard Lewis and Guarrera in accustomed places as Fiordiligi, Ferrando and Guglielmo. Schoeffler, the Vienna Opera's genial, veteran Alfonso joined the cast, and Katherine Hilgenberg, the Los Angeles mezzo, had her biggest opportunity to date as Dorabella. She held her own in this illustrious company, and there were indications experience might well bring out a portrayal of more size and sweep. Actually, though, a big role of totally serious nature would have been more appropriate for her talents.

Mary Costa's spunky comic style, with its contemporary inflections, helped produce as delightful a Despina as anyone could want. But those who might have thought that comedy was this artist's strongest point, had not yet heard her Violetta. She had not sung the part many times before her San Francisco performance of October 20, but she was in absolute and unrelenting command of it. She fired out jet-propelled tones of purity, punch and beauty, she handled the coloratura crisply and with facility, and she gave the role a touching, incisive sort of vocal characterization which brought it fully to life. The company could be proud of the growing list of Costa portrayals, but she did not let her status prevent her from being a good sport and repeating the relatively inconspicuous part of the Guardian of the Temple Gates in *Frau Ohne Schatten* besides her leading roles.

A parenthetical explanation about her slightly under top quality Micaela. She was indisposed, and actually fainted away after the performance.

As if one superior Violetta were not enough, Adler offered yet another at the regular series *Traviata* the following week when Anna Moffo took over. Rarely in company history have two such interesting and authoritative, yet wholly different, versions of a role been stated in such close succession. Actually the harshness of some of Moffo's *forte* singing in the upper register was worrisome, but if the vocalization was more slender than Costa's, there were some remarkable sustained *pianissimi*. The interpretation emphasized the mature, introspective possibilities of Violetta's personality while Costa had played up the ebullience, and seldom does an artist get quite so far into a character as Moffo did on this occasion.

The 1960 *Rosenkavalier* brought forth a new Ochs in Kurt Boehme, the distinguished Vienna and Munich bass. He was coarse but immediately lovable, and the audience at the first performance—there were three this year—gave him an ovation after the first act. Here was an Ochs with a battering ram belly and cheeks that shook like bowls full of jelly, a giggly, bumptious overgrown boy of an Ochs. He missed the pathos that lies in the part, but he did sing it gorgeously besides being a barrel of fun. Schwarzkopf's Marschallin seemed more youthful than ever—one wondered a bit why the passage of time worried her—and Stahlman's radiant Sophie was a joy to hear again. A member of the Frankfurt Opera since her last San Francisco appearances, she returned to find a place of deserved importance on the roster.

The *Traviata* and *Rosenkavalier* both benefited from the conducting of young Varviso, who has an exceedingly subtle, warm lyric touch, and directs with a discriminating neatness. The tender third act *Traviata* prelude, and the notably crisp, light, clean third act *Rosenkavalier* prelude—each in its different way reflected Varviso's talents. An occasional lack of ebullience in the Strauss can be forgotten in view of the relaxed, unrushed, exquisite overall spell. There was some lack of pace in Varviso's *Tosca* but also some remarkably effective slow tempos, and nobody has ever conducted the last scene of *Bohême* more touchingly here.

Yes, the conducting staff of 1960 was as close to the ideal as the company had ever offered. Molinari-Pradelli's and Ludwig's virtues have been discussed previously, but Ludwig's entry into the Italian repertory with *Boccanegra* was especially interesting, similarly Molinari's into the German with *Lohengrin*. Ludwig produced a rich brilliance of firm, round, elegant sounds without excess of volume. Clean attacks and maximum possible *marcato* phrasing were noteworthy, and if one sensed more control than passion, the interpretation was by no means lacking in expressive qualities. Molinari led an excellent *Lohengrin* christened with a warmly songful, forward-thrusting prelude.

Hans Georg Schaefer, a young German assistant conductor, led the children's matinees of *Gianni Schicchi* with a sense of firm climax and expansive but controlled lyricism. In addition to singing Wozzeck and the *Boccanegra* Paolo, Geraint Evans was the season's Schicchi. His enactment was dashing, large-voiced, quick-witted and non-buffo. And, as usual, his English diction was superb.

Frau Ohne Schatten returned in large part because Rysanek, the queen of the world's Empresses, could renew her San Francisco association in 1960. No more beautiful singing has ever been heard in the Opera House. After the Strauss and *Aida* one could add up the assets: warm, elegant tone, flawless musicianship, clarity and security of projection, conviction of acting, and a new, slim beauty of face and figure. If this was not perfection, it was as close as humanly possible. Schoeffler's great Barak was a boon to the *Frau*, but not Parly's garbled, miscast Emperor. Dalis and Schech were in their usual spots. It was unfortunate that the second performance came on the heels of a marathon rehearsal of *Wozzeck*: the brass was not in shape for Strauss.

The Rysanek *Aida* was a sellout, so Adler added an extra one to give San Franciscans a look at Floriana Cavalli, Tebaldi's replacement for Los Angeles performances of *Tosca, Bohême* and *Boccanegra*—Amara, the substitute in San Francisco, had to return to the Met. A very good-looking young woman, she came to the American stage with starring engagements at the Rome and Naples Operas behind her. Certain re-finements were in order—her low tones could be rather raw, her phrasing graceless, and she slithered around the stage registering the most self-conscious sort of agony—but her voice was so large and limpid and full of rich beauty that an exciting performance resulted.

Originally Konya was the only singer on the roster scheduled for an American debut, but the non-appearance of Tebaldi precipitated Cavalli's arrival in this country, and the cancellation of Jurinac, scheduled for Octavian and Elsa, resulted in the engagements of Hertha Toepper and Ingrid Bjoner, both new to the United States. Toepper, a valued member of the Munich Opera, was a fine Octavian, full in voice and sharp in action, in the second and third *Rosenkavalier* —Frances Bible returned for the first. Bjoner, a young blonde Norwegian, broke short her honeymoon to take over the Elsas. She sang with complete assurance and a radiantly lyric soprano, suitable for the lighter Wagner roles rather than the Isoldes and Brünnhildes. A member of the Düsseldorf Opera, she had sung in Vienna, Munich, Stuttgart and Berlin—after a brush with the relative obscurity of a pharmacological career.

Successful American debuts are fine, but there is a special importance about successful returns to America of relatively unknown American talents singing in Europe. Robert Anderson of the Augsburg Opera made news this year with his clean, beautiful singing in a variety of roles including Telramund, Ramfis, Pietro, the Spirit Messenger in *Frau Ohne Schatten* and José Castro in *Fanciulla*. Considering the deep velvet of his bass voice, the assignment of the higher-lying Telramund was not in Anderson's best interests, but he sang the part without the wobble and growl that sometimes afflict it. Speaking of young Americans, Janis Martin, a mezzo from nearby Sacramento— Dick Johnson's town—made an exceptionally good impression in such bits as the *Aida* priestess, Annina in *Traviata* and Teresa in *Sonnambula*. And Frances McCann, a Los Angeles soprano, was a decidedly superior Frasquita in *Carmen*. Altogether there were eighteen Californians on the roster. Another of them, a likeable and vocally competent baritone from Los Angeles named Ned Romero, took over the old Cehanovsky territory.

The Carmen herself for 1960 was Jean Madeira, who had sung the role with the Cosmopolitan. She was strangely disappointing considering her reputation as a leading exponent of this problematical character. The deep voice, rich as the Philadelphia Orchestra string section, sounded beautiful, but the portrayal, at least on this occasion, was too healthy, good-natured and two-dimensional. Why Adler recast Zanasi as Escamillo, a role in which he was vocally and dramatically uncomfortable, is a question. But, thankfully, there were few questionable castings. Zanasi, after an insufficiently oily and powerful Scarpia in the second *Tosca*, went on to rugged but commendable portrayals of Marcello and Amonasro. Weede returned in his finest post-Broadway form for the first *Aida*.

The revival of Kerz' 1955 *Lohengrin* production reminded one how beautiful the second act projection of the fortress is, and the misty morning light as the crowd comes in was a beautiful effect. The swan returned this year, a stationary emblem-like object behind a scrim. Even though it looked, as one critic said, like a Mexican postage stamp, a fairly satisfactory compromise was struck between the old-fashioned creaky swan boat and the ultra-modern invisibility.

The San Francisco Ballet offered a couple of productions of its own during the year's proceedings: Lew Christensen's riotous *Con Amore*, which followed the *Schicchi* at the children's matinees, and *Variations de Ballet*, a Balanchine-Christensen concoction which followed *Sonnambula*—unfortunately as an anti-climax because of the flimsy Glazunoff music.

While the operatic dramas were being played onstage, another drama of a sort was taking place on a poster in the outer lobby. It showed a thermometer, the mercury registering the progress of the largest fund drive in company history. In order to curb the dangers of a cumulative deficit, the goal was set at an unprecedented $150,000, sans the traditional attraction of subtracting one's contribution from the year's guarantor assessment. Expenses for the 1959 season, Miller reported, were $1,474,803—the figure in 1947 had been $728,842— and even after very healthy ticket sales (average capacity: ninety-seven per cent), a fund drive, guarantor assessments and guaranteed out-of-town performances, the total income for the year still left a deficit of $60,454. A carryover of $10,016 from 1958 also remained as the 1960 season opened and the new drive began. So the situation, if not grave, was potentially dangerous. Ticket sales were flourishing, though—there were no such troublesome sellers as *Orfeo* and *L'Amore* —and the drive got off to a solid start—ultimately netting $122,000, $40,000 more than the 1959 drive. Miller pointed out that the San Francisco's normal deficit is about $250,000 whereas the Chicago Opera's, in a fairly similar situation, is about $450,000. Chicago's season is slightly longer than the home activities of the San Francisco, and the opera house in the midwest city has a higher capacity (3,593), but there is not the financial advantage of touring to the huge Shrine Auditorium.[17] Moreover, Chicago tends to pay its big artists higher fees, and the average capacity attendance dipped below ninety per cent in 1959.

The San Francisco Opera, then, had every intention of continuing its policy of maximum economy and artistic interest. Only if public support refused to accept the challenge would a lowering of the artists-and-repertoire excitement quotient take place.

The highly successful season in the south brought some alterations from the published San Francisco casts, Cavalli and Kirsten sharing Tosca, Weede and Gobbi Scarpia, Cavalli and Moffo Mimi, Evans and Romero Schaunard. Zampieri, who had added Don José in Sacramento, was the Rodolfo in one Los Angeles *Bohême* and the Pinkerton of *Madama Butterfly*, given only in that city. The pressure of engagements had kept Leontyne Price from availability except during the southern series, but she did sing the second Cio-Cio-San of her career in Los Angeles November 8—her first was in Vienna. Rysanek was indisposed for her Los Angeles Aida and replaced by Mary Curtis-

[17] At the time of writing, a new Los Angeles Music Center fully equipped for opera could be expected to be ready for the San Francisco Opera's 1963 season. With a capacity about 150 less (!) than the Opera House, the Center has obviously raised questions as to the future financial feasibility of operating in such an aesthetically superior theater. Higher prices, more performances, a guarantee—these have been thought of.

Verna, the Mary Curtis of the 1952 roster. Tozzi was indisposed for his Rodolfo in the San Diego *Sonnambula* and replaced by Ferruccio Mazzoli, summoned from the Chicago Opera. Besides his major assignments, Konya took over the *Rosenkavalier* Italian Singer for one performance.

One of the remarkable deceptions of operatic history took place in a *Cosi* performance at the Shrine. The Act 1 quintet, "Sento o Dio," was turned into a quartet as Guarrera missed his entrance. But Lewis played ventriloquist for his absent partner at the beginning, singing Guglielmo's lines, and later on, when Ferrando and Guglielmo are supposed to sing together, Schoeffler took over the missing baritone's part. When Guarrera saw an unobtrusive opportunity for going on stage, he cheerily did so and the performance continued at full complement.

Perhaps the most exciting news of the Los Angeles season was the size and enthusiasm of the *Wozzeck* audience. Such an esoteric opera seen by a multitude in the blatantly unintimate surroundings of the Shrine may seem incongruous. But the facts of the matter are now pleasant history.

14

THE COSMOPOLITAN STORY

At the end of the chapter titled *The Pacific Story*, it was suggested that a collision between the San Francisco Opera and the Cosmopolitan was not impossible. Stars became increasingly important to the Shindell-managed operation. In 1956 some older singers of large fame such as Sayao, Baccaloni and Baum were on his roster, along with Brenda Lewis, Herva Nelli, Regina Resnik and Cesare Bardelli. With these artists at $3.50 top the Cosmopolitan filled houses while the Pacific, with less lustre at $2.50 top, did not do so well. Obviously there wasn't room for *three* companies altogether, and the Pacific died. Cosmopolitan continued on its course of bigger and better stars, the production aspects remaining at a generally unimaginative, old-fashioned, low-budget level. Eccentricities of production—like a real trained bear in *Bohême*—were sometimes thrown in as extras, but dubious ones they were.

Milanov, Valletti and Vinay came in 1957, and *Turandot*, planned for that year's fall season by the San Francisco company, was scooped off the shelf and placed in the Cosmopolitan's late winter proceedings. The rising Cornell MacNeil was added in 1958, and the following year Tucker came along, to be paid $2,500 per performance. This was $750 more than the San Francisco's top price, and considerably more than the Metropolitan pays most of its top artists. There was, of course, the problem of inducing singers of Tucker's repute to appear with a company of small reputation, but this sheer financial abandon reached unbelievable proportions in 1960 when Bjoerling was paid $4,000 a night.

There were eight performances in 1959, a dozen in 1960, and 1961 plans called for more than that. A fantastic list of tenors was lined up: Bjoerling, Tucker, Del Monaco, DiStefano and Carlo Bergonzi. Not to mention Birgit Nilsson, Simionato, Stevens and Fausto Cleva. Nilsson was to get $5,000 (!), Del Monaco $3,500, Stevens $3,000 and Bergonzi $2,500. This season never came to pass, however.

Most of these artists had appeared with the San Francisco, and Shindell tried to persuade others from Adler's stable to run in his league at stratospheric fees. Meanwhile, a largely new audience was hearing performances that often boasted fine singing but rarely the delights of good ensemble or true spirit from the conductor's stand. Repertoire remained almost totally standard, and since the budget was not weighted in favor of much rehearsal time, no operas outside the San Francisco's repertoire—barring *Hänsel and Gretel*—were presented. Members of the San Francisco Opera Chorus formed the Cosmopolitan Chorus, and the new company had to stick to what they knew.

The Cosmopolitan developed some new opera lovers and served the public—but if the stars in the later years were caviar, the production was peanuts, and often this did not constitute a well-balanced operatic meal.

The San Francisco company was suspicious of the Cosmopolitan's aspirations and was not about to let the smaller troupe use its scenery as suggested. Obviously the mixture of big stars, big company scenery and small company prices was a danger. As Miller said when his company was accused of trying to stifle the Cosmopolitan, "It's necessary to protect our interests since low-priced opera comes into direct competition with our lower scale seats."

While Shindell continued to raise his fees, and the top ticket price rose to $4.90 (the San Francisco's price for balcony seats on Thursday and Saturday nights is now $3.75), Campbell McGregor, holder of the Cosmopolitan purse strings, left the purse wide open. So the deficit was approximately $70,000 in 1959, and more in 1960. Mr. McGregor picked up the tab, as he liked to do. Shortly after the 1948 rejuvenation of the Pacific company, McGregor had discouraged a broad base of backing, and the single angel idea continued when he founded the Cosmopolitan. The Company's fortunes, then, depended on one man alone. Without him, Cosmopolitan could not exist, short of drastic reorganization.

On April 11, 1960, just after the season's close, the explosion came. McGregor announced he was withdrawing his financial support. The decision came as a surprise to just about everybody. Members of the board of directors met April 26 and voted to liquidate. There was no choice at that point.

One of the more concerned directors, Mrs. Leon Cuenin, spoke of the possibility of reorganizing. Neither the name of the company nor the scenery, it developed, would be available to her. As Mrs. Cuenin told the press: "Early last season I tried to organize a group of sponsors to assume some of the financial responsibility. I wanted a basis upon which the company could survive in case anything happened to Mr. McGregor. But when he heard about it he hit the ceiling. He said, 'When I die, Cosmopolitan dies.' "

The sudden ending of the Cosmopolitan is typical of the meteoric history of this organization. It provided what may well be the most interesting case of operatic rivalry in American history since the days when Gatti-Casazza and Hammerstein were operating a few blocks away from each other in New York. (The San Francisco and the Cosmopolitan both performed under the same roof.)

When Mrs. Cuenin with her friend Mrs. William Woods Adams called a meeting of persons interested in opera on June 16, 1960, the purpose was to form a second company to succeed the Cosmopolitan, albeit with more modest intentions. But at least two persons—William Kent III, a young businessman and opera lover, and the author—left the meeting with the feeling that San Francisco could afford more opera performances but not more companies and the possible attendant rivalry. James Schwabacher, a San Francisco business executive, and professional singer and music commentator, felt the same way. As the result of discussion among the three, Schwabacher suggested that a sponsoring group be formed to raise money and go to the San Francisco Opera and ask that it produce a spring season of appropriate character. There was obviously no point in having two separate sets of scenery, and music and administrative staff when the San Francisco Opera had all at its disposal.

Kent approached Miller, who said he was interested in the idea of a spring season but had not wanted to add any new financial burdens to the regular guarantors. But what if the money were raised independently by a new group, asked Kent? After a good deal of caution, Miller agreed that if a new group raised $40,000—$30,000 of it to cover the deficit of six performances in 1961 and $10,000 of it as a head-start for 1962 or a cushion against error in budgeting for 1961—well, then, the matter could probably be worked out. Meanwhile, Schwabacher talked to Adler, who had long been interested in producing spring seasons. And Mrs. Cuenin was interested in forgetting old rivalries and joining in a united operatic front for San Francisco— to provide a double bill of yearly artistic fare, as it were, aimed at servicing two different needs: that for biggest-league international opera in the fall, and that for low-budget yet imaginative opera in the spring.

By July 13 the official announcement was ready. Spring Opera of San Francisco had been organized. It would raise money to initiate spring seasons produced by the San Francisco Opera. Kent was named chairman of the Spring Opera executive committee, and a small artistic advisory committee was set up to consult with Adler in maintaining the appropriate policy for the spring. Repertoire would be mostly standard, it was decided, but fresh, light revivals were also indicated —and new productions when possible. Obviously, California singers would have more opportunities than the Cosmopolitan had seen fit to dispense. There would be no expensive stars.

In August, Shindell launched a surprise solicitation for funds to start a Cosmos Opera presenting his big stars, and the literature implied that the Spring Opera program was doomed to failure. But a promised financial status report did not materialize and no Cosmos season was forthcoming in San Francisco. On December 19 the directors of the San Francisco Opera Association unanimously approved collaboration with the Spring Opera and the task of raising the last two fifths of the goal was undertaken. As the year ended the future was not sure, but it seemed likely indeed that ultimately the Spring Opera season would grow in size and provide the San Francisco Opera with a way of taking more of its worthwhile productions out of the warehouse in a given year than has been the case. At all events, with the springtime affiliate launched, San Francisco could boast of an intelligent effort to take care of its unusually wide operatic needs. The line from Pacific to Cosmopolitan to Spring Opera appeared to be happily drawn, and for the public it had started off in a happy new direction.

Specifically, Spring Opera opened a six-opera, seven-performance season at the Opera House on May 2 with a graceful, stylish and consistently well-balanced production of Gounod's *Romeo and Juliet*. It greatly pleased a near-sellout audience and realized the fondest hopes of the founders. The utter believability and girlish charm of Lee Venora as Juliet, the elegant, free-topped lyricism of Richard Verreau, the youthful light baritone of Richard Fredricks, the glowingly sonorous bass of John Macurdy as Friar Lawrence: these were exciting elements in a performance which benefited greatly from Joseph Rosenstock's crisp, tender conducting—in the same class as Steinberg's classic *Faust*—and the tight, suspenseful stage direction of Allen Fletcher. Six West Coast singers were on stage that night, notably Janis Martin, Donald Drain and Margot Blum, and the season as a whole stressed opportunities for young singers from all over the United States. The 1937 *Romeo* set, modern for its day, looked fresh.

The season continued with a youthful *Bohême* freshly staged by

Matthew Farruggio.[1] It started Venora and George Shirley, a young Negro with a tenor voice of glowing dark timbre and a style as polished and elegant as Verreau's. The Spring Opera had engaged him a few months *before* he won the Metropolitan Auditions and a contract at that house. *Martha*, performed in a commendably non-streamlined English translation, was hardly brilliant vocally, but the utter lack of pretension in Fletcher's staging, and the helpful mixture of economy and imagination in the scenic trappings—there were no "built" sets—were noteworthy. *Traviata* brought home local girl Mary Gray from the West Berlin Opera for a successful enactment of Violetta, and Henry Lewis, a young conductor from Los Angeles (Marilyn Horne's husband, as a matter of fact) offered what may be the most sensitive and sparkling *Traviata* ever heard at the War Memorial. The possibilities for continuity between fall and spring seasons were stressed in Miss Horne's assignment as Carmen in a vivid performance of the old favorite staged by Irving Guttman of the Vancouver Opera.

The standards were high, and with few exceptions they were attained throughout the season. But the greatest praise must be reserved for the totally new production of *The Magic Flute* staged by San Francisco's Vincent Porcaro. Working with a unit set including some steps, a smiling scrim and a central pavilion, and utilizing a wide range of lighting effects, he kept his show moving with effortless pace. He reconciled the disconcerting counterpoints of the fantastic libretto by keeping the folk comedy from getting raucous and the solemnity from turning dull. There were all manner of delightful bits of business, in particular the little animals tiptoeing around the stage as Tamino played his flute, and the wooden dance of Monostatos' bow-legged cohorts, not to mention the dragon from Chinatown. The use of boys for the three genie was a happy thought which may be credited to Adler, and the eighteenth-century costuming can be defended as a logical enough escape from the exotic mish-mash of geography implied by the libretto. It remains to be stated that the witty, precise conducting of Rosenstock resulted in some of the best Mozart ever heard in the Opera House, and the cast—led by Doris Yarick, Luisa De Sett, Shirley, Drain, Macurdy, Spiro Malas, Robert Schmorr, Gwen Curatilo, Patricia Cann, Martin and Blum—was almost uniformly excellent.

The season was happily concluded. Four houses were sold out, and one came within one hundred seats of capacity, making the score of

---

[1] The sets were the old pre-Jenkins ones, but Farruggio, Adler's chief aide, was proclaimed a hero for "chopping down" the third act tree many a Mimi had hid behind. A more earthy pile of crates became her barrier.

success high. Spring Opera had proven a revolutionary point: that low-budget opera can be well-balanced and stylish, and even theatrically electrifying in performance. The budget rerouted the money from Bjoerling-type fees for rehearsals, and the sacrifice was slim indeed as one vocal discovery after another took to the stage. There was a pointed message for the fall season: no longer would the occasional importation of a second-rater from abroad be justified when young Americans of quality were available. Actually, the difference between the fall and spring seasons, it developed, would be more a difference of repertoire than vocal level. Obviously, the reduced forces of the Spring Opera would not be appropriate for a *Meistersinger*, a *Boris*, an *Aida* or a *Wozzeck*, but the special qualities of the spring ensemble indicated that intimate French operas and Mozart *singspiels*, in particular, had found a good home—an Opéra-Comique or Volksoper quality pervaded the whole happy experiment.

15 ✷

FINALE

The San Francisco Opera went into 1961 with a long record of achievement.

One could list, for instance, the American premieres of Strauss' *Die Frau Ohne Schatten*, Poulenc's *The Dialogues of the Carmelites*, Ravel's *L'Enfant et les Sortileges*, Walton's *Troilus and Cressida*, Orff's *Die Kluge* and Cherubini's *The Portuguese Inn*, all works of value. And the American stage premieres of Honegger's *Joan of Arc at the Stake*, Orff's *Carmina Burana* and Cherubini's *Medea*, such notable rare revivals as those of Boito's *Mefistofele*, the complete Puccini *Trittico* and Ravel's *L'Heure Espagnole*.

One could also list the American debuts of Ingrid Bjoner, Inge Borkh, Rosanna Carteri, Floriana Cavalli, Boris Christoff, Anselmo Colzani, Mario Del Monaco, Geraint Evans, Leyla Gencer, Tito Gobbi, Sena Jurinac, Sandor Konya, Richard Lewis, Max Lichtegg, Janine Micheau, Giuseppe Modesti, Birgit Uilsson, Rolando Panerai, Gotthelf Pistor, Leonie Rysanek, Giulietta Simionato, Ebe Stignani, Rita Streich, Giuseppe Taddei, Renata Tebaldi, Hertha Toepper, Rosina Torri, Cesare Valletti, Arnold Van Mill, Gaetano Viviani, and Giuseppe Zantieri. And there have been other new singers. Not to mention conductors Leopold Ludwig, Francesco Molinari-Pradelli, Georg Solti and Silvio Varviso.

One could note the promoting of such California singers as Josephine Tumminia, George Stinson, Dorothy Warenskjold, Claramae Turner, Katherine Hilgenberg and Heinz Blankenburg, and the opportunities given Americans from Europe like Richard Martell, Eugene Tobin and Robert Anderson.

One could mention the important place given by the San Francisco to star singers such as Leontyne Price, Eileen Farrell, Mary Costa and Elisabeth Schwarzkopf, who had not sung at the Met.

One could recall Jeritza's first Salome in America, the first *Siegfried* Brünnhilde of Flagstad's career, Martinelli's first Otello, Tibbett's first

Iago, Tebaldi's first Amelia, Price's first Elvira, Kirsten's first Tosca, Peerce's first Turiddu, Vinay's first Tristan, Albanese's first Desdemona, and then Journet's thousandth Mephistopheles, Lehmann's last Marschallin.

Naturally, one could also cite the omissions, the mistakes, the lapses. This book has taken them up. But the amount of growth and the regularity of uninterrupted activity are not to be questioned. Today the company has more new spirit, look and ideas than ever before—it is pressing onward to modernize as fully as possible. In 1960 more than half the productions were either brand new or less than six years old.

In 1961 the San Francisco Opera is presenting Norman Dello Joio's "Blood Moon," its first American opera since *Emperor Jones*, and its first world premiere. Thanks to the Ford Foundation, financial help for the special new undertaking will be available. Under the terms of a $950,000 appropriation, the San Francisco Opera has joined the two companies of New York and the one of Chicago in a plan whereby at least eighteen new operas will be produced in the next eight years. The hope is that the Metropolitan, Chicago and San Francisco will each produce one every other year; there will be more at the City Center. The foundation money is not a grant but an allotment. It can be used for extra rehearsal costs, stage production costs and to compensate the box office for additional revenue it might take in with a tried and popular bill. (Probably San Francisco audiences would be curious about such undertakings, however, and Ford money might well not be needed on that account.)

It might be pointed out that the generous Ford project reflected an interest originally displayed by Adler in a letter to the foundation written in January, 1958. He has always been especially interested in doing new things, and in doing old things in new ways. All this doing takes time. That is why the Opera House is available to the company a month before the season now—Adler has seen to that. The tight schedule of performances has always meant that a great deal must be done in a short time, but the possibilities for rehearsing novelties are somewhat greater than in the old days.

The production picture is bright. But this does not mean the company feels it has all the facilities needed to lubricate the engine of modernization properly. The Opera House is a beautiful house, in many respects commodious for the patron, producer and performer. The company enjoys it. But lighting equipment needs replacement, the freight elevators are inadequate for materials which now have to be precariously hoisted to the flies, and would that the architects had found a place and the trustees the money for a rehearsal stage. Another building close by with shops, warehouse and rehearsal space would be an ideal modern answer to many present and future needs, and there is a possibility such a structure will be built to the west of the Opera House at some future date.

What about the public? There can be no question, judging from the few empty seats, that interest in opera in San Francisco, Los Angeles and other communities visited by the company is running high. The 1960 schedule included thirty performances in San Francisco, eighteen in Los Angeles, three in San Diego, and one each in Berkeley and Sacramento. The total of fifty-three is nearly twice that of the Chicago Opera, the second largest company outside New York. There is no reason to believe this is too many. Average capacity at home was ninety-six per cent. On the highest price level, a long line waits for openings in the boxes in San Francisco: they don't occur often. Orchestra seats in the Opera House are now $10 for regular series performances, $7.75 other evenings.[1] The balcony is $4 for regular series performances, $3.75 other evenings. At all ranges there is a sure audience to virtually sell out two performances of any opera except such occasional rarities as *Louise* and *Orfeo*. *Bohème* can sell more, but also *Don Carlo*. Casting tips balances.

The purpose of the San Francisco Opera has always been to offer an international festival season—a policy nicely complemented now by that of the Volksoper-like Spring Opera. The senior company's purpose in 1961 was, more than ever, to do important things, to be on the operatic map as a creative outpost. The prospectus for the 1961 season bore witness to this spirit, with its inclusion of Dello Joio's opera in world premiere performances; Benjamin Britten's *A Midsummer Night's Dream*—this a United States premiere with sets on loan from the Vancouver Festival; the company's first performances of Verdi's *Nabucco*, made possible by a gift from the America-Italy Society of San Francisco and the Festival of Faith and Freedom Foundation; and a new production of Mozart's *The Marriage of Figaro* designed by Bauer-Ecsy. A number of American debuts were listed. The number of American singers from Europe swelled.

Artistic matters aside, the 1961 season will probaby take its place in the annals as one of the most precious, for the very reason that it almost did not come to pass. During the month of April, 1961, the San Francisco Opera went through what may well be the most agonizing crisis in its history: a protracted union-management dispute. The deficit after the *Ring* cycle of 1935 cast some shadow, the 1939 artists'

[1] Top price in Los Angeles is $7.

list was reduced by the procrastinations of the Italian government, the entrance of the United States into the Second World War brought doubts about going on, the Metropolitan invasion of Los Angeles in the late forties was difficult, and the Flagstad affair seriously threatened the 1949 season. But somehow the company had never missed its date with a fond audience. In April, 1961 one began to wonder, though, if the capacity for weathering storms had not reached the breaking point.

The company had hoped to announce its plans for the autumn about the first of April. But negotiations with The American Guild of Musical Artists (AGMA), representing the chorus, ballet and salaried singers, resulted in no contract after three months of intermittent talks. The Association was willing to grant a salary increase, but not the union's demand for unemployment insurance.

Repeatedly AGMA demanded the unemployment insurance. Just as assertively the Association repeated its stand. Such coverage, optional according to state law for a non-profit institution, must be paid to all company employees if it is paid to one, and, as Miller stated in a letter to the Board of Governors on March 29, "Our current income and potential resources of all sorts could not meet an increase of expenditure of this magnitude." And, furthermore, he noted: "Only a small number of AGMA members and other opera employees would benefit from this insurance coverage since most are protected through employment elsewhere."

The president told the governors AGMA had held up necessary rehearsals during the negotiations and, he concluded, if the demands were not promptly and substantially reduced, he would be forced to recommend, most reluctantly, the suspension of operations for 1961.

The cloud hung over the Opera House for three and a half weeks. The talks stopped for several days, an editorial called for Mayor Christopher—a savior in the 1949 Flagstad crisis—to move in, and the agony continued. Talks resumed, were fruitless again. Symphony men started worrying about the fate of the autumn employment which gives them a vital income for almost three months' work outside of the orchestra's season. A society editor wondered in print what would happen to the social season: it would be impossible to decide when it begins if there was no opera to open it.

Miller had set April 20 as deadline. The April 21 papers carried dismal stories of the talks having broken down on the unemployment insurance argument, and cancellation seemed sure. Miller, characteristically firm, called in his board and the season was officially cancelled by unanimous vote. More than that, if a contract for 1962 were not negotiated by September 1, 1961, the San Francisco Opera would be dissolved. It looked as if perhaps this book would serve as an obituary.

Yet San Franciscans considered such a turn of events—cancellation or dissolution—impossible, unthinkable. After all, they said, San Francisco is "The City That Knows How." The cliche proved as meaningful as ever when Mayor Christopher went into sudden action.

The announcement had come in the morning. The same afternoon Christopher called Miller and Adler into his office, then AGMA representatives. The following day, Saturday, April 22, a meeting of both sides began at 12:15 P.M. in the Mayor's office. There was discussion until about 3 P.M. and then the negotiators suggested a recess until the following day. Christopher answered, in effect, "Keep talking." And at 5:15 he emerged, weary but happy, to announce that an agreement had been reached—the Association had raised its salary increase offer from 5.5 to 6 per cent and the union had waived its unemployment insurance demand.

The crisis was over, reaffirming the deep belief of San Francisco's many opera fans that the death, or indisposition, of the company was unthinkable. Thirty-eight and still growing with pioneering vitality, the San Francisco Opera pulled itself together and faced the future with confidence.

There is no reason to believe the future does not promise excitements to equal those of the past. There will be disappointments, of course, and crises, no doubt, but the rhythm of achievement would be marked *crescendo*. That was the challenge, and, one strongly suspects, the challenge the company wanted.

COMPLETE
SAN FRANCISCO CASTS
1923—1960

CASTS—1923 SEASON

September 26: LA BOHEME (Puccini)   (gross: $14,592)
MIMI: Mario, RODOLFO: Martinelli, MARCELLO: Gandolfi, COLLINE: Didur, SCHAUNARD: D'Angelo, MUSETTA: Young, BENOIT: Ananian, ALCINDORO: Ananian, PARPIGNOL: Paltrinieri, SERGEANT: Corral, OFFICER: Alibertini, CONDUCTOR: Merola.

September 27: ANDREA CHENIER (Giordano)   (gross: $10,276)
MADELEINE: Saroya, ANDREA CHENIER: Gigli,[1] GERARD: DeLuca, MATHIEU: Didur,

[1] Harold Rosenthal, in his book *Two Centuries of Opera at Covent Garden*, points out that Gigli invariably chose *Chenier* for his debut in every major house. He did bow in this role in San Francisco in 1923 and upon his return after long absence in 1938. And in London in 1930.

FLEVILLE: D'Angelo, ROUCHER: D'Angelo, DUMAS: D'Angelo, ABBE: Paltrinieri, SPY: Paltrinieri, SCHMIDT: Ananian, FOUQUIER-TINVILLE: Ananian, COUNTESS: Johnstone, MADELON: Fernanda, BERSI: Lazelle, CONDUCTOR: Merola.

September 29, matinee: IL TABARRO (Puccini)   (gross: $12,320)
GIORGETTA: Saroya, LUIGI: Tokatyan, MICHELE: Gandolfi, TINCA: Paltrinieri, TALPA: Didur, SONG VENDOR: Frediani, FRUGOLA: Fernanda, CONDUCTOR: Merola.
         followed by: SUOR ANGELICA (Puccini)
SUOR ANGELICA: Saroya, PRINCESS: Fernanda, ABBESS: Johnstone, MISTRESS OF NOVICES: Eybel, ALMS COLLECTOR: Lazelle, SISTER GENEVIEVE: Young, SISTER OSMINA: Christoph, NOVICE: Monotti, CONVERTS: Ferguson, Badger, CONDUCTOR: Merola.
         followed by: GIANNI SCHICCHI (Puccini)
GIANNI SCHICCHI: DeLuca, RINUCCIO: Tokatyan, LAURETTA: Epton, SIMONE: Didur, BETTO: Ananian, GHERARDO: Paltrinieri, MARCO: D'Angelo, SPINELLOCCIO: Gillette, NOTARY: Frediani, PINELLINO: Corral, GUCCIO: Alibertini, ZITA: Fernanda, NELLA: Young, LA CIESCA: Lazelle, CONDUCTOR: Merola.

September 29: LA BOHEME (Puccini)   (gross: $12,500)
Same cast.

October 1: MEFISTOFELE (Boito)   (gross: $9,925)
MEFISTOFELE: Didur, FAUST: Gigli, MARGHERITA: Saroya, ELENA: Saroya, WAGNER: Paltrinieri, MARTHA: Fernanda, PANTALIS: Fernanda, CONDUCTOR: Merola.

October 2: TOSCA (Puccini)   (gross: $13,590)
TOSCA: Saroya, CAVARADOSSI: Martinelli, SCARPIA: DeLuca, SPOLETTA: Paltrinieri, SACRISTAN: Ananian, ANGELOTTI: D'Angelo, SCIARRONE: Corral, JAILOR: Alibertini, SHEPHERD: Johnstone, CONDUCTOR: Merola.
October 4: ROMEO AND JULIET (Gounod)   (gross: $12,126)
ROMEO: Gigli, JULIET: Mario, MERCUTIO: DeLuca, TYBALT: Paltrinieri, CAPULET: Didur, FRIAR LAWRENCE: D'Angelo, GREGORIO: Ananian, BENVOGLIO: Frediani, DUKE OF VERONA: Gillette, STEPHANO: Young, GERTRUDE: Johnstone, CONDUCTOR: Merola.
October 6 matinee: GIANNI SCHICCHI (Puccini)   (gross: $12,581)
Same cast except: RINUCCIO: Paltrinieri, GHERARDO: Frediani, NOTARY: Ordini.
    followed by: I PAGLIACCI (Leoncavallo)
CANIO: Martinelli, TONIO: DeLuca, NEDDA: Mario, SILVIO: Gandolfi, BEPPE: Paltrinieri, CONDUCTOR: Merola.
October 6: ANDREA CHENIER (Giordano)   (gross: $9,030)
Same cast except: GERARD: Gandolfi, SCHMIDT.
October 8: RIGOLETTO (Verdi)   (gross: $16,822)
GILDA: Mario, DUKE: Gigli, RIGOLETTO: DeLuca, MADDALENA: Fernanda, SPARAFUCILE: Didur, MONTERONE: D'Angelo, BORSA: Paltrinieri, MARULLO: Ananian, CEPRANO: Gillette, COUNTESS CEPRANO: Olmsted, GIOVANNA: Monotti, PAGE: Ferguson, CONDUCTOR: Merola.

CASTS—1924 SEASON

September 22: ANDREA CHENIER (Giordano)   (gross: $16,179)
MADELEINE: Muzio, ANDREA CHENIER: Gigli, GERARD: DeLuca, MATHIEU: Ananian, FLEVILLE: D'Angelo, ROUCHER: Seri, DUMAS: Gillette, ABBE: Oliviero, SPY: Oliviero, SCHMIDT: Gillette, FOUQUIER-TINVILLE: D'Angelo, COUNTESS: Shaffner, MADELON: Eybel, BERSI: DeVol, CONDUCTOR: Merola.
September 24: LA BOHEME (Puccini)   (gross: $13,132)
MIMI: Mario, RODOLFO: Gigli, MARCELLO: Picco, COLLINE: Seri, SCHAUNARD: D'Angelo, MUSETTA: Young, BENOIT: Ananian, ALCINDORO: Ananian, CONDUCTOR: Merola.
September 26: MADAMA BUTTERFLY (Puccini)   (gross: $11,345)
CIO-CIO-SAN: Sabanieeva, PINKERTON: Mojica, SHARPLESS: Picco, SUZUKI: I. Marlowe, GORO: Oliviero, BONZE: Ananian, YAMADORI: D'Angelo, COMMISSIONER: Gillette, KATE PINKERTON: Clifford, CONDUCTOR: Merola.
September 27: RIGOLETTO (Verdi)   (gross: $17,073)
GILDA: Mario, DUKE: Gigli, RIGOLETTO: DeLuca, MADDALENA: Bruntsch, SPARAFUCILE: Seri, MONTERONE: D'Angelo, BORSA: Oliviero, MARULLO: Ananian, CEPRANO: Gillette, COUNTESS CEPRANO: Olmsted, GIOVANNA: Monotti, PAGE: Ferguson, CONDUCTOR: Merola.
September 28, matinee: LA BOHEME (Puccini)   (gross: $3,355)
Same cast except: MIMI: Donnelly, RODOLFO: Mojica.
September 29: MANON (Massenet)   (gross: $14,500)
MANON: Sabanieeva, CHEVALIER DES GRIEUX: Schipa, LESCAUT: Picco, GUILLOT: A. Ferrier, DE BRETIGNY: D'Angelo, COUNT DES GRIEUX: Ananian, POUSETTE: Young, JAVOTTE: Newsom, ROSETTE: Shaffner, SERVANT: Moncla, GUARDS: Frediani, Feduloff, CONDUCTOR: Merola.
September 30: TOSCA (Puccini)   (gross: $16,021)
TOSCA: Muzio, CAVARADOSSI: Gigli, SCARPIA: DeLuca, SPOLETTA: Oliviero, SACRISTAN: Ananian, ANGELOTTI: Seri, SCIARRONE: D'Angelo, JAILOR: Gillette, SHEPHERD: Eybel, CONDUCTOR: Merola.

October 2: L'AMICO FRITZ (Mascagni)   (gross: $11,809)
SUZEL: Sabanieeva, FRITZ: Schipa, RABBINO: DeLuca, HANEZO: Ananian, FEDERICO: Oliviero, CATERINA: DeVol, BEPPE: Eybel, CONDUCTOR: Merola.
followed by: GIANNI SCHICCHI (Puccini)
GIANNI SCHICCHI: DeLuca, RINUCCIO: Mojica, LAURETTA: Donnelly, SIMONE: Seri, BETTO: Ananian, GHERARDO: Oliviero, MARCO: D'Angelo, SPINELLOCCIO: Gillette, NOTARY: A. Ferrier, PINELLINO: Frediani, GUCCIO: Alibertini, ZITA: Bruntsch, NELLA: Young, LA CIESCA: Lazelle, GHERARDINO: Olive Jones, CONDUCTOR: Merola.
October 3: Testimonial for Merola. *Madama Butterfly,* Act 1; *Manon, Act* 2; *Tosca,* Act 3; *Gianni Schicchi.* (Same casts.)
October 4: LA TRAVIATA (Verdi)   (gross: $19,615)
VIOLETTA: Muzio, ALFREDO: Schipa, GERMONT: DeLuca, GASTON: Oliviero, BARON DOUPHOL: D'Angelo, MARQUIS D'OBIGNY: Ananian, DR. GRENVIL: Seri, FLORA: Young, ANNINA: Monotti, CONDUCTOR: Merola.

CASTS—1925 SEASON

September 19: MANON (Massenet)
MANON: Torri, CHEVALIER DES GRIEUX: Schipa, LESCAUT: Nicolich, GUILLOT: Oliviero, DE BRETIGNY: Argall, COUNT DES GRIEUX: Journet, POUSETTE: Young, JAVOTTE: Newsom, ROSETTE: Cross, INNKEEPER: Vogel, SERGEANT: Frediani, CONDUCTOR: Merola.
September 21: SAMSON AND DELILAH (Saint-Saens)
SAMSON: Ansseau, DELILAH: D'Alvarez, HIGH PRIEST: Journet, ABIMELECH: Nicolich, OLD HEBREW: Vogel, MESSENGER: Oliviero, PHILISTINES: Frediani, Argall, CONDUCTOR: Cimini.
September 24: THE BARBER OF SEVILLE (Rossini)
ROSINA: DeHidalgo, COUNT ALMAVIVA: Schipa, FIGARO: Stracciari, BARTOLO: Trevisan, BASILIO: Journet, FIORELLO: Oliviero, OFFICER: Oliviero, BERTHA: Marlo, CONDUCTOR: Cimini.
September 26, matinee: ANIMA ALLEGRA (Vittadini)
CONSUELO: Torri, PEDRO: Cortis, DON ELIGIO: Trevisan, DONNA SACRAMENTO: Witter, CORALITO: Young, FRASQUITA: Elkus, CARMEN: Monotti, MARIQUITA: Golcher, LUCIO: Attilio Vannucci, TONIO: Oliviero, DIEGO: Nicolich, GYPSY: Argall, YOUNG MAN: Frediani, RAMMIREZ: Alibertini, CANTOR: Regoli, AURORA: Michelini, CONDUCTOR: Merola.
September 26: SAMSON AND DELILAH (Saint-Saens)
Same cast.
September 28: LA TRAVIATA (Verdi)   (Auspices Italy America Society)
VIOLETTA: DeHidalgo, ALFREDO: Schipa, GERMONT: Stracciari, GASTON: Oliviero, BARON DOUPHOL: Nicolich, MARQUIS D'OBIGNY: Argall, DR. GRENVIL: Trevisan, FLORA: Young, ANNINA: Monotti, CONDUCTOR: Merola.
September 30: MARTHA (Flotow)
LADY HARRIET: DeHidalgo, LIONEL: Schipa, PLUNKETT: Journet, SIR TRISTAN: Trevisan, SHERIFF: Wright, NANCY: Marlo, MOLLY: Badger, POLLY: Ferguson, BETTY: Monotti, FARMER'S WIFE: Darrow, CONDUCTOR: Cimini.
October 1: THE BARBER OF SEVILLE (Rossini) (Testimonal for Merola)
Same cast.
October 2: L'AMORE DEI TRE RE (Montemezzi)
FIORA: Torri, AVITO: Ansseau, MANFREDO: Stracciari, ARCHIBALDO: Journet, FLAMINIO: Oliviero, YOUTH: Frediani, OLD WOMAN: Marlo, YOUNG GIRL: Newsom, SERVANT: Farncroft, CONDUCTOR: Merola.

October 3, matinee: MANON (Massenet)
Same cast.
October 3: AIDA (Verdi)
AIDA: Muzio, AMNERIS: D'Alvarez, RHADAMES: Cortis, AMONASRO: Formichi, RAMFIS: Journet, KING: Nicolich, MESSENGER: Oliviero, PRIESTESS: Eybel, CONDUCTOR: Merola.
October 4, matinee: TOSCA (Puccini)
TOSCA: Muzio, CAVARADOSSI: Ansseau, SCARPIA: Stracciari, SPOLETTA: Oliviero, SACRISTAN: Trevisan, ANGELOTTI: Nicolich, SCIARRONE: Nicolich, JAILOR: Alibertini, SHEPHERD: Eybel, CONDUCTOR: Merola.

CASTS—1926 SEASON

September 21: MARTHA (Flotow)
LADY HARRIET: Macbeth, LIONEL: Schipa, PLUNKETT: Journet, SIR TRISTAN: Trevisan, SHERIFF: Wright, NANCY: Marlo, FARMER'S WIFE: Polidori, CONDUCTOR: Cimini.
September 23: FAUST (Gounod)
MARGUERITE: Donnelly, FAUST: Althouse, MEPHISTOPHELES: Journet, VALENTIN: Defrere, WAGNER: Nicolich, SIEBEL: Badger, MARTHE: Marlo, CONDUCTOR: Merola.
September 25: THE BARBER OF SEVILLE (Rossini)
ROSINA: Macbeth, COUNT ALMAVIVA: Schipa, FIGARO: Bonelli, BARTOLO: Trevisan, BASILIO: Journet, FIORELLO: Oliviero, OFFICER: Oliviero, BERTHA: Marlo, CONDUCTOR: Cimini.
September 27: SAMSON AND DELILAH (Saint-Saens)
SAMSON: C. Marshall, DELILAH: Homer, HIGH PRIEST: Journet, ABIMELECH: Nicolich, OLD HEBREW: Vogel, MESSENGER: Oliviero, PHILISTINE: Frediani, CONDUCTOR: Cimini.
September 28: MANON LESCAUT (Puccini)
MANON LESCAUT: Muzio, CHEVALIER DES GRIEUX: Cortis, LESCAUT: Defrere, GERONTE: Trevisan, EDMONDO: Oliviero, DANCING MASTER: Oliviero, LAMPLIGHTER: Oliviero, HAIRDRESSER: Frediani, CAPTAIN: Vogel, MUSICIAN: Fremont, CONDUCTOR: Merola.
September 29: RIGOLETTO (Verdi)
GILDA: Melius, DUKE: Schipa, RIGOLETTO: Bonelli, MADDALENA: Marlo, SPARAFUCILE: Journet, MONTERONE: Nicolich, BORSA: Oliviero, MARULLO: Vogel, CEPRANO: Alibertini, COUNTESS CEPRANO: E. Smith, GIOVANNA: Farncroft, CONDUCTOR: Cimini.
October 1: AIDA (Verdi)
AIDA: Muzio, AMNERIS: Meisle, RHADAMES: Cortis, AMONASRO: Bonelli, RAMFIS: Journet, KING: Nicolich, MESSENGER: Regoli, PRIESTESS: Knierr, CONDUCTOR: Merola.
October 2: FRA DIAVOLO (Auber)
FRA DIAVOLO: Schipa, ZERLINA: Macbeth, LORD RICHBURG: Trevisan, LADY PAMELA: Marlo, LORENZO: Bulotti, MATTEO: Vogel, BEPPO: Oliviero, GIACOMO: Lazzari, CONDUCTOR: Cimini.
October 3, matinee: LA BOHEME (Puccini)
MIMI: Muzio, RODOLFO: Cortis, MARCELLO: Bonelli, COLLINE: Journet, SCHAUNARD: Nicolich, MUSETTA: Donnelly, BENOIT: Trevisan, ALCINDORO: Trevisan, CONDUCTOR: Merola.
October 4: TOSCA (Puccini)
TOSCA: Muzio, CAVARADOSSI: Cortis, SCARPIA: Journet, SPOLETTA: Oliviero,

SACRISTAN: Trevisan, ANGELOTTI: Nicolich, SCIARRONE: Nicolich, JAILOR: Alibertini, SHEPHERD: Huff, CONDUCTOR: Merola.

October 5: LUCIA DI LAMMERMOOR (Donizetti)
LUCIA: Melius, LORD HENRY: Bonelli, EDGARDO: Schipa, LORD ARTHUR: Regoli, RAYMOND: Nicolich, ALICE: Badger, NORMAN: Carcione, CONDUCTOR: Cimini.

October 6: IL TROVATORE (Verdi)
LEONORA: Muzio, AZUCENA: Meisle, MANRICO: Lindi, COUNT DI LUNA: Bonelli, FERRANDO: Nicolich, RUIZ: Messina, OLD GYPSY: Guenter, INEZ: Knierr, CONDUCTOR: Merola.

CASTS—1927 SEASON

September 15: MANON LESCAUT (Puccini)
MANON LESCAUT: Peralta, CHEVALIER DES GRIEUX: Martinelli, LESCAUT: Scotti, GERONTE: D'Angelo, EDMONDO: Bada, DANCING MASTER: Oliviero, CAPTAIN: Sperry, MUSICIAN: Fremont, SERGEANT: Guenter, INNKEEPER: Alibertini, CONDUCTOR: Merola.

September 16: TRISTAN AND ISOLDE (Wagner)
ISOLDE: Alsen, BRANGÄNE: Meisle, TRISTAN: Laubenthal, KING MARKE: Patton, KURWENAL: Amato, MELOT: Picco, SHEPHERD: Oliviero, SAILOR'S VOICE: Bada, STEERSMAN: D'Angelo, CONDUCTOR: Hertz.

September 17: TOSCA (Puccini)
TOSCA: Roselle, CAVARADOSSI: Chamlee, SCARPIA: Scotti, SPOLETTA: Bada, SACRISTAN: Defrere, ANGELOTTI: D'Angelo, SCIARRONE: D'Angelo, JAILOR: Alibertini, SHEPHERD: Huff, CONDUCTOR: Merola.

September 19: TURANDOT (Puccini)
TURANDOT: Roselle, LIU: Donnelly, CALAF: Tokatyan, TIMUR: Pinza, PING: Picco, PANG: Bada, PONG: Oliviero, EMPEROR ALTOUM: Pilcher, MANDARIN: Sperry, PRINCE OF PERSIA: Kostin, MAIDS: Susulich, Chapman, CONDUCTOR: Merola.

September 20: ROMEO AND JULIET (Gounod)
ROMEO: Chamlee, JULIET: Macbeth, MERCUTIO: Defrere, TYBALT: Bada, CAPULET: D'Angelo, FRIAR LAWRENCE: Pinza, GREGORIO: Keaumoku, BENVOGLIO: Carcione, DUKE OF VERONA: Sperry, STEPHANO: Estabrook, GERTRUDE: Ferguson, CONDUCTOR: Merola.

September 22: IL TROVATORE (Verdi)
LEONORA: Roselle, AZUCENA: Meisle, MANRICO: Martinelli, COUNT DI LUNA: Picco, FERRANDO: D'Angelo, RUIZ: Messina, OLD GYPSY: Tulagin, INEZ: E. Smith, CONDUCTOR: Cimini.

September 24: CAVALLERIA RUSTICANA (Mascagni)
SANTUZZA: Peralta, TURIDDU: Chamlee, ALFIO: Amato, LOLA: Marlo, MAMMA LUCIA: Karkova, CONDUCTOR: Cimini.
followed by: I PAGLIACCI (Leoncavallo)
CANIO: Martinelli, TONIO: Amato, NEDDA: Roselle, SILVIO: Picco, BEPPE: Bada, CONDUCTOR: Cimini.

September 25, matinee: TRISTAN AND ISOLDE (Wagner)
Same cast.

September 27: FALSTAFF (Verdi)
SIR JOHN FALSTAFF: Scotti, MISTRESS FORD: Peralta, MISTRESS PAGE: Marlo, DAME QUICKLY: Bourskaya, ANNE: Donnelly, FENTON: Tokatyan, FORD: Tibbett, DR. CAIUS: Bada, BARDOLPH: Oliviero, PISTOL: D'Angelo, CONDUCTOR: Merola.

September 28: AIDA (Verdi)
AIDA: Roselle, AMNERIS: Bourskaya, RHADAMES: Martinelli, AMONASRO: Amato, RAMFIS: Pinza, KING: D'Angelo, MESSENGER: Carcione, PRIESTESS: Knierr, CONDUCTOR: Cimini.

September 29: LA CENA DELLE BEFFE (Giordano)
GINEVRA: Peralta, LISABETTA: Donnelly, NERI: Tibbett, GIANNETTO: Tokatyan, GABRIELLO: Bada, TORNAQUINCI: D'Angelo, FAZIO: Picco, TRINCA: Oliviero, DOTTORE: Sperry, CALANDRA: Pisani, LAPO: Dini, LALDOMINE: Deeley, FIAM-METTA: Leo, CINTIA: Marlo, SINGER: Attilio Vannucci, CONDUCTOR: Cimini.

September 30: LA BOHEME (Puccini)
MIMI: Macbeth, RODOLFO: Chamlee, MARCELLO: Picco, COLLINE: Pinza, SCHAU-NARD: Defrere, MUSETTA: Seymour, BENOIT: Oliviero, ALCINDORO: Oliviero, SERGEANT: Alibertini, OFFICER: Wright, CONDUCTOR: Cimini.

October 1: CARMEN (Bizet)
CARMEN: Bourskaya, MICAELA: Donnelly, DON JOSE: Martinelli, ESCAMILLO: Defrere, ZUNIGA: D'Angelo, DANCAIRO: Oliviero, REMENDADO: Bada, MORALES: Picco, FRASQUITA: Leo, MERCEDES: Fremont, CONDUCTOR: Merola.

October 2, matinee: TURANDOT (Puccini)
Same cast.

CASTS—1928 SEASON

September 15: AIDA (Verdi)
AIDA: Rethberg, AMNERIS: Telva, RHADAMES: E. Johnson, AMONASRO: Tibbett, RAMFIS: Pinza, KING: D'Angelo, MESSENGER: Oliviero, PRIESTESS: Knierr, CON-DUCTOR: Merola.

September 17: LA CENA DELLE BEFFE (Giordano)
GINEVRA: Vettori, LISABETTA: Donnelly, NERI: Tibbett, GIANNETTO: Tokatyan, GABRIELLO: Bada, TORNAQUINCI: D'Angelo, FAZIO: Picco, TRINCA: Oliviero, DOTTORE: Sperry, CALANDRA: Guenter, LAPO: Dini, LALDOMINE: Elliott, FIAM-METTA: Stadtegger, CINTIA: Forno, SINGER: Attilio Vannucci, CONDUCTOR: Cimini.

September 19: TOSCA (Puccini)
TOSCA: Jeritza, CAVARADOSSI: Tokatyan, SCARPIA: Tibbett, SPOLETTA: Bada, SACRISTAN: Malatesta, ANGELOTTI: D'Angelo, SCIARRONE: D'Angelo, JAILOR: Alibertini, SHEPHERD: Huff, CONDUCTOR: Merola.

September 21: MADAMA BUTTERFLY (Puccini)
CIO-CIO-SAN: Rethberg, PINKERTON: Barra, SHARPLESS: Picco, SUZUKI: Telva, GORO: Oliviero, BONZE: D'Angelo, YAMADORI: Malatesta, COMMISSIONER: Sperry, KATE PINKERTON: Sewall, CONDUCTOR: Cimini.

September 22: TURANDOT (Puccini)
TURANDOT: Jeritza, LIU: Vettori, CALAF: Tokatyan, TIMUR: D'Angelo, PING: Picco, PANG: Bada, PONG: Oliviero, EMPEROR ALTOUM: Attilio Vannucci, MAN-DARIN: Sperry, PRINCE OF PERSIA: Bonnecaze, CONDUCTOR: Merola.

September 24: L'AMORE DEI TRE RE (Montemezzi)
FIORA: Vettori, AVITO: E. Johnson, MANFREDO: Tibbett, ARCHIBALDO: Pinza, FLAMINIO: Bada, YOUTH: Frediani, OLD WOMAN: Elliott, YOUNG GIRL: Sewall, SERVANT: Gionas, CONDUCTOR: Pelletier.

September 25: FEDORA (Giordano)
FEDORA: Jeritza, OLGA: Donnelly, LORIS: E. Johnson, DE SIRIEX: Danise, GRECH: D'Angelo, DESIRE: Oliviero, ROUVEL: Bada, BOROV: Picco, CIRILLO: Mercado, LOREK: Sperry, DMITRI: Gionas, LITTLE SAVOYARD: Ott, NICOLA: Alibertini, SERGIO: Frediani, CONDUCTOR: Merola.

September 27: ANDREA CHENIER (Giordano)
MADELEINE: Rethberg, ANDREA CHENIER: Barra, GERARD: Danise, MATHIEU: Malatesta, FLEVILLE: D'Angelo, ROUCHER: Picco, DUMAS: Sperry, ABBE: Oliviero, SPY: Bada, SCHMIDT: Sperry, FOUQUIER-TINVILLE: D'Angelo, COUNTESS: Grun-inger, MADELON: Telva, BERSI: Post, CONDUCTOR: Merola.

September 29, matinee: TOSCA (Puccini)
Same cast except: CAVARADOSSI: Barra, SCARPIA: Danise.
September 29: FAUST (Gounod)
MARGUERITE: Rethberg, FAUST: Tokatyan, MEPHISTOPHELES: Pinza, VALENTIN: Picco, WAGNER: D'Angelo, SIEBEL: Florence, MARTHE: Ferguson, CONDUCTOR: Cimini.
October 1: CARMEN (Bizet)
CARMEN: Jeritza, DON JOSE: Tokatyan, ESCAMILLO: Pinza, MICAELA: Donnelly, ZUNIGA: D'Angelo, DANCAIRO: Picco, REMENDADO: Bada, MORALES: Mercado, FRASQUITA: Chirot, MERCEDES: Ivey, CONDUCTOR: Pelletier.
October 3: CAVALLERIA RUSTICANA (Mascagni)
SANTUZZA: Vettori, TURIDDU: Barra, ALFIO: Mercado, LOLA: Gruninger, MAMMA LUCIA: Emery, CONDUCTOR: Cimini.
            followed by: I PAGLIACCI (Leoncavallo)
CANIO: E. Johnson, TONIO: Tibbett, NEDDA: Vettori, SILVIO: Mercado, BEPPE: Oliviero, PEASANTS: Dini, Wright, CONDUCTOR: Cimini.

CASTS—1929 SEASON

September 12: RIGOLETTO (Verdi)
GILDA: Mario, DUKE: Lauri-Volpi, RIGOLETTO: DeLuca, MADDALENA: Gruninger, SPARAFUCILE: Rothier, MONTERONE: D'Angelo, BORSA: Oliviero, MARULLO: Picco, CEPRANO: Sperry, COUNTESS CEPRANO: Perdue, GIOVANNA: E. Smith, PAGE: M. Smith, CONDUCTOR: Merola.
September 14, matinee: HANSEL AND GRETEL (Humperdinck)
HANSEL: Ivey, GRETEL: Mario, WITCH: Meisle, GERTRUDE: Gruninger, PETER: Sandrini, SANDMAN: Sewall, DEWMAN: Rivero, CONDUCTOR: K. Riedel.
September 14: THE ELIXIR OF LOVE (Donizetti)
ADINA: Morgana, NEMORINO: Schipa, BELCORE: Picco, DR. DULCAMARA: Malatesta, GIANNETTA: Bruni, CONDUCTOR: Cimini.
September 16: IL TROVATORE (Verdi)
LEONORA: Rethberg, AZUCENA: Meisle, MANRICO: Lauri-Volpi, COUNT DI LUNA: Danise, FERRANDO: Rothier, RUIZ: Oliviero, OLD GYPSY: Alibertini, INEZ: Romaine, CONDUCTOR: Merola.
September 18: THE BARBER OF SEVILLE (Rossini)
ROSINA: Morgana, COUNT ALMAVIVA: Schipa, FIGARO: DeLuca, BARTOLO: Malatesta, BASILIO: Rothier, FIORELLO: Sperry, OFFICER: Oliviero, BERTHA: Ivey, CONDUCTOR: Cimini.
September 20: LA BOHEME (Puccini)
MIMI: Rethberg, RODOLFO: Barra, MARCELLO: Danise, COLLINE: Rothier, SCHAUNARD: Picco, MUSETTA: Young, BENOIT: Sandrini, ALCINDORO: Malatesta, PARPIGNOL: Oliviero, CONDUCTOR: Cimini.
September 21: GIANNI SCHICCHI (Puccini)
GIANNI SCHICCHI: DeLuca, RINUCCIO: Barra, LAURETTA: Morgana, SIMONE: D'Angelo, BETTO: Picco, GHERARDO: Oliviero, MARCO: Sandrini, SPINELLOCCIO: Malatesta, NOTARY: A. Ferrier, PINELLINO: Alibertini, GUCCIO: Germanetti, ZITA: Gruninger, NELLA: Young, LA CIESCA: Ivey, CONDUCTOR: Merola.
            followed by: I PAGLIACCI (Leoncavallo)
CANIO: Lauri-Volpi, TONIO: DeLuca, NEDDA: Morgana, SILVIO: Picco, BEPPE: Oliviero, CONDUCTOR: Cimini.
September 23: MARTHA (Flotow)
LADY HARRIET: Mario, LIONEL: Schipa, PLUNKETT: DeLuca, SIR TRISTAN: Malatesta, SHERIFF: D'Angelo, NANCY: Ivey, MAIDS: Huff, Twigg, Treweck, FARMER: Wright, SERVANT: Sigond, CONDUCTOR: K. Riedel.

September 25: AIDA (Verdi)
AIDA: Rethberg, AMNERIS: Meisle, RHADAMES: Lauri-Volpi, AMONASRO: Danise, RAMFIS: Rothier, KING: Sandrini, MESSENGER: Oliviero, PRIESTESS: Post, CONDUCTOR: Merola.

September 27: DON PASQUALE (Donizetti)
NORINA: Morgana, ERNESTO: Schipa, DR. MALATESTA: DeLuca, DON PASQUALE: Malatesta, NOTARY: Oliviero, CONDUCTOR: Dell'Orefice.

September 28: FAUST (Gounod)
MARGUERITE: Rethberg, FAUST: Lauri-Volpi, MEPHISTOPHELES: Rothier, VALENTIN: Danise, WAGNER: Sandrini, SIEBEL: Torres, MARTHE: Ferguson, CONDUCTOR: Pelletier.

September 30: MANON (Massenet)
MANON: Mario, CHEVALIER DES GRIEUX: Schipa, LESCAUT: DeLuca, GUILLOT: Oliviero, DE BRETIGNY: Picco, COUNT DES GRIEUX: Rothier, INNKEEPER: A. Ferrier, CONDUCTOR: Merola.

CASTS—1930 SEASON

September 11: MANON (Massenet)
MANON: Mario, CHEVALIER DES GRIEUX: Gigli, LESCAUT: Picco, GUILLOT: Oliviero, DE BRETIGNY: Sandrini, COUNT DES GRIEUX: D'Angelo, POUSETTE: Elmassian, JAVOTTE: Hodge, ROSETTE: Ferguson, SERVANT: Torres, GUARD: Steger, CONDUCTOR: Merola.

September 12: SALOME (Strauss)
SALOME: Jeritza, HEROD: Rayner, JOKANAAN: J. C. Thomas, HERODIAS: Manski, NARRABOTH: J. Riedel, PAGE: Gruninger, SOLDIERS: D'Angelo, Sandrini, NAZARENES: T. Williams, Horton, JEWS: Paltrinieri, Oliviero, Caravacci, Steger, Picco, CONDUCTOR: Merola.

September 13: LA TRAVIATA (Verdi)
VIOLETTA: Clairbert, ALFREDO: Gigli, GERMONT: Viviani, GASTON: Paltrinieri, BARON DOUPHOL: D'Angelo, MARQUIS D'OBIGNY: Picco, DR. GRENVIL: Sandrini, FLORA: Bruni, ANNINA: Cioni, CONDUCTOR: Merola.

September 15: THE GIRL OF THE GOLDEN WEST (Puccini)
MINNIE: Jeritza, DICK JOHNSON: Jagel, JACK RANCE: Viviani, JAKE WALLACE: T. Williams, NICK: Oliviero, ASHBY: D'Angelo, SONORA: Picco, TRIN: Paltrinieri, SID: A. Ferrier, HANDSOME: Cozzi, HARRY: Caravacci, JOE: Fadem, HAPPY: Sellon, LARKENS: Sandrini, JOSE CASTRO: Sandrini, BILLY JACKRABBIT: Sandrini, WOWKLE: Marlo, CONDUCTOR: Merola.

September 17: LA BOHEME (Puccini)
MIMI: Mario, RODOLFO: Gigli, MARCELLO: Viviani, COLLINE: Pinza, SCHAUNARD: Picco, MUSETTA: Farncroft, BENOIT: Sandrini, ALCINDORO: Sandrini, PARPIGNOL: Oliviero, SERGEANT: Alibertini, CONDUCTOR: Dell'Orefice.

September 19: L'ENFANT ET LES SORTILÈGES (Ravel)
BOY: Mario, FIRE: Farncroft, PRINCESS: Farncroft, LARK: Farncroft, MOTHER: Gruninger, BUTTERFLY: Gruninger, ARMCHAIR: D'Angelo, TREE: D'Angelo, CLOCK: Picco, TOMCAT: Picco, TEAPOT: Oliviero, ARITHMETIC: A. Ferrier, FROG: Paltrinieri, SHEPHERD: Caravacci, SHEPHERDESSES: Kovaleff, Torres, SQUIRREL: Torres, LOUIS XV CHAIR: Torres, CAT: Ferguson, BAT: Dimitrieff, OWL: Gionas, CHINESE CUP: Strause, CONDUCTOR: Merola.

followed by: HANSEL AND GRETEL (Humperdinck)
HANSEL: Marlo, GRETEL: Mario, WITCH: Manski, GERTRUDE: Gruninger, PETER: Sandrini, SANDMAN: Zickhardt, DEWMAN: Elmassian, CONDUCTOR: K. Riedel.

September 20: CAVALLERIA RUSTICANA (Mascagni)
SANTUZZA: Jeritza, TURIDDU: Jagel, ALFIO: Picco, LOLA: Gruninger, MAMMA LUCIA: Gambi, CONDUCTOR: Dell'Orefice.
followed by: I PAGLIACCI (Leoncavallo)
CANIO: Rayner, TONIO: J. C. Thomas, NEDDA: Jeritza, SILVIO: Picco, BEPPE: Paltrinieri, PEASANTS: Alibertini, Dini, CONDUCTOR: Dell'Orefice.
September 22: MIGNON (Thomas)
MIGNON: Mario, PHILINE: Clairbert, WILHELM MEISTER: Gigli, LOTHARIO: Pinza, LAERTE: Paltrinieri, ANTONIO: Sandrini, GIARNO: Sandrini, FREDERIC: Marlo, CONDUCTOR: Pelletier.
September 23: TANNHÄUSER (Wagner)
ELISABETH: Jeritza, VENUS: Manski, TANNHÄUSER: Rayner, WOLFRAM: J. C Thomas. LANDGRAVE: Pinza, WALTHER: Paltrinieri, BITEROLF: Sandrini, HEINRICH: Oliviero, REINMAR: D'Angelo, SHEPHERD: Elmassian, CONDUCTOR: K. Riedel.
September 25: FAUST (Gounod)
MARGUERITE: Hampton, FAUST: Jagel, MEPHISTOPHELES: Pinza, VALENTIN: J. C. Thomas, WAGNER: Sandrini, SIEBEL: Torres, MARTHE: Ferguson, CONDUCTOR: Pelletier.
September 27, matinee: SALOME (Strauss)
Same cast.
September 27: LUCIA DI LAMMERMOOR (Donizetti)
LUCIA: Clairbert, LORD HENRY: Viviani, EDGARDO: Gigli, LORD ARTHUR: Oliviero, RAYMOND: D'Angelo, ALICE: Gambi, NORMAN: Paltrinieri, CONDUCTOR: Merola.

CASTS—1931 SEASON

September 10: MAROUF (Rabaud)
PRINCESS SAAMCHEDDINE: Gall, MAROUF: Chamlee, FATIMAH: Gruninger, SULTAN: D'Angelo, VIZIER: Sandrini, ALI: Picco, THE FELLAH: Windheim, MERCHANTS: Windheim, T. Williams, THE KADI: T. Williams, AHMAD: D'Angelo, DONKEY DRIVER: Oliviero, SEA CAPTAIN: Oliviero, MUZZEINS: Oliviero, Simondet, POLICEMEN: Julian, Radic, CONDUCTOR: Merola.
September 12: AIDA (Verdi)
AIDA: Rethberg, AMNERIS: Petrova, RHADAMES: Martinelli, AMONASRO: Danise, RAMFIS: D'Angelo, KING: Sandrini, MESSENGER: Oliviero, PRIESTESS: Linne, CONDUCTOR: Merola.
September 14: LOHENGRIN (Wagner)
ELSA: Müller, ORTRUD: Petrova, LOHENGRIN: Pistor, TELRAMUND: Schorr, KING HENRY: D'Angelo, HERALD: Gabor, CONDUCTOR: Blechschmidt.
September 16: ANDREA CHENIER (Giordano)
MADELEINE: Rethberg, ANDREA CHENIER: Martinelli, GERARD: Danise, MATHIEU: Sandrini, FLEVILLE: D'Angelo, ROUCHER: Picco, DUMAS: Picco, ABBE: Windheim, SPY: Oliviero, SCHMIDT: Sandrini, FOUQUIER-TINVILLE: D'Angelo, COUNTESS: Gruninger, MADELON: Petrova, BERSI: Ferguson, CONDUCTOR: Merola.
September 18: MADAMA BUTTERFLY (Puccini)
CIO-CIO-SAN: Müller, PINKERTON: Chamlee, SHARPLESS: deSegurola, SUZUKI: Petrova, GORO: Oliviero, BONZE: D'Angelo, YAMADORI: Sandrini, COMMISSIONER: Picco, KATE PINKERTON: D. Murphy, REGISTRAR: Alibertini, CONDUCTOR: Pelletier.
September 19: A MASKED BALL (Verdi)
AMELIA: Rethberg, ULRICA: Silva, OSCAR: Farncroft, RICCARDO: Martinelli, RENATO:

Danise, SAM: D'Angelo, TOM: Sandrini, JUDGE: Edmunds, SERVANT: Julian, CONDUCTOR: Cimini.

September 21: TOSCA (Puccini)
TOSCA: Gall, CAVARADOSSI: Chamlee, SCARPIA: Danise, SPOLETTA: Oliviero, SACRISTAN: Sandrini, ANGELOTTI: D'Angelo, SCIARRONE: Picco, JAILOR: Picco, SHEPHERD: Gruninger, CONDUCTOR: Cimini.

September 23: TANNHÄUSER (Wagner)
ELISABETH: Rethberg, VENUS: Castleton, TANNHÄUSER: Pistor, WOLFRAM: Schorr, LANDGRAVE: Pinza, WALTHER: Windheim, BITEROLF: Gabor, HEINRICH: Oliviero, REINMAR: D'Angelo, SHEPHERD: McLaughlin, CONDUCTOR: Blechschmidt.

September 25: LA BOHEME (Puccini)
MIMI: Müller, RODOLFO: Chamlee, MARCELLO: deSegurola, COLLINE: Pinza, SCHAUNARD: Picco, MUSETTA: Farncroft, BENOIT: Oliviero, ALCINDORO: Sandrini, PARPIGNOL: Oliviero, SERGEANT: Alibertini, OFFICER: G. Miller, CONDUCTOR: Dell'Orefice.

September 26: IL TROVATORE (Verdi)
LEONORA: Rethberg, AZUCENA: Silva, MANRICO: Martinelli, COUNT DI LUNA: Danise, FERRANDO: D'Angelo, RUIZ: Oliviero, OLD GYPSY: Alibertini, INEZ: Strause, CONDUCTOR: Merola.

September 28: DIE MEISTERSINGER (Wagner)
EVA: Müller, MAGDALENA: Gruninger, WALTHER: Pistor, HANS SACHS: Schorr, POGNER: Pinza, DAVID: Windheim, BECKMESSER: Gabor, KOTHNER: Picco, NIGHT WATCHMAN: Sandrini, VOGELGESANG: Steger, NACHTIGALL: D'Angelo, ZORN: Horton, EISSLINGER: Oliviero, MOSER: Simondet, ORTEL: T. Williams, SCHWARZ: Sellon, FOLTZ: Sandrini, CONDUCTOR: Blechschmidt.

September 29: CARMEN (Bizet)
CARMEN: Petrova, MICAELA: Farncroft, DON JOSE: Martinelli, ESCAMILLO: Pinza, ZUNIGA: D'Angelo, DANCAIRO: Picco, REMENDADO: Oliviero, MORALES: Gabor, FRASQUITA: Elmassian, MERCEDES: Gruninger, CONDUCTOR: Pelletier.

CASTS—1932 SEASON

October 15: TOSCA (Puccini)
TOSCA: Muzio, CAVARADOSSI: Borgioli, SCARPIA: Gandolfi, SPOLETTA: Windheim, SACRISTAN: D'Angelo, ANGELOTTI: Argall, SCIARRONE: D'Angelo, JAILOR: Sperry, SHEPHERD: Gruninger, CONDUCTOR: Merola.

October 17: LUCIA DI LAMMERMOOR (Donizetti)
LUCIA: Pons, LORD HENRY: Gandolfi, EDGARDO: Merli, LORD ARTHUR: R. Marlowe, RAYMOND: D'Angelo, ALICE: Bruni, NORMAN: Lanfranconi, CONDUCTOR: Merola.

October 18: DIE MEISTERSINGER (Wagner)
EVA: Müller, MAGDALENA: MacNevin, WALTHER: Chamlee, HANS SACHS: Schorr, POGNER: Pinza, DAVID: Windheim, BECKMESSER: Gabor, KOTHNER: Gandolfi, NIGHT WATCHMAN: Argall, VOGELGESANG: R. Marlowe, NACHTIGALL: D'Angelo, ZORN: Horton, EISSLINGER: Argall, MOSER: Simondet, ORTEL: T. Williams, SCHWARZ: Tibbe, FOLTZ: Eldredge, CONDUCTOR: Blechschmidt.

October 20: RIGOLETTO (Verdi)
GILDA: Pons, DUKE: Borgioli, RIGOLETTO: Bonelli, MADDALENA: Gruninger, SPARAFUCILE: Pinza, MONTERONE: D'Angelo, BORSA: Windheim, MARULLO: Argall, CEPRANO: Alibertini, COUNTESS CEPRANO: Linne, GIOVANNA: Bruni, PAGE: Dimitrieff, CONDUCTOR: Merola.

October 22, matinee: HANSEL AND GRETEL (Humperdinck)
HANSEL: Lothrop, GRETEL: Mario, WITCH: Meisle, GERTRUDE: MacNevin, PETER:

Gabor, SANDMAN: Sewall, DEWMAN: Malinoff, CONDUCTOR: Blechschmidt.
    followed by: LA VALSE and BOLERO ballets (Ravel)
THE DANCER (Bolero): E. Reed, CONDUCTOR: Merola.
October 22: CAVALLERIA RUSTICANA (Mascagni)
SANTUZZA: Muzio, TURIDDU: Chamlee, ALFIO: Gandolfi, LOLA: Gruninger,
MAMMA LUCIA: Gambi, CONDUCTOR: Merola.
    followed by: I PAGLIACCI (Leoncavallo)
CANIO: MacKenzie, TONIO: Bonelli, NEDDA: Muzio, SILVIO: Argall, BEPPE: Lan-
franconi, CONDUCTOR: Cimini.
October 23, matinee: LUCIA DI LAMMERMOOR (Donizetti)
Same cast except EDGARDO: Borgioli.
October 25: LOHENGRIN (Wagner)
ELSA: Müller, ORTRUD: Meisle, LOHENGRIN: Chamlee, TELRAMUND: Schorr, KING
HENRY: D'Angelo, HERALD: Gabor, CONDUCTOR: Blechschmidt.
October 27: FAUST (Gounod)
MARGUERITE: Mario, FAUST: Borgioli, MEPHISTOPHELES: Pinza, VALENTIN: Bonelli,
WAGNER: D'Angelo, SIEBEL: Malova, MARTHE: Gruninger, CONDUCTOR: Blech-
schmidt.
October 29: IL TROVATORE (Verdi)
LEONORA: Muzio, AZUCENA: Meisle, MANRICO: MacKenzie, COUNT DI LUNA:
Bonelli, FERRANDO: D'Angelo, RUIZ: Lanfranconi, OLD GYPSY: Alibertini, INEZ:
Strause, CONDUCTOR: Cimini.
October 30, matinee: DIE MEISTERSINGER (Wagner)
Same cast.
November 1: LA TRAVIATA (Verdi)
VIOLETTA: Muzio, ALFREDO: Borgioli, GERMONT: Bonelli, GASTON: Windheim,
BARON DOUPHOL: Argall, MARQUIS D'OBIGNY: Alibertini, DR. GRENVIL: D'Angelo,
FLORA: Malova, ANNINA: McLaughlin, CONDUCTOR: Merola.

CASTS—1933 SEASON

November 3: SAMSON AND DELILAH (Saint-Saens)
SAMSON: Martinelli, DELILAH: Van Gordon, HIGH PRIEST: Pinza, ABIMELECH:
D'Angelo, OLD HEBREW: Belarsky, MESSENGER: Oliviero, PHILISTINES: Simondet,
Eldredge, CONDUCTOR: Merola.
November 6: LE COQ D'OR (Rimsky-Korsakoff)
    Dance Pantomime with Vocal Accompaniment
Singers: QUEEN: Hardy, KING DODON: Stewart, ASTROLOGER: R. Marlowe, GEN-
ERAL: Eldredge, AMELFA: Leonard, VOICE OF COCK: Eybel, PRINCE GUIDON:
Frediani, BOYARS: Albert Vannucci, Levi, Dancers: QUEEN: Ruiz, KING DODON:
Bolm, ASTROLOGER: Bratoff, GENERAL: Vasilieff, AMELFA: Paulini, PRINCE GUIDON:
Charisse, PRINCE AFRON: Cooke, BOYARS: Kolodin, Romanoff, CONDUCTOR: Pel-
letier.
November 8: AIDA (Verdi)
AIDA: Muzio, AMNERIS: Meisle, RHADAMES: Martinelli, AMONASRO: Bonelli, RAM-
FIS: Pinza, KING: D'Angelo, MESSENGER: Oliviero, PRIESTESS: Folli, CONDUCTOR:
Merola.
November 10: TRISTAN AND ISOLDE (Wagner)
ISOLDE: Kappel, BRANGÄNE: Meisle, TRISTAN: Althouse, KING MARKE: Pinza, KUR-
WENAL: Bonelli, MELOT: Gandolfi, SHEPHERD: Oliviero, SAILOR'S VOICE: R. Mar-
lowe, STEERSMAN: D'Angelo, CONDUCTOR: Hertz.
November 12, matinee: SAMSON AND DELILAH (Saint-Saens)
Same cast.

November 14: MANON (Massenet)
MANON: Bori, CHEVALIER DES GRIEUX: Borgioli, LESCAUT: Gandolfi, GUILLOT: Oliviero, DE BRETIGNY: Stewart, COUNT DES GRIEUX: D'Angelo, CONDUCTOR: Pelletier.

November 17: THE SECRET OF SUZANNE (Wolf-Ferrari)
COUNTESS SUZANNE: Morgana, COUNT GIL: Gandolfi, SANTE: D'Angelo, CONDUCTOR: Dell'Orefice.

followed by: THE EMPEROR JONES (Gruenberg)
BRUTUS JONES: Tibbett, HENRY SMITHERS: R. Marlowe, OLD NATIVE WOMAN: Leonard, PULLMAN PORTER: E. Anderson, CONGO WITCH DOCTOR: Charisse, CONDUCTOR: Pelletier.

November 19, matinee: TRISTAN AND ISOLDE (Wagner)
Same cast.

November 21: CAVALLERIA RUSTICANA (Mascagni)
SANTUZZA: Muzio, TURIDDU: Borgioli, ALFIO: Gandolfi, LOLA: Leonard, MAMMA LUCIA: Strause, CONDUCTOR: Dell'Orefice.

followed by: I PAGLIACCI (Leoncavallo)
CANIO: Martinelli, TONIO: Tibbett, NEDDA: Bori, SILVIO: Gandolfi, BEPPE: Oliviero, PEASANTS: Alibertini, Frediani, CONDUCTOR: Merola.

November 24: LA TRAVIATA (Verdi)
VIOLETTA: Muzio, ALFREDO: Borgioli, GERMONT: Tibbett, GASTON: Oliviero, BARON DOUPHOL: Gandolfi, MARQUIS D'OBIGNY: Eldredge, DR. GRENVIL: D'Angelo, FLORA: Eybel, ANNINA: McLaughlin, CONDUCTOR: Merola.

November 26, matinee: LE COQ D'OR (Rimsky-Korsakoff)
Same cast.

November 28: LA BOHEME (Puccini)
MIMI: Bori, RODOLFO: Borgioli, MARCELLO: Bonelli, COLLINE: Pinza, SCHAUNARD: Gandolfi, MUSETTA: Hardy, BENOIT: Oliviero, ALCINDORO: D'Angelo, PARPIGNOL: Oliviero, CONDUCTOR: Merola.

November 30, matinee: THE SECRET OF SUZANNE (Wolf-Ferrari)
followed by: THE EMPEROR JONES (Gruenberg)
Same cast.

December 1: LA FORZA DEL DESTINO (Verdi)
LEONORA: Muzio, DON ALVARO: Martinelli, DON CARLO: Bonelli, PADRE GUARDIANO: Pinza, FRA MELITONE: Gandolfi, PREZIOSILLA: Leonard, MARQUIS OF CALATRAVA: D'Angelo, ALCADE: Eldredge, TRABUCCO: Oliviero, CURRA: Strause, SURGEON: D'Angelo, CONDUCTOR: Merola.

December 2: MANON (Massenet)
Same cast.

CASTS—1934 SEASON

November 14:[1] THE BARTERED BRIDE (Smetana)
MARIE: Rethberg, JENIK: Chamlee, KEZAL: D'Angelo, VASHEK: Windheim, KRUSCHINA: Gandolfi, LUDMILA: E. Smith, MICHA: Howell, HATA: Gruninger, SPRINGER: Taenzler, ESMERALDA: Clark, MUFF: Ellis, CONDUCTOR: Hertz.

November 16: TOSCA (Puccini)
TOSCA: Lehmann, CAVARADOSSI: Borgioli, SCARPIA: Gandolfi, SPOLETTA: Windheim, SACRISTAN: D'Angelo, ANGELOTTI: Howell, SCIARRONE: D'Angelo, JAILOR: Alibertini, SHEPHERD: Gruninger, CONDUCTOR: Merola.

[1] San Francisco openings had moved up the calendar as the Metropolitan was beginning its seasons later in the year.

November 17: CARMEN (Bizet)
CARMEN: Vallin, MICAELA: Clark, DON JOSE: Chamlee, ESCAMILLO: Pinza, ZUNIGA: D'Angelo, DANCAIRO: Ellis, REMENDADO: Windheim, MORALES: Howell, FRASQUITA: E. Smith, MERCEDES: Gruninger, CONDUCTOR: Merola.

November 19: MANON (Massenet)
MANON: Bori, CHEVALIER DES GRIEUX: Crooks, LESCAUT: Gandolfi, GUILLOT: Windheim, DE BRETIGNY: Howell, COUNT DES GRIEUX: D'Angelo, POUSETTE: McLaughlin, JAVOTTE: Strause, ROSETTE: Schiller, SERVANT: Lanz, INNKEEPER: A. Ferrier, GUARDS: Simondet, Frediani, CONDUCTOR: Cimini.

November 22: MADAMA BUTTERFLY (Puccini)
CIO-CIO-SAN: Lehmann, PINKERTON: Borgioli, SHARPLESS: Gandolfi, SUZUKI: Marlo, GORO: Windheim, BONZE: D'Angelo, YAMADORI: D'Angelo, COMMISSIONER: Howell, KATE PINKERTON: Glando, REGISTRAR: Alibertini, CONDUCTOR: Cimini.

November 26: TANNHÄUSER (Wagner)
ELISABETH: Rethberg, VENUS: Eybel, TANNHÄUSER: Melchior, WOLFRAM: Bonelli, LANDGRAVE: Pinza, WALTHER: Windheim, BITEROLF: Gandolfi, HEINRICH: R. Marlowe, REINMAR: D'Angelo, SHEPHERD: Clark, CONDUCTOR: Hertz.

November 28: LA TRAVIATA (Verdi)
VIOLETTA: Bori, ALFREDO: Crooks, GERMONT: Bonelli, GASTON: Windheim, BARON DOUPHOL: Gandolfi, MARQUIS D'OBIGNY: Howell, DR. GRENVIL: D'Angelo, FLORA: Badger, ANNINA: McLaughlin, CONDUCTOR: Merola.

November 30: FAUST (Gounod)
MARGUERITE: Vallin, FAUST: Crooks, MEPHISTOPHELES: Pinza, VALENTIN: Bonelli, WAGNER: Howell, SIEBEL: Clark, MARTHE: Gruninger, CONDUCTOR: Merola.

December 1: MANON (Massenet)
Same cast.

December 2, matinee: MADAMA BUTTERFLY (Puccini)
Same cast except: CIO-CIO-SAN: Rethberg, PINKERTON: Chamlee.

December 3: LA RONDINE (Puccini)
MAGDA: Bori, RUGGERO: Borgioli, LISETTE: Clark, PRUNIER: Windheim, RAMBALDO: D'Angelo, PERICHAUD: Howell, GOBIN: Frediani, CREBILLON: Alibertini, YVETTE: Folli, BIANCA: E. Smith, SUZY: Strause, VOICE: Nostrom, CONDUCTOR: Merola.

December 4: LAKMÉ (Delibes)
LAKMÉ: Hardy, GERALD: Chamlee, FREDERIC: Gandolfi, NILAKANTHA: Pinza, HADJI: Simondet, MALLIKA: Gruninger, MRS. BENSON: J. G. Ferrier, ELLEN: Clark, ROSE: Strause, A SEPOY: Howell, CHINESE VENDOR: Frediani, CONDUCTOR: Merola.

December 5: OTELLO (Verdi)
DESDEMONA: Rethberg, OTELLO: Melchior, IAGO: Bonelli, CASSIO: R. Marlowe, RODERIGO: Frediani, LODOVICO: D'Angelo, MONTANO: Alibertini, HERALD: Howell, EMILIA: Gruninger, CONDUCTOR: Merola.

December 7: MIGNON (Thomas)
MIGNON: Bori, PHILINE: Hardy, WILHELM MEISTER: Borgioli, LOTHARIO: Pinza, LAERTE: Windheim, GIARNO: D'Angelo, FREDERIC: Marlo, CONDUCTOR: CIMINI.

December 8: TANNHÄUSER (Wagner)
Same cast except: WOLFRAM: Eddy, SHEPHERD: McLaughlin.

CASTS—1935 SEASON

November 1: DAS RHEINGOLD (Wagner)
WOTAN: Schorr, DONNER: Gandolfi, FROH: R. Marlowe, LOGE: Clemens, ALBERICH: Schützendorf, MIME: Windheim, FASOLT: Baromeo, FAFNER: Beattie, FRICKA:

Eybel, FREIA: Manski, ERDA: Meisle, WOGLINDE: Omeron, WELLGUNDE: J. Merrill, FLOSSHILDE: Doe, CONDUCTOR: Bodanzky.

November 4: DIE WALKÜRE (Wagner)
BRÜNNHILDE: Flagstad, SIEGLINDE: Rethberg, FRICKA: Meisle, SIEGMUND: *Melchior* WOTAN: Schorr, HUNDING: Baromeo, HELMWIGE: Manski, GERHILDE: Eybel, ORT-LINDE: J. Merrill, SIEGRUNE: Gerdau, ROSSWEISSE: Leandre, WALTRAUTE: Doe, GRIMGERDE: Callahan, SCHWERTLEITE: Gruninger, CONDUCTOR: Bodanzky.

November 6: SIEGFRIED (Wagner)
BRÜNNHILDE: Flagstad, SIEGFRIED: Melchior, WANDERER: Schorr, FAFNER: Baro-meo, ALBERICH: Schützendorf, MIME: Windheim, ERDA: Meisle, VOICE OF THE FOREST BIRD: Hardy, CONDUCTOR: Bodanzky.

November 9, at 5 p.m.: DIE GÖTTERDÄMMERUNG (Wagner)
BRÜNNHILDE: Flagstad, SIEGFRIED: Melchior, GUNTHER: Schorr, GUTRUNE: Manski, HAGEN: List, ALBERICH: Schützendorf, WALTRAUTE: Meisle, NORNS: Doe, Meisle, Manski, WOGLINDE: Kroph, WELLGUNDE: J. Merrill, FLOSSHILDE: Doe, VASSALS: Braunstein, B. Martin, CONDUCTOR: Bodanzky.

November 11: AIDA (Verdi)
AIDA: Rethberg, AMNERIS: Meisle, RHADAMES: Martinelli, AMONASRO: Eddy, RAMFIS: Pinza, KING: Beattie, MESSENGER: Windheim, PRIESTESS: Watt, CON-DUCTOR: Merola.

November 13: DIE WALKÜRE (Wagner)
Same cast except: HUNDING: List.

November 16: MARTHA (Flotow)
LADY HARRIET: Jepson, LIONEL: Schipa, PLUNKETT: Shefoff, SIR TRISTAN: D'Angelo, SHERIFF: Beattie, NANCY: Glade, MAIDS: Ferguson, Nostrom, Isariotis, FARMER: Baldacci, FARMER's WIFE: Callahan, CONDUCTOR: Lert.

November 18: LA JUIVE (Halevy)
RACHEL: Rethberg, ELEAZAR: Martinelli, CARDINAL: Pinza, LEOPOLD: Clemens, EUDOXIA: Hardy, RUGGIERO: Howell, TOWN CRIER: Howell, EXECUTIONER: Guen-ter, ALBERT: Wright, CONDUCTOR: Lert.

November 22: WERTHER (Massenet)
CHARLOTTE: Glade, WERTHER: Schipa, SOPHIE: Young, ALBERT: Gandolfi, BAILIFF: D'Angelo, SCHMIDT: R. Marlowe, JOHANN: Howell, BRUHLMANN: Albert Van-nucci, KATCHEN: Lanz, CONDUCTOR: Merola.

November 23: AIDA (Verdi)
Same cast except: AMNERIS: Glade, AMONASRO: Bonelli.

November 25: THE BARBER OF SEVILLE (Rossini)
ROSINA: Tumminia, COUNT ALMAVIVA: Schipa, FIGARO: Bonelli, BARTOLO: D'Angelo, BASILIO: Pinza, FIORELLO: Howell, OFFICER: Windheim, BERTHA: Gruninger, CONDUCTOR: Merola.

November 27: LA BOHEME (Puccini)
MIMI: Jepson, RODOLFO: Martinelli, MARCELLO: Bonelli, COLLINE: Pinza, SCHAUN-ARD: Gandolfi, MUSETTA: E. Smith, BENOIT: D'Angelo, ALCINDORO: D'Angelo, PARPIGNOL: Mennucci, CONDUCTOR: Lert.

November 29: RIGOLETTO (Verdi)
GILDA: Hardy, DUKE: Schipa, RIGOLETTO: Bonelli, MADDALENA: Gruninger, SPARA-FUCILE: Pinza, MONTERONE: Beattie, BORSA: Rossini, MARULLO: Howell, CEPRANO: Alibertini, COUNTESS CEPRANO: Sholl, GIOVANNA: Callahan, PAGE: Giragossiantz, CONDUCTOR: Merola.

December 2, matinee: MARTHA (Flotow)
Same cast except: NANCY: Gruninger.

December 2: SUOR ANGELICA (Puccini)
SUOR ANGELICA: Gahagan, PRINCESS: O'Dea, ABBESS: Hartman, MISTRESS OF

NOVICES: Steed, SISTER GENEVIEVE: Young, NOVICES: Callahan, Fremont, CONVERTS: Schiller, Ferguson, CONDUCTOR: Merola.

followed by: LE COQ D'OR (Rimsky-Korsakoff)
Dance Pantomime with Vocal Accompaniment
Singers: QUEEN: Hardy, KING DODON: Beattie, ASTROLOGER: R. Marlowe, GENERAL: Oliver Jones, AMELFA: Gruninger, VOICE OF COCK: Eybel, PRINCE GUIDON: Friberg, BOYERS: Albert Vannucci, Alibertini, *Dancers:* QUEEN: Ruiz, KING DODON: Bolm, ASTROLOGER: Bratoff, GENERAL: Vasilieff, AMELFA: Lauche, PRINCE GUIDON: Romanoff, PRINCE AFRON: Block, CONDUCTOR: Merola.

CASTS—1936 SEASON

REGULAR SERIES
October 30: LA JUIVE (Halevy)
RACHEL: Rethberg, ELEAZAR: Martinelli, CARDINAL: Pinza, LEOPOLD: Clemens, EUDOXIA: Boerner, RUGGIERO: Howell, TOWN CRIER: Burr, EXECUTIONER: Guenter, ALBERT: Wright, CONDUCTOR: Merola.
November 2: TRISTAN AND ISOLDE (Wagner)
ISOLDE: Flagstad, BRANGÄNE: Meisle, TRISTAN: Melchior, KING MARKE: List, KURWENAL: Schorr, MELOT: Gabor, SHEPHERD: Clemens, SAILOR'S VOICE: Oliviero, STEERSMAN: D'Angelo, CONDUCTOR: Reiner.
November 4: CARMEN (Bizet)
CARMEN: Castagna, MICAELA: Tumminia, DON JOSE: Kullman, ESCAMILLO: Pinza, ZUNIGA: D'Angelo, DANCAIRO: R. Russell, REMENDADO: Oliviero, MORALES: Howell, FRASQUITA: Kroph, MERCEDES: Doe, CONDUCTOR: Papi.
November 6: RIGOLETTO (Verdi)
GILDA: Tumminia, DUKE: Kullman, RIGOLETTO: Tibbett, MADDALENA: Gruninger, SPARAFUCILE: Pinza, MONTERONE: Cordon, BORSA: Oliviero, MARULLO: Howell, CEPRANO: Oliver Jones, COUNTESS CEPRANO: Esther Green, GIOVANNA: Hackett, PAGE: Lawlor, CONDUCTOR: Papi.
November 7 at 5 p.m.: DIE GÖTTERDÄMMERUNG (Wagner)
BRÜNNHILDE: Flagstad, SIEGFRIED: Melchior, GUNTHER: Schorr, GUTRUNE: Manski, HAGEN: List, ALBERICH: Gabor, WALTRAUTE: Meisle, NORNS: Doe, O'Dea, Manski, WOGLINDE: Kroph, WELLGUNDE: J. Merrill, FLOSSHILDE: Doe, CONDUCTOR: Reiner.
November 9: THE MARRIAGE OF FIGARO (Mozart)
SUSANNA: Rethberg, COUNTESS: Boerner, CHERUBINO: Vanna, FIGARO: Pinza, COUNT: Askam, BARTOLO: D'Angelo, BASILIO: Clemens, MARCELLINA: Callahan, BARBARINA: Monte, ANTONIO: Oliver Jones, CONDUCTOR: Lert.
November 11: I PAGLIACCI (Leoncavallo)
CANIO: Martinelli, TONIO: Tibbett, NEDDA: Vanna, SILVIO: Howell, BEPPE: Oliviero, CONDUCTOR: Papi.

followed by: GIANNI SCHICCHI (Puccini)
GIANNI SCHICCHI: Tibbett, RINUCCIO: Kullman, LAURETTA: Tumminia, SIMONE: Cordon, BETTO: Gabor, GHERARDO: Oliviero, MARCO: D'Angelo, SPINELLOCCIO: Oliver Jones, NOTARY: Gandolfi, PINELLINO: Sherrill, GUCCIO: Wright, ZITA: Doe, NELLA: Esther Green, LA CIESCA: J. Merrill, GHERARDINO: Lawlor, CONDUCTOR: Papi.
November 13: DIE WALKÜRE (Wagner)
BRÜNNHILDE: Flagstad, SIEGLINDE: Lehmann, FRICKA: Meisle, SIEGMUND: Melchior, WOTAN: Schorr, HUNDING: List, HELMWIGE: Manski, GERHILDE: Glando, ORTLINDE:

J. Merrill, SIEGRUNE: Watt, ROSSWEISSE: Esther Green, WALTRAUTE: Doe, GRIM-GERDE: Callahan, SCHWERTLEITE: Gruninger, CONDUCTOR: Reiner.

November 16: LA FORZA DEL DESTINO (Verdi)

LEONORA: Rethberg, DON ALVARO: Martinelli, DON CARLO: Morelli, PADRE GUARD-IANO: Pinza, FRA MELITONE: Gandolfi, PREZIOSILLA: Doe, MARQUIS OF CALATRAVA: D'Angelo, ALCADE: Howell, TRABUCCO: Oliviero, CURRA: Callahan, SURGEON: Burr, CONDUCTOR: Papi.

November 18: TOSCA (Puccini)

TOSCA: Lehmann, CAVARADOSSI: Kullman, SCARPIA: Tibbett, SPOLETTA: Oliviero, SACRISTAN: D'Angelo, ANGELOTTI: Cordon, SCIARRONE: Howell, JAILOR: Burr, SHEPHERD: Fremont, CONDUCTOR: Papi.

November 20: OTELLO (Verdi)

DESDEMONA: Rethberg, OTELLO: Martinelli, IAGO: Tibbett, CASSIO: Clemens, RODERIGO: R. Russell, LODOVICO: D'Angelo, MONTANO: Howell, HERALD: Burr, EMILIA: Gruninger, CONDUCTOR: Merola.

POPULAR SERIES

October 31: THE BARBER OF SEVILLE (Rossini)

ROSINA: Tumminia, COUNT ALMAVIVA: Kullman, FIGARO: Morelli, BARTOLO: D'Angelo, BASILIO: Pinza, FIORELLO: Oliviero, OFFICER: Oliver Jones, BERTHA: Gruninger, CONDUCTOR: Merola.

November 14, matinee: IL TROVATORE (Verdi)

LEONORA: Rethberg, AZUCENA: Castagna, MANRICO: Martinelli, COUNT DI LUNA: Morelli, FERRANDO: D'Angelo, RUIZ: Oliviero, OLD GYPSY: Burr, INEZ: Maschio, CONDUCTOR: Papi.

November 21: DAS RHEINGOLD (Wagner)

WOTAN: Schorr, DONNER: Gandolfi, FROH: L. George, LOGE: Clemens, ALBERICH: Gabor, MIME: Oliviero, FASOLT: Cordon, FAFNER: List, FRICKA: Manski, FREIA: J. Merrill, ERDA: O'Dea, WOGLINDE: Kroph, WELLGUNDE: J. Merrill, FLOSSHILDE: Doe, CONDUCTOR: K. Riedel.

EXTRA PERFORMANCES

November 15, matinee: CARMEN (Bizet)
Same cast.

November 17: TRISTAN AND ISOLDE (Wagner)
Same cast except: BRANGÄNE: Doe.

November 22, matinee: DIE WALKÜRE (Wagner)
Same cast.

CASTS—1937 SEASON

REGULAR SERIES

October 15: AIDA (Verdi)

AIDA: Cigna, AMNERIS: Castagna, RHADAMES: Martinelli, AMONASRO: Bonelli, RAMFIS: List, KING: Cordon, MESSENGER: Oliviero, PRIESTESS: Balfour, CONDUC-TOR: Merola.

October 18: LA BOHEME (Puccini)

MIMI: Bovy, RODOLFO: Kullman, MARCELLO: Bonelli, COLLINE: Pinza, SCHAUN-ARD: Cehanovsky, MUSETTA: Boerner, BENOIT: Oliviero, ALCINDORO: Oliver Jones, PARPIGNOL: Mancini, SERGEANT: Alibertini, OFFICER: Lorenzini, CONDUCTOR: Papi.

October 20: A MASKED BALL (Verdi)

AMELIA: Cigna, ULRICA: Castagna, OSCAR: Boerner, RICCARDO: Martinelli, RENATO:

Bonelli, SAM: List, TOM: Cordon, SILVANO: Cehanovsky, JUDGE: Oliviero, CON-
DUCTOR: Papi.

October 25: TRISTAN AND ISOLDE (Wagner)
ISOLDE: Flagstad, BRANGÄNE: Meisle, TRISTAN: Melchior, KING MARKE: Hofmann,
KURWENAL: Huehn, MELOT: Cehanovsky, SHEPHERD: Clemens, SAILOR'S VOICE:
Clemens, STEERSMAN: Cordon, CONDUCTOR: Reiner.

October 27: MADAMA BUTTERFLY
CIO-CIO-SAN: Tentoni, PINKERTON: Kullman, SHARPLESS: Huehn, SUZUKI: Cornish,
GORO: Oliviero, BONZE: Cordon, YAMADORI: Howell, COMMISSIONER: Lorenzini,
KATE PINKERTON: Hackett, REGISTRAR: Alibertini, CONDUCTOR: Papi.

October 29: LAKMÉ (Delibes)
LAKMÉ: Pons, GERALD: Maison, FREDERIC: Cehanovsky, NILAKANTHA: Pinza,
HADJI: A. Ferrier, MALLIKA: Beatty, MRS. BENSON: Callahan, ELLEN: Kroph,
ROSE: Hackett, CONDUCTOR: Cimini.

November 1: ROMEO AND JULIET (Gounod)
ROMEO: Maison, JULIET: Bovy, MERCUTIO: Askam, TYBALT: R. Russell, CAPULET:
Cordon, FRIAR LAWRENCE: List, GREGORIO: Howell, BENVOGLIO: Oliviero, DUKE OF
VERONA: Shefoff, STEPHANO: Esther Green, GERTRUDE: Cornish, CONDUCTOR:
Merola.

November 5: LOHENGRIN (Wagner)
ELSA: Flagstad, ORTRUD: Meisle, LOHENGRIN: Melchior, TELRAMUND: Huehn,
KING HENRY: Hofmann, HERALD: Cehanovsky, CONDUCTOR: Reiner.

November 8: FIDELIO (Beethoven)
LEONORE: Flagstad, FLORESTAN: Maison, ROCCO: List, DON PIZARRO: Hofmann,
DON FERNANDO: Huehn, MARZELLINE: Boerner, JACQUINO: Clemens, PRISONERS:
L. George, Sherrill, CONDUCTOR: Reiner.

November 10: MANON (Massenet)
MANON: Bovy, CHEVALIER DES GRIEUX: Maison, LESCAUT: Bonelli, GUILLOT:
Oliviero, DE BRETIGNY: Cehanovsky, COUNT DES GRIEUX: Cordon, POUSETTE:
Kroph, JAVOTTE: Landan, ROSETTE: Luscombe, INNKEEPER: A. Ferrier, SERVANT:
Robert, GUARDS: Loughery, Bernhard, CONDUCTOR: Cimini.

November 13: NORMA (Bellini)
NORMA: Cigna, ADALGISA: Castagna, POLLIONE: Martinelli, OROVESO: Pinza, FLAVIO:
Oliviero, CLOTILDE: Cornish, CONDUCTOR: Merola.

POPULAR SERIES

October 23: FAUST (Gounod)
MARGUERITE: Boerner, FAUST: Martinelli, MEPHISTOPHELES: Pinza, VALENTIN:
Askam, WAGNER: Howell, SIEBEL: Beatty, MARTHE: Callahan, CONDUCTOR:
Cimini.

October 30: LA TRAVIATA (Verdi)
VIOLETTA: Cigna, ALFREDO: Kullman, GERMONT: Bonelli, GASTON: Oliviero, BARON
DOUPHOL: Cehanovsky, MARQUIS D'OBIGNY: Howell, DR. GRENVIL: Cordon, FLORA:
Kroph, ANNINA: Hathaway, CONDUCTOR: Merola.

November 6: RIGOLETTO (Verdi)
GILDA: Tumminia, DUKE: Kullman, RIGOLETTO: Bonelli, MADDALENA: Cornish,
SPARAFUCILE: Cordon, MONTERONE: Shefoff, BORSA: Oliviero, MARULLO: Ceha-
novsky, CEPRANO: Alibertini, COUNTESS CEPRANO: Wishart, GIOVANNA: Hackett,
PAGE: Cozzens, CONDUCTOR: Papi.

REPEAT SERIES

October 26: AIDA (Verdi)
Same cast except: RAMFIS: Pinza.

October 31, matinee: TRISTAN AND ISOLDE (Wagner)
Same cast.

November 3: LAKMÉ (Delibes)
Same cast.
November 11: LOHENGRIN (Wagner)
Same cast.

CASTS—1938 SEASON

REGULAR SERIES

October 7: ANDREA CHENIER (Giordano)
MADELEINE: Rethberg, ANDREA CHENIER: Gigli, GERARD: Bonelli, MATHIEU: D'Angelo, FLEVILLE: Howell, ROUCHER: Cehanovsky, DUMAS: Cordon, ABBE: Oliviero, SPY: Oliviero, SCHMIDT: Gabor, FOUQUIER-TINVILLE: Gabor, COUNTESS: Doe, MADELON: Doe, BERSI: Kroph, CONDUCTOR: Merola.

October 10: DON GIOVANNI (Mozart)
DONNA ANNA: Rethberg, DONNA ELVIRA: Jessner, ZERLINA: Favero, DON GIOVANNI: Pinza, LEPORELLO: Baccaloni, DON OTTAVIO: Borgioli, COMMENDATORE: Cordon, MASETTO: D'Angelo, CONDUCTOR: Reiner.

October 12: MARTHA (Flotow)
LADY HARRIET: Favero, LIONEL: Gigli, PLUNKETT: D'Angelo, SIR TRISTAN: Baccaloni, SHERIFF: Cordon, NANCY: Doe, MAIDS: Allison, Lawlor, S. Browne, FARMER: Palumbo, FARMER'S WIFE: Gambi, CONDUCTOR: Papi.

October 14: DIE MEISTERSINGER (Wagner)
EVA: Jessner, MAGDALENA: Thorborg, WALTHER: Kullman, HANS SACHS: Schorr, POGNER: Gauld, DAVID: Laufkötter, BECKMESSER: Gabor, KOTHNER: Huehn, NIGHT WATCHMAN: Cehanovsky, VOGELGESANG: Clemens, NACHTIGALL: D'Angelo, ZORN: L. George, EISSLINGER: Oliviero, MOSER: Hague, ORTEL: Cehanovsky, SCHWARZ: Cordon, FOLTZ: Howell, CONDUCTOR: Reiner.

October 17: CAVALLERIA RUSTICANA (Mascagni)
SANTUZZA: Stignani, TURIDDU: Ziliani, ALFIO: Tagliabue, LOLA: Doe, MAMMA LUCIA: Votipka, CONDUCTOR: Merola.
          followed by: DON PASQUALE (Donizetti)
NORINA: Favero, ERNESTO: Borgioli, DR. MALATESTA: Bonelli, DON PASQUALE: Baccaloni, NOTARY: Oliviero, CONDUCTOR: Papi.

October 19: PELLÉAS ET MÉLISANDE (Debussy)
MÉLISANDE: Micheau, PELLÉAS: Cathelat, GOLAUD: Gauld, ARKEL: D'Angelo, GENEVIEVE: Doe, YNIOLD: Jamison, DOCTOR: A. Ferrier, CONDUCTOR: Leinsdorf.

October 21: LUCIA DI LAMMERMOOR (Donizetti)
LUCIA: Pons, LORD HENRY: Tagliabue, EDGARDO: Masini, LORD ARTHUR: L. George, RAYMOND: Cordon, ALICE: Votipka, NORMAN: Oliviero, CONDUCTOR: Papi.

October 24: ELEKTRA (Strauss)
ELEKTRA: Pauly, CHRYSOTHEMIS: Jessner, KLYTEMNESTRA: Thorborg, AEGISTHUS: Laufkötter, ORESTES: Huehn, ORESTES' TUTOR: Cordon, CONFIDANTE: Markham, TRAINBEARER: Lawlor, YOUNG SERVANT: Clemens, OLD SERVANT: Youngs, OVERSEER: Ponitz, MAIDSERVANTS: Doe, Kroph, Avakian, Votipka, Cornish, CONDUCTOR: Reiner.

October 28: LA FORZA DEL DESTINO (Verdi)
LEONORA: Rethberg, DON ALVARO: Gigli, DON CARLO: Bonelli, PADRE GUARDIANO: Pinza, FRA MELITONE: Baccaloni, PREZIOSILLA: Doe, MARQUIS OF CALATRAVA: D'Angelo, ALCADE: Howell, TRABUCCO: Oliviero, CURRA: Votipka, SURGEON: D'Angelo, CONDUCTOR: Papi.

October 31: LA BOHEME (Puccini)
MIMI: Favero, RODOLFO: Masini, MARCELLO: Tagliabue, COLLINE: Pinza, SCHAUN-

ARD: Cehanovsky, MUSETTA: Jamison, BENOIT: Oliviero, ALCINDORO: D'Angelo, PARPIGNOL: Walti, CONDUCTOR: Papi.

November 3: LE COQ D'OR (Rimsky-Korsakoff)
QUEEN: Pons, KING DODON: Pinza, ASTROLOGER: Massue, GENERAL: Cordon, AMELFA: Doe, VOICE OF COCK: Votipka, CONDUCTOR: Papi.

POPULAR SERIES

October 15: ANDREA CHENIER (Giordano)
Same cast except: GERARD: Tagliabue.
October 22: CAVALLERIA RUSTICANA (Mascagni)
Same cast except: TURIDDU: Masini.
                    followed by: DON PASQUALE (Donizetti)
Same cast.
October 29: LUCIA DI LAMMERMOOR (Donizetti)
Same cast.

EXTRA PERFORMANCES

October 20: DON GIOVANNI (Mozart)
Same cast.
October 23, matinee: THE BARBER OF SEVILLE (Rossini)
ROSINA: Micheau, COUNT ALMAVIVA: Borgioli, FIGARO: Tagliabue, BARTOLO: Baccaloni, BASILIO: Cordon, FIORELLO: Oliviero, OFFICER: Oliviero, BERTHA: Gruninger, CONDUCTOR: Merola.
October 26: DIE MEISTERSINGER (Wagner)
Same cast.
October 30, matinee: ELEKTRA (Strauss)
Same cast.
November 1: LA FORZA DEL DESTINO (Verdi)
Same cast except: DON CARLO: Tagliabue.

CASTS—1939 SEASON

REGULAR SERIES

October 13: MANON (Massenet)
MANON: Sayao, CHEVALIER DES GRIEUX: Schipa, LESCAUT: Bonelli, GUILLOT: A. Ferrier, DE BRETIGNY: Cehanovsky, COUNT DES GRIEUX: Cordon, GUARDS: Edwards, Noonan, MAID: Ritter, CONDUCTOR: Merola.
October 17: DIE WALKÜRE (Wagner)
BRÜNNHILDE: M. Lawrence, SIEGLINDE: Flagstad, FRICKA: Meisle, SIEGMUND: Melchior, WOTAN: Huehn, HUNDING: Cordon, HELMWIGE: Sharpe, GERHILDE: Votipka, ORTLINDE: Ponitz, SIEGRUNE: Paulee, ROSSWEISSE: S. Browne, WALTRAUTE: Glaz, GRIMGERDE: Avakian, SCHWERTLEITE: Cornish, CONDUCTOR: Leinsdorf.
October 18: MADAMA BUTTERFLY (Puccini)
CIO-CIO-SAN: Novotna, PINKERTON: Bartlett, SHARPLESS: Huehn, SUZUKI: Glaz, GORO: Oliviero, BONZE: Shiffeler, YAMADORI: Harvey, COMMISSIONER: Noonan, KATE PINKERTON: Hackett, REGISTRAR: Alibertini, CONDUCTOR: Papi.
October 20: TRISTAN AND ISOLDE (Wagner)
ISOLDE: Flagstad, BRANGÄNE: Meisle, TRISTAN: Melchior, KING MARKE: Kipnis, KURWENAL: Huehn, MELOT: Cehanovsky, SHEPHERD: Oliviero, SAILOR'S VOICE: L. George, STEERSMAN: D'Angelo, CONDUCTOR: McArthur.
October 23: RIGOLETTO (Verdi)
GILDA: Pons, DUKE: Jagel, RIGOLETTO: Tibbett, MADDALENA: Glaz, SPARAFUCILE:

Cordon, MONTERONE: Shiffeler, BORSA: Oliviero, MARULLO: Cehanovsky, CEPRANO: Wellman, COUNTESS CEPRANO: Chinn, GIOVANNA: Votipka, PAGE: Lawlor, CONDUCTOR: Papi.

October 25: LUCIA DI LAMMERMOOR (Donizetti)
LUCIA: Pons, LORD HENRY: Ballarini, EDGARDO: Schipa, LORD ARTHUR: L. George, RAYMOND: Cordon, ALICE: Votipka, NORMAN: Oliviero, CONDUCTOR: Papi.

October 27: OTELLO (Verdi)
DESDEMONA: Rethberg, OTELLO: Martinelli, IAGO: Tibbett, CASSIO: Oliviero, RODERIGO: Walti, LODOVICO: D'Angelo, MONTANO: Cehanovsky, HERALD: Navarro, EMILIA: Votipka, CONDUCTOR: Merola.

October 30: LA TRAVIATA (Verdi)
VIOLETTA: Novotna, ALFREDO: Martini, GERMONT: Tibbett, GASTON: Oliviero, BARON DOUPHOL: Cehanovsky, MARQUIS D'OBIGNY: Noonan, DR. GRENVIL: D'Angelo, FLORA: Votipka, ANNINA: Ritter, CONDUCTOR: Merola.

November 1: THE BARBER OF SEVILLE (Rossini)
ROSINA: Pons, COUNT ALMAVIVA: Martini: FIGARO: Bonelli, BARTOLO: D'Angelo, BASILIO: Cordon, FIORELLO: Oliviero, OFFICER: Oliviero, BERTHA: Glaz, CONDUCTOR: Papi.

November 3: FIDELIO (Beethoven)
LEONORE: Flagstad, FLORESTAN: Melchior, ROCCO: Kipnis, DON PIZARRO: Destal, DON FERNANDO: Huehn, MARZELLINE: Boerner, JACQUINO: Clemens, PRISONERS: Walti, Garden, CONDUCTOR: Leinsdorf.

POPULAR SERIES

October 21: I PAGLIACCI (Leoncavallo)
CANIO: Stinson, TONIO: Bonelli, NEDDA: Boerner, SILVIO: Cehanovsky, BEPPE: Oliviero, CONDUCTOR: Merola.
followed by: CAVALLERIA RUSTICANA (Mascagni)
SANTUZZA: Giannini, TURIDDU: Jagel, ALFIO: Cehanovsky, LOLA: Avakian, MAMMA LUCIA: Votipka, CONDUCTOR: Papi.

October 24: DIE WALKÜRE (Wagner)
Same cast except: BRÜNNHILDE: Flagstad, SIEGLINDE: M. Lawrence, FRICKA: Glaz, WOTAN: Destal, CONDUCTOR: McArthur.

October 29, matinee: RIGOLETTO (Verdi)
Same cast except: MADDALENA: Gaihle.

November 4: IL TROVATORE (Verdi)
LEONORA: Rethberg, AZUCENA: Meisle, MANRICO: Martinelli, COUNT DI LUNA: Bonelli, FERRANDO: Cordon, RUIZ: Oliviero, OLD GYPSY: Alibertini, INEZ: Votipka, CONDUCTOR: Papi.

EXTRA PERFORMANCES

October 31: I PAGLIACCI (Leoncavallo)
Same cast.
followed by: COPPELIA ballet (Delibes)
SWANHILDA: J. Reed, FRANTZ: W. Christensen, COPPELIUS: Riggins, BURGOMEISTER: Crockett, CONDUCTOR: Van Den Burg.

November 2: TRISTAN AND ISOLDE (Wagner)
Same cast except: BRANGÄNE: Glaz.

CHILDREN'S PERFORMANCE

November 3, matinee: MADAMA BUTTERFLY (Puccini)
Same cast except: SHARPLESS: Cehanovsky.

CASTS—1940 SEASON

REGULAR SERIES

October 12: THE MARRIAGE OF FIGARO (Mozart)
SUSANNA: Sayao, COUNTESS: Rethberg, CHERUBINO: Stevens, FIGARO: Pinza, COUNT: Brownlee, BARTOLO: Pechner, BASILIO: DePaolis, MARCELLINA: Petina, BARBARINA: Monte, ANTONIO: Cehanovsky, DON CURZIO: Ballagh, CONDUCTOR: Leinsdorf.

October 14: LAKMÉ (Delibes)
LAKMÉ: Pons, GERALD: Jobin, FREDERIC: Cehanovsky, NILAKANTHA: Kipnis, HADJI: A. Ferrier, MALLIKA: Petina, MRS. BENSON: Votipka, ELLEN: Andreotti, ROSE: Paulee, CONDUCTOR: Merola.

October 16: DER ROSENKAVALIER (Strauss)
MARSCHALLIN: Lehmann, BARON OCHS: Kipnis, OCTAVIAN: Stevens, SOPHIE: Bokor, FANINAL: Olitzki, TENOR: Naya, MARIANNE: Ponitz, VALZACCHI: DePaolis, ANNINA: Sten, POLICE COMMISSIONER: Alvary, NOTARY: Lorenz, LANDLORD: L. George, MILLINER: Simpson, ANIMAL VENDOR: Lieber, MARSCHALLIN'S MAJORDOMO: L. George, FANINAL'S MAJOR-DOMO: Walti, ORPHANS: Lawlor, Hackett, B. Ward, CONDUCTOR: Leinsdorf.

October 18: LA BOHEME (Puccini)
MIMI: Sayao, RODOLFO: Bjoerling, MARCELLO: Brownlee, COLLINE: Pinza, SCHAUNARD: Cehanovsky, MUSETTA: Bokor, BENOIT: DePaolis, ALCINDORO: Alvary, PARPIGNOL: Walti, SERGEANT: Alibertini, OFFICER: Lorenzini, CONDUCTOR: Papi.

October 21: DON GIOVANNI (Mozart)
DONNA ANNA: Rethberg, DONNA ELVIRA: Zebranska, ZERLINA: Bokor, DON GIOVANNI: Pinza, LEPORELLO: Kipnis, DON OTTAVIO: DePaolis, COMMENDATORE: Alvary, MASETTO: Cehanovsky, CONDUCTOR: Leinsdorf.

October 23: A MASKED BALL (Verdi)
AMELIA: Rethberg, ULRICA: Sten, OSCAR: Bokor, RICCARDO: Bjoerling, RENATO: Bonelli, SAM: Alvary, TOM: Sellon, SILVANO: Cehanovsky, JUDGE: Walti, SERVANT: Garden, CONDUCTOR: Papi.

October 25: CARMEN (Bizet)
CARMEN: M. Lawrence, MICAELA: Osborne, DON JOSE: Jobin, ESCAMILLO: Pinza, ZUNIGA: Alvary, DANCAIRO: Cehanovsky, REMENDADO: DePaolis, MORALES: Noonan, FRASQUITA: Votipka, MERCEDES: Avakian, CONDUCTOR: Merola.

October 28: RIGOLETTO (Verdi)
GILDA: Pons, DUKE: Naya, RIGOLETTO: Weede, MADDALENA: Avakian, SPARAFUCILE: Alvary, MONTERONE: Shiffeler, BORSA: DePaolis, MARULLO: Cehanovsky, CEPRANO: Wellman, COUNTESS CEPRANO: Wishart, GIOVANNA: Votipka, PAGE: Lawlor, CONDUCTOR: Papi.

October 29: AIDA (Verdi)
AIDA: Rethberg, AMNERIS: Sten, RHADAMES: Jagel, AMONASRO: Weede, RAMFIS: Pinza, KING: Alvary, MESSENGER: Walti, PRIESTESS: Ponitz, CONDUCTOR: Papi.

November 1: MANON (Massenet)
MANON: Sayao, CHEVALIER DES GRIEUX: Schipa, LESCAUT: Brownlee, GUILLOT: DePaolis, DE BRETIGNY: Cehanovsky, COUNT DES GRIEUX: Alvary, SERVANT: Ritter, GUARDS: Ballagh, Noonan, CONDUCTOR: Merola.

POPULAR SERIES

October 20, matinee: LAKMÉ (Delibes)
Same cast.
October 27, matinee: DER ROSENKAVALIER (Strauss)
Same cast.

October 29: LA BOHEME (Puccini)
Same cast.
November 2: CARMEN (Bizet)
Same cast.

CHILDREN'S PERFORMANCES

October 31, matinee: CARMEN (Bizet)
Same cast.
November 1, matinee: AIDA (Verdi)
Same cast except: AMNERIS: Zebranska, RHADAMES: Stinson.

CASTS—1941 SEASON

REGULAR SERIES

October 13: DON PASQUALE (Donizetti)
NORINA: Sayao, ERNESTO: Perulli, DR. MALATESTA: Brownlee, DON PASQUALE: Baccaloni, NOTARY: A. Marlowe, CONDUCTOR: Papi.
October 14: DER ROSENKAVALIER (Strauss)
MARSCHALLIN: Lehmann, BARON OCHS: Kipnis, OCTAVIAN: Stevens, SOPHIE: Bokor, FANINAL: Olitzki, TENOR: L. George, MARIANNE: Ponitz, VALZACCHI: Laufkötter, ANNINA: Petina, POLICE COMMISSIONER: Alvary, NOTARY: Lorenz, LANDLORD: L. George, MILLINER: Simpson, ANIMAL VENDOR: Lieber, MARSCHALLIN'S MAJOR-DOMO: Schoen, FANINAL'S MAJOR-DOMO: Walti, ORPHANS: Lawlor, Hersch, Hackett, CONDUCTOR: Leinsdorf.
October 16: THE DAUGHTER OF THE REGIMENT (Donizetti)
MARIE: Pons, TONIO: Jobin, SULPICE: Baccaloni, MARQUISE DE BIRKENFELD: Petina, HORTENSIUS: Alvary, CORPORAL: Cehanovsky, NOTARY: Riggins, PEASANT: Schoen, DUCHESSE DE KRAKENTHORP: Spence, YOUNG DUKE: N. Thompson, CONDUCTOR: Papi.
October 18: TOSCA (Puccini)
TOSCA: Roman, CAVARADOSSI: Kullman, SCARPIA: Brownlee, SPOLETTA: A. Marlowe, SACRISTAN: Baccaloni, ANGELOTTI: Alvary, SCIARRONE: Cehanovsky, JAILOR: Lorenz, SHEPHERD: Ritter, CONDUCTOR: Merola.
October 20: MADAMA BUTTERFLY (Puccini)
CIO-CIO-SAN: Albanese, PINKERTON: Jagel, SHARPLESS: Brownlee, SUZUKI: Petina, GORO: Windheim, BONZE: Alvary, YAMADORI: Cehanovsky, COMMISSIONER: Wellman, KATE PINKERTON: Ritter, REGISTRAR: Alibertini, CONDUCTOR: Papi.
October 22: THE BARBER OF SEVILLE (Rossini)
ROSINA: Sayao, COUNT ALMAVIVA: Perulli, FIGARO: Tibbett, BARTOLO: Baccaloni, BASILIO: Pinza, FIORELLO: Cehanovsky, OFFICER: A. Marlowe, BERTHA: Petina, CONDUCTOR: Merola.

October 24: TANNHÄUSER (Wagner)
ELISABETH: Roman, VENUS: Branzell, TANNHÄUSER: Melchior, WOLFRAM: Huehn, LANDGRAVE: Kipnis, WALTHER: Walti, BITEROLF: Hines, HEINRICH: A. Marlowe, REINMAR: Strelkoff, SHEPHERD: Carroll, PAGES: Spence, Carroll, Avakian, Hopkins, CONDUCTOR: Leinsdorf.
October 27: CARMEN (Bizet)
CARMEN: Swarthout, MICAELA: Albanese, DON JOSE: Jobin, ESCAMILLO: Weede, ZUNIGA: Alvary, DANCAIRO: Cehanovsky, REMENDADO: Laufkötter, MORALES: Cehanovsky, FRASQUITA: Votipka, MERCEDES: Avakian, CONDUCTOR: Leinsdorf.
October 29: L'AMORE DEL TRE RE (Montemezzi)
FIORA: G. Moore, AVITO: Kullman, MANFREDO: Weede, ARCHIBALDO: Pinza,

FLAMINIO: A. Marlowe, YOUTH: Walti, OLD WOMAN: Avakian, YOUNG GIRL: Jurs, SERVANT: Votipka, VOICE: Ritter, CONDUCTOR: Montemezzi.
November 1: SIMON BOCCANEGRA (Verdi)
SIMON BOCCANEGRA: Tibbett, AMELIA: Roman, FIESCO: Pinza, ADORNO: Jagel, PAOLO: Brownlee, PIETRO: Alvary, CAPTAIN: A. Marlowe, MAIDSERVANT: Votipka, CONDUCTOR: Leinsdorf.

POPULAR SERIES
October 19, matinee: RIGOLETTO (Verdi)
GILDA: Pons, DUKE: Peerce, RIGOLETTO: Tibbett, MADDALENA: Petina, SPARAFUCILE: Alvary, MONTERONE: Hines, BORSA: A. Marlowe, MARULLO: Cehanovsky, CEPRANO: Wellman, COUNTESS CEPRANO: Markham, GIOVANNA: Votipka, PAGE: Lawlor, CONDUCTOR: Papi.
October 23: MADAMA BUTTERFLY (Puccini)
Same cast.
October 28: THE DAUGHTER OF THE REGIMENT (Donizetti)
Same cast.
October 30: TANNHÄUSER (Wagner)
Same cast.

CHILDREN'S PERFORMANCES
October 24, 31, matinees: THE BARBER OF SEVILLE (Rossini)
Same cast except: FIGARO: Weede.

CASTS—1942 SEASON

REGULAR SERIES
October 9: AIDA (Verdi)
AIDA: Roman, AMNERIS: Castagna, RHADAMES: Jagel, AMONASRO: Weede, RAMFIS: Pinza, KING: Alvary, MESSENGER: Walti, PRIESTESS: Votipka, CONDUCTOR: Merola.
October 12: THE DAUGHTER OF THE REGIMENT (Donizetti)
MARIE: Pons, TONIO: Jobin, SULPICE: Baccaloni, MARQUISE DE BIRKENFELD: Petina, HORTENSIUS: Alvary, CORPORAL: Cehanovsky, NOTARY: Riggins, PEASANT: Walti, DUCHESSE DE KRAKENTHORP: Hopkins, YOUNG DUKE: Krauter, CONDUCTOR: Cimara.
October 14: LA TRAVIATA (Verdi)
VIOLETTA: Sayao, ALFREDO: Peerce, GERMONT: Bonelli, GASTON: DePaolis, BARON DOUPHOL: Cehanovsky, MARQUIS D'OBIGNY: Alvary, DR. GRENVIL: Beattie, FLORA: Votipka, ANNINA: Ritter, CONDUCTOR: Cleva.
October 16: THE BARTERED BRIDE (Smetana)
MARIE: Antoine, JENIK: Kullman, KEZAL: Beattie, VASHEK: Windheim, KRUSCHINA: Cehanovsky, LUDMILA: Votipka, MICHA: Alvary, HATA: Wysor, SPRINGER: Shiffeler, ESMERALDA: Engel, MUFF: Harvey, CONDUCTOR: W. Herbert.
October 19: CARMEN (Bizet)
CARMEN: Petina, MICAELA: Albanese, DON JOSE: Jobin, ESCAMILLO: Brownlee, ZUNIGA: Alvary, DANCAIRO: Cehanovsky, REMENDADO: DePaolis, MORALES: Cehanovsky, FRASQUITA: Votipka, MERCEDES: Carroll, CONDUCTOR: Merola.
October 21: FAUST (Gounod)
MARGUERITE: Albanese, FAUST: Kullman, MEPHISTOPHELES: Pinza, VALENTIN: Brownlee, WAGNER: Cehanovsky, SIEBEL: Osborne, MARTHE: Votipka, CONDUCTOR: Cleva.
October 23: L'AMORE DEI TRE RE (Montemezzi)
FIORA: Tennyson, AVITO: Kullman, MANFREDO: Weede, ARCHIBALDO: Pinza,

FLAMINIO: DePaolis, YOUTH: Walti, OLD WOMAN: Wysor, YOUNG GIRL: Lawlor, SERVANT: McCarthy, VOICE: C. Turner, CONDUCTOR: Montemezzi.

October 26: DIE FLEDERMAUS (Johann Strauss)
ROSALINDA: Bokor, ADELE: Antoine, PRINCE ORLOFSKY: Petina, ALFRED: R. Marshall, EISENSTEIN: Windheim, FRANK: Beattie, DR. FALKE: Brownlee, DR. BLIND: Alvary, FROSCH: Lockhart, MOLLY: Carroll, IVAN: R. Marvin, CONDUCTOR: W. Herbert.

October 28: A MASKED BALL (Verdi)
AMELIA: Roman, ULRICA: Castagna, OSCAR: Bokor, RICCARDO: Jagel, RENATO: Bonelli, SAM: Alvary, TOM: Beattie, SILVANO: Cehanovsky, JUDGE: Walti, SERVANT: Wellman, CONDUCTOR: Cleva.

October 30: LE COQ D'OR (Rimsky-Korsakoff)
QUEEN: Antoine, KING DODON: Baccaloni, ASTROLOGER: DePaolis, GENERAL: Beattie, AMELFA: Wysor, VOICE OF COCK: Votipka, PRINCE GUIDON: Walti, PRINCE AFRON: Palumbo, CONDUCTOR: Merola.

POPULAR SERIES

October 18, matinee: LUCIA DI LAMMERMOOR (Donizetti)
LUCIA: Pons, LORD HENRY: Bonelli, EDGARDO: Peerce, LORD ARTHUR: DePaolis, RAYMOND: Alvary, ALICE: Votipka, NORMAN: Walti, CONDUCTOR: Cimara.

October 25, matinee: AIDA (Verdi)
Same cast.

October 27: THE BARBER OF SEVILLE (Rossini)
ROSINA: Sayao, COUNT ALMAVIVA: Kullman, FIGARO: Brownlee, BARTOLO: Baccaloni, BASILIO: Pinza, FIORELLO: Cehanovsky, OFFICER: DePaolis, BERTHA: Petina, CONDUCTOR: Cleva.

October 31: FAUST (Gounod)
Same cast.

EXTRA PERFORMANCE

October 22: THE DAUGHTER OF THE REGIMENT (Donizetti) (Auspices France Forever)
Same cast.

CASTS—1943 SEASON

October 7: SAMSON AND DELILAH (Saint-Saens)
SAMSON: Jobin, DELILAH: Thorborg, HIGH PRIEST: Warren, ABIMELECH: Cehanovsky, OLD HEBREW: Alvary, MESSENGER: DePaolis, PHILISTINES: Garris, Wellman, CONDUCTOR: Merola.

October 11: LA FORZA DEL DESTINO (Verdi)
LEONORA: Milanov, DON ALVARO: Jagel, DON CARLO: Warren, PADRE GUARDIANO: Pinza, FRA MELITONE: Baccaloni, PREZIOSILLA: Petina, MARQUIS OF CALATRAVA: Alvary, ALCADE: Alvary, TRABUCCO: DePaolis, CURRA: Votipka, SURGEON: Cehanovsky, CONDUCTOR: Merola.

October 13: CAVALLERIA RUSTICANA (Mascagni)
SANTUZZA: Giannini, TURIDDU: Kullman, ALFIO: Cehanovsky, LOLA: C. Johnson, MAMMA LUCIA: Votipka, CONDUCTOR: Adler.
followed by: I PAGLIACCI (Leoncavallo)
CANIO: Jobin, TONIO: J. C. Thomas, NEDDA: Albanese, SILVIO: Valentino, BEPPE: DePaolis, PEASANTS: Wellman, Mennucci, CONDUCTOR: Cimara.

October 15: THE GIRL OF THE GOLDEN WEST (Puccini)
MINNIE: Kirk, DICK JOHNSON: Jagel, JACK RANCE: Weede, JAKE WALLACE:

Alexander, NICK: DePaolis, ASHBY: Alvary, SONORA: Cehanovsky, TRIN: Garris, SID: Lorenzini, HANDSOME: Wellman, HARRY: R. Evans, JOE: Francis Oliver, HAPPY: Lourenzo, LARKENS: T. Thompson, JOSE CASTRO: Goodwin, BILLY JACKRABBIT: Goodwin, WOWKLE: C. Johnson, CONDUCTOR: Cleva.

October 18: LUCIA DI LAMMERMOOR (Donizetti)
LUCIA: Pons, LORD HENRY: Warren, EDGARDO: Peerce, LORD ARTHUR: Garris, RAYMOND: Alvary, ALICE: Votipka, NORMAN: R. Evans, CONDUCTOR: Cimara.

October 20: LA BOHEME (Puccini)
MIMI: Albanese, RODOLFO: Kullman, MARCELLO: Valentino, COLLINE: Pinza, SCHAUNARD: Cehanovsky, MUSETTA: Osborne, BENOIT: Baccaloni, ALCINDORO: Baccaloni, SERGEANT: Alibertini, OFFICER: Lorenzini, CONDUCTOR: Merola.

October 22: IL TROVATORE (Verdi)
LEONORA: Milanov, AZUCENA: Thorborg, MANRICO: Baum, COUNT DI LUNA: Weede, FERRANDO: Silva, RUIZ: Garris, OLD GYPSY: Guenter, INEZ: Votipka, CONDUCTOR: Cleva.

October 25: RIGOLETTO (Verdi)
GILDA: Pons, DUKE: Peerce, RIGOLETTO: Petroff, MADDALENA: C. Johnson, SPARAFUCILE: Alvary, MONTERONE: London (Burnson), BORSA: DePaolis, MARULLO: Cehanovsky, CEPRANO: Wellman, COUNTESS CEPRANO: Markham, GIOVANNA: Votipka, PAGE: Lawlor, CONDUCTOR: Cimara.

October 27: DON GIOVANNI (Mozart)
DONNA ANNA: Milanov, DONNA ELVIRA: Kirk, ZERLINA: Albanese, DON GIOVANNI: Pinza, LEPORELLO: Baccaloni, DON OTTAVIO: Kullman, COMMENDATORE: Silva, MASETTO: Alvary, CONDUCTOR: Beecham.

October 29: DON PASQUALE (Donizetti)
NORINA: Albanese, ERNESTO: Garris, DR. MALATESTA: Petroff, DON PASQUALE: Baccaloni, NOTARY: DePaolis, CONDUCTOR: Cimara.

POPULAR SERIES

October 10, matinee: LA TRAVIATA (Verdi)
VIOLETTA: Albanese, ALFREDO: Kullman, GERMONT: Valentino, GASTON: DePaolis, BARON DOUPHOL: Cehanovsky, MARQUIS D'OBIGNY: Lorenzini, DR. GRENVIL: Alvary, FLORA: Votipka, ANNINA: Lawlor, CONDUCTOR: Cleva.

October 17, matinee: LA FORZA DEL DESTINO (Verdi)
Same cast except: DON ALVARO: Baum.

October 24: CARMEN (Bizet)
CARMEN: Petina, MICAELA: Gonzales, DON JOSE: Jobin, ESCAMILLO: Pinza, ZUNIGA: Alvary, DANCAIRO: Cehanovsky, REMENDADO: DePaolis, MORALES: Cehanovsky, FRASQUITA: Votipka, MERCEDES: C. Johnson, CONDUCTOR: Beecham.

October 28: RIGOLETTO (Verdi)
Same cast except: RIGOLETTO: J. C. Thomas.

October 30: CAVALLERIA RUSTICANA (Mascagni)
Same cast except: TURIDDU: Baum.
        followed by: I PAGLIACCI (Leoncavallo)
Same cast except: TONIO: Weede.

EXTRA PERFORMANCES

October 24, matinee: LA BOHEME (Puccini)
Same cast except: COLLINE: Silva.

October 26: SAMSON AND DELILAH (Saint-Saens)
Same cast except: ABIMELECH: Silva.

CASTS—1944 SEASON

REGULAR SERIES

September 29: AIDA (Verdi)
AIDA: Roman, AMNERIS: Harshaw, RHADAMES: Jagel, AMONASRO: Warren, RAM-
FIS: Pinza, KING: Alvary, MESSENGER: DePaolis, PRIESTESS: Votipka, CONDUCTOR:
Merola.

October 3: MARTHA (Flotow)
LADY HARRIET: Albanese, LIONEL: Landi, PLUNKETT: Alvary, SIR TRISTAN: Bac-
caloni, SHERIFF: Goodwin, NANCY: Glaz, MAIDS: Gianopulos, Lawlor, Levon,
FARMER: B. Martin, FARMER'S WIFE: Gambi, LACKEYS: Wahlin, Guenter, Doan,
Albert Vannucci, CONDUCTOR: Merola.

October 6: LAKMÉ (Delibes)
LAKMÉ: Pons, GERALD: Jobin, FREDERIC: Cehanovsky, NILAKANTHA: Silva, HADJI:
Garris, MALLIKA: Glaz, MRS. BENSON: Votipka, ELLEN: Karpelenia, ROSE:
Avakian, A SEPOY: DeLugg, CHINESE VENDOR: Tallone, ASTROLOGER: B. Martin,
CONDUCTOR: Cimara.

October 10: MANON (Massenet)
MANON: Albanese, CHEVALIER DES GRIEUX: Kullman, LESCAUT: Valentino, GUILLOT:
DePaolis, DE BRETIGNY: Cehanovsky, COUNT DES GRIEUX: Alvary, SERVANT: Levon,
GUARDS: Bernhard, Wellman, CONDUCTOR: Cimara.

October 13: THE SECRET OF SUZANNE (Wolf-Ferrari)
COUNTESS SUZANNE: MacWatters, COUNT GIL: H. Thompson, SANTE: DePaolis,
CONDUCTOR: Adler.

followed by: SALOME (Strauss)
SALOME: Djanel, HEROD: Jagel, JOKANAAN: Shafer, HERODIAS: Harshaw, NARRA-
BOTH: Garris, PAGE: Glaz, SOLDIERS: Cehanovsky, Wellman, NAZARENES: Alvary,
Nelson, JEWS: Garris, Berton, DePaolis, Tissier, Goodwin, SLAVE: Heitman,
CAPPADOCIAN: Sanders, HENCHMAN: G. Anderson, CONDUCTOR: Sebastian.

October 16: FALSTAFF (Verdi)
SIR JOHN FALSTAFF: Baccaloni, MISTRESS FORD: Della Chiesa, MISTRESS PAGE:
Glaz, DAME QUICKLY: Harshaw, ANNE: Albanese, FENTON: Landi, FORD: Petroff,
DR. CAIUS: Garris, BARDOLPH: DePaolis, PISTOL: Alvary, CONDUCTOR: Steinberg.

October 18: FAUST (Gounod)
MARGUERITE: Della Chiesa, FAUST: Jobin, MEPHISTOPHELES: Pinza, VALENTIN:
Warren, WAGNER: Cehanovsky, SIEBEL: Glaz, MARTHE: Votipka, CONDUCTOR:
Steinberg.

October 20: A MASKED BALL (Verdi)
AMELIA: Roman, ULRICA: Harshaw, OSCAR: MacWatters, RICCARDO: Peerce,
RENATO: Warren, SAM: Alvary, TOM: Goodwin, SILVANO: Cehanovsky, JUDGE:
Tallone, SERVANT: Lorenzini, CONDUCTOR: Steinberg.

October 24: THE TALES OF HOFFMANN (Offenbach)
HOFFMANN: Jobin, OLYMPIA: MacWatters, GIULIETTA: Djanel, ANTONIA: Al-
banese, COPPELIUS: Pinza, DAPERTUTTO: Valentino, DR. MIRACLE: Pinza, NICK-
LAUSSE: Glaz, VOICE OF ANTONIA'S MOTHER: C. Turner, SPALANZANI: DePaolis,
SCHLEMIL: Cehanovsky, CRESPEL: Alvary, FRANTZ: DePaolis, COCHENILLE: Garris,
PITICHINACCIO: Garris, NATHANAEL: Tissier, HERMANN: Wellman, LUTHER: San-
ders, CONDUCTOR: Merola.

October 27: CARMEN (Bizet)
CARMEN: Stevens, MICAELA: MacWatters, DON JOSE: Kullman, ESCAMILLO:
Valentino, ZUNIGA: Alvary, DANCAIRO: Cehanovsky, REMENDADO: DePaolis,
MORALES: Cehanovsky, FRASQUITA: Votipka, MERCEDES: Avakian, CONDUCTOR:
Sebastian.

POPULAR SERIES

October 5: LA BOHEME (Puccini)
MIMI: Albanese, RODOLFO: Kullman, MARCELLO: Valentino, COLLINE: Pinza, SCHAUNARD: Cehanovsky, MUSETTA: MacWatters, BENOIT: Baccaloni, ALCINDORO: Baccaloni, SERGEANT: Alibertini, OFFICER: Lorenzini, CONDUCTOR: Merola.
October 11: LUCIA DI LAMMERMOOR (Donizetti)
LUCIA: Pons, LORD HENRY: Petroff, EDGARDO: Peerce, LORD ARTHUR: Garris, RAYMOND: Alvary, ALICE: Votipka, NORMAN: Tissier, CONDUCTOR: Cimara.
October 15, matinee: AIDA (Verdi)
Same cast.
October 19: THE SECRET OF SUZANNE (Wolf-Ferrari)
Same cast.
followed by: SALOME (Strauss)
Same cast.
October 26: FALSTAFF (Verdi)
Same cast.

EXTRA PERFORMANCES

October 1, matinee: LA FORZA DEL DESTINO (Verdi)
LEONORA: Roman, DON ALVARO: Jagel, DON CARLO: Warren, PADRE GUARDIANO: Pinza, FRA MELITONE: Baccaloni, PREZIOSILLA: Glaz, MARQUIS OF CALATRAVA: Alvary, ALCADE: Alvary, TRABUCCO: DePaolis, CURRA: Votipka, SURGEON: Cehanovsky, CONDUCTOR: Merola.
October 8, matinee: MARTHA (Flotow)
Same cast, CONDUCTOR: K. Riedel.
October 17: RIGOLETTO (Verdi)
GILDA: Pons, DUKE: Peerce, RIGOLETTO: Warren, MADDALENA: Glaz, SPARAFUCILE: Silva, MONTERONE: Alvary, BORSA: DePaolis, MARULLO: Cehanovsky, CEPRANO: Wellman, COUNTESS CEPRANO: Markham, GIOVANNA: Votipka, PAGE: Lawlor, CONDUCTOR: Cimara.
October 22, matinee: MANON (Massenet)
Same cast.
October 28: THE TALES OF HOFFMANN (Offenbach)
Same cast.

CASTS—1945 SEASON

REGULAR SERIES

September 25: CARMEN (Bizet)
CARMEN: Stevens, MICAELA: Steber, DON JOSE: Jobin, ESCAMILLO: Harrell, ZUNIGA: Olitzki, DANCAIRO: Cehanovsky, REMENDADO: DePaolis, MORALES: Cehanovsky, FRASQUITA: Votipka, MERCEDES: C. Turner, CONDUCTOR: Merola.
September 28: LA BOHEME (Puccini)
MIMI: Albanese, RODOLFO: Kullman, MARCELLO: Harrell, COLLINE: Pinza, SCHAUNARD: Cehanovsky, MUSETTA: Conner, BENOIT: Baccaloni, ALCINDORO: Baccaloni, SERGEANT: Alibertini, OFFICER: Lorenzini, CONDUCTOR: Merola.
October 2: DER ROSENKAVALIER (Strauss)
MARSCHALLIN: Lehmann, BARON OCHS: Alvary, OCTAVIAN: Stevens, SOPHIE: Steber, FANINAL: Olitzki, TENOR: Landi, MARIANNE: Votipka, VALZACCHI: DePaolis, ANNINA: Glaz, POLICE COMMISSIONER: Harrell, NOTARY: Goodwin, LANDLORD: Garris, MILLINER: King, ANIMAL VENDOR: Lieber, MARSCHALLIN'S MAJOR-DOMO: Tissier, FANINAL'S MAJOR-DOMO: Tallone, ORPHANS: Lawlor,

Hersch, Sanderson, FOOTMEN: Guenter, Tallone, MacKay, F. Williams, CON-
DUCTOR: Sebastian.

October 5: TRISTAN AND ISOLDE (Wagner)
ISOLDE: Traubel, BRANGÄNE: Glaz, TRISTAN: Melchior, KING MARKE: Alvary,
KURWENAL: Janssen, MELOT: Olitzki, SHEPHERD: Garris, SAILOR'S VOICE: Garris,
STEERSMAN: Goodwin, CONDUCTOR: Steinberg.

October 9: DIE WALKÜRE (Wagner)
BRÜNNHILDE: Traubel, SIEGLINDE: Djanel, FRICKA: Harshaw, SIEGMUND: Mel-
chior, WOTAN: Janssen, HUNDING: Alvary, HELMWIGE: Ragusa, GERHILDE:
Votipka, ORTLINDE: Demers, SIEGRUNE: Glaz, ROSSWEISSE: B. Anderson, WAL-
TRAUTE: Calcagno, GRIMGERDE: C. Turner, SCHWERTLEITE: Harshaw, CONDUCTOR:
Steinberg.

October 12: BORIS GODOUNOFF (Moussorgsky)
BORIS: Pinza, DIMITRI: Jagel, MARINA: Della Chiesa, PIMEN: Alvary, SHOUISKY:
DePaolis, VARLAAM: Baccaloni, MISSAIL: Nystrom, TCHELKALOFF: Cehanovsky,
FEODOR: Glaz, XENIA: Castellani, NURSE: Harshaw, INNKEEPER: C. Turner,
SIMPLETON: Garris, POLICE OFFICER: Mills, FRONTIER GUARD SERGEANT: Spelvinski,
BOYAR-IN-WAITING: Tissier, LOVITZKY: Goodwin, TCHERNIAKOVSKY: Mills, BOYAR:
Lieber, PEASANTS: Bruni, Calcagno, B. Martin, Lourenzo, CONDUCTOR: Sebastian.

October 16: DON GIOVANNI (Mozart)
DONNA ANNA: Roman, DONNA ELVIRA: Della Chiesa, ZERLINA: Albanese, DON
GIOVANNI: Pinza, LEPORELLO: Baccaloni, DON OTTAVIO: Landi, COMMENDATORE:
Mills, MASETTO: Harrell, CONDUCTOR: Steinberg.

October 19: LUCIA DI LAMMERMOOR (Donizetti)
LUCIA: Pons, LORD HENRY: Petroff, EDGARDO: Peerce, LORD ARTHUR: Garris,
RAYMOND: Alvary, ALICE: Votipka, NORMAN: Tallone, CONDUCTOR: Cimara.

October 23: THE SPANISH HOUR (Ravel)
CONCEPCION: Albanese, GONZALVE: Garris, TORQUEMADA: DePaolis, RAMIRO:
Harrell, DON INIGO GOMEZ: Baccaloni, CONDUCTOR: Merola.

followed by: SALOME (Strauss)
SALOME: Djanel, HEROD: Jagel, JOKANAAN: Janssen, HERODIAS: Harshaw, NAR-
RABOTH: Garris, PAGE: Glaz, SOLDIERS: Cehanovsky, Mills, NAZARENES: Alvary,
Nelson, JEWS: Tallone, Nystrom, DePaolis, Tissier, Goodwin, SLAVE: Heit-
man, CAPPADOCIAN: Sanders, HENCHMAN: Galt, CONDUCTOR: Sebastian.

October 26: RIGOLETTO (Verdi)
GILDA: Pons, DUKE: Peerce, RIGOLETTO: Petroff, MADDALENA: Glaz, SPARAFUCILE:
Alvary, MONTERONE: Mills, BORSA: DePaolis, MARULLO: Cehanovsky, CEPRANO:
Nelson, COUNTESS CEPRANO: Calcagno, GIOVANNA: Ragusa, PAGE: Lawlor, CON-
DUCTOR: Cimara.

POPULAR SERIES

October 4: THE TALES OF HOFFMANN (Offenbach)
HOFFMANN: Jobin, OLYMPIA: Corvello, GIULIETTA: Djanel, ANTONIA: Albanese,
COPPELIUS: Pinza, DAPERTUTTO: Valentino, DR. MIRACLE: Pinza, NICKLAUSSE:
Glaz, VOICE OF ANTONIA'S MOTHER: C. Turner, SPALANZANI: DePaolis, SCHLEMIL:
Olitzki, CRESPEL: Alvary, FRANTZ: DePaolis, COCHENILLE: Garris, PITICHINACCIO:
Garris, NATHANAEL: Tissier, HERMANN: Mills, LUTHER: Sanders, CONDUCTOR:
Merola.

October 11: CARMEN (Bizet)
Same cast.

October 18: DER ROSENKAVALIER (Strauss)
Same cast except: SOPHIE: Conner.

October 22: BORIS GODOUNOFF (Moussorgsky)
Same cast.

October 25: DON GIOVANNI (Mozart)
Same cast except: DONNA ELVIRA: Steber, ZERLINA: Conner, MASETTO: Alvary.

EXTRA PERFORMANCES

September 30, matinee: LA TRAVIATA (Verdi)
VIOLETTA: Albanese, ALFREDO: Kullman, GERMONT: Valentino, GASTON: DePaolis,
BARON DOUPHOL: Cehanovsky, MARQUIS D'OBIGNY: Olitzki, DR. GRENVIL: Good-
win, FLORA: Ragusa, ANNINA: Lawlor, CONDUCTOR: Merola.
October 7, matinee: CAVALLERIA RUSTICANA (Mascagni)
SANTUZZA: Della Chiesa, TURIDDU: Kullman, ALFIO: Petroff, LOLA: Glaz, MAMMA
LUCIA: Votipka, CONDUCTOR: Adler.
          followed by: I PAGLIACCI (Leoncavallo)
CANIO: Jobin, TONIO: Valentino, NEDDA: Albanese, SILVIO: Harrell, BEPPE: De-
Paolis, PEASANTS: Sanders, Tallone, CONDUCTOR: Adler.
October 14, matinee: TRISTAN AND ISOLDE (Wagner)
Same cast except: BRANGÄNE: Harshaw.
October 17: LA TRAVIATA (Verdi)
Same cast, CONDUCTOR: Cimara.
October 21, matinee: THE BARBER OF SEVILLE (Rossini)
ROSINA: Reggiani, COUNT ALMAVIVA: Landi, FIGARO: Valentino, BARTOLO: Bac-
caloni, BASILIO: Pinza, FIORELLO: DePaolis, OFFICER: Tallone, BERTHA: C. Turner,
CONDUCTOR: Cimara.
October 24: LA BOHEME (Puccini)
Same cast except: MIMI: Della Chiesa, MARCELLO: Valentino.
October 27: AIDA (Verdi)
AIDA: Roman, AMNERIS: Harshaw, RHADAMES: Jagel, AMONASRO: Petroff, RAM-
FIS: Pinza, KING: Alvary, MESSENGER: DePaolis, PRIESTESS: Votipka, CONDUC-
TOR: Kritz.

CASTS—1946 SEASON

REGULAR SERIES

September 17: LOHENGRIN (Wagner)
ELSA: Varnay, ORTRUD: Harshaw, LOHENGRIN: Svanholm, TELRAMUND: Cza-
plicki, KING HENRY: Moscona, HERALD: Harrell, PAGES: Zubiri, Connors, Sander-
son, Hessling, CONDUCTOR: Steinberg.
September 20: LA TRAVIATA (Verdi)
VIOLETTA: Albanese, ALFREDO: Peerce, GERMONT: Valentino, GASTON: DePaolis,
BARON DOUPHOL: Cehanovsky, MARQUIS D'OBIGNY: Olitzki, DR. GRENVIL: Ligeti,
FLORA: Votipka, ANNINA: Lawlor, CONDUCTOR: Merola.
September 24: ROMEO AND JULIET (Gounod)
ROMEO: Jobin, JULIET: Sayao, MERCUTIO: Brownlee, TYBALT: DePaolis, CAPULET:
Schon, FRIAR LAWRENCE: Moscona, GREGORIO: Harvey, BENVOGLIO: Tissier, DUKE
OF VERONA: Ligeti, STEPHANO: E. Knapp, GERTRUDE: Votipka, CONDUCTOR:
Breisach.
September 27: BORIS GODOUNOFF (Moussorgsky)
BORIS: Pinza, DIMITRI: Berini, MARINA: Glaz, PIMEN: Alvary, SHOUISKY: DePaolis,
VARLAAM: Baccaloni, MISSAIL: Tissier, TCHELKALOFF: Cehanovsky, FEODOR: E.
Knapp, XENIA: Demers, NURSE: Harshaw, INNKEEPER: Repp, SIMPLETON: Garris,
POLICE OFFICER: Ligeti, FRONTIER GUARD SERGEANT: Schon, BOYAR-IN-WAITING:
Tallone, LOVITZKY: Ligeti, TCHERNIAKOVSKY: Olitzki, BOYAR: Rooney, PEASANTS:
Bruni, Calcagno, B. Martin, Lourenzo, CONDUCTOR: Sebastian.

October 1: LAKMÉ (Delibes)
LAKMÉ: Pons, GERALD: Jobin, FREDERIC: Cehanovsky, NILAKANTHA: Moscona, HADJI: Garris, MALLIKA: Glaz, MRS. BENSON: Votipka, ELLEN: Zubiri, ROSE: E. Knapp, A SEPOY: Doan, CHINESE VENDOR: Tallone, ASTROLOGER: B. Martin, CONDUCTOR: Cimara.

October 3: LA FORZA DEL DESTINO (Verdi)
LEONORA: Roman, DON ALVARO: Baum, DON CARLO: Valentino, PADRE GUARDIANO: Pinza, FRA MELITONE: Baccaloni, PREZIOSILLA: Glaz, MARQUIS OF CALATRAVA: Alvary, ALCADE: Ligeti, TRABUCCO: DePaolis, CURRA: Votipka, SURGEON: Cehanovsky, CONDUCTOR: Merola.

October 8: DER ROSENKAVALIER (Strauss)
MARSCHALLIN: Lehmann, BARON OCHS: Alvary, OCTAVIAN: Novotna, SOPHIE: Connor, FANINAL: Olitzki, TENOR: Baum, MARIANNE: Votipka, VALZACCHI: DePaolis, ANNINA: Glaz, POLICE COMMISSIONER: Harrell, NOTARY: Harvey, LANDLORD: Garris, MILLINER: King, ANIMAL VENDOR: Daneluz, MARSCHALLIN'S MAJORDOMO: Tissier, FANINAL'S MAJOR-DOMO: Tallone, ORPHANS: Lawlor, Sanderson, Calcagno, FOOTMEN: Guenter, Tallone, Erich Lawrence, E. Vannucci, CONDUCTOR: Sebastian.

October 11: FIDELIO (Beethoven)
LEONORE: Resnik, FLORESTAN: Berini, ROCCO: Alvary, DON PIZARRO: Schon, DON FERNANDO: Harrell, MARZELLINE: Conner, JACQUINO: Garris, PRISONERS: Nesbitt, Harvey, CONDUCTOR: Breisach.

October 15: MADAMA BUTTERFLY (Puccini)
CIO-CIO-SAN: Albanese, PINKERTON: Kullman, SHARPLESS: Brownlee, SUZUKI: Glaz, GORO: DePaolis, BONZE: Alvary, YAMADORI: Cehanovsky, COMMISSIONER: Olitzki, KATE PINKERTON: Eloise Farrell, REGISTRAR: Harvey, CONDUCTOR: Merola.

October 18: THE MARRIAGE OF FIGARO (Mozart)
SUSANNA: Sayao, COUNTESS: Roman, CHERUBINO: Novotna, FIGARO: Pinza, COUNT: Brownlee, BARTOLO: Baccaloni, BASILIO: DePaolis, MARCELLINA: Glaz, BARBARINA: Zubiri, ANTONIO: Ligeti, DON CURZIO: Garris, PEASANT GIRLS: Demers, Viti, CONDUCTOR: Steinberg.

POPULAR SERIES

September 19: CARMEN (Bizet)
CARMEN: Djanel, MICAELA: Conner, DON JOSE: Jobin, ESCAMILLO: Czaplicki, ZUNIGA: Alvary, DANCAIRO: Cehanovsky, REMENDADO: DePaolis, MORALES: Cehanovsky, FRASQUITA: Votipka, MERCEDES: Glaz, CONDUCTOR: Breisach.

September 26: LA BOHEME (Puccini)
MIMI: Sayao, RODOLFO: Kullman, MARCELLO: Valentino, COLLINE: Pinza, SCHAUNARD: Cehanovsky, MUSETTA: SaEarp, BENOIT: Baccaloni, ALCINDORO: Baccaloni, SERGEANT: Lorenzini, OFFICER: E. Vannucci, CONDUCTOR: Merola.

October 9: LOHENGRIN (Wagner)
Same cast.

October 10: LUCIA DI LAMMERMOOR (Donizetti)
LUCIA: Pons, LORD HENRY: Petroff, EDGARDO: Peerce, LORD ARTHUR: Tissier, RAYMOND: Alvary, ALICE: Votipka, NORMAN: Tallone, CONDUCTOR: Cimara.

October 17: FIDELIO (Beethoven)
Same cast.

EXTRA PERFORMANCES

September 22, matinee: DON PASQUALE (Donizetti)
NORINA: Albanese, ERNESTO: Garris, DR. MALATESTA: Brownlee, DON PASQUALE: Baccaloni, NOTARY: DePaolis, CONDUCTOR: Kritz.

September 29, matinee: CARMEN (Bizet)
Same cast except: MICAELA: F. George, ESCAMILLO: Harrell, ZUNIGA: Olitzki.

September 30: LA TRAVIATA (Verdi)
Same cast except: GERMONT: Harrell.
October 6, matinee: LAKMÉ (Delibes)
Same cast.
October 7: BORIS GODOUNOFF (Moussorgsky)
Same cast.
October 13, matinee: DER ROSENKAVALIER (Strauss)
Same cast except: TENOR: Nesbitt, LANDLORD: Tallone.
October 14: LA BOHEME (Puccini)
Same cast except: MIMI: Roman, RODOLFO: Bjoerling, MARCELLO: Harrell, COL-
LINE: Moscona, CONDUCTOR: Cimara.
October 16: IL TROVATORE (Verdi)
LEONORA: Roman, AZUCENA: Harshaw, MANRICO: Bjoerling, COUNT DI LUNA:
Valentino, FERRANDO: Moscona, RUIZ: Tissier, OLD GYPSY: E. Vannucci, INEZ:
Viti, CONDUCTOR: Adler.
October 19: RIGOLETTO (Verdi)
GILDA: Pons, DUKE: Peerce, RIGOLETTO: Tibbett, MADDALENA: E. Knapp, SPARA-
FUCILE: Alvary, MONTERONE: Ligeti, BORSA: Tissier, MARULLO: Cehanovsky,
CEPRANO: Harvey, COUNTESS CEPRANO: Heitman, GIOVANNA: Calcagno, PAGE:
Lawlor, CONDUCTOR: Cimara.
October 20, matinee: MADAMA BUTTERFLY (Puccini)
Same cast.

CHILDREN'S PERFORMANCES

October 4, matinee: CARMEN (Bizet)
Same cast as September 19 except: MICAELA: F. George, ZUNIGA: Olitzki,
MERCEDES: E. Knapp.
October 11, matinee: DON PASQUALE (Donizetti)
Same cast except: DR. MALATESTA: Valentino.

CASTS—1947 SEASON

REGULAR SERIES

September 16: LA TRAVIATA (Verdi)
VIOLETTA: Albanese, ALFREDO: Peerce, GERMONT: Warren, GASTON: DePaolis,
BARON DOUPHOL: Cehanovsky, MARQUIS D'OBIGNY: Olitzki, DR. GRENVIL: Ligeti,
FLORA: Votipka, ANNINA: Lawlor, CONDUCTOR: Merola.
September 19: DON GIOVANNI (Mozart)
DONNA ANNA: Roman, DONNA ELVIRA: Quartararo, ZERLINA: Albanese, DON GIO-
VANNI: Pinza, LEPORELLO: Baccaloni, DON OTTAVIO: Kullman, COMMENDATORE:
Ligeti, MASETTO: Alvary, CONDUCTOR: Breisach.
September 22: MADAMA BUTTERFLY (Puccini)
CIO-CIO-SAN: Albanese, PINKERTON: Peerce, SHARPLESS: Valentino, SUZUKI: Glaz,
GORO: DePaolis, BONZE: Alvary, YAMADORI: Cehanovsky, COMMISSIONER: Olitzki,
KATE PINKERTON: Votipka, REGISTRAR: Harvey, CONDUCTOR: Cimara.
September 26: DIE GÖTTERDÄMMERUNG (Wagner)
BRÜNNHILDE: Traubel, SIEGFRIED: Svanholm, GUNTHER: Czaplicki, GUTRUNE:
Resnik, HAGEN: Alvary, ALBERICH: Olitzki, WALTRAUTE: Harshaw, NORNS: Glaz,
C. Turner, Votipka, WOGLINDE: Hartzell, WELLGUNDE: Popper, FLOSSHILDE:
Glaz, VASSALS: Guenter, Benson, Daneluz, CONDUCTOR: Steinberg.
September 30: LA GIOCONDA (Ponchielli)
LA GIOCONDA: Roman, LAURA: Thebom, LA CIECA: Harshaw, ENZO: Baum,
BARNABA: Warren, ALVISE: Moscona, ZUANE: Benson, ISEPO: Tallone, PILOT·

206 THE SAN FRANCISCO OPERA

Nelson, MONK: Ligeti, CANTOR: McVey, VOICES: Alibertini, Tallone, CONDUCTOR: Marzollo.

October 3: LOUISE (Charpentier)
LOUISE: Kirsten, JULIEN: Jobin, MOTHER: C. Turner, FATHER: Pinza, RAGPICKER: Lazzari, JUNKMAN: Ligeti, YOUNG RAGPICKER: Baldwin, STREET SWEEPER: Turnbull, NEWSPAPER GIRL: Hessling, MILKWOMAN: E. Browne, COALPICKER: Spry, STREET ARAB: Zubiri, BIRDFOOD VENDOR: Bish, ARTICHOKE VENDOR: Votipka, WATERCRESS VENDOR: Popper, CHAIR MENDER: Popper, OLD CLOTHES MAN: Tallone, GREEN PEA VENDOR: Daneluz, CARROT VENDOR: Nesbitt, RAG VENDOR: Cehanovsky, POLICEMEN: Harvey, Lorenzini, NOCTAMBULIST: DePaolis, KING OF FOOLS: DePaolis, SONG WRITER: Cehanovsky, PHILOSOPHERS: Olitzki, B. Martin, PAINTER: Davis, SCULPTOR: McVey, POET: Erich Lawrence, STUDENT: Schmidling, IRMA: Hartzell, CAMILLE: Gray, GERTRUDE: Popper, APPRENTICE: Zubiri, ELISE: Coryell, BLANCHE: Phillips, SUZANNE: Lawlor, FOREWOMAN: Heitman, MARGUERITE: Campbell, MADELEINE: Harper, CONDUCTOR: Breisach.

October 7: OTELLO (Verdi)
DESDEMONA: Albanese, OTELLO: Svanholm, IAGO: Tibbett, CASSIO: DePaolis, RODERIGO: Chabay, LODOVICO: Lazzari, MONTANO: Cehanovsky, HERALD: Nelson, EMILIA: Votipka, CONDUCTOR: Steinberg.

October 10: PELLÉAS ET MÉLISANDE (Debussy)
MÉLISANDE: Sayao, PELLÉAS: Singher, GOLAUD: Tibbett, ARKEL: Alvary, GENEVIEVE: Harshaw, YNIOLD: Zubiri, DOCTOR: Ligeti, CONDUCTOR: Pelletier.

October 14: L'AMORE DEI TRE RE (Montemezzi)
FIORA: Kirsten, AVITO: Kullman, MANFREDO: Weede, ARCHIBALDO: Pinza, FLAMINIO: DePaolis, YOUTH: Nesbitt, OLD WOMAN: C. Turner, YOUNG GIRL: Lawlor, SERVANT: Turnbull, VOICE: Baldwin, CONDUCTOR: Montemezzi.

October 17: LUCIA DI LAMMERMOOR (Donizetti)
LUCIA: Tumminia, LORD HENRY: Valentino, EDGARDO: Peerce, LORD ARTHUR: Chabay, RAYMOND: Alvary, ALICE: Votipka, NORMAN: Tallone, CONDUCTOR: Cimara.

POPULAR SERIES

September 18: ROMEO AND JULIET (Gounod)
ROMEO: Jobin, JULIET: Sayao, MERCUTIO: Singher, TYBALT: DePaolis, CAPULET: Ligeti, FRIAR LAWRENCE: Moscona, GREGORIO: Harvey, BENVOGLIO: Tallone, DUKE OF VERONA: Cehanovsky, STEPHANO: Glaz, GERTRUDE: C. Turner, CONDUCTOR: Pelletier.

September 25: AIDA (Verdi)
AIDA: Roman, AMNERIS: Thebom, RHADAMES: Baum, AMONASRO: Warren, RAMFIS: Moscona, KING: Alvary, MESSENGER: Chabay, PRIESTESS: Votipka, CONDUCTOR: Breisach.

October 2: TRISTAN AND ISOLDE (Wagner)
ISOLDE: Traubel, BRANGÄNE: Thebom, TRISTAN: Svanholm, KING MARKE: Alvary, KURWENAL: Czaplicki, MELOT: Olitzki, SHEPHERD: Chabay, SAILOR'S VOICE: Chabay, STEERSMAN: Ligeti, CONDUCTOR: Steinberg.

October 9: DIE GÖTTERDÄMMERUNG (Wagner)
Same cast.

October 16: LA GIOCONDA (Ponchielli)
Same cast except: LA GIOCONDA: Resnik.

EXTRA PERFORMANCES

September 21, matinee: FAUST (Gounod)
MARGUERITE: Claudia Pinza, FAUST: Jobin, MEPHISTOPHELES: Pinza, VALENTIN:

Valdengo, WAGNER: Cehanovsky, SIEBEL: Glaz, MARTHE: C. Turner, CONDUCTOR: Pelletier.

September 28, matinee: LA BOHEME (Puccini)
MIMI: Sayao, RODOLFO: Peerce, MARCELLO: Valentino, COLLINE: Moscona, SCHAUNARD: Cehanovsky, MUSETTA: Hartzell, BENOIT: Baccaloni, ALCINDORO: Baccaloni, PARPIGNOL: Tallone, SERGEANT: Lorenzini, OFFICER: E. Vannucci, CONDUCTOR: Merola.

October 5, matinee: THE MARRIAGE OF FIGARO (Mozart)
SUSANNA: Sayao, COUNTESS: Quartararo, CHERUBINO: Thebom, FIGARO: Pinza, COUNT: Singher, BARTOLO: Baccaloni, BASILIO: DePaolis, MARCELLINA: Glaz, BARBARINA: Zubiri, ANTONIO: Ligeti, DON CURZIO: Chabay, PEASANT GIRLS: Phillips, Gray, CONDUCTOR: Steinberg.

October 12, matinee: RIGOLETTO (Verdi)
GILDA: Pons, DUKE: Peerce, RIGOLETTO: Tibbett, MADDALENA: C. Turner, SPARAFUCILE: Lazzari, MONTERONE: Ligeti, BORSA: Chabay, MARULLO: Cehanovsky, CEPRANO: Harvey, COUNTESS CEPRANO: Heitman, GIOVANNA: Votipka, PAGE: Lawlor, CONDUCTOR: Cimara.

October 19, matinee: LOUISE (Charpentier)
Same cast.

ADDED PERFORMANCES

September 24: ROMEO AND JULIET (Gounod)
Same cast.

October 4, matinee: LA TRAVIATA (Verdi)
Same cast except: ALFREDO: Kullman, CONDUCTOR: Adler.

October 6: FAUST (Gounod)
Same cast except: VALENTIN: Weede.

October 8: DON GIOVANNI (Mozart)
Same cast except: DONNA ELVIRA: Resnik, ZERLINA: Conner.

October 13: TRISTAN AND ISOLDE (Wagner)
Same cast except: BRANGÄNE: Harshaw.

October 15: LA BOHEME (Puccini)
Same cast except: COLLINE: Lazzari.

October 18: MADAMA BUTTERFLY (Puccini)
Same cast except: PINKERTON: Kullman.

CHILDREN'S PERFORMANCES

October 10, matinee: LA TRAVIATA (Verdi)
Same cast as September 16 except: VIOLETTA: Conner, ALFREDO: Kullman, GERMONT: Valentino.

October 17, matinee: LA TRAVIATA (Verdi)
Same cast as September 16 except: VIOLETTA: Conner, ALFREDO: Kullman, GERMONT: Tibbett, CONDUCTOR: Adler.

CASTS—1948 SEASON

REGULAR SERIES

September 14: FALSTAFF (Verdi)
SIR JOHN FALSTAFF: Baccaloni, MISTRESS FORD: Resnik, MISTRESS PAGE: Glaz, DAME QUICKLY: Stignani, ANNE: Albanese, FENTON: Lichtegg, FORD: Weede, DR. CAIUS: Garris, BARDOLPH: DePaolis, PISTOL: Alvary, CONDUCTOR: Steinberg.

September 17: MANON (Massenet)
MANON: Sayao, CHEVALIER DES GRIEUX: Jobin, LESCAUT: Valentino, GUILLOT: De-

Paolis, DE BRETIGNY: Cehanovsky, COUNT DES GRIEUX: Alvary, POUSETTE: Hartzell, JAVOTTE: Zubiri, ROSETTE: Sanderson, SERVANT: Alver, INNKEEPER: Olitzki, GUARDS: Curzi, Lorenzini, CONDUCTOR: Breisach.

September 21: DIE MEISTERSINGER (Wagner)
EVA: Varnay, MAGDALENA: Glaz, WALTHER: Kullman, HANS SACHS: Janssen, POGNER: Moscona, DAVID: Garris, BECKMESSER: Olitzki, KOTHNER: Duno, NIGHT WATCHMAN: Sharretts, VOGELGESANG: Walti, NACHTIGALL: Uppman, ZORN: DePaolis, EISSLINGER: Chabay, MOSER: Schwabacher, ORTEL: Cehanovsky, SCHWARZ: Ligeti, FOLTZ: J. Ford, CONDUCTOR: Steinberg.

September 24: LA FORZA DEL DESTINO (Verdi)
LEONORA: Menkes, DON ALVARO: Baum, DON CARLO: Warren, PADRE GUARDIANO: Pinza, FRA MELITONE: Baccaloni, PREZIOSILLA: C. Turner, MARQUIS OF CALATRAVA: Alvary, ALCADE: J. Ford, TRABUCCO: DePaolis, CURRA: Baldwin, SURGEON: Cehanovsky, CONDUCTOR: Merola.

September 28: CAVALLERIA RUSTICANA (Mascagni)
SANTUZZA: Stignani, TURIDDU: Binci, ALFIO: Valentino, LOLA: Glaz, MAMMA LUCIA: C. Turner, CONDUCTOR: Marzollo.
       followed by: I PAGLIACCI (Leoncavallo)
CANIO: Baum, TONIO: Weede, NEDDA: Albanese, SILVIO: Cehanovsky, BEPPE: Chabay, PEASANTS: Benson, Curzi, CONDUCTOR: Cimara.

October 1: BORIS GODOUNOFF (Moussorgsky)
BORIS: Pinza, DIMITRI: Kullman, MARINA: Heidt, PIMEN: Alvary, SHOUISKY: DePaolis, RANGONI: Duno, VARLAAM: Baccaloni, MISSAIL: Chabay, TCHELKALOFF: Cehanovsky, FEODOR: Zubiri, XENIA: Hartzell, NURSE: C. Turner, INNKEEPER: Beal, SIMPLETON: Garris, POLICE OFFICER: J. Ford, FRONTIER GUARD SERGEANT: Ligeti, BOYAR-IN-WAITING: Walti, LOVITZKY: Olitzki, TCHERNIAKOVSKY: J. Ford, BOYAR: Rooney, CONDUCTOR: Leinsdorf.

October 5: CARMEN (Bizet)
CARMEN: Heidt, MICAELA: Conner, DON JOSE: Kullman, ESCAMILLO: Valdengo, ZUNIGA: Alvary, DANCAIRO: Cehanovsky, REMENDADO: DePaolis, MORALES: Uppman, FRASQUITA: Hartzell, MERCEDES: C. Turner, CONDUCTOR: Leinsdorf.

October 8: MADAMA BUTTERFLY (Puccini)
CIO-CIO-SAN: Kirsten, PINKERTON: Peerce, SHARPLESS: Valdengo, SUZUKI: Glaz, GORO: DePaolis, BONZE: Alvary, YAMADORI: Cehanovsky, COMMISSIONER: Olitzki, KATE PINKERTON: Gray, REGISTRAR: Harvey, CONDUCTOR: Cimara.

October 11: THE ELIXIR OF LOVE (Donizetti)
ADINA: Sayao, NEMORINO: Tagliavini, BELCORE: Gobbi, DR. DULCAMARA: Baccaloni, GIANNETTA: Hartzell, CONDUCTOR: Breisach.

October 14: SIEGFRIED (Wagner)
BRÜNNHILDE: Varnay, SIEGFRIED: Svanholm, WANDERER: Janssen, FAFNER: Ligeti, ALBERICH: Olitzki, MIME: Garris, ERDA: Beal, VOICE OF THE FOREST BIRD: Hartzell, CONDUCTOR: Leinsdorf.

POPULAR SERIES

September 16: LA TRAVIATA (Verdi)
VIOLETTA: Albanese, ALFREDO: Peerce, GERMONT: Valdengo, GASTON: DePaolis, BARON DOUPHOL: Cehanovsky, MARQUIS D'OBIGNY: Olitzki, DR. GRENVIL: Ligeti, FLORA: Gray, ANNINA: Lawlor, CONDUCTOR: Cimara.

September 23: LA BOHEME (Puccini)
MIMI: Sayao, RODOLFO: Peerce, MARCELLO: Valentino, COLLINE: Tajo, SCHAUNARD: Cehanovsky, MUSETTA: Hartzell, BENOIT: Baccaloni, ALCINDORO: Baccaloni, PARPIGNOL: Curzi, SERGEANT: Lorenzini, OFFICER: Benson, CONDUCTOR: Merola.

September 30: IL TROVATORE (Verdi)
LEONORA: Menkes, AZUCENA: Elmo, MANRICO: Baum, COUNT DI LUNA: Warren,

FERRANDO: Moscona, RUIZ: Chabay, OLD GYPSY: Benson, INEZ: Baldwin, CON-
DUCTOR: Marzollo.

October 7: FALSTAFF (Verdi)
Same cast except: DAME QUICKLY: Elmo, ANNE: Warenskjold.

October 16: OTELLO (Verdi)
DESDEMONA: Albanese, OTELLO: Svanholm, IAGO: Warren, CASSIO: DePaolis,
RODERIGO: Chabay, LODOVICO: Ligeti, MONTANO: Cehanovsky, HERALD: Nelson,
EMILIA: C. Turner, CONDUCTOR: Steinberg.

NON-SUBSCRIPTION PERFORMANCES

September 19, matinee: DON GIOVANNI (Mozart)
DONNA ANNA: Resnik, DONNA ELVIRA: Claudia Pinza, ZERLINA: Sayao, DON GIO-
VANNI: Pinza, LEPORELLO: Baccaloni, DON OTTAVIO: Lichtegg, COMMENDATORE:
Ligeti, MASETTO: Alvary, CONDUCTOR: Breisach.

September 22: THE BARBER OF SEVILLE (Rossini)
ROSINA: Conner, COUNT ALMAVIVA: Garris, FIGARO: Valdengo, BARTOLO: Bac-
caloni, BASILIO: Tajo, FIORELLO: DePaolis, OFFICER: Chabay, BERTHA: C. Turner,
CONDUCTOR: Breisach.

September 26, matinee: RIGOLETTO (Verdi)
GILDA: Conner, DUKE: Peerce, RIGOLETTO: Warren, MADDALENA: Glaz, SPARAFU-
CILE: Alvary, MONTERONE: Ligeti, BORSA: DePaolis, MARULLO: Cehanovsky,
CEPRANO: Harvey, COUNTESS CEPRANO: Heitman, GIOVANNA: Baldwin, PAGE:
Lawlor, CONDUCTOR: Adler.

September 29: DON GIOVANNI (Mozart)
Same cast except: LEPORELLO: Tajo.

October 2, matinee: THE BARBER OF SEVILLE (Rossini)
Same cast except: FIGARO: Gobbi, FIORELLO: Cehanovsky.

October 3, matinee: LA GIOCONDA (Ponchielli)
LA GIOCONDA: Varnay, LAURA: Stignani, LA CIECA: C. Turner, ENZO: Baum,
BARNABA: Valentino, ALVISE: Moscona, ZUANE: McVey, ISEPO: Curzi, PILOT:
Nelson, MONK: Ligeti, CANTOR: Benson, VOICES: Alibertini, Attarian, CONDUCTOR:
Marzollo.

October 4: MANON (Massenet)
Same cast except: COUNT DES GRIEUX: Moscona.

October 6: LA FORZA DEL DESTINO (Verdi)
Same cast except: DON CARLO: Weede, CONDUCTOR: Marzollo.

October 10, matinee: DIE MEISTERSINGER (Wagner)
Same cast except: WALTHER: Svanholm.

October 12: LA BOHEME (Puccini)
Same cast except: MIMI: Albanese, RODOLFO: Bjoerling, MARCELLO: Gobbi.

October 13: BORIS GODOUNOFF (Moussorgsky) (Portola Festival performance)
Same cast.

October 15: LA TRAVIATA (Verdi)
Same cast except: VIOLETTA: Kirsten, ALFREDO: Tagliavini, GERMONT: Weede,
GASTON: Chabay, FLORA: Zubiri.

October 17: CARMEN (Bizet)
Same cast except: MICAELA: Warenskjold, DON JOSE: Jobin.

CHILDREN'S PERFORMANCES

October 8, matinee: LA BOHEME (Puccini)
Same cast as September 23 except: MIMI: Albanese, RODOLFO: Kullman, MAR-
CELLO: Gobbi, BENOIT: Olitzki, ALCINDORO: Olitzki.

October 15, matinee: LA BOHEME (Puccini)
Same cast as September 23 except: RODOLFO: Bjoerling, MUSETTA: Zubiri, CONDUCTOR: Kritz.

CASTS—1949 SEASON

REGULAR SERIES

September 20: TOSCA (Puccini)
TOSCA: Barbato, CAVARADOSSI: Bjoerling, SCARPIA: Tibbett, SPOLETTA: DePaolis, SACRISTAN: Baccaloni, ANGELOTTI: Ligeti, SCIARRONE: Cehanovsky, JAILOR: Guenter, SHEPHERD: D. Walker, CONDUCTOR: Cleva.

September 22: FAUST (Gounod)
MARGUERITE: Albanese, FAUST: Jobin, MEPHISTOPHELES: Tajo, VALENTIN: Mascherini, WAGNER: McVey, SIEBEL: Glaz, MARTHE: C. Turner, CONDUCTOR: Merola.

September 27: DON GIOVANNI (Mozart)
DONNA ANNA: Bampton, DONNA ELVIRA: Novotna, ZERLINA: Albanese, DON GIOVANNI: Tajo, LEPORELLO: Baccaloni, DON OTTAVIO: Peerce, COMMENDATORE: Ligeti, MASETTO: Cehanovsky, CONDUCTOR: Breisach.

September 30: TRISTAN AND ISOLDE (Wagner)
ISOLDE: Flagstad, BRANGÄNE: Thebom, TRISTAN: Svanholm, KING MARKE: Szekely, KURWENAL: Janssen, MELOT: Cehanovsky, SHEPHERD: Chabay, SAILOR'S VOICE: Chabay, STEERSMAN: McVey, CONDUCTOR: Steinberg.

October 4: AIDA (Verdi)
AIDA: Barbato, AMNERIS: Thebom, RHADAMES: Svanholm, AMONASRO: Weede, RAMFIS: Moscona, KING: Ligeti, MESSENGER: Chabay, PRIESTESS: Graf, CONDUCTOR: Steinberg.

October 7: MANON LESCAUT (Puccini)
MANON LESCAUT: Albanese, CHEVALIER DES GRIEUX: Bjoerling, LESCAUT: Mascherini, GERONTE: Baccaloni, EDMONDO: Curzi, DANCING MASTER: DePaolis, LAMPLIGHTER: Chabay, CAPTAIN: Ligeti, MUSICIAN: Glaz, INNKEEPER: Harvey, CONDUCTOR: Cleva.

October 11: DIE WALKÜRE (Wagner)
BRÜNNHILDE: Flagstad, SIEGLINDE: Bampton, FRICKA: Thebom, SIEGMUND: Svanholm, WOTAN: Sharretts, HUNDING: Szekely, HELMWIGE: Wilcox, GERHILDE: Spry, ORTLINDE: Chauveau, SIEGRUNE: Glaz, ROSSWEISSE: Baldwin, WALTRAUTE: Ostrowski, GRIMGERDE: Thornbury, SCHWERTLEITE: D. Walker, CONDUCTOR: Steinberg.

October 14: THE TALES OF HOFFMANN (Offenbach)
HOFFMANN: Jobin, OLYMPIA: Graf, GIULIETTA: Novotna, ANTONIA: Albanese, COPPELIUS: Baccaloni, DAPERTUTTO: Tibbett, DR. MIRACLE: Tibbett, NICKLAUSSE: Glaz, VOICE OF ANTONIA'S MOTHER: D. Walker, SPALANZANI: DePaolis, SCHLEMIL: Cehanovsky, CRESPEL: Ligeti, FRANTZ: DePaolis, COCHENILLE: Chabay, PITICHINACCIO: Chabay, NATHANAEL: Curzi, HERMANN: Trevor, LUTHER: Harvey, LINDORF: Cehanovsky, ANDRES: Chabay, STELLA: Lagorio, CONDUCTOR: Breisach.

October 18: SAMSON AND DELILAH (Saint-Saens)
SAMSON: Jobin, DELILAH: Thebom, HIGH PRIEST: Weede, ABIMELECH: Cehanovsky, OLD HEBREW: Ligeti, MESSENGER: Peters, PHILISTINE: Nelson, CONDUCTOR: Cleva.

October 21: LUCIA DI LAMMERMOOR (Donizetti)
LUCIA: Pons, LORD HENRY: Valentino, EDGARDO: Tagliavini, LORD ARTHUR: Chabay, RAYMOND: Ligeti, ALICE: Zubiri, NORMAN: Curzi, CONDUCTOR: Merola.

POPULAR MATINEE SERIES

September 25: LA BOHEME (Puccini)
MIMI: Albanese, RODOLFO: Bjoerling, MARCELLO: Mascherini, COLLINE: Moscona,
SCHAUNARD: Cehanovsky, MUSETTA: Hartzell, BENOIT: Baccaloni, ALCINDORO:
Baccaloni, PARPIGNOL: Curzi, SERGEANT: Lorenzini, OFFICER: Harvey, CONDUC-
TOR: Kritz.
October 2: FAUST (Gounod)
Same cast except: MARGUERITE: Quartararo, FAUST: Bjoerling, MEPHISTOPHELES:
Moscona, MARTHE: Ostrowski, CONDUCTOR: Adler.
October 9: DON GIOVANNI (Mozart)
Same cast.
October 16: MANON LESCAUT (Puccini)
Same cast except: LESCAUT: Valentino.
October 23: DIE WALKÜRE (Wagner)
Same cast except: WOTAN: Janssen.

POPULAR EVENING SERIES

September 24: CARMEN (Bizet)
CARMEN: Heidt, MICAELA: Graf, DON JOSE: Vinay, ESCAMILLO: Valentino,
ZUNIGA: Ligeti, DANCAIRO: Cehanovsky, REMENDADO: DePaolis, MORALES: Ceha-
novsky, FRASQUITA: Hartzell, MERCEDES: C. Turner, CONDUCTOR: Breisach.
September 29: TOSCA (Puccini)
Same cast except: CAVARADOSSI: Tagliavini.
October 6: TRISTAN AND ISOLDE (Wagner)
Same cast except: BRANGÄNE: Glaz.
October 13: AIDA (Verdi)
Same cast except: RAMFIS: Szekely.
October 20: THE TALES OF HOFFMANN (Offenbach)
Same cast except: OLYMPIA: O'Connell, GIULIETTA: Thebom, ANTONIA: War-
enskjold.

EXTRA PERFORMANCES

October 8: TOSCA (Puccini)
Same cast as September 20 except: CAVARADOSSI: Tagliavini.
October 15: TRISTAN AND ISOLDE (Wagner)
Same cast as September 30.
October 19: LA BOHEME (Puccini)
Same cast except: RODOLFO: Tagliavini, MARCELLO: Valentino.

CHILDREN'S PERFORMANCES

October 6, matinee: FAUST (Gounod)
Same cast as September 22 except: MARGUERITE: Quartararo, VALENTIN: Weede,
SIEBEL: Hartzell, MARTHE: Ostrowski, CONDUCTOR: Adler.
October 13, matinee: FAUST (Gounod)
Same cast as September 22 except: MARGUERITE: Quartararo, FAUST: Bjoerling,
MEPHISTOPHELES: Moscona, MARTHE: Glaz, CONDUCTOR: Adler.

CASTS—1950 SEASON

REGULAR SERIES

September 26: AIDA (Verdi)
AIDA: Tebaldi, AMNERIS: Nikolaidi, RHADAMES: Del Monaco, AMONASRO: Weede,

RAMFIS: Tajo, KING: Ligeti, MESSENGER: Curzi, PRIESTESS: Graf, CONDUCTOR: Cleva.

September 29: THE MARRIAGE OF FIGARO (Mozart)
SUSANNA: Sayao, COUNTESS: Quartararo, CHERUBINO: Glaz, FIGARO: Tajo, COUNT: Brownlee, BARTOLO: Baccaloni, BASILIO: DePaolis, MARCELLINA: C. Turner, BARBARINA: Chauveau, ANTONIO: Cehanovsky, DON CURZIO: Norville, PEASANT GIRLS: Lanyon, Brubaker, CONDUCTOR: Perlea.

October 3: TRISTAN AND ISOLDE (Wagner)
ISOLDE: Flagstad, BRANGÄNE: Glaz, TRISTAN: Vinay, KING MARKE: Ernster, KURWENAL: Sigurd Bjoerling, MELOT: Cehanovsky, SHEPHERD: Schwabacher, SAILOR'S VOICE: Norville, STEERSMAN: J. Ford, CONDUCTOR: Perlea.

October 6: ANDREA CHENIER (Giordano)
MADELEINE: Albanese, ANDREA CHENIER: Del Monaco, GERARD: Weede, MATHIEU: R. Herbert, FLEVILLE: Sze, ROUCHER: Cehanovsky, DUMAS: Sze, ABBE: Norville, SPY: DePaolis, SCHMIDT: J. Ford, FOUQUIER-TINVILLE: Ligeti, COUNTESS: C. Turner, MADELON: D. Walker, BERSI: Ostrowski, CONDUCTOR: Cleva.

October 10: OTELLO (Verdi)
DESDEMONA: Tebaldi, OTELLO: Vinay, IAGO: Valdengo, CASSIO: DePaolis, RODERIGO: Schwabacher, LODOVICO: Ligeti, MONTANO: Cehanovsky, HERALD: B. Nelson, EMILIA: Ostrowski, CONDUCTOR: Cleva.

October 13: THE MAGIC FLUTE (Mozart)
PAMINA: Warenskjold, QUEEN OF THE NIGHT: Barabas, TAMINO: Kullman, PAPAGENO: Brownlee, SARASTRO: Ernster, SPEAKER: Sze, PAPAGENA: G. Williams, MONOSTATOS: Norville, PRIESTS: J. Ford, Schwabacher, LADIES: Lauppe, Chauveau, C. Turner, SLAVES: Harvey, Bond, Louw, GUARDS: Curzi, Ligeti, YOUTHS: O'Connell, Sanderson, Baldwin, CONDUCTOR: Breisach.

October 17: THE BARBER OF SEVILLE (Rossini)
ROSINA: Pons, COUNT ALMAVIVA: Conley, FIGARO: Mascherini, BARTOLO: Baccaloni, BASILIO: Tajo, FIORELLO: Cehanovsky, OFFICER: DePaolis, BERTHA: C. Turner, AMBROSIO: Harvey, CONDUCTOR: Rescigno.

October 20: SUOR ANGELICA (Puccini)
SUOR ANGELICA: Albanese, PRINCESS: C. Turner, ABBESS: Thornbury, MISTRESS OF NOVICES: D. Walker, ALMS COLLECTOR: Baldwin, SISTER GENEVIEVE: Chauveau, SISTER OSMINA: Throndson, SISTER MONITOR: Ostrowski, SISTER DOLCINA: Hurd, NURSING SISTER: Stephens, NOVICES: Pappas, Lanyon, LAY SISTERS: Welton, G. Nelson, SISTERS: Barbano, Bruni, Andreatta, CONDUCTOR: Adler.

followed by: SALOME (Strauss)
SALOME: B. Lewis, HEROD: Jagel, JOKANAAN: Sigurd Bjoerling, HERODIAS: C. Turner, NARRABOTH: Fredericks, PAGE: Glaz, SOLDIERS: Cehanovsky, J. Ford, NAZARENES: Ligeti, Peters, JEWS: Norville, Curzi, DePaolis, Schwabacher, Sze, SLAVE: Baldwin, CAPPADOCIAN: R. Nelson, HENCHMAN: Louw, CONDUCTOR: Breisach.

October 24: MANON LESCAUT (Puccini)
MANON LESCAUT: Kirsten, CHEVALIER DES GRIEUX: Del Monaco, LESCAUT: Valdengo, GERONTE: R. Herbert, EDMONDO: Curzi, DANCING MASTER: DePaolis, LAMPLIGHTER: Norville, CAPTAIN: J. Ford, MUSICIAN: Glaz, INNKEEPER: Harvey, SERGEANT: McVey, CONDUCTOR: Cleva.

October 27, at 5 p.m.: PARSIFAL (Wagner)
KUNDRY: Flagstad, PARSIFAL: Kullman, AMFORTAS: Sigurd Bjoerling, GURNEMANZ: Ernster, KLINGSOR: R. Herbert, TITUREL: Ligeti, VOICE: D. Walker, KNIGHTS: Curzi, J. Ford, ESQUIRES: Graf, Glaz, Norville, Schwabacher, FLOWER MAIDENS: Graf, Chauveau, Glaz, O'Connell, Stephens, Ostrowski, CONDUCTOR: Perlea.

SUNDAY MATINEE SERIES
October 1: AIDA (Verdi)
Same cast except: KING: Sze.
October 8: LA BOHEME (Puccini)
MIMI: Sayao, RODOLFO: DiStefano, MARCELLO: Mascherini, COLLINE: Tajo, SCHAU-NARD: Cehanovsky, MUSETTA: Graf, BENOIT: Baccaloni, ALCINDORO: Baccaloni, PARPIGNOL: Curzi, SERGEANT: Lorenzini, OFFICER: Harvey, CONDUCTOR: Kritz.
October 15: ANDREA CHENIER (Giordano)
Same cast.
October 22: THE BARBER OF SEVILLE (Rossini)
Same cast.
October 29: PARSIFAL (Wagner)
Same cast.

MIDWEEK EVENING SERIES
September 28: LUCIA DI LAMMERMOOR (Donizetti)
LUCIA: Pons, LORD HENRY: Mascherini, EDGARDO: DiStefano, LORD ARTHUR: Curzi, RAYMOND: Ligeti, ALICE: Chauveau, NORMAN: Norville, CONDUCTOR: Breisach.
October 4: THE MARRIAGE OF FIGARO (Mozart)
Same cast except: CHERUBINO: Warenskjold.
October 12: TRISTAN AND ISOLDE (Wagner)
Same cast except: KING MARKE: Ligeti.
October 19: OTELLO (Verdi)
Same cast.
October 26: SUOR ANGELICA (Puccini)
Same cast.
                    followed by: SALOME (Strauss)
Same cast except: JOKANAAN: R. Herbert.

EXTRA PERFORMANCES
October 2: LUCIA DI LAMMERMOOR (Donizetti)
Same cast except: LORD HENRY: Valentino, EDGARDO: Conley.
October 11: THE MAGIC FLUTE (Mozart) (California Masonic Centennial performance)
Same cast except: PAMINA: Graf.
October 28: LA BOHEME (Puccini)
Same cast except: MARCELLO: Valentino.

CHILDREN'S PERFORMANCES
October 19, matinee: MADAMA BUTTERFLY (Puccini)
CIO-CIO-SAN: Kirsten, PINKERTON: Conley, SHARPLESS: Valentino, SUZUKI: Glaz, GORO: DePaolis, BONZE: Sze, YAMADORI: Cehanovsky, COMMISSIONER: J. Ford, KATE PINKERTON: Chauveau, REGISTRAR: Harvey, CONDUCTOR: Rescigno.
October 26, matinee: MADAMA BUTTERFLY (Puccini)
Same cast except: SUZUKI: Ostrowski.

CASTS—1951 SEASON

REGULAR SERIES
September 18: OTELLO (Verdi)
DESDEMONA: Nelli, OTELLO: Vinay, IAGO: Valdengo, CASSIO: Schwabacher, RODE-RIGO: Curzi, LODOVICO: Ligeti, MONTANO: Cehanovsky, HERALD: Trevor, EMILIA: Ostrowski, CONDUCTOR: Cleva.

September 21: ROMEO AND JULIET (Gounod)
ROMEO: Bjoerling, JULIET: Sayao, MERCUTIO: R. Herbert, TYBALT: Schwabacher, CAPULET: Ligeti, FRIAR LAWRENCE: Moscona, GREGORIO: Harvey, BENVOGLIO: Curzi, DUKE OF VERONA: Ernster, STEFANO: Glaz, GERTRUDE: Ostrowski, CONDUCTOR: Breisach.

September 25: DER ROSENKAVALIER (Strauss)
MARSCHALLIN: Roman, BARON OCHS: Alvary, OCTAVIAN: Thebom, SOPHIE: Graf, FANINAL: R. Herbert, TENOR: Conley, MARIANNE: Chauveau, VALZACCHI: DePaolis, ANNINA: Glaz, POLICE COMMISSIONER: Ligeti, NOTARY: Harvey, LANDLORD: Curzi, MILLINER: Brubaker, ANIMAL VENDOR: Thomson, MARSCHALLIN'S MAJOR-DOMO: Andersen, FANINAL'S MAJOR-DOMO: Schwabacher, ORPHANS: Lanyon, Baldwin, Lagorio, FOOTMEN: T. Miller, Guenter, Rossi, Trevor, CONDUCTOR: Leinsdorf.

September 28: LA FORZA DEL DESTINO (Verdi)
LEONORA: Nelli, DON ALVARO: Baum, DON CARLO: Weede, PADRE GUARDIANO: Moscona, FRA MELITONE: Baccaloni, PREZIOSILLA: C. Turner, MARQUIS OF CALATRAVA: Alvary, ALCADE: Sze, TRABUCCO: DePaolis, CURRA: Baldwin, SURGEON: Cehanovsky, CONDUCTOR: Adler.

October 2: BORIS GODOUNOFF (Moussorgsky)
BORIS: Rossi-Lemeni, DIMITRI: Fredericks, MARINA: Thebom, PIMEN: Moscona, SHOUISKY: DePaolis, RANGONI: Ligeti, VARLAAM: Baccaloni, MISSAIL: Curzi, TCHELKALOFF: Cehanovsky, FEODOR: Chauveau, XENIA: Hartzell, NURSE: Wilkins, INNKEEPER: Ostrowski, SIMPLETON: Schwabacher, POLICE OFFICER: Sze, FRONTIER GUARD SERGEANT: Porta, BOYAR-IN-WAITING: Ernest Lawrence, LOVITZKY: Sze, TCHERNIAKOVSKY: Cehanovsky, BOYAR: White, PEASANTS: McIntosh, Eloise Farrell, Guenter, Novi, CONDUCTOR: Leinsdorf.

October 5: LA TRAVIATA (Verdi)
VIOLETTA: Pons, ALFREDO: Peerce, GERMONT: Valdengo, GASTON: DePaolis, BARON DOUPHOL: Cehanovsky, MARQUIS D'OBIGNY: Sze, DR. GRENVIL: Ligeti, FLORA: Chauveau, ANNINA: Baldwin, CONDUCTOR: Cleva.

October 8: LA BOHEME (Puccini)
MIMI: Sayao, RODOLFO: Bjoerling, MARCELLO: Valdengo, COLLINE: Moscona, SCHAUNARD: Cehanovsky, MUSETTA: Graf, BENOIT: Baccaloni, ALCINDORO: Baccaloni, PARPIGNOL: Curzi, SERGEANT: Lorenzini, OFFICER: Harvey, CONDUCTOR: Breisach.

October 12: TOSCA (Puccini)
TOSCA: Kirsten, CAVARADOSSI: Bjoerling, SCARPIA: Weede, SPOLETTA: DePaolis, SACRISTAN: Baccaloni, ANGELOTTI: Ligeti, SCIARRONE: Cehanovsky, JAILOR: Sze, SHEPHERD: Throndson, CONDUCTOR: Cleva.

October 16: MANON (Massenet)
MANON: Sayao, CHEVALIER DES GRIEUX: Vroons, LESCAUT: Valentino, GUILLOT: DePaolis, DE BRETIGNY: Cehanovsky, COUNT DES GRIEUX: Alvary, POUSETTE: Hartzell, JAVOTTE: Chauveau, ROSETTE: Baldwin, SERVANT: Lanyon, GUARDS: Andersen, Lorenzini, TRAVELERS: Hurd, S. L. Knapp, CONDUCTOR: Cleva.

October 19: FIDELIO (Beethoven)
LEONORE: Varnay, FLORESTAN: Svanholm, ROCCO: Ernster, DON PIZARRO: Janssen, DON FERNANDO: Ligeti, MARZELLINE: Graf, JACQUINO: Schwabacher, PRISONERS: Ernest Lawrence, Sze, CONDUCTOR: Wallenstein.

SUNDAY MATINEE SERIES

September 23: OTELLO (Verdi)
Same cast.

September 30: DER ROSENKAVALIER (Strauss)
Same cast except: SOPHIE: Warenskjold, TENOR: Fredericks.

October 7: BORIS GODOUNOFF (Moussorgsky)
Same cast except: MARINA: C. Turner, PIMEN: Alvary.
October 14: LA BOHEME (Puccini)
Same cast except: COLLINE: Rossi-Lemeni, MUSETTA: Hartzell.
October 21: MANON (Massenet)
Same cast except: COUNT DES GRIEUX: Moscona.

THURSDAY EVENING SERIES

September 20: CARMEN (Bizet)
CARMEN: Thebom, MICAELA: Warenskjold, DON JOSE: Vinay, ESCAMILLO: Valdengo, ZUNIGA: Alvary, DANCAIRO: Cehanovsky, REMENDADO: DePaolis, MORALES: Andersen, FRASQUITA: Hartzell, MERCEDES: Ostrowski, CONDUCTOR: Breisach.
September 27: ROMEO AND JULIET (Gounod)
Same cast except: JULIET: Anna Lisa Bjoerling, FRIAR LAWRENCE: Alvary.
October 4: LA FORZA DEL DESTINO (Verdi)
Same cast except: PADRE GUARDIANO: Rossi-Lemeni.
October 11: LA TRAVIATA (Verdi)
Same cast except: ALFREDO: Conley.
October 18: TOSCA (Puccini)
Same cast except: CAVARADOSSI: Peerce, SCARPIA: R. Herbert.

EXTRA PERFORMANCES

September 29: MADAMA BUTTERFLY (Puccini)
CIO-CIO-SAN: Kirsten, PINKERTON: Conley, SHARPLESS: Valentino, SUZUKI: Glaz, GORO: DePaolis, BONZE: Sze, YAMADORI: Cehanovsky, COMMISSIONER: Trevor, KATE PINKERTON: Chauveau, REGISTRAR: Harvey, CONDUCTOR: Rescigno.
October 13: PARSIFAL (Wagner)
KUNDRY: Varnay, PARSIFAL: Svanholm, AMFORTAS: Janssen, GURNEMANZ: Ernster, KLINGSOR: R. Herbert, TITUREL: Ligeti, VOICE: C. Turner, KNIGHTS: Curzi, Sze, ESQUIRES: Graf, Glaz, Ernest Lawrence, Schwabacher, FLOWER MAIDENS: Graf, Chauveau, Glaz, Hartzell, Stephens, Ostrowski, CONDUCTOR: Leinsdorf.
October 20: RIGOLETTO (Verdi)
GILDA: Pons, DUKE: Bjoerling, RIGOLETTO: Weede, MADDALENA: Glaz, SPARAFUCILE: Alvary, MONTERONE: Ligeti, BORSA: DePaolis, MARULLO: Cehanovsky, CEPRANO: Harvey, COUNTESS CEPRANO: Chauveau, GIOVANNA: Baldwin, PAGE: Lanyon, CONDUCTOR: Cimara.

CHILDREN'S PERFORMANCES

October 4, matinee: CARMEN (Bizet)
Same cast except: MICAELA: Graf, ESCAMILLO: R. Herbert, ZUNIGA: Ligeti.
October 11, matinee: CARMEN (Bizet)
Same cast as September 20 except: MICAELA: Graf, DON JOSE: Svanholm, ESCAMILLO: R. Herbert.
October 18, matinee: CARMEN (Bizet)
Same cast as September 20 except: CARMEN: C. Turner, DON JOSE: Baum, CONDUCTOR: Kritz.

CASTS—1952 SEASON

REGULAR SERIES

September 16: TOSCA (Puccini)
TOSCA: Kirsten, CAVARADOSSI: Del Monaco, SCARPIA: Weede, SPOLETTA: DePaolis, SACRISTAN: Baccaloni, ANGELOTTI: Ligeti, SCIARRONE: Cehanovsky, JAILOR: Andersen, SHEPHERD: Throndson, CONDUCTOR: Cleva.

September 20: MEFISTOFELE (Boito)
MEFISTOFELE: Rossi-Lemeni, FAUST: Tagliavini, MARGHERITA: Sayao, ELENA: Fenn, WAGNER: Assandri, MARTHA: Votipka, PANTALIS: Roggero, NEREO: Curzi, CONDUCTOR: Cleva.

September 23: AIDA (Verdi)
AIDA: Curtis, AMNERIS: Thebom, RHADAMES: Del Monaco, AMONASRO: Valdengo, RAMFIS: Tajo, KING: Ligeti, MESSENGER: Schwabacher, PRIESTESS: Roggero, CONDUCTOR: Adler.

September 26: IL TABARRO (Puccini)
GIORGETTA: B. Lewis, LUIGI: Del Monaco, MICHELE: Weede, TINCA: Assandri, TALPA: Moscona, SONG VENDOR: Curzi, FRUGOLA: C. Turner, LOVERS: Chauveau, Schwabacher, CONDUCTOR: Curiel.

followed by: SUOR ANGELICA (Puccini)
SUOR ANGELICA: Curtis, PRINCESS: C. Turner, ABBESS: Throndson, MISTRESS OF NOVICES: D. Walker, ALMS COLLECTORS: Andreatta, Baldwin, SISTER GENEVIEVE: Roggero, SISTER OSMINA: Sherry Stevens, SISTER MONITOR: Votipka, SISTER DOLCINA: Johanson, NURSING SISTER: Frances Oliver, NOVICES: Marion, Larsen, LAY SISTERS: Kantor, Hoots, SISTERS: Brubaker, Barbano, S. L. Knapp, CONDUCTOR: Adler.

followed by: GIANNI SCHICCHI (Puccini)
GIANNI SCHICCHI: Tajo, RINUCCIO: Conley, LAURETTA: Warenskjold, SIMONE: Alvary, BETTO: Cehanovsky, GHERARDO: DePaolis, MARCO: Gbur, SPINELLOCCIO: Louw, NOTARY: Ligeti, PINELLINO: Harvey, GUCCIO: Andersen, ZITA: C. Turner, NELLA: Chauveau, LA CIESCA: Votipka, GHERARDINO: Andreatta, CONDUCTOR: Kritz.

September 30: DER ROSENKAVALIER (Strauss)
MARSCHALLIN: B. Lewis, BARON OCHS: Alvary, OCTAVIAN: Thebom, SOPHIE: Warenskjold, FANINAL: R. Herbert, TENOR: Ernest Lawrence, MARIANNE: Votipka, VALZACCHI: DePaolis, ANNINA: Roggero, POLICE COMMISSIONER: Gbur, NOTARY: Harvey, LANDLORD: Curzi, MILLINER: Brubaker, ANIMAL VENDOR: Daneluz, MARSCHALLIN'S MAJOR-DOMO: Andersen, FANINAL'S MAJOR-DOMO: Schwabacher, ORPHANS: Marion, Hoots, Baldwin, FOOTMEN: T. Miller, Guenter, Rossi, L. Ford, CONDUCTOR: Breisach.

October 3: IL TROVATORE (Verdi)
LEONORA: Nelli, AZUCENA: C. Turner, MANRICO: Del Monaco, COUNT DI LUNA: Guarrera, FERRANDO: Moscona, RUIZ: Assandri, OLD GYPSY: Lovasich, INEZ: Votipka, CONDUCTOR: Breisach.

October 7: THE DAUGHTER OF THE REGIMENT (Donizetti)
MARIE: Pons, TONIO: Ernest Lawrence, SULPICE: Baccaloni, MARQUISE DE BIRKENFELD: C. Turner, HORTENSIUS: Alvary, CORPORAL: Cehanovsky, NOTARY: Harvey, PEASANT: Schwabacher, DUCHESSE DE KRAKENTHORP: Chauveau, CONDUCTOR: Cimara.

October 10: LA BOHEME (Puccini)
MIMI: Sayao, RODOLFO: Peerce, MARCELLO: Valentino, COLLINE: Tajo, SCHAUNARD: Cehanovsky, MUSETTA: Fenn, BENOIT: Baccaloni, ALCINDORO: Baccaloni, PARPIGNOL: Curzi, SERGEANT: Lorenzini, OFFICER: Harvey, CONDUCTOR: Merola.

October 14: DON GIOVANNI (Mozart)
DONNA ANNA: Curtis, DONNA ELVIRA: B. Lewis, ZERLINA: Sayao, DON GIOVANNI: Rossi-Lemeni, LEPORELLO: Tajo, DON OTTAVIO: Peerce, COMMENDATORE: Ligeti, MASETTO: Alvary, CONDUCTOR: Breisach.

October 17: L'AMORE DEI TRE RE (Montemezzi)
FIORA: Kirsten, AVITO: B. Sullivan, MANFREDO: Weede, ARCHIBALDO: Rossi-Lemeni, FLAMINIO: Assandri, YOUTH: Curzi, OLD WOMAN: Votipka, YOUNG GIRL: Larsen, SERVANT: S. L. Knapp, VOICE: Baldwin, CONDUCTOR: Cleva.

SUNDAY MATINEE SERIES

September 21: TOSCA (Puccini)
Same cast except: CAVARADOSSI: Conley.
September 28: AIDA (Verdi)
Same cast except: AIDA: Nelli, KING: Gbur.
October 5: DER ROSENKAVALIER (Strauss)
Same cast except: TENOR: Fredericks.
October 12: THE DAUGHTER OF THE REGIMENT (Donizetti)
Same cast.
October 19: DON GIOVANNI (Mozart)
Same cast except: DON OTTAVIO: Conley, MASETTO: R. Herbert.

WEDNESDAY EVENING SERIES

September 17: RIGOLETTO (Verdi)
GILDA: Pons, DUKE: Peerce, RIGOLETTO: Valdengo, MADDALENA: C. Turner, SPARA-
FUCILE: Moscona, MONTERONE: Gbur, BORSA: DePaolis, MARULLO: Cehanovsky,
CEPRANO: Harvey, COUNTESS CEPRANO: Chauveau, GIOVANNA: Baldwin, PAGE:
Brubaker, CONDUCTOR: Cimara.
September 24: MEFISTOFELE (Boito)
Same cast.
October 1: IL TABARRO (Puccini)
Same cast except: LUIGI: Fredericks.
          followed by: SUOR ANGELICA (Puccini)
Same cast.
          followed by: GIANNI SCHICCHI (Puccini)
Same cast.
October 8: IL TROVATORE (Verdi)
Same cast except: LEONORA: Curtis, AZUCENA: Barbieri.
October 15: LA BOHEME (Puccini)
Same cast except: MIMI: Warenskjold, RODOLFO: Tagliavini, MARCELLO: Val-
dengo, COLLINE: Moscona, MUSETTA: B. Lewis, CONDUCTOR: Kritz.

EXTRA PERFORMANCES

October 4: LA TRAVIATA (Verdi)
VIOLETTA: Pons, ALFREDO: Conley, GERMONT: Weede, GASTON: DePaolis, BARON
DOUPHOL: Cehanovsky, MARQUIS D'OBIGNY: Gbur, DR. GRENVIL: Ligeti, FLORA:
Chauveau, ANNINA: Baldwin, CONDUCTOR: Cimara.
October 11, matinee: MEFISTOFELE (Boito)
Same cast as September 20 except: FAUST: Del Monaco.
October 16: CAVALLERIA RUSTICANA (Mascagni)
SANTUZZA: Barbieri, TURIDDU: Peerce, ALFIO: R. Herbert, LOLA: Roggero,
MAMMA LUCIA: Votipka, CONDUCTOR: Adler.
          followed by: I PAGLIACCI (Leoncavallo)
CANIO: Del Monaco, TONIO: Guarrera, NEDDA: Sayao, SILVIO: Valentino, BEPPE:
Assandri, PEASANTS: Harvey, Frost, CONDUCTOR: Kritz.
October 18: AIDA (Verdi)
Same cast as September 23 except: AIDA: Nelli, AMNERIS: Barbieri, RAMFIS:
Moscona, KING: Gbur.

CHILDREN'S PERFORMANCES

October 1, matinee: CAVALLERIA RUSTICANA (Mascagni)
Same cast except: SANTUZZA: Nelli, LOLA: Chauveau.
          followed by: I PAGLIACCI (Leoncavallo)
Same cast except: TONIO: Valentino, NEDDA: Fenn, SILVIO: Cehanovsky.

October 8, matinee: CAVALLERIA RUSTICANA (Mascagni)
Same cast as October 16 except: TURIDDU: Conley, LOLA: Chauveau.
                followed by: I PAGLIACCI (Leoncavallo)
Same cast as October 16 except: CANIO: Fredericks, TONIO: Valentino, SILVIO:
Cehanovsky, BEPPE: Curzi.
October 15, matinee: CAVALLERIA RUSTICANA (Mascagni)
Same cast as October 16 except: TURIDDU: Conley.
                followed by: I PAGLIACCI (Leoncavallo)
Same cast as October 16 except: CANIO: Fredericks, NEDDA: Fenn.

CASTS—1953 SEASON

REGULAR SERIES

September 15: MEFISTOFELE (Boito)
MEFISTOFELE: Rossi-Lementi, FAUST: Peerce, MARGHERITA: Albanese, ELENA: Sills,
WAGNER: Assandri, MARTHA: Wilkins, PANTALIS: Roggero, NEREO: Curzi, CON-
DUCTOR: Cleva.
September 19: WERTHER (Massenet)
CHARLOTTE: Simionato, WERTHER: Valletti, SOPHIE: Warenskjold, ALBERT:
Lombardi, BAILIFF: Alvary, SCHMIDT: Curzi, JOHANN: Cehanovsky, BRUHLMANN:
Andersen, KATCHEN: Roehr, CONDUCTOR: Serafin.
September 22: LA TRAVIATA (Verdi)
VIOLETTA: Kirsten, ALFREDO: Poleri, GERMONT: Mascherini, GASTON: DePaolis,
BARON DOUPHOL: Cehanovsky, MARQUIS D'OBIGNY: Gbur, DR. GRENVIL: Ligeti,
FLORA: Chauveau, ANNINA: Currier, CONDUCTOR: Cleva.
September 25: THE CREATURES OF PROMETHEUS ballet (Beethoven)
PROMETHEUS: Paxman, FIRE: V. Johnson, ZEUS: Feinberg, WOMAN: N. Johnson,
MAN: Barallobre, ATHENA: Johnston, APOLLO: Mallozzi, TERPSICHORE: Arnold,
APHRODITE: Bailey, MELPOMENE: Bering, QUEEN: Shore, KING: Sage, THALIA:
Coler, BACCHUS: Ludlow, CONDUCTOR: Curiel.
                followed by: ELEKTRA (Strauss)
ELEKTRA: Borkh, CHRYSOTHEMIS: Faull, KLYTEMNESTRA: Klose, AEGISTHUS: Su-
thaus, ORESTES: Schoeffler, ORESTES' TUTOR: Ligeti, CONFIDANTE: Eloise Farrell,
TRAINBEARER: Roehr, OLD SERVANT: Gbur, OVERSEER: Chauveau, MAIDSERVANTS:
Roggero, Wilkins, Moudry, Sills, Hartzell, CONDUCTOR: Solti.
September 29: BORIS GODOUNOFF (Moussorgsky)
BORIS: Rossi-Lemeni, DIMITRI: B. Sullivan, MARINA: Simionato, PIMEN: Alvary,
SHOUISKY: DePaolis, RANGONI: Bardelli, VARLAAM: Baccaloni, MISSAIL: Curzi,
TCHELKALOFF: Cehanovsky, FEODOR: Chauveau, XENIA: Hartzell, NURSE: Wilkins,
INNKEEPER: Moudry, SIMPLETON: Mason, POLICE OFFICER: Gbur, FRONTIER
GUARD SERGEANT: Ligeti, BOYAR-IN-WAITING: Assandri, LOVITZKY: Gbur, TCHERNI-
AKOVSKY: Cehanovsky, BOYAR: White, CONDUCTOR: Serafin.
October 2: TRISTAN AND ISOLDE (Wagner)
ISOLDE: Grob-Prandl, BRANGÄNE: Klose, TRISTAN: Suthaus, KING MARKE: Ernster,
KURWENAL: Schoeffler, MELOT: Cehanovsky, SHEPHERD: Mason, SAILOR'S VOICE:
Curzi, STEERSMAN: Gbur, CONDUCTOR: Solti.
October 6: TURANDOT (Puccini)
TURANDOT: Borkh, LIU: Albanese, CALAF: Turrini, TIMUR: Tajo, PING: Lombardi,
PANG: Assandri, PONG: Curzi, EMPEROR ALTOUM: DePaolis, MANDARIN: Gbur,
PRINCE OF PERSIA: Daneluz, MAIDS: Gotelli, D. Petersen, CONDUCTOR: Cleva.
October 9: THE BARBER OF SEVILLE (Rossini)
ROSINA: Simionato, COUNT ALMAVIVA: Valletti, FIGARO: Guarrera, BARTOLO:
Baccaloni, BASILIO: Rossi-Lemeni, FIORELLO: DePaolis, OFFICER: Assandri,
BERTHA: Moudry, CONDUCTOR: Serafin.

October 13: DIE WALKÜRE (Wagner)
BRÜNNHILDE: Grob-Prandl, SIEGLINDE: Borkh, FRICKA: Klose, SIEGMUND: Suthaus, WOTAN: Schoeffler, HUNDING: Ernster, HELMWIGE: Faull, GERHILDE: Sills, ORTLINDE: Chauveau, SIEGRUNE: Moudry, ROSSWEISSE: Roggero, WALTRAUTE: Eloise Farrell, GRIMGERDE: D. Petersen, SCHWERTLEITE: Wilkins, CONDUCTOR: Solti.

October 16: A MASKED BALL (Verdi)
AMELIA: Grob-Prandl, ULRICA: Klose, OSCAR: B. Gibson, RICCARDO: Turrini, RENATO: Mascherini, SAM: Alvary, TOM: Ligeti, SILVANO: Cehanovsky, JUDGE: Assandri, SERVANT: Lorenzini, CONDUCTOR: Serafin.

SUNDAY MATINEE SERIES

September 20: MEFISTOFELE (Boito)
Same cast.

September 27: MADAMA BUTTERFLY (Puccini)
CIO-CIO-SAN: Albanese, PINKERTON: B. Sullivan, SHARPLESS: Bardelli, SUZUKI: Roggero, GORO: DePaolis, BONZE: Alvary, YAMADORI: Cehanovsky, COMMISSIONER: Gbur, KATE PINKERTON: Chauveau, REGISTRAR: Harvey, CONDUCTOR: Adler.

October 4: BORIS GODOUNOFF (Moussorgsky)
Same cast.

October 11: TURANDOT (Puccini)
Same cast except: LIU: Warenskjold.

October 18: DIE WALKÜRE (Wagner)
Same cast.

WEDNESDAY EVENING SERIES

September 16: LA BOHEME (Puccini)
MIMI: Kirsten, RODOLFO: Poleri, MARCELLO: Bardelli, COLLINE: Tajo, SCHAUNARD: Cehanovsky, MUSETTA: Hartzell, BENOIT: Baccaloni, ALCINDORO: Baccaloni, SERGEANT: Lorenzini, OFFICER: Harvey, CONDUCTOR: Curiel.

September 23: DON GIOVANNI (Mozart)
DONNA ANNA: Faull, DONNA ELVIRA: Sills, ZERLINA: B. Gibson, DON GIOVANNI: Rossi-Lemeni, LEPORELLO: Tajo, DON OTTAVIO: Peerce, COMMENDATORE: Ernster, MASETTO: Alvary, CONDUCTOR: Serafin.

September 30: THE CREATURES OF PROMETHEUS ballet (Beethoven)
                followed by: ELEKTRA (Strauss)
Same cast.

October 7: TRISTAN AND ISOLDE (Wagner)
Same cast except: KING MARKE: Ligeti.

October 14: LA TRAVIATA (Verdi)
Same cast except: VIOLETTA: Albanese, ALFREDO: Peerce.

EXTRA PERFORMANCES

September 26: CARMEN (Bizet)
CARMEN: C. Turner, MICAELA: Warenskjold, DON JOSE: Poleri, ESCAMILLO: Guarrera, ZUNIGA: Alvary, DANCAIRO: Cehanovsky, REMENDADO: DePaolis, MORALES: Andersen, FRASQUITA: Hartzell, MERCEDES: Roggero, CONDUCTOR: Cleva.

October 17: LA BOHEME (Puccini)
Same cast except: MIMI: Albanese, RODOLFO: Peerce, MARCELLO: Mascherini.

CHILDREN'S PERFORMANCES

September 30, matinee: THE BARBER OF SEVILLE (Rossini)
Same cast as October 9 except: ROSINA: B. Gibson, FIGARO: Mascherini, BASILIO: Tajo, BERTHA: Wilkins, CONDUCTOR: Kritz.

October 7, matinee: THE BARBER OF SEVILLE (Rossini)
Same cast as October 9 except: ROSINA: B. Gibson, FIGARO: Mascherini, BASILIO: Tajo, BERTHA: Wilkins, CONDUCTOR: Kritz.
October 14, matinee: THE BARBER OF SEVILLE (Rossini)
Same cast as October 9 except: BASILIO: Tajo, CONDUCTOR: Kritz.

CASTS—1954 SEASON

REGULAR SERIES

September 17: RIGOLETTO (Verdi)
GILDA: Robin, DUKE: Tucker, RIGOLETTO: Warren, MADDALENA: C. Turner, SPARAFUCILE: Moscona, MONTERONE: Palangi, BORSA: DePaolis, MARULLO: Cehanovsky, CEPRANO: Harvey, COUNTESS CEPRANO: Hall, GIOVANNA: Elinor Warren, PAGE: Currier, CONDUCTOR: Cleva.
September 21: LA FORZA DEL DESTINO (Verdi)
LEONORA: Martinis, DON ALVARO: Tucker, DON CARLO: Warren, PADRE GUARDIANO: Siepi, FRA MELITONE: Baccaloni, PREZIOSILLA: C. Turner, MARQUIS OF CALATRAVA: Ligeti, ALCADE: Palangi, TRABUCCO: DePaolis, CURRA: Elinor Warren, SURGEON: Andersen, CONDUCTOR: Cleva.
September 24: THE PORTUGUESE INN (Cherubini)
RODRIGO: Alvary, DONNA GABRIELA: Carteri, ROSELBO: R. Herbert, DON CARLOS: Curzi, PEDRILLO: Cehanovsky, INIGO: DePaolis, INES: Caselle, CONDUCTOR: Curiel.
followed by: SALOME (Strauss)
SALOME: Borkh, HEROD: Kullman, JOKANAAN: Welitsch, HERODIAS: C. Turner, NARRABOTH: B. Sullivan, PAGE: Nadell, SOLDIERS: Cehanovsky, Palangi, NAZA-RENES: Ligeti, Andersen, JEWS: Curzi, Assandri, DePaolis, Mason, Harvey, SLAVE: Scott, CAPPADOCIAN: Enns, CONDUCTOR: Szenkar.
September 28: MANON (Massenet)
MANON: Kirsten, CHEVALIER DES GRIEUX: Prandelli, LESCAUT: R. Herbert, GUILLOT: DePaolis, DE BRETIGNY: Cehanovsky, COUNT DES GRIEUX: Alvary, POUSETTE: Caselle, JAVOTTE: Elinor Warren, ROSETTE: Nadell, SERVANT: Pappas, INNKEEPER: Harvey, GUARDS: Andersen, Lorenzini, CONDUCTOR: Monteux.
October 1: TOSCA (Puccini)
TOSCA: Kirsten, CAVARADOSSI: Peerce, SCARPIA: Weede, SPOLETTA: DePaolis, SACRISTAN: Baccaloni, ANGELOTTI: Ligeti, SCIARRONE: Cehanovsky, JAILOR: Palangi, SHEPHERD: Rosenblatt, CONDUCTOR: Cleva.
October 5: THE FLYING DUTCHMAN (Wagner)
DUTCHMAN: Hotter, SENTA: Borkh, ERIC: B. Sullivan, DALAND: Alvary, STEERS-MAN: Curzi, MARY: Elinor Warren, CONDUCTOR: Szenkar.
October 8: TURANDOT (Puccini)
TURANDOT: Martinis, LIU: Albanese, CALAF: Turrini, TIMUR: Moscona, PING: Guarrera, PANG: Assandri, PONG: Curzi, EMPEROR ALTOUM: DePaolis, MANDARIN: Palangi, PRINCE OF PERSIA: Bruce, MAIDS: Gotelli, D. Petersen, CONDUCTOR: Cleva.
October 12: THE MARRIAGE OF FIGARO (Mozart)
SUSANNA: Carteri, COUNTESS: Albanese, CHERUBINO: Warenskjold, FIGARO: Siepi, COUNT: Hotter, BARTOLO: Baccaloni, BASILIO: DePaolis, MARCELLINA: Elinor Warren, BARBARINA: Caselle, ANTONIO: Cehanovsky, DON CURZIO: Curzi, CON-DUCTOR: Szenkar.
October 15: IL TABARRO (Puccini)
GIORGETTA: Martinis, LUIGI: B. Sullivan, MICHELE: Weede, TINCA: Assandri, TALPA: Moscona, SONG VENDOR: Curzi, FRUGOLA: C. Turner, LOVERS: Currier, W. Petersen, CONDUCTOR: Curiel.
followed by: JOAN OF ARC AT THE STAKE (Honegger)

JOAN: McGuire, FRIAR DOMINIC: L. Marvin, PORCUS: Kullman, VIRGIN: Duval,
ST. MARGARET: Hall, ST. CATHERINE: Nadell, HERALDS: Mason, R. Herbert,
Palangi, CLERIC: Curzi, JUDGE: Ligeti, MONK: Assandri, VOICE IN THE PROLOGUE:
Hall, VOICES: Andersen, Flynn, CHILD: Ursino, ASS: S. Walker, DUKE OF BEDFORD:
Sage, JOHN OF LUXEMBOURG: Paxman, REYNOLD OF CHARTRES: Carvajal, WILLIAM
OF FLAVY: Ross, GRINDER TRUSTY: Ross, MOTHER OF BARRELS: McDonald, YOUNG
PEASANT: Franklyn, OLD PEASANT: Hagopian, PERROT: Hatch, JAILORS: J. Sullivan,
Verdell, CONDUCTOR: Monteux.
October 19: FIDELIO (Beethoven)
LEONORE: Borkh, FLORESTAN: Turrini, ROCCO: Alvary, DON PIZARRO: Hotter, DON
FERNANDO: Welitsch, MARZELLINE: Warenskjold, JACQUINO: Curzi, PRISONERS:
Millar, Enns, CONDUCTOR: Monteux.

SUNDAY MATINEE SERIES
September 19: LA BOHEME (Puccini)
MIMI: Carteri, RODOLFO: Peerce, MARCELLO: Guarrera, COLLINE: Moscona,
SCHAUNARD: Cehanovsky, MUSETTA: Duval, BENOIT: Baccaloni, ALCINDORO: Bac-
caloni, PARPIGNOL: Assandri, SERGEANT: Lorenzini, OFFICER: Harvey, CONDUCTOR:
Mueller.
September 26: RIGOLETTO (Verdi)
Same cast except: DUKE: B. Sullivan, MADDALENA: Nadell, SPARAFUCILE: Ligeti,
COUNTESS CEPRANO: Roehr, CONDUCTOR: Kritz.
October 3: MANON (Massenet)
Same cast except: MANON: Carteri.
October 10: THE FLYING DUTCHMAN (Wagner)
Same cast.
October 17: THE MARRIAGE OF FIGARO (Mozart)
Same cast.

THURSDAY EVENING SERIES
September 23: LUCIA DI LAMMERMOOR (Donizetti)
LUCIA: Robin, LORD HENRY: Guarrera, EDGARDO: Peerce, LORD ARTHUR: Curzi,
RAYMOND: Moscona, ALICE: Elinor Warren, NORMAN: Assandri, CONDUCTOR:
Barbini.
September 30: LA FORZA DEL DESTINO (Verdi)
Same cast except: DON ALVARO: Turrini.
October 7: THE PORTUGUESE INN (Cherubini)
Same cast.
                    followed by: SALOME (Strauss)
Same cast.
October 14: TURANDOT (Puccini)
Same cast except: TURANDOT: Borkh, LIU: Warenskjold.
October 21: IL TABARRO (Puccini)
Same cast.
        followed by: JOAN OF ARC AT THE STAKE (Honegger)
Same cast.

EXTRA PERFORMANCES
September 18: MADAMA BUTTERFLY (Puccini)
CIO-CIO-SAN: Albanese, PINKERTON: Prandelli, SHARPLESS: R. Herbert, SUZUKI:
Nadell, GORO: DePaolis, BONZE: Ligeti, YAMADORI: Cehanovsky, COMMISSIONER:
Palangi, KATE PINKERTON: Hall, REGISTRAR: Harvey, CONDUCTOR: Kritz.
October 16: A GALA NIGHT AT THE OPERA
I Pagliacci, PROLOGUE: Weede, *La Boheme,* ACT I: Carteri, Tucker, Guarrera,

Siepi, Cehanovsky, Baccaloni, *Forza Del Destino*, OVERTURE AND MONASTERY
SCENE: Martinis, Moscona, Baccaloni, *Manon*, COURS LA REINE SCENE: Kirsten,
R. Herbert, DePaolis, Cehanovsky, Alvary, Caselle, Elinor Warren, Nadell,
Rigoletto, ACT 3: Robin, Tucker, Warren, Palangi, Assandri, Cehanovsky,
Harvey, Currier, CONDUCTORS: Mueller, Cleva, Monteux, Kritz.
October 20: TOSCA (Puccini)
Same cast except: TOSCA: Albanese, CAVARADOSSI: Tucker.

CHILDREN'S PERFORMANCES
October 7, matinee: RIGOLETTO (Verdi)
Same cast as September 17 except: DUKE: Prandelli, RIGOLETTO: Weede, MAD-
DALENA: Nadell, BORSA: Assandri, COUNTESS CEPRANO: Roehr, CONDUCTOR: Kritz.
October 14, matinee: RIGOLETTO (Verdi)
Same cast as September 17 except: DUKE: Prandelli, MADDALENA: Nadell, SPARA-
FUCILE: Alvary, BORSA: Assandri, COUNTESS CEPRANO: Roehr, CONDUCTOR: Kritz.
October 18, matinee: RIGOLETTO (Verdi)
Same cast as September 17 except: DUKE: Prandelli, RIGOLETTO: Weede, MAD-
DALENA: Nadell, BORSA: Assandri, COUNTESS CEPRANO: Roehr, CONDUCTOR: Kritz.

CASTS—1955 SEASON

REGULAR SERIES
September 15: AIDA (Verdi)
AIDA: Tebaldi, AMNERIS: C. Turner, RHADAMES: Turrini, AMONASRO: Warren,
RAMFIS: Tozzi, KING: Ligeti, MESSENGER: Assandri, PRIESTESS: Roggero, CON-
DUCTOR: Cleva.
September 20: DER ROSENKAVALIER (Strauss)
MARSCHALLIN: Schwarzkopf, BARON OCHS: Edelmann, OCTAVIAN: Bible, SOPHIE:
Warenskjold, FANINAL: R. Herbert, TENOR: Manton, MARIANNE: Roehr, VAL-
ZACCHI: DePaolis, ANNINA: Roggero, POLICE COMMISSIONER: Palangi, NOTARY:
Harvey, LANDLORD: Lachona, MILLINER: McArt, ANIMAL VENDOR: Assandri,
MARSCHALLIN'S MAJOR-DOMO: Segale, FANINAL'S MAJOR-DOMO: Hague, ORPHANS:
Crader, D. Walker, Hilgenberg, FOOTMEN: Frost, Booth, Guenter, Toolatjan,
CONDUCTOR: Leinsdorf.
September 23: LOUISE (Charpentier)
LOUISE: Kirsten, JULIEN: B. Sullivan, MOTHER: C. Turner, FATHER: R. Herbert,
RAGPICKER: Alvary, JUNKMAN: Ligeti, YOUNG RAGPICKER: Roggero, STREET
SWEEPER: D. Walker, NEWSPAPER GIRL: Ronec, MILKWOMAN: West, COALPICKER:
Roehr, STREET ARAB: McArt, BIRDFOOD VENDOR: Scott, ARTICHOKE VENDOR: Kar-
ras, WATERCRESS VENDOR: Bible, CHAIR MENDER: Bible, OLD CLOTHES MAN: De-
Paolis, CARROT VENDOR: Assandri, RAG VENDOR: Cehanovsky, POLICEMEN: Blank-
enburg, Palangi, NOCTAMBULIST: Lachona, KING OF FOOLS: Lachona, SONG WRITER:
Cehanovsky, PHILOSOPHERS: Andersen, Harvey, PAINTER: J. Taylor, SCULPTOR:
Booth, POET: Petit, STUDENT: Segale, IRMA: Crader, CAMILLE: Gordon, GERTRUDE:
Hilgenberg, APPRENTICE: McArt, ELISE: Allen, BLANCHE: Garnier, SUZANNE:
S. L. Knapp, FOREWOMAN: Avery, MARGUERITE: Gotelli, MADELEINE: Covington,
CONDUCTOR: Morel.
September 27: MACBETH (Verdi)
LADY MACBETH: Borkh, MACBETH: Weede, BANQUO: Tozzi, MACDUFF: Fredericks,
MALCOLM: Assandri, LADY-IN-WAITING: Roehr, MEDIC: Palangi, SERVANT: Ander-
sen, ASSASSIN: Blankenburg, HERALD: A. Turner, APPARITIONS: P. Murphy,
Gotelli, R. Moore, CONDUCTOR: Cleva.

September 30: DON GIOVANNI (Mozart)
DONNA ANNA: Albanese, DONNA ELVIRA: Schwarzkopf, ZERLINA: Carteri, DON GIO-
VANNI: Siepi, LEPORELLO: Alvary, DON OTTAVIO: Peerce, COMMENDATORE: Ligeti,
MASETTO: R. Herbert, CONDUCTOR: Leinsdorf.
October 4: ANDREA CHENIER (Giordano)
MADELEINE: Tebaldi, ANDREA CHENIER: Tucker, GERARD: Warren, MATHIEU:
Alvary, FLEVILLE: Cehanovsky, ROUCHER: Blankenburg, DUMAS: Palangi, ABBE:
Assandri, SPY: DePaolis, SCHMIDT: Harvey, FOUQUIER-TINVILLE: Ligeti, COUNT-
ESS: Hilgenberg, MADELON: Roggero, BERSI: Roggero, CONDUCTOR: Cleva.
October 7: TROILUS AND CRESSIDA (Walton)
TROILUS: R. Lewis, CRESSIDA: Kirsten, DIOMEDE: Weede, CALKAS: Tozzi, PANDA-
RUS: McChesney, ANTENOR: Palangi, EVADNE: Bible, HORASTE: Blankenburg,
PRIESTS: Hammons, Andersen, TROJAN LADIES: Gordon, San Miguel, Gotelli,
WATCHMEN: Toolatjan, Manning, W. Petersen, SOLDIERS: Daneluz, Mayock,
CONDUCTOR: Leinsdorf.
October 11: LE COQ D'OR (Rimsky-Korsakoff)
QUEEN: Dobbs, KING DODON: Alvary, ASTROLOGER: Manton, GENERAL: Tozzi,
AMELFA: Roggero, VOICE OF COCK: Roehr, PRINCE GUIDON: Fredericks, PRINCE
AFRON: Blankenburg, BOYARS: Frost, Andersen, CONDUCTOR: Leinsdorf.
            followed by: I PAGLIACCI (Leoncavallo)
CANIO: Turrini, TONIO: Warren, NEDDA: Albanese, SILVIO: MacNeil, BEPPE: As-
sandri, PEASANTS: Mayock, Hammons, CONDUCTOR: Barbini.
October 14: LOHENGRIN (Wagner)
ELSA: Borkh, ORTRUD: Rankin, LOHENGRIN: B. Sullivan, TELRAMUND: Welitsch,
KING HENRY: Edelmann, HERALD: MacNeil, PAGES: Crader, McArt, Roehr, Hil-
genberg, CONDUCTOR: Cleva.
October 18: FAUST (Gounod)
MARGUERITE: Carteri, FAUST: Peerce, MEPHISTOPHELES: Siepi, VALENTIN: MacNeil,
WAGNER: Palangi, SIEBEL: Bible, MARTHE: Hilgenberg, CONDUCTOR: Morel.

SATURDAY EVENING SERIES

September 17: CARMEN (Bizet)
CARMEN: Rankin, MICAELA: Carteri, DON JOSE: R. Lewis, ESCAMILLO: MacNeil,
ZUNIGA: Alvary, DANCAIRO: Cehanovsky, REMENDADO: DePaolis, MORALES:
Blankenburg, FRASQUITA: Roehr, MERCEDES: Roggero, CONDUCTOR: Morel.
September 24: DER ROSENKAVALIER (Strauss)
Same cast except: TENOR: Fredericks.
October 1: MACBETH (Verdi)
Same cast.
October 8: ANDREA CHENIER (Giordano)
Same cast.
October 15: LE COQ D'OR (Rimsky-Korsakoff)
Same cast.
            followed by: I PAGLIACCI (Leoncavallo)
Same cast except: TONIO: Weede, SILVIO: Blankenburg.

THURSDAY EVENING SERIES

September 22: AIDA (Verdi)
Same cast except: AMNERIS: Rankin.
September 29: LOUISE (Charpentier)
Same cast.
October 6: DON GIOVANNI (Mozart)
Same cast.

October 13: TROILUS AND CRESSIDA (Walton)
Same cast.
October 20: LOHENGRIN (Wagner)
Same cast.

EXTRA PERFORMANCES

October 16, matinee: AIDA (Verdi)
Same cast as September 15.
October 19: TOSCA (Puccini)
TOSCA: Tebaldi, CAVARADOSSI: Tucker, SCARPIA: Weede, SPOLETTA: DePaolis, SACRISTAN: Cehanovsky, ANGELOTTI: Ligeti, SCIARRONE: Palangi, JAILOR: Blanken-burg, SHEPHERD: Roggero, CONDUCTOR: Curiel.

CHILDREN'S PERFORMANCES

October 6, matinee: CARMEN (Bizet)
Same cast except: MICAELA: Warenskjold, DON JOSE: Fredericks, ZUNIGA: Palangi, CONDUCTOR: Mueller.
October 13, matinee: CARMEN (Bizet)
Same cast as September 17 except: CARMEN: C. Turner, DON JOSE: Fredericks, ESCAMILLO: R. Herbert, CONDUCTOR: Mueller.
October 17, matinee: CARMEN (Bizet)
Same cast as September 17 except: MICAELA: Warenskjold, ESCAMILLO: R. Herbert, CONDUCTOR: Mueller.

CASTS—1956 SEASON

REGULAR SERIES

September 13: MANON LESCAUT (Puccini)
MANON LESCAUT: Kirsten, CHEVALIER DES GRIEUX: Bjoerling, LESCAUT: Quilico, GERONTE: Alvary, EDMONDO: Curzi, DANCING MASTER: DePaolis, LAMPLIGHTER: Assandri, CAPTAIN: Palangi, MUSICIAN: Roggero, SERGEANT: Andersen, CON-DUCTOR: De Fabritiis.
September 18: THE FLYING DUTCHMAN (Wagner)
DUTCHMAN: Hotter, SENTA: Rysanek, ERIC: Suthaus, DALAND: Alvary, STEERS-MAN: Curzi, MARY: Hilgenberg, CONDUCTOR: Steinberg.
September 21: FALSTAFF (Verdi)
SIR JOHN FALSTAFF: Warren, MISTRESS FORD: Schwarzkopf, MISTRESS PAGE: Rog-gero, DAME QUICKLY: Dominguez, ANNE: Schuh, FENTON: Campora, FORD: Guar-rera, DR. CAIUS: Assandri, BARDOLPH: DePaolis, PISTOL: Moscona, CONDUCTOR: Steinberg.
September 25: BORIS GODOUNOFF (Moussorgsky)
BORIS: Christoff, DIMITRI: R. Lewis, MARINA: Dominguez, PIMEN: Moscona, SHOUISKY: Curzi, RANGONI: Hotter, VARLAAM: Alvary, MISSAIL: Lachona, TCHEL-KALOFF: Cehanovsky, FEODOR: Nadell, XENIA: Crader, NURSE: Wilkins, INN-KEEPER: Hilgenberg, SIMPLETON: Manton, POLICE OFFICER: Palangi, FRONTIER GUARD SERGEANT: Ligeti, LOVITZKY: Kenig, TCHERNIAKOVSKY: Quilico, BOYAR: Assandri, PEASANTS: Covington, Eloise Farrell, Lovasich, CONDUCTOR: Steinberg.
September 28: FRANCESCA DA RIMINI (Zandonai)
FRANCESCA: Gencer, PAOLO: Martell, GIOVANNI: Colzani, MALATESTINO: Curzi, SAMARITANA: Crader, BIANCOFIORE: Gray, GARSENDA: McArt, ALTICHIARA: Rog-gero, DONELLA: Nadell, OSTASIO: Palangi, SER TOLDO BERARDENGO: DePaolis, JESTER: Blankenburg, BOWMAN: Lachona, TOWER WARDEN: Kenig, SMARAGDI: Hilgen-berg, VOICE OF A PRISONER: Assandri, CONDUCTOR: De Fabritiis.

October 2: COSI FAN TUTTE (Mozart)
FIORDILIGI: Schwarzkopf, DORABELLA: Rankin, DESPINA: Munsel, FERRANDO: R. Lewis, GUGLIELMO: Guarrera, DON ALFONSO: Alvary, CONDUCTOR: Schwieger.

October 5: DIE WALKÜRE (Wagner)
BRÜNNHILDE: Nilsson, SIEGLINDE: Rysanek, FRICKA: Rankin, SIEGMUND: Suthaus, WOTAN: Hotter, HUNDING: Moscona, HELMWIGE: Velsir, GERHILDE: Ronson, ORTLINDE: Althof, SIEGRUNE: Hilgenberg, ROSSWEISSE: Roggero, WALTRAUTE: Krooskos, GRIMGERDE: D. Petersen, SCHWERTLEITE: Nadell, CONDUCTOR: Schwieger.

October 9: SIMON BOCCANEGRA (Verdi)
SIMON BOCCANEGRA: Warren, AMELIA: Tebaldi, FIESCO: Christoff, ADORNO: Turrini, PAOLO: Blankenburg, PIETRO: Palangi, CAPTAIN: Assandri, MAIDSERVANT: Krooskos, CONDUCTOR: De Fabritiis.

October 12: THE ELIXIR OF LOVE (Donizetti)
ADINA: Munsel, NEMORINO: Campora, BELCORE: Quilico, DR. DULCAMARA: Tajo, GIANNETTA: McArt, CONDUCTOR: Curiel.

October 16: LA BOHEME (Puccini)
MIMI: Albanese, RODOLFO: Peerce, MARCELLO: Quilico, COLLINE: Tajo, SCHAUNARD: Blankenburg, MUSETTA: Gray, BENOIT: Cehanovsky, ALCINDORO: DePaolis, PARPIGNOL: Assandri, CONDUCTOR: Kritz.

SATURDAY EVENING SERIES

September 15: TOSCA (Puccini)
TOSCA: Tebaldi, CAVARADOSSI: Martell, SCARPIA: Warren, SPOLETTA: DePaolis, SACRISTAN: Cehanovsky, ANGELOTTI: Palangi, SCIARRONE: Cehanovsky, JAILOR: Harvey, SHEPHERD: Hilgenberg, CONDUCTOR: Curiel.

September 22: THE FLYING DUTCHMAN (Wagner)
Same cast.

September 29: BORIS GODOUNOFF (Moussorgsky)
Same cast.

October 6: COSI FAN TUTTE (Mozart)
Same cast.

October 13: SIMON BOCCANEGRA (Verdi)
Same cast.

THURSDAY EVENING SERIES

September 20: MANON LESCAUT (Puccini)
Same cast.

September 27: FALSTAFF (Verdi)
Same cast.

October 4: FRANCESCA DA RIMINI (Zandonai)
Same cast.

October 11: DIE WALKÜRE (Wagner)
Same cast except: HUNDING: Alvary.

October 18: THE ELIXIR OF LOVE (Donizetti)
Same cast.

EXTRA PERFORMANCES

September 16, matinee: IL TROVATORE (Verdi)
LEONORA: Farrell, AZUCENA: Dominguez, MANRICO: Bjoerling, COUNT DI LUNA: Colzani, FERRANDO: Moscona, RUIZ: Assandri, OLD GYPSY: Lovasich, INEZ: Krooskos, CONDUCTOR: De Fabritiis.

September 23, matinee: TOSCA (Puccini)
Same cast except: CAVARADOSSI: Bjoerling, SCARPIA: Colzani, SCIARRONE: Blankenburg.
October 7, matinee: MADAMA BUTTERFLY (Puccini)
CIO-CIO-SAN: Albanese, PINKERTON: Campora, SHARPLESS: Quilico, SUZUKI: Roggero, GORO: DePaolis, BONZE: Ligeti, YAMADORI: Cehanovsky, COMMISSIONER: Palangi, KATE PINKERTON: Covington, REGISTRAR: Harvey, CONDUCTOR: Kritz.
October 14, matinee: COSI FAN TUTTE (Mozart)
Same cast.
October 17: AIDA (Verdi)
AIDA: Rysanek, AMNERIS: Rankin, RHADAMES: Martell, AMONASRO: Colzani, RAMFIS: Moscona, KING: Ligeti, MESSENGER: Assandri, PRIESTESS: Hilgenberg, CONDUCTOR: De Fabritiis.

CHILDREN'S PERFORMANCES
October 10, matinee: MADAMA BUTTERFLY (Puccini)
Same cast except: PINKERTON: R. Lewis, SHARPLESS: Colzani.
October 11, matinee: MADAMA BUTTERFLY (Puccini)
Same cast as October 7 except: CIO-CIO-SAN: Kirsten, PINKERTON: Curzi, SHARPLESS: Guarrera, SUZUKI: Nadell.
October 16, matinee: MADAMA BUTTERFLY (Puccini)
Same cast as October 7 except: CIO-CIO-SAN: Kirsten, PINKERTON: R. Lewis, SHARPLESS: Guarrera, GORO: Assandri.

CASTS—1957 SEASON

REGULAR SERIES
September 17: TURANDOT (Puccini)
TURANDOT: Rysanek, LIU: Albanese, CALAF: Tobin, TIMUR: Moscona, PING: Blankenburg, PANG: Assandri, PONG: Curzi, EMPEROR ALTOUM: Fried, PRINCE OF PERSIA: Malone, MAIDS: Cadwallader, D. Petersen, CONDUCTOR: Molinari-Pradelli.
September 20: DIALOGUES OF THE CARMELITES (Poulenc)
BLANCHE: Kirsten, PRIORESS: C. Turner, NEW PRIORESS: Price, MOTHER MARIE: Thebom, SISTER CONSTANCE: Stahlman, MARQUIS DE LA FORCE: R. Herbert, CHEVALIER: Crain, MOTHER JEANNE: Hilgenberg, SISTER MATHILDE: D. Petersen, FATHER CONFESSOR: Curzi, COMMISSIONERS: Fried, Palangi, JAILOR: Presnell, GOVERNESS: West, THIERRY: Kenig, M. JAVELINOT: Enns, FIRST OFFICER: Reitan, FANATIC WOMAN: S. L. Knapp, WOMEN: Berrar, B. Johnson, OLD MAN: Wagner, CONDUCTOR: Leinsdorf.
September 24: A MASKED BALL (Verdi)
AMELIA: Rysanek, ULRICA: C. Turner, OSCAR: Stahlman, RICCARDO: Peerce, RENATO: R. Merrill, SAM: Alvary, TOM: Moscona, SILVANO: Blankenburg, JUDGE: Fried, SERVANT: Kenig, CONDUCTOR: Steinberg.
September 27: LUCIA DI LAMMERMOOR (Donizetti)
LUCIA: Gencer, LORD HENRY: Borghi, EDGARDO: Raimondi, LORD ARTHUR: Curzi, RAYMOND: Alvary, ALICE: Burlingham, NORMAN: Assandri, CONDUCTOR: Molinari-Pradelli.
October 1: DER ROSENKAVALIER (Strauss)
MARSCHALLIN: Schwarzkopf, BARON OCHS: Edelmann, OCTAVIAN: Bible, SOPHIE: Streich, FANINAL: R. Herbert, TENOR: Crain, MARIANNE: Andrew, VALZACCHI: Fried, ANNINA: Hilgenberg, POLICE COMMISSIONER: Presnell, NOTARY: Harvey, LANDLORD: Curzi, MILLINER: McArt, ANIMAL VENDOR: Assandri, MARSCHALLIN'S MAJOR-DOMO: Kenig, FANINAL'S MAJOR-DOMO: J. Thomas, ORPHANS: M. L. Hoff-

man, San Miguel, D. Petersen, FOOTMEN: Hubbard, Booth, Guenter, Woellhaf, CONDUCTOR: Leinsdorf.

October 8: ARIADNE AUF NAXOS (Strauss)
ARIADNE, PRIMA DONNA: Rysanek, BACCHUS, TENOR: R. Lewis, COMPOSER: H. George, ZERBINETTA: Streich, MUSIC TEACHER: R. Herbert, MAJOR-DOMO: Louw, ARLECCHINO: Blankenburg, SCARAMUCCIO: Manton, TRUFFALDINO: Alvary, BRIGHELLA: Curzi, NAIAD: Stahlman, DRYAD: C. Turner, ECHO: M. Gibson, DANCING MASTER: Fried, WIGMAKER: Kenig, LACKEY: Palangi, OFFICER: Presnell, CONDUCTOR: Steinberg.

October 11: MACBETH (Verdi)
LADY MACBETH: Rysanek, MACBETH: Taddei, BANQUO: Alvary, MACDUFF: Crain, MALCOLM: J. Thomas, LADY-IN-WAITING: Burlingham, MEDIC: Enns, SERVANT: Andersen, ASSASSIN: Kenig, HERALD: Lovasich, APPARITIONS: P. Murphy, Covington, Fernandez, CONDUCTOR: Molinari-Pradelli.

October 15: TOSCA (Puccini)
TOSCA: Kirsten, CAVARADOSSI: Peerce, SCARPIA: Taddei, ANGELOTTI: Palangi, SPOLETTA: Assandri, SACRISTAN: R. Herbert, SCIARRONE: Presnell, JAILOR: Enns, SHEPHERD: Fernandez, CONDUCTOR: Leinsdorf.

October 18: AIDA (Verdi)
AIDA: Price, AMNERIS: Thebom, RHADAMES: Tobin, AMONASRO: R. Merrill, RAMFIS: Moscona, KING: Palangi, MESSENGER: Fried, PRIESTESS: Andrew, CONDUCTOR: Molinari-Pradelli.

October 22: COSI FAN TUTTE (Mozart)
FIORDILIGI: Schwarzkopf, DORABELLA: Merriman, DESPINA: Streich, FERRANDO: R. Lewis, GUGLIELMO: Blankenburg, DON ALFONSO: Alvary, CONDUCTOR: Leinsdorf.

SATURDAY EVENING SERIES

September 21: TURANDOT (Puccini)
Same cast.
September 28: A MASKED BALL (Verdi)
Same cast except: AMELIA: Nelli.
October 5: LUCIA DI LAMMERMOOR (Donizetti)
Same cast except: EDGARDO: Peerce, RAYMOND: Moscona
October 12: ARIADNE AUF NAXOS (Strauss)
Same cast.
October 19: TOSCA (Puccini)
Same cast except: CAVARADOSSI: Crain.

THURSDAY EVENING SERIES

September 19: LA TRAVIATA (Verdi)
VIOLETTA: Gencer, ALFREDO: Raimondi, GERMONT: R. Merrill, GASTON: Assandri, BARON DOUPHOL: Kenig, MARQUIS D'OBIGNY: Presnell, DR. GRENVIL: Palangi, FLORA: McArt, ANNINA: Hilgenberg, CONDUCTOR: Curiel.
September 26: DIALOGUES OF THE CARMELITES (Poulenc)
Same cast.
October 3: DER ROSENKAVALIER (Strauss)
Same cast except: TENOR: Tobin.
October 10: MADAMA BUTTERFLY (Puccini)
CIO-CIO-SAN: Albanese, PINKERTON: Raimondi, SHARPLESS: Borghi, SUZUKI: Hilgenberg, GORO: Assandri, BONZE: Palangi, YAMADORI: Blankenburg, COMMISSIONER: Enns, KATE PINKERTON: Howe, REGISTRAR: Harvey, CONDUCTOR: Kritz.
October 17: MACBETH (Verdi)
Same cast.

EXTRA PERFORMANCES

October 13, matinee: DER ROSENKAVLIER (Strauss)
Same cast as October 1 except: SOPHIE: Stahlman, TENOR: Manton.
October 16: DIALOGUES OF THE CARMELITES (Poulenc)
(special performance for International Industrial Development
Conference under Time-Life auspices)
Same cast.
October 20, matinee: LA TRAVIATA (Verdi)
Same cast except: VIOLETTA: Albanese.
October 21: AÏDA (Verdi)
Same cast except: AIDA: Rysanek, AMNERIS: C. Turner.
October 23: AÏDA (Verdi)
Same cast as October 18 except: AMNERIS: C. Turner
October 24: COSI FAN TUTTE (Mozart)
Same cast.

CHILDREN'S PERFORMANCES

October 4, matinee: LA TRAVIATA (Verdi)
Same cast as September 19 except: VIOLETTA: Albanese, ALFREDO: Crain, GER-
MONT: Borghi.
October 10, matinee: LA TRAVIATA (Verdi)
Same cast as September 19 except: ALFREDO: Curzi.
October 17, matinee: LA TRAVIATA (Verdi)
Same cast as September 19 except: ALFREDO: Curzi, GERMONT: Borghi.

CASTS—1958 SEASON

REGULAR SERIES

September 12: MEDEA (Cherubini)
MEDEA: Farrell, JASON: R. Lewis, CREON: Modesti, GLAUCE: Stahlman, NERIS: C.
Turner, CAPTAIN: Enns, HANDMAIDENS: Moynagh, Blum, CONDUCTOR: Fournet.
September 16: DON CARLO (Verdi)
ELISABETH: Gencer, EBOLI: Dalis, DON CARLO: Ferraro, RODRIGO: Guarrera,
PHILIP II: Tozzi, GRAND INQUISITOR: Modesti, FRIAR: Elyn, COUNTESS OF MONDE-
CAR: Moynagh, COUNT LERMA: Assandri, ROYAL HERALD: R. Thomas, COUNTESS
OF AREMBERG: Broughton, CELESTIAL VOICE: Daniel, CONDUCTOR: Sebastian.
September 19: LA BOHEME (Puccini)
MIMI: Della Casa, RODOLFO: Raimondi, MARCELLO: Panerai, COLLINE: Alvary,
SCHAUNARD: Gillaspy, MUSETTA: Ratti, BENOIT: Wentworth, ALCINDORO: As-
sandri, PARPIGNOL: R. Thomas, SERGEANT: Lorenzini, OFFICER: Harvey, CONDUC-
TOR: Fournet.
September 26: IL TROVATORE (Verdi)
LEONORA: Price, AZUCENA: C. Turner, MANRICO: Bjoerling, COUNT DI LUNA:
Quilico, FERRANDO: Elyn, RUIZ: Assandri, OLD GYPSY: Enns, INEZ: Blum, CON-
DUCTOR: Sebastian.
September 30: THE BARTERED BRIDE (Smetana)
MARIE: Schwarzkopf, JENIK: R. Lewis, KEZAL: Tozzi, VASHEK: Fried, KRUSCHINA:
Eugene Green, LUDMILA: C. Ward, MICHA: Wentworth, HATA: Hilgenberg,
SPRINGER: Hager, ESMERALDA: Moynagh, MUFF: Harvey, CONDUCTOR: Ludwig.
October 3: THE WISE MAIDEN (Orff)
KING: Winters, PEASANT'S DAUGHTER: Price, PEASANT: Alvary, JAILOR: Wagner,
MAN WITH DONKEY: Manton, MAN WITH MULE: Eugene Green, TRAMPS: R.

Thomas, Gillaspy, Wentworth, CONDUCTOR: Ludwig.

followed by: CARMINA BURANA (Orff)
BURGUNDIAN TROUBADOUR: Guarrera, OLD POET: Guarrera, DRINKERS: Guarrera, Manton, BURGUNDIAN LADY: Malbin, YOUNG COUPLE IN LOVE: Blum, Eugene Green, COQUETTES: Oldt, C. Ward, Moynagh, FRIENDS OF TROUBADOUR: R. Thomas, Fried, Gillaspy, Eugene Green, Elyn, Enns, PAGES OF THE LADY: Carilli, Cherney, Dong, Fromer, Kattge, Wong, CONDUCTOR: Ludwig.

October 7: LA FORZA DEL DESTINO (Verdi)
LEONORA: Rysanek, DON ALVARO: Ferraro, DON CARLO: Weede, PADRE GUARDIANO: Modesti, FRA MELITONE: Wentworth, PREZIOSILLA: C. Ward, MARQUIS OF CALATRAVA: Elyn, ALCADE: Enns, TRABUCCO: Assandri, CURRA: Hilgenberg, SURGEON: Harvey, CONDUCTOR: Sebastian.

October 10: GIANNI SCHICCHI (Puccini)
GIANNI SCHICCHI: Taddei, RINUCCIO: R. Miller, LAURETTA: Stahlman, SIMONE: Alvary, BETTO: Wentworth, GHERARDO: Assandri, MARCO: Gillaspy, SPINELLOCCIO: Eugene Green, NOTARY: Elyn, PINELLINO: Harvey, GUCCIO: Enns, ZITA: Hilgenberg, NELLA: Moynagh, LA CIESCA: C. Ward, GHERARDINO: Fromer, CONDUCTOR: Curiel.

followed by: ELEKTRA (Strauss)
ELEKTRA: Goltz, CHRYSOTHEMIS: Della Casa, KLYTEMNESTRA: C. Turner, AEGISTHUS: Feiersinger, ORESTES: Van Mill, ORESTES' TUTOR: Elyn, CONFIDANTE: Blum, TRAINBEARER: Oldt, YOUNG SERVANT: R. Thomas, OLD SERVANT: Enns, OVERSEER: C. Ward, MAIDSERVANTS: A. Taylor, Groves, Hilgenberg, Moynagh, Daniel, CONDUCTOR: Ludwig.

October 14: TANNHÄUSER (Wagner)
ELISABETH: Rysanek, VENUS: G. Hoffman, TANNHÄUSER: Feiersinger, WOLFRAM: Winters, LANDGRAVE: Van Mill, WALTHER: R. Miller, BITEROLF: Elyn, HEINRICH: Fried, REINMAR: Enns, SHEPHERD: Stahlman, CONDUCTOR: Ludwig.

October 17: MANON (Massenet)
MANON: Gencer, CHEVALIER DES GRIEUX: R. Lewis, LESCAUT: Quilico, GUILLOT: Fried, DE BRETIGNY: Gillaspy, COUNT DES GRIEUX: Alvary, POUSETTE: Stahlman, JAVOTTE: Moynagh, ROSETTE: Blum, INNKEEPER: Eugene Green, SERVANT: Pappas, GUARDS: R. Thomas, Enns, SERGEANT: Andersen, ATTENDANT: Lorenzini, CONDUCTOR: Fournet.

October 21: THE MARRIAGE OF FIGARO (Mozart)
SUSANNA: Ratti, COUNTESS: Schwarzkopf, CHERUBINO: C. Ward, FIGARO: Panerai, COUNT: Modesti, BARTOLO: Wentworth, BASILIO: Fried, MARCELLINA: Hilgenberg, BARBARINA: Moynagh, ANTONIO: Eugene Green, DON CURZIO: Manton, PEASANT GIRLS: Oldt, Blum, CONDUCTOR: Adler.

SATURDAY EVENING SERIES

September 13: THE BARBER OF SEVILLE (Rossini)
ROSINA: Ratti, COUNT ALMAVIVA: R. Miller, FIGARO: Panerai, BARTOLO: Baccaloni, BASILIO: Tozzi, FIORELLO: Gillaspy, OFFICER: Assandri, BERTHA: Hilgenberg, CONDUCTOR: Curiel.

September 20: DON CARLO (Verdi)
Same cast.

September 27: LA BOHEME (Puccini)
Same cast.

October 4: THE BARTERED BRIDE (Smetana)
Same cast.

October 11: IL TROVATORE (Verdi)
Same cast except: AZUCENA: Dalis, INEZ: Groves.

October 18: TANNHÄUSER (Wagner)
Same cast.

THURSDAY EVENING SERIES

September 18: MEDEA (Cherubini)
Same cast.
September 25: RIGOLETTO (Verdi)
GILDA: Gencer, DUKE: Raimondi, RIGOLETTO: Weede, MADDALENA: C. Ward,
SPARAFUCILE: Alvary, MONTERONE: Elyn, BORSA: Assandri, MARULLO: Enns,
CEPRANO: Gillaspy, COUNTESS CEPRANO: Blum, GIOVANNA: Hilgenberg, PAGE:
Moynagh, CONDUCTOR: Fournet.
October 2: LA BOHEME (Puccini)
Same cast as September 19 except: RODOLFO: Bjoerling, COLLINE: Tozzi.
October 9: THE WISE MAIDEN (Orff)
Same cast.
            followed by: CARMINA BURANA (Orff)
Same cast.
October 16: GIANNI SCHICCHI (Puccini)
Same cast.
            followed by: ELEKTRA (Strauss)
Same cast except: KLYTEMNESTRA: Dalis.
October 23: THE MARRIAGE OF FIGARO (Mozart)
Same cast.

EXTRA PERFORMANCES

October 12, matinee: THE BARTERED BRIDE (Smetana)
Same cast.
October 19, matinee: DON CARLO (Verdi)
Same cast except: ELISABETH: Goltz, EBOLI: Hoffman, PHILIP II: Van Mill,
GRAND INQUISITOR: Alvary, FRIAR: Enns.
October 20: RIGOLETTO (Verdi) (East Bay Night)
Same cast except: MADDALENA: C. Turner.
October 22: TANNHÄUSER (Wagner)
Same cast.

CHILDREN'S PERFORMANCES

October 2, matinee: LA BOHEME (Puccini)
Same cast as September 19 except: MIMI: Moynagh, MARCELLO: Quilico,
MUSETTA: Stahlman, CONDUCTOR: Kritz.
October 16, matinee: LA BOHEME (Puccini)
Same cast as September 19 except: MIMI: Malbin, RODOLFO: Ferraro, MARCELLO:
Guarrera, COLLINE: Elyn, ALCINDORO: Eugene Green.
October 22, matinee: LA BOHEME (Puccini)
Same cast as September 19 except: MARCELLO: Quilico, MUSETTA: Stahlman,
ALCINDORO: Eugene Green.

CASTS—1959 SEASON[2]

REGULAR SERIES

September 11: AIDA (Verdi)
AIDA: Price, AMNERIS: Dalis, RHADAMES: Vickers, AMONASRO: Weede, RAMFIS:

[2] For the first time, several operas (*Butterfly, L'Amore dei Tre Re* and *Don Giovanni*) appeared on the Regular Series *after* having been introduced on one of the other series.

Tozzi, KING: Palangi, MESSENGER: R. Thomas, PRIESTESS: Hilgenberg, CONDUC-
TOR: Molinari-Pradelli.

September 15: ORFEO (Gluck)
ORFEO: Thebom, EURIDICE: Amara, AMOR: Moynagh, CONDUCTOR: Varviso.

September 17: DIE FRAU OHNE SCHATTEN (Strauss)
EMPRESS: Lang, EMPEROR: Feiersinger, BARAK: Yahia, BARAK'S WIFE: Schech,
NURSE: Dalis, SPIRIT MESSENGER: Elyn, GUARDIAN OF TEMPLE GATES: Costa, ONE-
ARMED MAN: Alvary, ONE-EYED MAN: Eugene Green, HUNCHBACK: Manton,
FALCON'S VOICE: Moynagh, YOUTH: R. Thomas, SPIRITS: Hilgenberg, Winden,
NIGHT WATCHMEN: Quilico, Andersen, McGuckin, SERVANTS: Foster, Moynagh,
Blum, SOLO VOICES: Foster, Costa, Moynagh, E. Evans, Blum, Hilgenberg, CON-
DUCTOR: Ludwig.

September 22: MADAMA BUTTERFLY (Puccini)
CIO-CIO-SAN: Jurinac, PINKERTON: Zampieri, SHARPLESS: Zanasi, SUZUKI: E. Evans,
GORO: Assandri, BONZE: Elyn, YAMADORI: Fried, COMMISSIONER: Eugene Green,
KATE PINKERTON: Blum, REGISTRAR: Harvey, CONDUCTOR: Basile.

September 25: ANDREA CHENIER (Giordano)
MADELEINE: Tucci, ANDREA CHENIER: Del Monaco, GERARD: Weede, MATHIEU:
Alvary, FLEVILLE: Elyn, ROUCHER: Quilico, DUMAS: Palangi, ABBE: R. Thomas,
SPY: Assandri, SCHMIDT: Woellhaf, FOUQUIER-TINVILLE: Eugene Green, COUNTESS:
A. Taylor, MADELON: Hilgenberg, BERSI: E. Evans, CONDUCTOR: Molinari-
Pradelli.

September 29: CARMEN (Bizet)
CARMEN: Lane, MICAELA: Amara, DON JOSE: Vickers, ESCAMILLO: Guarrera,
ZUNIGA: Alvary, DANCAIRO: Fried, REMENDADO: R. Thomas, MORALES: Eugene
Green, FRASQUITA: Moynagh, MERCEDES: E. Evans, CONDUCTOR: Basile.

October 6: DIE MEISTERSINGER (Wagner)
EVA: Jurinac, MAGDALENA: Hilgenberg, WALTHER: Feiersinger, HANS SACHS:
Schoeffler, POGNER: Tozzi, DAVID: Curzi, BECKMESSER: G. Evans, KOTHNER:
Winters, NIGHT WATCHMAN: Elyn, VOGELGESANG: Manton, NACHTIGALL: Eugene
Green, ZORN: R. Thomas, EISSLINGER: Dal Poggetto, MOSER: Fried, ORTEL: Mc-
Guckin, SCHWARZ: Palangi, FOLTZ: Elyn, CONDUCTOR: Ludwig.

October 9: L'AMORE DEI TRE RE (Montemezzi)
FIORA: Kirsten, AVITO: Zampieri, MANFREDO: Guarrera, ARCHIBALDO: Tozzi,
FLAMINIO: R. Thomas, YOUTH: Fried, OLD WOMAN: E. Evans, YOUNG GIRL: Cann,
SERVANT: Blum, CONDUCTOR: Molinari-Pradelli.

October 13: DANSES CONCERTANTES ballet (Stravinsky)
PRINCIPALS: N. Johnson, Drew, Fuerstner, Herrin, Bailey, Stowell, Vollmar,
Carter, V. Johnson, Smuin, CONDUCTOR: Murray.

followed by: ARIADNE AUF NAXOS (Strauss)
ARIADNE, PRIMA DONNA: Farrell, BACCHUS, TENOR: R. Lewis, COMPOSER: Jurinac,
ZERBINETTA: Streich, MUSIC TEACHER: G. Evans, MAJOR DOMO: Symonds,
ARLECCHINO: Uppman, SCARAMUCCIO: Manton, TRUFFALDINO: Alvary, BRIGHELLA:
Curzi, NAIAD: Alarie, DRYAD: Hilgenberg, ECHO: Moynagh, DANCING MASTER:
Fried, WIGMAKER: Assandri, LACKEY: Palangi, OFFICER: R. Thomas, CONDUCTOR:
Ludwig.

October 16: OTELLO (Verdi)
DESDEMONA: Tucci, OTELLO: Del Monaco, IAGO: Zanasi, CASSIO: Zampieri,
RODERIGO: Fried, LODOVICO: Yahia, MONTANO: Elyn, HERALD: Eugene Green,
EMILIA: Hilgenberg, CONDUCTOR: Molinari-Pradelli.

October 20: DON GIOVANNI (Mozart)
DONNA ANNA: Jurinac, DONNA ELVIRA: Price, ZERLINA: Alarie, DON GIOVANNI:
London, LEPORELLO: Alvary, DON OTTAVIO: R. Lewis, COMMENDATORE: Yahia,
MASETTO: Uppman, CONDUCTOR: Ludwig.

SATURDAY EVENING SERIES

September 12: MADAMA BUTTERFLY (Puccini)
Same cast except: CIO-CIO-SAN: Kirsten, PINKERTON: Gismondo.
September 19: I PAGLIACCI (Leoncavallo)
CANIO: Vickers, TONIO: Weede, NEDDA: Amara, SILVIO: Quilico, BEPPE: Fried,
PEASANTS: Eugene Green, R. Thomas, CONDUCTOR: Basile.
        followed by: CARMINA BURANA (Orff)
BURGUNDIAN TROUBADOUR: Guarrera, OLD POET: Guarrera, DRINKERS: Guarrera,
Manton, BURGUNDIAN LADY: Costa, YOUNG COUPLE IN LOVE: Winden, Elyn,
THREE COQUETTES: Foster, Blum, Moynagh, FRIENDS OF TROUBADOURS: R. Thomas,
Fried, Dal Poggetto, Eugene Green, Elyn, Palangi, PAGES OF THE LADY: Carilli,
Dong, Fromer, R. Goodwin, R. Murphy, Waring, CONDUCTOR: Varviso.
September 26: ORFEO (Gluck)
Same cast.
October 3: DON GIOVANNI (Mozart)
Same cast except: DON GIOVANNI: Yahia, COMMENDATORE: Tozzi.
October 10: ANDREA CHENIER (Giordano)
Same cast.
October 17: DANSES CONCERTANTES ballet (Stravinsky)
Same cast.
        followed by: ARIADNE AUF NAXOS (Strauss)
Same cast.

THURSDAY EVENING SERIES

September 17: L'AMORE DEI TRE RE (Montemezzi)
Same cast.
September 24: AIDA (Verdi)
Same cast except: AMONASRO: Winters, RAMFIS: Yahia.
October 1: CARMEN (Bizet)
Same cast except: MICAELA: Costa, ESCAMILLO: Zanasi.
October 8: DIE MEISTERSINGER (Wagner)
Same cast except: POGNER: Yahia.
October 15: DIE FRAU OHNE SCHATTEN (Strauss)
Same cast.
October 22: OTELLO (Verdi)
Same cast.

EXTRA PERFORMANCES

October 2: AIDA (Verdi)
Same cast as September 11 except: AIDA: Amara, RHADAMES: Del Monaco,
AMONASRO: Quilico, KING: Elyn.
October 19: LA BOHEME (Puccini)
MIMI: Albanese, RODOLFO: Gismondo, MARCELLO: Uppman, COLLINE: Alvary,
SCHAUNARD: G. Evans, MUSETTA: Costa, BENOIT: Baccaloni, ALCINDORO: Bac-
caloni, PARPIGNOL: Assandri, SERGEANT: Lorenzini, OFFICER: Harvey, CONDUC-
TOR: Varviso.
October 21: DIE MEISTERSINGER (Wagner)
Same cast as October 6 except: POGNER: Yahia.

CHILDREN'S PERFORMANCES

October 15, matinee: I PAGLIACCI (Leoncavallo)
Same cast except: TONIO: Winters, NEDDA: Mari, SILVIO: Uppman, BEPPE: Curzi,
CONDUCTOR: W. Martin.

October 19, matinee: I PAGLIACCI (Leoncavallo)
Same cast as September 19 except: CANIO: Feiersinger, TONIO: Winters, NEDDA: Mari, SILVIO: Guarrera, BEPPE: Curzi, CONDUCTOR: W. Martin.
October 20, matinee: I PAGLIACCI (Leoncavallo)
Same cast as September 19 except: NEDDA: Mari, SILVIO: Guarrera, BEPPE: Manton, CONDUCTOR: Basile.

CASTS—1960 SEASON

REGULAR SERIES

September 16: TOSCA (Puccini)
TOSCA: Kirsten, CAVARADOSSI: Zampieri, SCARPIA: Gobbi, SPOLETTA: Fried, SACRISTAN: Baccaloni, ANGELOTTI: Foldi, SCIARRONE: Romero, JAILOR: Standard, SHEPHERD: Waring, CONDUCTOR: Varviso.
September 20: DIE FRAU OHNE SCHATTEN (Strauss)
EMPRESS: Rysanek, EMPEROR: Parly, BARAK: Schoeffler, BARAK'S WIFE: Schech, NURSE: Dalis, SPIRIT MESSENGER: R. Anderson, GUARDIAN OF TEMPLE GATES: Costa, ONE-ARMED MAN: Alvary, ONE-EYED MAN: Wentworth, HUNCHBACK: Manton, FALCON'S VOICE: McCann, YOUTH: G. Russell, SPIRITS: J. Martin, Blum, NIGHT WATCHMEN: Drain, Standard, Romero, SERVANTS: Starr, McCann, Blum, SOLO VOICES: Starr, Costa, McCann, J. Martin, Blum, Hilgenberg, CONDUCTOR: Ludwig.
September 23: THE GIRL OF THE GOLDEN WEST (Puccini)
MINNIE: Kirsten, DICK JOHNSON: Konya, JACK RANCE: Gobbi, JAKE WALLACE: Standard, NICK: Fried, ASHBY: Alvary, SONORA: Romero, TRIN: Manton, SID: Harvey, HANDSOME: Drain, HARRY: G. Russell, JOE: Hoskinson, HAPPY: Foldi, LARKENS: Andersen, JOSE CASTRO: R. Anderson, BILLY JACKRABBIT: Wentworth, WOWKLE: Hilgenberg, CONDUCTOR: Molinari-Pradelli.
September 27: SIMON BOCCANEGRA (Verdi)
SIMON BOCCANEGRA: Gobbi, AMELIA: Amara, FIESCO: Tozzi, ADORNO: Zampieri, PAOLO: G. Evans, PIETRO: R. Anderson, CAPTAIN: G. Russell, MAIDSERVANT: J. Martin, CONDUCTOR: Ludwig.
October 4: WOZZECK (Berg)
WOZZECK: G. Evans, MARIE: Horne, CAPTAIN: R. Lewis, DOCTOR: Alvary, DRUM MAJOR: Parly, ANDRES: Manton, MARGRET: Blum, ARTISANS: Wentworth, Romero, FOOL: Fried, SOLDIERS: Booth, Pierre, CHILD: Garay, CONDUCTOR: Ludwig.
October 7: DER ROSENKAVALIER (Strauss)
MARSCHALLIN: Schwarzkopf, BARON OCHS: Boehme, OCTAVIAN: Toepper, SOPHIE: Stahlman, FANINAL: Wentworth, TENOR: Manton, MARIANNE: McCann, VALZAC-CHI: Fried, ANNINA: Hilgenberg, POLICE COMMISSIONER: Foldi, NOTARY: Harvey, LANDLORD: Hoskinson, MILLINER: Curatilo, ANIMAL VENDOR: Caperello, MAR-SCHALLIN'S MAJOR-DOMO: Andersen, FANINAL'S MAJOR-DOMO: G. Russell, OR-PHANS: Liagre, Blum, J. Martin, FOOTMEN: Hoskinson, Drain, Booth, Standard, CONDUCTOR: Varviso.
October 1: LA SONNAMBULA (Bellini)
AMINA: Moffo, ELVINO: Monti, RODOLFO: Tozzi, LISA: Stahlman, TERESA: J. Martin, ALESSIO: Foldi, NOTARY: Manton, CONDUCTOR: Molinari-Pradelli.
        followed by: VARIATIONS DE BALLET (Glazounoff)
PRINCIPALS: Vollmar, Bailey, Drew, Herrin, CONDUCTOR: DeRosa.
October 14: LA BOHEME (Puccini)
MIMI: Amara, RODOLFO: Konya, MARCELLO: Zanasi, COLLINE: Alvary, SCHAU-NARD: Romero, MUSETTA: Costa, BENOIT: Baccaloni, ALCINDORO: Baccaloni, PARPIGNOL: G. Russell, SERGEANT: Standard, OFFICER: Drain, CONDUCTOR: Varviso.

October 18: COSI FAN TUTTE (Mozart)
FIORDILIGI: Schwarzkopf, DORABELLA: Hilgenberg, DESPINA: Costa, FERRANDO: R. Lewis, GUGLIELMO: Guarrera, DON ALFONSO: Schoeffler, CONDUCTOR: Adler.
October 21: LOHENGRIN (Wagner)
ELSA: Bjoner, ORTRUD: Dalis, LOHENGRIN: Konya, TELRAMUND: R. Anderson, KING HENRY: Boehme, HERALD: Wentworth, PAGES: Liagre, Curatilo, Blum, J. Martin, CONDUCTOR: Molinari-Pradelli.
October 25: LA TRAVIATA (Verdi)
VIOLETTA: Moffo, ALFREDO: Peerce, GERMONT: Weede, GASTON: G. Russell, BARON: DOUPHOL: Romero, MARQUIS D'OBIGNY: Standard, DR. GRENVIL: Foldi, FLORA: Blum, ANNINA: J. Martin, CONDUCTOR: Varviso.

SATURDAY EVENING SERIES

September 17: CARMEN (Bizet)
CARMEN: Madeira, MICAELA: Costa, DON JOSE: Vickers, ESCAMILLO: Zanasi, ZUNIGA: Alvary, DANCAIRO: Fried, REMENDADO: Manton, MORALES: Romero, FRASQUITA: McCann, MERCEDES: Hilgenberg, CONDUCTOR: Molinari-Pradelli.
September 24: DIE FRAU OHNE SCHATTEN (Strauss)
Same cast.
October 1: THE GIRL OF THE GOLDEN WEST (Puccini)
Same cast.
October 8: WOZZECK (Berg)
Same cast.
October 15: COSI FAN TUTTE (Mozart)
Same cast.
October 22: LA BOHEME (Puccini)
Same cast except: RODOLFO: Peerce.

THURSDAY EVENING SERIES

September 22: TOSCA (Puccini)
Same cast except: TOSCA: Amara, SCARPIA: Zanasi.
September 29: DER ROSENKAVALIER (Strauss)
Same cast except: OCTAVIAN: Bible.
October 6: SIMON BOCCANEGRA (Verdi)
Same cast.
October 13: LA SONNAMBULA (Bellini)
Same cast.
      followed by: VARIATIONS DE BALLET (Glazounoff)
Same cast.
October 20: LA TRAVIATA (Verdi)
Same cast except: VIOLETTA: Costa, ALFREDO: Zampieri.
October 27: LOHENGRIN (Wagner)
Same cast.

EXTRA PERFORMANCES

September 30: AIDA (Verdi)
AIDA: Rysanek, AMNERIS: Dalis, RHADAMES: Vickers, AMONASRO: Weede, RAM-FIS: Tozzi, KING: Foldi, MESSENGER: G. Russell, PRIESTESS: J. Martin, CONDUCTOR: Molinari-Pradelli.
October 16: DER ROSENKAVALIER (Strauss)
Same cast as October 7 except: TENOR: Parly.
October 24: AIDA (Verdi)
Same cast except: AIDA: Cavalli, RHADAMES: Konya, AMONASRO: Zanasi, RAMFIS: R. Anderson.

October 26: WOZZECK (Berg)
Same cast.

CHILDREN'S PERFORMANCES

October 18, matinee: GIANNI SCHICCHI (Puccini)
GIANNI SCHICCHI: G. Evans, RINUCCIO: Parly, LAURETTA: Stahlman, SIMONE: Alvary, BETTO: Wentworth, GHERARDO: Manton, MARCO: Romero, SPINELLOC-CIO: Foldi, NOTARY: R. Anderson, PINELLINO: Harvey, GUCCIO: Standard, ZITA: Horne, NELLA: McCann, LA CIESCA: J. Martin, CONDUCTOR: Schaefer.
   followed by: CON AMORE ballet (Rossini)
CAPTAIN: Bailey, THIEF: Drew, MISTRESS: Lawler, MASTER: Herrin, DANDY: Ohman, SAILOR: Smuin, STUDENT: Orr, AMOR: Wallace, CONDUCTOR: DeRosa.
October 25, 26, matinees: GIANNI SCHICCHI (Puccini)
Same cast except: ZITA: Hilgenberg.
   followed by: CON AMORE ballet (Rossini)
Same cast.

REPERTOIRE[1]

1923—1961

AUBER
Fra Diavolo. 1926
BEETHOVEN
Fidelio. 1937, 1939, 1946, 1951, 1954, 1961
BELLINI
Norma. 1937
La Sonnambula. 1960
BERG
Wozzeck. 1960
BIZET
Carmen. 1927-28, 1931, 1934, 1936, 1940-46, 1948-49, 1951, 1953, 1955, 1959-60.
BOITO
Mefistofele. 1923, 1952-53
BRITTEN
A Midsummer Night's Dream. 1961
CHARPENTIER
Louise. 1947, 1955
CHERUBINI
Medea. 1958
The Portuguese Inn. 1954
DEBUSSY
Pelléas et Mélisande. 1938, 1947
DELIBES
Lakmé. 1934, 1937, 1940, 1944, 1946
DELLO JOIO
Blood Moon. 1961
DONIZETTI
The Daughter of the Regiment. 1941-42, 1952
Don Pasquale. 1929, 1938, 1941, 1943, 1946
The Elixir of Love. 1929, 1948, 1956
Lucia di Lammermoor. 1926 1930, 1932, 1938-39, 1942-47, 1949-50, 1954, 1957, 1961
FLOTOW
Martha. 1925-26, 1929, 1935, 1938, 1944
GIORDANO
Andrea Chenier. 1923-24, 1928, 1931, 1938, 1950, 1955, 1959
La Cena Delle Beffe. 1927-28
Fedora. 1928

[1] Very occasionally an opera has been given only outside San Francisco during a particular season. If so, that year is not listed after the opera's name.

GLUCK
Orfeo. 1959
GOUNOD
Faust. 1926, 1928-30, 1932, 1934, 1937, 1942, 1944, 1947, 1949, 1955
Romeo and Juliet. 1923, 1927, 1937, 1946-47, 1951
GRUENBERG
The Emperor Jones. 1933
HALEVY
La Juive. 1935-36
HONEGGER
Joan of Arc at the Stake. 1954
HUMPERDINCK
Hansel and Gretel. 1929-30, 1932
LEONCAVALLO
I Pagliacci. 1923, 1927-30, 1932-33, 1936, 1939, 1943, 1945, 1948, 1952, 1955, 1959
MASCAGNI
L'Amico Fritz. 1924
Cavalleria Rusticana. 1927-28, 1930, 1932-33, 1938-39, 1943, 1945, 1948, 1952
MASSENET
Manon. 1924-25, 1929-30, 1933-34, 1937, 1939-40, 1944, 1948, 1951, 1954, 1958
Werther. 1935, 1953
MONTEMEZZI
L'Amore dei Tre Re. 1925, 1928, 1941-42, 1947, 1952, 1959
MOUSSORGSKY
Boris Godounoff. 1945-46, 1948, 1951, 1953, 1956, 1961
MOZART
Cosi Fan Tutte. 1956-57, 1960
Don Giovanni. 1938, 1940, 1943, 1945, 1947-49, 1952-53, 1955, 1959
The Magic Flute. 1950
The Marriage of Figaro. 1936, 1940, 1946-47, 1950, 1954, 1958, 1961
OFFENBACH
The Tales of Hoffmann. 1944-45, 1949
ORFF
Carmina Burana. 1958-59
The Wise Maiden. 1958
PONCHIELLI
La Gioconda. 1947-48
POULENC
Dialogues of the Carmelites. 1957
PUCCINI
La Boheme. 1923-24, 1926-27, 1929-31, 1933, 1935, 1937-38, 1940, 1943-1954, 1956, 1958-60
Gianni Schicchi. 1923, 1929, 1936, 1952, 1958, 1960
The Girl of the Golden West. 1930, 1943, 1960
Madama Butterfly. 1924, 1928, 1931, 1934, 1937, 1939, 1941, 1946-48, 1950-51, 1953-54, 1956-57, 1959, 1961
Manon Lescaut. 1926-27, 1949-50, 1956
La Rondine. 1934
Suor Angelica. 1923, 1935, 1950, 1952
Il Tabarro. 1923, 1952, 1954
Tosca. 1923-28, 1931-32, 1934, 1936, 1941, 1949, 1951-52, 1954-57, 1960
(Il Trittico. 1923, 1952)
Turandot. 1927-28, 1953-54, 1957, 1961

RABAUD
Marouf. 1931
RAVEL
L'Enfant et les Sortilèges. 1930
The Spanish Hour. 1945
RIMSKY-KORSAKOFF
Le Coq d'Or. 1933, 1935, 1938, 1942, 1955
ROSSINI
The Barber of Seville. 1925-26, 1929, 1935-36, 1938-39, 1941-42, 1945, 1948,
1950, 1953, 1958
SAINT-SAENS
Samson and Delilah. 1925-26, 1933, 1943, 1949
SMETANA
The Bartered Bride. 1934, 1942, 1958
STRAUSS, JOHANN
Die Fledermaus. 1942
STRAUSS, RICHARD
Ariadne auf Naxos. 1957, 1959
Elektra. 1938, 1953, 1958
Die Frau Ohne Schatten. 1959-60
Der Rosenkavalier. 1940-41, 1945-46, 1951-52, 1955, 1957, 1960
Salome. 1930, 1944-45, 1950, 1954
THOMAS
Mignon. 1930, 1934
VERDI
Aida. 1925-29, 1931, 1933, 1935, 1937, 1940, 1942, 1944-45, 1947, 1949-50,
1952, 1955-57, 1959-60
Don Carlo. 1958
Falstaff. 1927, 1944, 1948, 1956
La Forza del Destino. 1933, 1936, 1938, 1943-44, 1946, 1948, 1951, 1954, 1958
Macbeth. 1955, 1957
A Masked Ball. 1931, 1937, 1940, 1942, 1944, 1953, 1957, 1961
Nabucco. 1961
Otello. 1934, 1936, 1939, 1947-48, 1950-51, 1959
Rigoletto. 1923-24, 1926, 1929, 1932, 1935-37, 1939-41, 1943-48, 1951-52, 1954,
1958, 1961
Simon Boccanegra. 1941, 1956, 1960
La Traviata. 1924-25, 1930, 1932-34, 1937, 1939, 1942-43, 1945-48, 1951-53,
1957, 1960
Il Trovatore. 1926-27, 1929, 1931-32, 1936, 1939, 1943, 1946, 1948, 1952, 1956,
1958
VITTADINI
Anima Allegra. 1925
WAGNER
The Flying Dutchman. 1954, 1956
Die Götterdämmerung. 1935-36, 1947
Lohengrin. 1931-32, 1937, 1946, 1955, 1960
Die Meistersinger. 1931-32, 1938, 1948, 1959, 1961
Parsifal. 1950-51
Das Rheingold. 1935-36
Siegfried. 1935, 1948
Tannhäuser. 1930-31, 1934, 1941, 1958
Tristan and Isolde. 1927, 1933, 1936-37, 1939, 1945, 1947, 1949-50, 1953
Die Walküre. 1935-36, 1939, 1945, 1949, 1953, 1956

WALTON
Troilus and Cressida. 1955
WOLF-FERRARI
The Secret of Suzanne. 1933, 1944
ZANDONAI
Francesca da Rimini. 1956

BALLETS

BEETHOVEN
The Creatures of Prometheus. 1953
DELIBES
Coppelia. 1939
GLAZOUNOFF
Variations de Ballet. 1960
RAVEL
Bolero. 1932
La Valse. 1932
ROSSINI
Con Amore. 1960
STRAVINSKY
Danses Concertantes. 1959

INDEX OF PERFORMERS

(The dates in parenthesis refer to the San Francisco seasons in which the artist was listed as a featured singer, conductor, etc. 'S' stands for Stanford season.)

Adler, Kurt Herbert (1943-53, 1958, 1960)
Agni, R. (S)
Alarie, Pierrette (1959)
Albanese, Licia (1941-50, 1953-57, 1959)
Alexander, Nicolai (1943)
Alibertini, Evaristo (1923-35, 1937, 1939-41, 1943-45, 1947-48)
Allen, Janette (1955)
Allison, Catherine (1938)
Alsen, Elsa (1927)
Althof, Phyllis (1956)
Althouse, Paul (1926, 1933)
Alvary, Lorenzo (1940-48, 1951-60)
Alver, Sheril (1948)
Amara, Lucine (Armaganian, Lucy) (1959-60)
Amato, Pasquale (1927)
Ananian, Paolo (1923-24)
Andersen, Winther (1951-60)
Anderson, Britta (1945)
Anderson, Eugene (1933)
Anderson, Geary (1944)
Anderson, Robert (1960)
Andreatta, Carmen (1950, 1952)
Andreotti, Norma (1940)
Andrew, Milla (1957)
Ansseau, Fernand (1925)
Antoine, Josephine (1942)
Argall, Marsden (S, 1925, 1932)
Arnold, Bene (1953)
Askam, Perry (1936-37)
Assandri, Virginio (1952-59)
Attarian, James (1948)
Avakian, Alice (1938-41, 1944)

Avery, Eleanor (1955)
Baccaloni, Salvatore (1938, 1941-54, 1958-60)
Bada, Angelo (1927-28)
Badger, Flossita (1923, 1925-26, 1934)
Bailey, Sally (1953, 1959-60)
Baldacci, Otello (1935)
Baldwin, Eileen (1947-52)
Balfour, Jean (1937)
Ballagh, Robert (1940)
Ballarini, Stefan (1939)
Ballester, Vincente (S)
Bampton, Rose (1949)
Barabas, Sari (1950)
Barallobre, Ray (1953)
Barbano, Josephine (1950, 1952)
Barbato, Elisabetta (1949)
Barbieri, Fedora (1952)
Barbini, Ernesto (1954-55)
Bardelli, Cesare (1953)
Baromeo, Chase (1935)
Barra, Gennaro (1928-29)
Bartlett, Michael (1939)
Basile, Arturo (1959)
Baum, Kurt (1943, 1946-48, 1951)
Beal, Eula (1948)
Beattie, Douglas (1935, 1942)
Beatty, Helen (1937)
Beecham, Sir Thomas (1943)
Belarsky, Sidor (1933)
Benson, Norman (1947-48)
Bering, Christine (1953)
Berini, Mario (1946)
Bernhard, Alton (1937, 1944)
Berrar, Carol (1957)

Cross, Elsie (1925)
Curatilo, Gwen (1960)
Curiel, Glauco (1952-58)
Currier, Sharon (1952)
Curtis, Mary (Curtis-Verna, Mary) (1952)
Curzi, Cesare (1948-54, 1956-57, 1959)
Czaplicki, George (1946-47)

Dalis, Irene (1958-60)
D'Alvarez, Marguerite (1925)
Daneluz, Galliano (1946-47, 1952-53, 1955)
D'Angelo, Louis (1923-24, 1927-36, 1938-39)
Daniel, Ruth (1958)
Danise, Giuseppe (1928-29, 1931)
Darrow, Lois Viola (1925)
Davis, Floyd (1947)
Deeley, Ellen (1927)
DeFabritiis, Oliviero (1956)
Defrere, Desire (1926-27)
DeHidalgo, Elvira (1925)
Della Casa, Lisa (1958)
Della Chiesa, Vivian (1944-45)
Dell'Orefice, Antonio (1929-31, 1933)
Del Monaco, Mario (1950, 1952, 1959)
DeLuca, Giuseppe (1923-24, 1929)
DeLugg, Harry (1944)
Demers, Muriel (1945-46)
DePaolis, Alessio (1940, 1942-56)
DeSegurola, Andres (1931)
Destal, Fred (1939)
DeVol, Eva (1924)
Didur, Adamo (1923)
Dimitrieff, Zoia (1930, 1932)
Dini, Adolfo (1927-28, 1930)
DiRosa, Ottavio (1960)
DiStefano, Giuseppe (1950)
Djanel, Lily (1944-46)
Doan, Philip (1944, 1946)
Dobbs, Mattiwilda (1955)
Doe, Doris (1935-36, 1938)
Dominguez, Oralia (1956)
Dong, Galen (1958-59)
Donnelly, Myrtle (1924, 1926-28)
Drain, Donald (1960)
Drew, Roderick (1959-60)
Duno, Daniel (1948)
Duval, Franca (1954)

Eddy, Nelson (1934-35)
Edelmann, Otto (1955, 1957)
Edmunds, Robert (1931)

Edwards, Max (1939)
Eldredge, George (1932-33)
Elkus, Miriam (1925)
Elliott, Mary Taylor (1928)
Ellis, John (1934)
Elmassian, Zaruhi (1930-31)
Elmo, Cloe (1948)
Elyn, Mark (1958-59)
Emery, Marie DeForest (1928)
Engel, Peggy (1942)
Enns, Harold (1954, 1957-58)
Epton, Merle (1923)
Ernster, Dezso (1950-51, 1953)
Estabrook, Winifred (1927)
Evans, Edith (1959)
Evans, Geraint (1959-60)
Evans, Randall (1943)
Eybel, Querita (1923-25, 1933-35)

Fadem, Edward (1930)
Farncroft, Audrey (1925-26, 1930-31)
Farrell, Eileen (1956, 1958-59)
Farrell, Eloise (1946, 1951, 1953, 1956)
Faull, Ellen (1953)
Favero, Mafalda (1938)
Feduloff, N. (1924)
Feiersinger, Sebastian (1958-59)
Feinberg, Ronald (1953)
Fenn, Jean (1952)
Ferguson, DuBlois (1923-24, 1927-31, 1935)
Fernanda, Doria (S, 1923)
Fernandez, Alfredo (1957)
Ferraro, Piero Miranda (1958)
Ferrier, Andre (1924, 1929-30, 1934, 1937-40)
Ferrier, Jeanne Gustin (1934)
Flagstad, Kirsten (1935-37, 1939, 1949-50)
Florence, Rose (1928)
Flynn, John (1954)
Foldi, Andrew (1960)
Folli, Ester (1933-34)
Ford, John (1948, 1950)
Ford, Lloyd (1952)
Formichi, Cesare (1925)
Forno, Fedela (1928)
Foster, Nancy (1959)
Fournet, Jean (1958)
Franklyn, Roy (1954)
Fredericks, Walter (1950-52, 1955)
Frediani, Amerigo (1923-26, 1928, 1933-34)
Fremont, Irene (1926-27, 1935-36)

Jagel, Frederick (1930, 1939-45, 1950)
Jamison, Anne (1938)
Janssen, Herbert (1945, 1948-49, 1951)
Jepson, Helen (1935)
Jeritza, Maria (1928, 1930)
Jessner, Irene (1938)
Jobin, Raoul (1940-49)
Johansen, Barbara (1952)
Johnson, Barbara (1957)
Johnson, Christine (1943)
Johnson, Edward (1928)
Johnson, Nancy (1953, 1959)
Johnson, Virginia (1953, 1959)
Johnston, Patricia (1953)
Johnstone, Lela (1923)
Jones, Olive (1924)
Jones, Oliver (1935-37)
Journet, Marcel (1925-26)
Julian, Alexandre (1931)
Jurinac, Sena (1959)
Jurs, Evelyn (1941)

Kantor, Mary (1952)
Kappel, Gertrude (1933)
Karkova, Anna (1927)
Karpelenia, Helen (1944)
Karras, Sophie (1955)
Kattge, Gary (1958)
Keaumoku, Louis (1927)
Kenig, Murray (1956-57)
King, Marilynn (1945-46)
Kipnis, Alexander (1939-41)
Kirk, Florence (1943)
Kirsten, Dorothy (1947-48, 1950-57, 1959-60)
Klose, Margarete (1953)
Knapp, Eleanor (1946)
Knapp, Sybil Louise (1951-52, 1955, 1957)
Knierr, Marcella (1926-28)
Kolodin, Michael (1933)
Konya, Sandor (1960)
Kostin, Feodor (1927)
Kovaleff, Alexandra (1930)
Krauter, Marvin (1942)
Kritz, Karl (1945-46, 1949-54, 1956-58)
Krooskos, Christine (1956)
Kroph, Lina (1935-38)
Kullman, Charles (1936-38, 1941-48, 1950, 1954)

Lachona, Chris (1955-56)
Lagorio, Valerie (1949, 1951)

Landan, Charlotte (1937)
Landi, Bruno (1944-45)
Lane, Gloria (1959)
Lanfranconi, Terry (1932)
Lang, Edith (1959)
Lanyon, Sherrill (1950-51)
Lanz, Madelaine (1934-35)
Larsen, Karen (1952)
Laubenthal, Rudolf (1927)
Lauche, Clare (1935)
Laufkötter, Karl (1938, 1941)
Lauppe, Barbara (1950)
Lauri-Volpi, Giacomo (1929)
Lawler, Louise (1960)
Lawlor, Kathleen (1936, 1938-48)
Lawrence, Erich (1946-47)
Lawrence, Ernest (1951-52)
Lawrence, Marjorie (1939-40)
Lazelle, Rena (1923-24)
Lazzari, Virgilio (1926, 1947)
Leandre, Marie (1935)
Lehmann, Lotte (1934, 1936, 1940-41, 1945-46)
Leinsdorf, Erich (1938-41, 1948, 1951, 1955, 1957)
Leo, Cecile (1927)
Leonard, Myrtle (1933)
Lert, Richard (1935-36)
Levi, Alfred (1933)
Levon, Nevart (1944)
Lewis, Brenda (1950, 1952)
Lewis, Richard (1955-60)
Liagre, Jeannine (1960)
Lichtegg, Max (1948)
Lieber, Paul (1940-41, 1945)
Ligeti, Desire (1946-56)
Lindi, Aroldo (1926)
Linne, Charlotte (1931-32)
List, Emanuel (1935-37)
Lockhart, Gene (1942)
Lombardi, John (1953)
London, George (Burnson, George) (1943, 1959)
Lorenz, Walter (1940-41)
Lorenzini, Max (1937, 1940, 1943-54, 1958)
Lothrop, Marie (1932)
Loughery, Edward (1937)
Lourenzo, August (1943, 1945-46)
Louw, Allan (1950, 1952, 1957)
Lovasich, Edward (1952, 1956-57)
Ludlow, Conrad (1953)
Ludwig, Leopold (1958-60)
Luscombe, Grace (1937)

Navarro, Juan (1939)
Naya, Francisco (1940)
Nelli, Herva (1951-52, 1957)
Nelson, Greta (1950)
Nelson, Robin (1944-45, 1947-50)
Neri, Aristide (S)
Nesbitt, Kayton (1946-47)
Newsom, Mary (1924-25)
Nicolich, Antonio (1925-26)
Nikolaidi, Elena (1950)
Nilsson, Birgit (1956)
Noonan, Stanley (1939-40)
Norville, Hubert (1950)
Nostrom, Helen (1934-35)
Novi, Edward (1951)
Novotna, Jarmila (1939, 1946, 1949)
Nystrom, Herbert (1945)

O'Connell, Jo Ann (1949-50)
O'Dea, Margaret (1935-36)
Ohman, Frank (1960)
Oldt, Louise (1958)
Olitzki, Walter (1940-41, 1945-48)
Oliver, Frances (1952)
Oliver, Francis (1943)
Oliviero, Lodovico (1924-31, 1933, 1936-38)
Olmsted, Anita (1923-24)
Omeron, Grace (1935)
Ordini, G. (1923)
Orr, Terry (1960)
Osborne, Verna (1940, 1942-43)
Ostrowski, Alice (1949-51)
Ott, Hildegarde (1928)

Palangi, Carl (1954-57, 1959)
Paltrinieri, Gordano (1923, 1930)
Palumbo, Frank (1938, 1942)
Panerai, Rolando (1958)
Papi, Gennaro (1936-41)
Pappas, Pauline (1950, 1954)
Parly, Ticho (1960)
Patton, Fred (1927)
Paulee, Mona (1939-40)
Paulini, Philippa (1954)
Pauly, Rose (1938)
Paxman, Gordon (1953-54)
Pechner, Gerhard (1940)
Peerce, Jan (1941-49, 1951-57, 1960)
Pelletier, Wilfred (1928-31, 1933, 1947)
Peralta, Frances (1927)
Perdue, Lola (1929)
Perlea, Jonel (1950)

Perulli, Franco (1941)
Peters, Arthur (1949-50)
Petersen, Donna (1953-54, 1956-57)
Petersen, William (1954-55)
Petina, Irra (1940-43)
Petit, Joseph (1955)
Petroff, Ivan (1943-46)
Petrova, Faina (1931)
Phillips, Delphia (1947)
Picco, Millo (1924, 1927-31)
Pilcher, William (1927)
Pinza, Claudia (1947-48)
Pinza, Ezio (1927-28, 1930-38, 1940-48)
Pisani, Gioacchino (1927)
Pistor, Gotthelf (1931)
Poleri, David (1953)
Polidori, Violetta (1926)
Ponitz, Olive (1938-41)
Pons, Lily (1932, 1937-47, 1949-52)
Popper, Beta (1947)
Post, Valeria (1928-29)
Prandelli, Giacinto (1954)
Presnell, Harve (1957)
Price, Leontyne (1957-59)

Quartararo, Florence (1947, 1949-50)
Quilico, Louis (1956, 1958-59)

Radic, John (1931)
Ragusa, Anita (1945)
Raimondi, Gianni (1957-58)
Rankin, Nell (1955-56)
Ratti, Eugenia (1958)
Rayner, Sydney (1930)
Reed, Estelle (1932)
Reed, Janet (1939)
Reese, Constance (S)
Reggiani, Hilde (1945)
Regoli, Nazareth (1925-26)
Reiner, Fritz (1936-38)
Reitan, Roald (1957)
Repp, Ellen (1946)
Rescigno, Nicola (1950-51)
Resnik, Regina (1946-48)
Rethberg, Elisabeth (1928-29, 1931, 1934-36, 1938-40)
Riedel, Johann (1930)
Riedel, Karl (1929-30, 1936, 1944)
Riggins, Earl (1939, 1941-42)
Ritter, Margaret (1939-42)
Rivero, Adeline (1929)
Robert, Josephine (1937)

Susulich, Lina (1927)
Suthaus, Ludwig (1953, 1956)
Svanholm, Set (1946-49, 1951)
Swarthout, Gladys (1941)
Sze, Yi-Kwei (1950-51)
Szekely, Mihaly (1949)
Szenkar, Eugen (1954)

Taddei, Giuseppe (1957-58)
Taenzlar, Hans (1934)
Tagliabue, Carlo (1938)
Tagliavini, Ferruccio (1948-49, 1952)
Tajo, Italo (1948-50, 1952-53, 1956)
Tallone, George (1944-47)
Taylor, Alice (1959)
Taylor, John (1955)
Tebaldi, Renata (1950, 1955-56)
Telva, Marion (1928)
Tennyson, Jean (1942)
Tentoni, Rosa (1937)
Thebom, Blanche (1947, 1949, 1951-52, 1957, 1959)
Thomas, Jess (1957)
Thomas, John Charles (1930, 1943)
Thomas, Robert (1958-59)
Thompson, Hugh (1944)
Thompson, Norman (1941)
Thompson, Truman (1943)
Thomson, Austin (1951)
Thorborg, Kerstin (1938, 1943)
Thornbury, Destal (1949-50)
Throndson, Dorothy (1950-52)
Tibbe, Cuthbert (1932)
Tibbett, Lawrence (1927-28, 1933, 1936, 1939, 1941, 1946-47, 1949)
Tissier, Joseph (1944-46)
Tobin, Eugene (1957)
Toepper, Hertha (1960)
Tokatyan, Armand (1923, 1927-28)
Toolatjan, Vahan (1955)
Torres, Suzanne (1929-30)
Torri, Rosina (1925)
Tozzi, Giorgio (1955, 1958-60)
Traubel, Helen (1945, 1947)
Trevisan, Vittorio (1925-26)
Trevor, Demy (1949, 1951)
Treweck, Ruth (1929)
Tucci, Gabriella (1959)
Tucker, Richard (1954-55)
Tulagin, J. (1927)
Tumminia, Josephine (1935-37, 1947)
Turnbull, Mary Jane (1947)
Turner, Albert (1955)

Turner, Claramae (1942, 1944-45, 1947-55, 1957-58)
Turrini, Roberto (1953-56)
Twigg, Ethel (1929)

Uppman, Theodor (1948, 1959)
Ursino, James (1954)

Valdengo, Giuseppe (1947-48, 1950-52)
Valentino, Francesco (1943-52)
Valletti, Cesare (1953)
Vallin, Ninon (1934)
Van Den Burg, Willem (1939)
Van Gordon, Cyrena (1933)
Van Mill, Arnold (1958)
Vanna, Gina (1936)
Vannucci, Albert (1933, 1935, 1944)
Vannucci, Attilio (1925, 1927-28)
Vannucci, Edwin (1946-47)
Varnay, Astrid (1946, 1948, 1951)
Varviso, Silvio (1959-60)
Vasilieff, Nikolai (1933, 1935)
Velsir, Patricia (1956)
Verdell, Anthony (1954)
Vettori, Elda (1928)
Vickers, Jon (1959-60)
Vinay, Ramon (1949-51)
Viti, Geraldine (1946)
Viviani, Gaetano (1930)
Vogel, Victor (1925-26)
Vollmar, Jocelyn (1959-60)
Votipka, Thelma (1938-47, 1952)
Vroons, Frans (1951)

Wagner, James (1957-58)
Wahlin, Fred (1944)
Walker, Donna (1949-50, 1952, 1955)
Walker, Sidney (1954)
Wallace, Mimi (1960)
Wallenstein, Alfred (1951)
Walti, Paul (1938-42, 1948)
Ward, Barbara (1940)
Ward, Cecilia (1958)
Warenskjold, Dorothy (1948-55)
Waring, James (1959)
Warren, Elinor (1954)
Warren, Leonard (1943-44, 1947-48, 1954-56)
Weede, Robert (1940-43, 1947-52, 1954-55, 1958-60)
Welitsch, Alexander (1954-55)
Wellman, Edward (1939-44)
Welton, Joan (1950)

OFFICERS AND DIRECTORS
1923—1960

Wallace M. Alexander, 1924-36 (Vice President 1925-31; President 1932-36)
Frank B. Anderson, 1924-33
George Washington Baker Jr., 1943-49
Mrs. George S. Behrendt, 1959-60
Albert M. Bender, 1923

Robert I. Bentley, 1923-31 (President 1924-31)
Charles R. Blyth, 1937-58 (Vice President 1940-58)
Louise Boyd, 1923
Arthur Merrill Brown Jr., 1932-60 (Vice President)
Starr Bruce, 1949-60 (Secretary 1951-60)

George T. Cameron, 1932-55 (Treasurer 1942-55; Vice President 1951-55)
Edward W. Carter, 1956-60
Mrs. Norman Chandler, 1956-60
Charles Christin, 1923
Edward H. Clark Jr. (Vice President 1925-31)

Horace B. Clifton, 1923-39 (Vice Chairman 1923; Vice President 1924-39)
Mrs. Horace B. Clifton, 1923
William H. Crocker, 1924, 1932-36
William W. Crocker, 1937-60
George E. Crothers, 1923

Mary Dunham, 1923
Henry Duque, 1956-60
Milton H. Esberg, 1923-38
Charles K. Field, 1923
Mrs. William M. Fitzhugh, 1923

Mortimer Fleishhacker, 1924-52
Prentis Cobb Hale, 1955-60 (Vice President 1957-60)
Timothy Healy, 1923-45 (Chairman 1923; Vice President 1924)
Mrs. Timothy Healy (Marie Hicks Davidson), 1923
Marco F. Hellman, 1949-60 (Treasurer 1956-60)

Bruce Kelham, 1950-56
Mrs. Marcus Koshland, 1923
Edith Livermore, 1923

Sallie Maynard, 1923
William Gladstone Merchant, 1954-60

Mrs. James B. Miller, 1923 (Secretary)
Robert Watt Miller, 1932-41, 1946-60 (Vice President 1932-36; President 1937-
41, 1952-60)
Mrs. W. H. Mills, 1923
Edward F. Moffatt (Treasurer 1923-24; Secretary-Treasurer 1925-41; Secre-
tary 1942-46)
Kenneth Monteagle, 1942-60 (President 1942-51)

John Francis Neylan, 1932-59
Selby Oppenheimer, 1923
T. S. Petersen, 1955-60
Mrs. M. C. Porter, 1923
Paul Posz (Secretary 1947-50)

Mrs. Stanley Powell, 1940-60 (Vice President 1942-60)
Joseph D. Redding, 1925-26, 1928-29
Mrs. Henry Potter Russell, 1940-60
B. F. Schlesinger, 1923
William T. Sesnon, 1924-28

Mrs. William T. Sesnon, 1923
Mrs. Ernest Simpson, 1923
Mrs. M. C. Sloss, 1923
Ralph J. A. Stern, 1952-60
Mrs. Oliver Stine, 1923

Richard M. Tobin, 1930-42
Nion R. Tucker, 1934-49
Whitney Warren, 1960
A. W. Widenham, 1923 (Vice Chairman)
J. D. Zellerbach, 1950-60